Marriage
IN THE
Catholic
Tradition

Marriage

IN THE

Catholic Tradition

Scripture, Tradition, and Experience

EDITED BY

Todd A. Salzman, Thomas M. Kelly,

and John J. O'Keefe

A Herder & Herder Book
The Crossroad Publishing Company
New York

The Crossroad Publishing Company
16 Penn Plaza, 481 Eighth Avenue
New York, NY 10001

Printed in the United States of America

Library of Congress Cataloging-in-Publication Data

Marriage in the Catholic tradition : scripture, tradition, and experience / edited by Todd A. Salzman, Thomas M. Kelly, and John J. O'Keefe.
     p. cm.
   "A Herder & Herder book."
   Includes bibliographical references and index.
   ISBN 0-8245-2272-9 (alk. paper)
     1. Marriage – Religious aspects – Catholic Church. 2. Catholic Church – Doctrines. I. Salzman, Todd A. II. Kelly, Thomas M., 1969- III. O'Keefe, John J., 1961-
BX2250.M17 2004
234'.165'088282 – dc22

                                                               2004022303

1   2   3   4   5   6   7   8   9   10   10   09   08   07   06   05   04

To Michael G. Lawler

Maxima cum gratia amicitiaque

Contents

Part Three
MARRIAGE AND EXPERIENCE

Contributors

Florence Caffrey Bourg is a Visiting Professor of Theology, Loyola University, New Orleans. Recent publications: *Where Two or Three Are Gathered: Christian Families as Domestic Churches* (University of Notre Dame Press, 2004); "Domestic Church: A New Frontier in Ecclesiology," *Horizons* (2002); "The Family Home as the Place of Religious Formation," in *Religious Education of Boys and Girls,* ed. Lisa Sowle Cahill and Werner Jeanrond, *Concilium* (2002).

Aldegonde Brenninkmeijer-Werhahn is Director of the International Academy for Marital Spirituality (INTAMS), Brussels, Belgium, and Editor-in-Chief of *INTAMS Review.* Recent publications: *Christian Marriage Today* (Catholic University of America Press, 1997); *Threefold Vocation of Marriage* (Emmaüs Antwerpen, 1993); *Marriage for all Seasons* (Emmaüs Antwerpen, 1992).

Timothy J. Buckley, C.S.S.R., is Publishing Director of Redemptorist Publications, Chawton, Alton, Hampshire, England. Recent publication: *What Binds Marriage? Roman Catholic Theology in Practice,* revised and expanded edition (Continuum, 2002).

Lisa Sowle Cahill is J. Donald Monan Professor of Theology, Boston College. Recent publications: "Marriage: Developments in Catholic Theology and Ethics," *Theological Studies* (2003); *Family: A Christian Social Perspective* (Fortress, 2000).

Susan A. Calef is Assistant Professor of Theology at Creighton University. Recent publications: "By Grit and Grace: Women on the Early Christian Frontier," in *Practical Theology: Perspectives from the Plains,* ed. Michael G. Lawler and Gail S. Risch (Creighton University Press, 2000); "The Shape of Family and Family Values: 'The Bible Tells Me So,' or Does It?" in *Religion and Family: Historical, Social, and Theological Dimensions,* ed. Ronald Simkins and Gail S. Risch (Creighton University Press, 2005).

John J. Collins is Holmes Professor of Old Testament, Yale. Recent publications: *The Hebrew Bible: An Introduction* (Fortress, 2004); *The Apocalyptic Imagination,* 2nd ed. (Eerdmans, 1998); *Daniel: A Commentary on the Book of Daniel* (Fortress, 1993).

Raymond F. Collins is Warren-Blanding Professor of Religion and Ordinary Professor of New Testament, Catholic University of America. Recent publications: *The Many Faces of the Church: A Study in New Testament Ecclesiology* (Crossroad, 2003); *1 and 2 Timothy and Titus* (Westminster John Knox, 2002); *Sexual Ethics in the New Testament: Behavior and Belief* (Crossroad, 2000).

Bernard Cooke is Adjunct Professor, Loyola University, New Orleans, Institute for Ministry. Recent publication: *Power and the Spirit of God* (Oxford University Press, 2004).

Rev. Gregory M. Faulhaber is Vice Rector/Associate Professor of Moral Theology at Christ the King Seminary, East Aurora, New York. Recent publications: Pamphlet: Faulhaber et al., *We Are Catholic. Let It Show: Open Wide the Doors to Christ* (Diocese of Buffalo, 1999); *Politics, Law and the Church: An Examination of the Relationship between Catholicism and American Law* (University Press of America, 1996).

Joann Heaney-Hunter is Associate Professor of Theology at St. John's University, New York; she also serves as an advocate for the Diocesan Tribunal, Diocese of Rockville Centre, and as a member of the Diocesan Clergy Sex Abuse Review Board for the Diocese of Brooklyn, New York. Recent publications: "Dancing Together: The Family and the Trinity," "The Family as Reconciling Community," and *Unitas: Preparing for Sacramental Marriage.*

Thomas M. Kelly is Assistant Professor of Theology, Creighton University. Recent publications: "An Integrated Theology of Married Love," *LOGOS, A Journal of Catholic Thought and Culture* (2002); *Theology at the Void: The Retrieval of Experience* (Notre Dame, 2002).

Thomas Knieps-Port le Roi is research/staff member of the International Academy for Marital Spirituality (INTAMS) and editor of *INTAMS Review,* Brussels, Belgium. Recent publications: "Marriage and the Church: Theological Reflections on an Underrated Relationship," in *Celebrating Christian Marriage,* ed. A. Thatcher (T & T Clark–Continuum, 2002); *Die Unvertretbarkeit von Individualität: Der wissenschafts-philosophische Ort der Theologie nach Karl Rahners "Hörer des Wortes"* (Echter, 1995).

Michael G. Lawler is Professor of Theology, Graff Chair in Catholic Theological Studies, and Director of the Center for Marriage and the Family, Creighton University. Recent publications: *Marriage and the Catholic Church: Disputed Questions* (Liturgical Press, 2002); *Family: American and Christian* (Loyola Press, 1998).

Gerard Magill is Professor, Executive Director, and Department Chair in the Center for Health Care Ethics, Health Sciences, Saint Louis University.

Recent publications: *Genetics and Ethics: An Interdisciplinary Study,* editor (Saint Louis University Press, 2004); "The Ethics Weave in Human Genomics, Embryonic Stem Cell Research and Therapeutic Cloning," *Albany Law Review* (2002); "Organizational Ethics in Catholic Health Care," *Christian Bioethics* (2001).

Bruce J. Malina is Professor of Theology, Creighton University. Recent publications: *The Social Gospel of Jesus* (Fortress, 2001); *The New Jerusalem in the Book of Revelation* (Liturgical Press, 2000).

Enda McDonagh is Professor Emeritus of Moral Theology at Pontifical University, Maynooth, Ireland, and Chair on the Governing Body, University of Cork, Ireland. Recent publications: *The Reality of HIV and AIDS* with Ann Smith (Dublin and London, 2003); *Religion and Politics in Ireland,* editor (Dublin, 2003).

John J. O'Keefe is Associate Professor of Theology, Creighton University. Recent publications: "Incorruption, Anti-Origenism, and Incarnation: Eschatology in the Thought of Cyril of Alexandria," *The Theology of Cyril of Alexandria: A Critical Appreciation,* ed. Thomas G. Weinandy and Daniel A. Keating (T & T Clark, 2003); "A Letter that Killeth: Toward a Reassessment of Antiochene Exegesis," *Journal of Early Christian Studies* (2000).

R. R. Reno is Associate Professor of Theology, Creighton University. Recent publications: *In the Ruins of the Church* (Brazos, 2002); *Redemptive Change* (Trinity Press International, 2002).

Gail S. Risch is Lecturer in Theology and Researcher, Center for Marriage and Family, Creighton University. Recent publications: "Problematic Issues in the Early Years of Marriage: Content for Premarital Education," *Journal of Psychology and Theology* (2003); "Sexuality Education and the Catholic Teenager: A Report," *Catholic Education: A Journal of Theory and Practice* (2003).

William P. Roberts is Professor of Theology, University of Dayton. Publications: *Thorny Issues: Theological and Pastoral Reflections* (Nova Science Publishers, 2001); *Marriage: Sacrament of Hope and Challenge* (St. Anthony Messenger Press, 1983); *Partners in Intimacy: Living Christian Marriage Today* co-authored with wife, Challon Roberts (Paulist Press, 1988).

Julie Hanlon Rubio is Assistant Professor of Christian Ethics, Saint Louis University. Recent publications: *A Christian Theology of Marriage and Family* (Paulist, 2003); " 'Three in One Flesh': A Christian Reappraisal of Divorce in Light of Recent Studies," *Journal of Society of Christian Ethics* (2003); "The Dual Vocation of Christian Parents," *Theological Studies* (2002).

Todd A. Salzman is Associate Professor of Theology, Creighton University. Recent publications: *What Are They Saying about Catholic Ethical Method?* (Paulist, 2003); *Method and Catholic Moral Theology,* editor (Creighton University Press, 1999).

Ronald A. Simkins is Associate Professor of Theology and Classical and Near Eastern Studies, Creighton University. Recent publications: "Gender and the Body in Ancient Israel," in *Practical Theology: Perspectives from the Plains,* ed. Michael G. Lawler and Gail S. Risch (Creighton University Press, 2000); "Class and Gender in Early Israel," *Concepts of Class in Ancient Israel,* ed. M. Sneed (Scholars Press, 1999).

Wendy M. Wright is Professor of Theology and holder of the John C. Kenefick Chair in the Humanities, Creighton University. Recent publications: *Heart Speaks to Heart: The Salesian Tradition* (Darton, Longman, Todd/Orbis, 2004); *Seasons of a Family's Life: Cultivating a Contemplative Spirit at Home* (Jossey-Bass, 2003).

Introduction

The purpose of this anthology is to investigate marriage in the Catholic tradition as it originated in scripture, evolved historically and theologically in tradition, and is lived in the twenty-first century. To facilitate this exploration, this book is divided into three parts.

Part One:
Marriage in Scripture and Early Christianity

The first part of this book is about orientation. One of the hallmarks of the Catholic approach to understanding any topic is to begin at the beginning and to contextualize knowledge beneath the illuminating beam of historical inquiry. And so this collection begins, appropriately, with a consideration of marriage in scripture and early Christianity. To borrow an image from a travel journal, the study of the past can provoke an experience akin to arriving unprepared in a new and distant land. Citizens of that land might use words that a person understands — marriage, family, husband, wife — but the way they use these words may be completely unfamiliar. It is sometimes the case that the shock of difference can make a person more open to reception of new ideas that challenge long-held assumptions or, perhaps, provoke reflection for the first time.

The first three essays in this collection deal primarily with difference. Readers are likely to emerge from these texts amazed at the vast distance that separates the current romantic view of marriage from the otherness of our forbears in the faith. We are not like them, yet we come from them. This connection holds us fast, yet the difference is provocative and, perhaps for some, unnerving. The last four essays in this section emphasize difference as well but attempt in some way or other to use difference as a way to explicitly challenge. The discovery that people in our own tradition did not act and think exactly like we act and think can help us to reflect anew about a topic we have thought we understood well. The past, then, is both provocative and evocative.

The priority of difference strikes readers of John Collins's essay in the first paragraph (chap. 1). Collins wishes not only to illustrate the distance that separates us from the understanding of marriage present in the Old Testament; he also wishes to show how it differs considerably from the view of marriage that Jesus himself seems to have held. According to Collins, marriage in the Old Testament was not a sacrament celebrating a bond of love between a man and a woman, but a contractual arrangement designed to uphold and advance economic goods. The contract was arranged by the groom and the person who had authority over the bride — usually the bride's father — but the bride herself had no role in the arrangement. Collins points out that romantic love between a man and a woman was not unknown in the Old Testament; the classic example is the Song of Songs. That kind of love, however, was never the basis for a marriage contract. Perhaps more shocking to modern students of marriage is recognition that key figures in the Old Testament, including Abraham himself, practiced polygamy. Indeed, the Old Testament never condemns or forbids a man from marrying more than one woman.

Although Jesus may have condemned divorce, the Old Testament does not. According to Collins, divorce is clearly allowed and relatively easy to obtain, especially for men. Unlike the marriage contract itself and the practice of polygamy, the prophetic tradition of the Old Testament, in particular Hosea and Malachi, are highly critical of this easy acceptance of divorce. This tradition likely influenced the teachings of Jesus and subsequent Christian teaching about divorce.

In the second essay of the collection, Ronald Simkins also explores questions about marriage in the Old Testament (chap. 2). He, however, is eager to situate the Old Testament understanding of marriage within the broader cultural rubric of gender in ancient Israel. According to Simkins, gender identity was very closely tied to being married. While it is clear that in American culture, our identity as men and women is not tied to our marital status, Simkins argues that maleness and femaleness in ancient Israel were so tied. The key to understanding this close relationship between marriage and gender identity is procreation. Marriage was the social bond that allowed for procreation and the social construction of gender. In this system, the male gender dominates. The bulk of Simkins's essay contextualizes the development of this patriarchal system within the agrarian economy of ancient Israel. Whereas the modern understanding of procreation emphasizes the equal contribution of the man and the woman to the generation of new life, ancient Israelites imaged this generation to be similar to the sowing of seeds in the ground. The male provided the seed and the woman served as the soil. This imagery supported patriarchal views and, according to Simkins, is also the proper context for understanding the creation of male and female in the Genesis narrative.

The third essay in this collection also provokes by underscoring difference. Unlike the first two, the subject here is the New Testament and the question of "non-marriage" (chap. 3). The author, Bruce Malina, deliberately chose the term "non-marriage" to avoid the contemporary implications of the word "celibacy." Malina suggests that thinking of non-marriage in the New Testament as akin to what contemporary Christians mean by celibacy — an other-centered renunciation of marriage for religious reasons — masks the social context and complexity of non-marriage in the ancient world. According to Malina, non-marriage in the New Testament, like celibacy, could be for other-centered reasons, but it could also be for more egocentric reasons. In other words, not all non-married people in the New Testament are trying to make a statement (like John the Baptist, Jesus); some (like Paul and his circle) embrace it for practical reasons related to their particular circumstances. The only way to understand the full impact of these choices is to see them within the social system of the ancient world. These particular contexts and particular choices do not easily lend themselves to universal timeless truths about the meaning of non-marriage.

Like the first three essays, the final four in this first section seek to place marriage in context. In these, however, more of an explicit effort is made to use the fruits of historical inquiry to critique and challenge the present. Thus, Raymond Collins offers a close reading of the literary structure of 1 Corinthians 13 as a means to heighten Christian appreciation of this text (chap. 4). Since the text is already a favorite of modern weddings, Collins works to expose the radical and challenging character of Paul's message about love. Once recovered, that radical teaching can and should challenge all of those attempting to live a Christian marriage to strive to live up to this ideal.

In a similar way Susan Calef argues against the facile use of the Bible in certain Christian circles as a way to uphold uncritical — and in her view unbiblical — views of what does and does not constitute Christian marriage and family (chap. 5). The bulk of Calef's essay summarizes the key prophetic features of Jesus' life and ministry. Jesus preached a prophetic message about the reign of God, about the requirement to work for justice, to share one's possessions, to pray like it mattered, to have concern for the afflicted, and to have fellowship with the outcast. For Calef, this witness of Jesus should challenge Christian marriage and family life to move beyond complacent acceptance of the norms of contemporary culture. In other words, married and familied Christians are called to nothing less than to live according to the radical witness of Jesus himself.

Lisa Cahill's essay also seeks to challenge (chap. 6). Adopting a more feminist critique than does Calef, Cahill begins by acknowledging the real changes for the good that have occurred in the gender roles of married men and women. The changes, she explains, have even been formally incorporated into Catholic teaching. It is no longer desirable or appropriate to view the man as the dominant partner in a marital relationship. Cahill goes on to consider the complexity of the biblical witness, which does not unambiguously support the changes in marital relations that have occurred in the modern world. What are we to do with the texts suggesting women are not equal and should be submissive to their husbands, seeming to contradict the more modern view? Unlike Collins's and Calef's essays, which exploit the radical core of the biblical witness to challenge married Christians to embrace a deeper truth, Cahill uses modern interpretive methods to show how biblical teaching can remain even in a vastly changed social context.

Finally, John O'Keefe, in a way similar to Cahill and reminiscent of Malina, seeks to explain the historical tendency of the Roman Catholic

Church to view celibacy as a higher calling than marriage (chap. 7). O'Keefe contextualizes the privileging of celibacy in the world of nascent Christian monasticism and of ancient ascetical theories that, in the extreme, linked sexuality with the perpetuation of sin. Although marriage has generally been affirmed by the church as a positive good, it has generally been seen as a lesser good than celibacy precisely because of the church's ambivalent attitude toward sexuality. Finally, O'Keefe suggests that the cultural circumstances that produced the view that celibacy was superior have disappeared, paving the way for a more robust affirmation of the goodness of marriage than has previously been possible in the church.

Part Two:
Marriage and Tradition

Reflection on marriage in light of the Catholic theological tradition has never been richer than it is today. Lay and ordained people have delved into the intricacies of married life and love and have brought these realities into serious and thoughtful dialogue with the Catholic tradition. For many centuries a theology of marriage has been construed in idealized language abstracted from human experience that was more theological than marital. The contemporary conversation between marriage and the Catholic tradition attempts to bring the lived reality of marital life and love to bear upon a tradition that has not always respected it for what it is — a lifelong call to holiness through the asceticism of authentic relationship. The following essays grouped under the title "Marriage and Tradition" substantively engage the Catholic tradition and explore foundational theological concepts associated with marriage and sacrament, both affirming the tradition and challenging it to move toward a fuller theology of marriage. Arguing from tradition grounded in human experience, these essays make for a rich conversation that, far from being over, is just beginning.

In the first essay, Timothy Buckley, C.S.S.R., concentrates on the centrality of the marriage bond in traditional Catholic teaching (chap. 8). One of the difficulties in addressing this topic is the fact that the actual bond of marriage is not carefully or clearly defined in contemporary terms. Essentially the bond is a relationship that must inhere in the person to be real. In this sense, the bond is an *ontological* reality, something that deeply affects both the substance and direction of one's being. If that is so, how can the marriage bond be said to exist when, through the free consent of two people, it is decidedly ended? This article takes a fascinating look at the annulment process, perceptions of divorce and relationality according to Catholic theology, and the ongoing tension between a medieval frame of reference and a very contemporary problem — the ending of Catholic marriages and the church theology in place to deal with this reality.

In the second essay, William Roberts delineates the bias against marriage in the traditional theology of the Catholic Church with regard to vocations and states of life (chap. 9). The purpose of his essay is to reflect on Christian marriage as an authentic divine calling that is neither superior nor inferior to the complementary states of life of other Christian vocations. He begins in the theology of calling or vocation and works to understand what a call from God is and how one can discern it properly. He then grounds this call to marriage in our baptismal vows — specifically in our participation in Trinitarian life, dying to ourselves and rising to Christ — and relating our marital commitment toward the community in which we live. Marriage, according to Roberts, is an authentic and loving way to respond to God's love in the context of community. It is also an avenue to live out the vows of poverty, chastity, and obedience in ways that while not "traditional" are, nevertheless, authentic and life-giving.

In the third essay, Bernard Cooke illustrates the dynamic development related to the theology of marriage between the writing of *Casti Connubii* (1930) and *Gaudium et Spes* (1965) (chap. 10). Pope Pius XI's encyclical *Casti Connubii* was written with the purpose of reiterating, amid threats to traditional views of Christian marriage, the teaching that had been passed down unchanged — and considered unchangeable — for decades. This encyclical reflects the church's conflict with the state over which set of laws should govern marriage — ecclesiastical or civil. Further, its positions on women working outside the home, the primacy of the male gender within the marriage, and the absolute prohibition on all forms of birth control would markedly change both in content and tone with *Gaudium et Spes*.

The fourth essay, by Todd Salzman, explores the philosophical and theological perspectives on friendship, or *philia* (chap. 11). What is the relationship between *philia* and sacrament and how can Christian marriage be understood as the greatest friendship? Taking as his point of departure Aristotle's understanding of friendship in the *Nicomachean Ethics*, Salzman argues Christian ideas of friendship are qualitatively superior. Charting the development of Christian *philia* from Augustine through Aelred of Rievaulx and Thomas Aquinas, he maintains that *philia*, properly understood, is the most complete form of human-human love and God-human love. This has important consequences for traditional understandings of Christian marriage.

The fifth essay, by Joann Heaney-Hunter, argues toward a eucharistic spirituality of family (chap. 12). Heaney-Hunter understands Eucharist as partaking of the body of Christ within the body of Christ and so essentially a call to a life of sharing and service. Such an understanding of married life and love will emphasize the covenant aspect of familial relations. Covenant begins when a couple makes an unconditional commitment to each other. But other dimensions of family life are critical as well. For example, brokenness forms a significant element of contemporary family life — rising and dying are part of the family life cycle. Ultimately for Heaney-Hunter a joining of lives, of which sharing food is a metaphor, is the point where Eucharist and family intersect.

In the sixth essay, Thomas Knieps-Port le Roi argues that marriage in the Catholic tradition ought to have an ecclesial status and function (chap. 13). He does this by relating marriage not to celibacy but to the ordained ministry in the church. What are the ecclesiological implications of the sacrament of marriage? Knieps-Port le Roi maintains that sacramental marriage confers on the spouses a proper and true ministry that is not part of or subject to, but complementary to, hierarchical ministry. He will promote this view by concentrating on an understanding of church as sacrament for salvation.

In the final essay in this section, Thomas Kelly argues that in order to understand the mission of the laity in the context of church, one must understand it in terms of marriage—the primary vocation of the vast majority of laypeople (chap. 14). In order to understand that vocation, one must look carefully at the way marriage has been understood as a sacrament in traditional church teachings. What becomes evident is a serious contradiction between an active social mission for the family encouraged by the church and a passive notion of sacrament. Kelly suggests a new way of thinking about the sacrament of marriage that enables laypeople to envision the family as a transforming force in our society. With such an understanding, the sacrament of marriage and the reality of family can become the primary mode through which Catholic social thought encounters the world.

Part Three:
Marriage and Experience

Drawing from biblical resources and theological insights, the final part reflects on the lived experiences of cohabiting, engaged, and married couples in the twenty-first century. In so doing, these essays address many pressing issues that confront, challenge, nurture, sustain, and deepen the marital vocation. A growing phenomenon in society as well as the Catholic Church is the reality of cohabitation. Cohabitation is defined as couples who live together and share all aspects of the marital life including sexual relations, but who are not yet married. Studies indicate that between 50 and 80 percent of engaged Catholic couples cohabit. As a result, cohabitation and its implications for the marital relationship are a crucial consideration theologically and pastorally. In the first essay, Gail Risch, while recognizing the link between cohabitation and subsequent marital instability and higher rates of divorce documented by social scientists, ecclesial documents, and theologians, questions these conclusions based on more recent sociological scientific studies (chap. 15). In so doing, Risch demonstrates that this correlation is weakening and influences other than cohabitation, such as whether or not the couple intends to marry, their religious commitment, socioeconomic and educational levels, and family background, are more indicative of marital stability.

Once a couple becomes engaged and decides to marry, the period of marriage preparation is crucial for deepening one's personal, relational, and theological understanding of the marital vocation. Gregory Faulhaber explores these facets of immediate marital preparation (chap. 16). This preparation includes open and honest dialogue and assessment of the couple's understanding of love, commitment, sexuality, and marriage as sacrament. This period of preparation can solidify the commitment and resolve between the couple, but it can also make it evident that two people are not compatible for a lifelong commitment in the sacrament of marriage. Either way, the process of marriage preparation is an essential pastoral ministry within the church.

An essential component of marital preparation is to understand the meaning and nature of marital love. Enda McDonagh's essay explores the nature of Christian marital love in terms of vulnerability (chap. 17). Vulnerability is the painful openness to hurt that is a potential aspect of all relationships, human and divine. He applies this concept of vulnerability to friendship and marital sexuality. In both cases, there is a dialogical tension between total self-giving and separation. McDonagh argues that it is in and through the growth, development, and deepening of human relationships, in particular the marital relationship, that we further realize the meaning of vulnerability and our ability to embrace it as a lived reality.

Expanding vulnerability from spouses to family, Wendy Wright addresses family spirituality (chap. 18). The point of departure for her reflections is human experience. Spirituality is grounded in experience, guided by the spirit, and lived in community. One of the most sacred of these communities is the family, referred to frequently as the "domestic church." The domestic church is a sacred reality whereby we participate in, and strive to further realize, God's transforming love. It is within this most intimate, broken, and loving community that we learn what it truly means to be a disciple of Christ.

Family spirituality faces innumerable challenges in contemporary society, not least of which is balancing one's commitment to spouse and children as well as to the broader community, both of which are essential to the meaning and nature of Christian discipleship. In her essay, Julie Hanlon Rubio addresses this challenge in what she refers to as the dual vocation of Christian parenting; the dual vocations are as parent/spouse and as a contributor to the social common good (chap. 19). She provides scriptural and theological foundations validating both vocations as intrinsic to discipleship, highlights the challenges of living out this dual vocation, and provides creative approaches to fulfilling them.

As science, technology, and medicine develop, these impact the very nature of marriage in terms of its duration and longevity. In her essay, Aldegonde Brenninkmeijer-Werhahn investigates the growing phenomenon of aging marital relationships (chap. 20). These relationships bring with them both gift and blessing as well as pastoral challenges. In terms of the former, couples who celebrate their silver, or even golden anniversary, have a wealth of knowledge, insight, and understanding of a shared life of commitment, which can enlighten younger generations on the meaning and nature of marriage. On the other hand, living longer also creates pastoral challenges such as the complex dynamics of second and third marriages, and the emotional, psychological, relational, and physiological difficulties that accompany an aging couple and those who care for them. Brenninkmeijer-Werhahn argues that we must develop a theology of, and for, the aging to respond to this reality.

While secular society poses many challenges for Christian married couples, one in particular has profound implications on the meaning and nature of marriage as sacrament — the reality of baptized non-practicing Catholics. Through social and theological analyses, Florence Caffrey Bourg investigates this phenomenon and provides insight into how we can live with the tension between two realities; on the one hand, the need to uphold the meaning and integrity of marriage as sacrament, which implies that spouses have an active, living faith; on the other hand, the recognition that there are a large number of non-practicing Catholics who desire a sacramental Catholic marriage, and yet fall short of fully living marriage as a sacrament juridically defined (chap. 21). Bourg proposes a pastoral response to this challenge and comes to the conclusion that these marriages are still sacramental and need to be recognized as such.

Not only do marriages between non-practicing Catholics pose pastoral and sacramental theological challenges, but so too interchurch marriages, i.e., marriages between a Catholic and a Christian from a Protestant denomination. Michael Lawler explores both the theological (e.g., the issue of the non-Catholic spouse participating in Eucharist) and pastoral challenges of such marriages (chap. 22). Lawler sees in the interchurch couple the hopes, dreams, and struggles to become a "coupled-we," and notes the close parallels between this lived reality and the struggles to create unity between various Christian churches. Interchurch marriages can serve as a model and example in the journey toward Christian unity.

The next essay is a poignant reflection on the experiential challenges of an interreligious marriage. On the occasion of his daughter's bat mitzvah, R. Reno, a Christian, details some of the marital and familial challenges in his own marriage to Juliana, a Jew (chap. 23). The reflections are structured around his daughter Rachel's bat mitzvah and her recitation in Hebrew of the Ten Commandments. This essay highlights the tension between religious traditions, but more so, God's binding charity that permeates family bonds facilitating and creating unity and challenging the all too frequent disunity caused by different religious faiths.

The final essay in this section, by Gerard Magill, uses a sacramentality of marriage as a foundation for Catholic ethics in general and for health care ethics in particular (chap. 24). Arguing in three parts, Magill first discusses the shared experience of life and love between wife and husband in the sacramental meaning of marriage. He then illustrates how this reality is a helpful methodological and hermeneutical tool for approaching Catholic health care ethics. The final section uses this conceptual tool and applies it directly to the issue of surrogate parenthood for infertile couples to rescue abandoned frozen embryos.

While all the authors in this collection offer unique theological and pastoral perspectives, reflections, and nuances for understanding the meaning and nature of marriage in the Catholic tradition, what binds them is the desire to acknowledge, honor, and celebrate Michael G. Lawler's thirty-five years dedicated to the theological and pastoral study of marriage in the Catholic tradition. Through his teaching, scholarship — including over 20 books and over 125 scholarly articles — and the Center for Marriage and Family at Creighton University of which he is the current director, Lawler has been an inspiration for students and scholars alike. He has had a profound impact on the Catholic tradition's ongoing theological understanding of marriage and has substantially influenced that understanding both within the theological community and among the American bishops, priests, and laypeople. Not only is he a remarkable scholar, but he also models the vocation of discipleship in a genuine spirit of generosity and friendship with his family, friends, and colleagues. For these gifts, we thank Michael and dedicate this book to him.

Part One

MARRIAGE IN SCRIPTURE AND EARLY CHRISTIANITY

Chapter I

Marriage in the Old Testament

John J. Collins

From the beginning of creation "God made them male and female." "For this reason a man shall leave his father and mother and be joined to his wife, and the two shall become one flesh." So they are no longer two, but one flesh. Therefore what God has joined together, let no one separate.[1]

These words of Jesus in response to the Pharisees in the Gospel of Mark are often assumed to reflect the normative biblical view of marriage. But despite the allusions to the creation stories, in the beginning it was not so. Like most things in life, the understanding of marriage changed over time. Marriage in ancient Israel, as reflected in the Old Testament, was quite different from what it would later become in Christianity.

Marriage as Contract

Unlike Christian marriage, in ancient Israel the union of man and wife was not considered a sacrament and was not sanctified by a cultic act. Rather it was a contract to which the man and woman were parties, and members of the community were witnesses.[2] Numerous written marriage contracts survive from ancient Babylon. No actual contracts are preserved in the Bible, but we have some Jewish marriage contracts on papyri from Elephantine in the south of Egypt, where there was a Jewish garrison community in the fifth century B.C.E.[3] We also have some Jewish marriage contracts from the early second century C.E., which were found near the Dead Sea.[4] Throughout most of the biblical period, most people would not have had written contracts, but the terms of the agreement would be recited orally. Deuteronomy 24:1, 3 mentions a certificate of divorce. The first mention of a written marriage contract is in Tobit 7:13, where the bride's father is said to write out a marriage contract "according to the decree of the law of Moses," although there is no law about marriage contracts in the Torah as we know it.[5]

Surprisingly, there are no laws in the Old Testament that deal directly with marriage or divorce. The only description of a marriage ceremony is the one in Tobit. We have some more explicit documents from other parts of the ancient Near East. An Assyrian law describes the marriage ceremony of a woman who has been a concubine as follows:

If a man intends to veil his concubine, he shall assemble five or six of his comrades, and he shall veil her in their presence, he shall declare: "she is my wife"; she is his wife. A concubine who is not veiled in the presence of people, whose husband did not declare, "she is my wife," she is not a wife, she is indeed a concubine.[6]

The ceremony may have been different if the woman was not a concubine, and of course custom may have been different in Israel. Nonetheless, this brief passage illustrates the core of the marriage ceremony in the ancient Near East (and indeed at other times and places too): a solemn declaration in the presence of witnesses.

The Jewish marriage contracts from Elephantine typically show four steps in the constitution of a marriage:

1. The groom requests the hand of the bride from the person in authority over her, normally her father, or the master in the case of a slave girl.

2. He declares solemnly, "She is my wife and I am her husband." The formula often concludes with the words "from this day and forever." This does not, however, mean that the marriage is indissoluble, as the contract makes provision for divorce. The formula only means that the marriage is not envisioned as a temporary arrangement. It is open-ended.

3. The groom pays a *mohar,* or "bride price," to the person in authority over the bride.

4. The contract is drawn up. It specifies the contents of the bride's dowry, specifies what will happen in the event of divorce, and names the witnesses.

The contract was formally an agreement between the groom and the person with authority over the bride. The extant contracts contain no expression of the bride's assent, although it must have been required. In many cases, the bride would have been very young. The Talmud praises the man who arranges his children's marriage just before they attain puberty. That way it was easier to ensure that girls were virgins when they married. But even when the bride was mature, as is the case in at least one contract from Elephantine, the contract was still made with her father.

Modern Western people are likely to be somewhat scandalized by the phenomenon of the *mohar,* or "bride price," as it gives the impression that the groom is buying the wife.[7] (The *mohar* is mentioned in Gen. 34:12; Exod. 22:16; 1 Sam. 18:25; Jacob has to work for his wives in Gen. 29). That impression may be strengthened by the tenth commandment of the Decalogue in Exodus 20:17, which lists the neighbor's wife with his house, male or female slaves, ox, ass, and anything that belongs to him. Most scholars agree, however, that it would be too simple to describe this transaction as a purchase. Originally, it seems that the *mohar* was intended to compensate the father or master for the transfer of authority over the bride. In the Elephantine contracts, the *mohar* is added to the dowry and given to the woman, as a kind of trust fund, which would be returned to her in the event of divorce. By rabbinic times, the groom did not actually have to pay the *mohar,* but only to promise it, and it became payable in the event of divorce. There is no clear evidence of dowries in the biblical corpus.[8] The parents of the bride, however, sometimes gave her presents. When Tobias marries Sarah, her father gives him half of his possessions. At least in the later period, then, the *mohar* was converted into a security deposit for the woman in the event of divorce.

The importance of marriage contracts was recognized from early times in the ancient Near East. The Code of Hammurabi, from the eighteenth century B.C.E., declares: "if a man acquired a wife, but did not draw up the contracts for her, that woman is no wife" (paragraph 128). The Laws of Eshnunna, from around the same time, insist that the status of the wife depends on the existence of a formal contract between the husband and the wife's parents. Cohabitation did not constitute marriage. There is no direct evidence for marriage contracts in the preexilic period in Israel or Judah, although there is evidence for bills of divorce (Deut. 24:1, 3; Isa. 50:1; Jer. 3:8). Jeremiah 32:8–12 refers to a bill of sale. Writing, however, may have become reasonably widespread only in the seventh century B.C.E. or thereabouts. Prior to that, and also subsequently for many people, contracts may have been enacted orally. The prophet Hosea, who uses marriage and divorce as metaphors for the relation between Israel and Yahweh, presupposes the same formula for divorce that we find in the Elephantine papyri: "You are not my wife, and I am not your husband" (compare Hos. 2:2). When the prophet remarries in chapter 3, he pays fifteen shekels of silver, and measures of barley and wine, as a *mohar.* He insists that his wife not have intercourse with any other man. This is also a common provision in the contracts. Hosea makes no mention of a written contract, but he clearly presupposes a contractual view of marriage. By the time we get to the book of Tobit in the Hellenistic period, the written contract appears to be standard.

In one of the contracts from Elephantine, the couple already has a child when the contract is drawn up. In Egypt, in the Hellenistic period "unwritten marriages" were recognized. In many cases, couples drew up contracts only when a child was born, in order to establish the property rights. The Mishnah (second century C.E.) says that a woman is acquired in three ways, through "money, writ and intercourse" (*m. Kiddushin* 3:1). Normally all three were required, but it is likely that some people did not formalize their marriages by the written contract.

The marriage contracts embody a highly pragmatic, unsentimental view of marriage. Romantic love was not unknown in ancient Israel. It finds wonderful expression in the Canticle of Canticles. But it is not the basis of any marriage contract. The primary concern in these documents is to clarify the expectations of both parties and to make provision for the wife in the event of divorce. This kind of practical concern helps explain some other features of biblical law that may seem strange to the modern reader. According to Deuteronomy 22:28–29: "If a man meets a virgin who is not engaged, and seizes her and lies with her, and they are caught in the act, the man who lay with her shall give fifty shekels of silver to the young woman's father, and she shall become his wife. Because he violated her he shall not be permitted to divorce her as long as he lives." A modern reader might wonder whether the young woman would want to be married to her rapist. But a woman who had been raped might find it difficult to find another husband. The point of the law is that the rapist must provide for her. Again, the so-called "levirate law" in Deuteronomy 25:1–10 provides that if a man dies without an heir, his brother is supposed to marry his widow and raise up an heir for him. Whether he finds her attractive is not an issue; the needs of the family take precedence. Similar reasoning underlies the frequent insistence that people should marry within their tribe or clan (that is, marry people who are relatives, but who do not belong to the immediate family). The book of Numbers legislates that "every daughter who possesses an inheritance in any tribe of the Israelites shall marry one from the clan of her father's tribe, so that all Israelites may continue to possess their ancestral inheritance" (Num. 36:8). Even in the book of Tobit, which is one of the latest books in the Old Testament, Tobit tells his son, Tobias, to marry within his tribe. Tobias marries his cousin, Sarah, an only child. The angel Raphael, who accompanies Tobit, explains the situation to him: "He [her father, Raguel] has no male heir and no daughter except Sarah only, and you, as next of kin to her, have before all other men a hereditary claim on her. Also it is right for you to inherit her father's possessions. Moreover, the girl is sensible, brave and very beautiful, and her father is a good man" (Tob. 6:12). The property must be kept in the family. If the woman was beautiful, that was a bonus. The basis of the relationship was obligation to one's family and clan. The primacy of family obligations is also very much in evidence in the story of Ruth.

Polygamy

One of the ways in which Old Testament marriage differs most clearly from its Christian counterpart is that there is no requirement of monogamy. When Abraham's wife, Sarah, fails to produce an heir, she gives him her servant maid Hagar, and he has relations with her. Jacob marries two sisters, each of whom gives him her maid (Gen. 29:15–30; 30:1–9). Polygamy was practiced throughout the biblical period. Solomon is blamed for taking foreign wives, but this is not a condemnation of polygamy as such. It is often supposed that polygamy was practiced only by the wealthy, such as the Herodian family, who could afford to support several wives, but we do not actually know how widely it was practiced. The Mishnah allows a man to have as many as five wives if he could afford it, and permitted eighteen for kings. These numbers, of course, are theoretical and not reflective of actual practice. The practice was still known, however, in the time of Ben Sira in the early second century B.C.E. (Sir. 37:11). Recently new light was shed on the subject by a papyrus from the early second century C.E., found near the Dead Sea, in which two women dispute the inheritance of a dead man, each claiming that he was her husband, but with no mention of divorce. In early times, polygamy may have been encouraged by the nature of agrarian life, which needed plenty of hands for manual labor. This would not have been a factor in Second Temple Judaism. There were obvious problems with the practice. Jealousy between wives is a common problem (see already the wives of Jacob in Gen. 30:1). Deuteronomy legislates to protect the rights of the children of a wife less favored (Deut. 21:15–17). The women in the papyrus from the Dead Sea were involved in litigation over the husband's estate. Nonetheless, the Jewish historian Josephus, writing at the end of the first century C.E., states that "it is our ancestral custom that a man may have several wives at the same time."[9] Polygamy is never forbidden in the Old Testament.

Divorce

The Old Testament also differs from Catholic (though not from Protestant) tradition in its acceptance of divorce. The inference drawn by Jesus, that what God has joined together no one should take asunder, was seldom drawn in ancient Israel or Judah, and then only in the postexilic period. Most people did not think of marriage as a union effected by God, but as a contract between two human beings.

There is no legislation in the Bible that deals directly with divorce, just as there is none that deals directly with marriage.

The passage most often cited in connection with divorce is Deuteronomy 24:1–4. This law concerns the case of a woman who has been divorced and remarried. The point of the law is that she may not then return to her first husband. The broader significance of this passage arises from the incidental account of how the divorce comes about: "Suppose a man enters into marriage with a woman, but she does not please him because he finds something objectionable about her, and so he writes her a certificate of divorce, puts it in her hand, and sends her out of his house...." In the second case, the reference to "something objectionable" is dropped: "Then suppose the second man dislikes her, writes her a bill of divorce...and sends her out of his house." The phrase "dislikes her" (NRSV) is more appropriately translated as "repudiates her." The right of a man to divorce his wife is clearly assumed. The question is whether this right applies only in certain circumstances (if he finds "something objectionable" in her) or whether he can divorce her at will.

The contracts from Elephantine require no reason for divorce. They simply specify that "tomorrow or another day" if X should stand up in the congregation and say "I hate my wife/husband," certain financial obligations are entailed. There were, however, some things that would lead directly to divorce. One was adultery on the part of the wife. Oddly enough, this is not usually mentioned in the Babylonian contracts; it is simply assumed. Both the Babylonian and the biblical laws usually impose a death penalty for adultery (see, for example, Deut. 22:22). The contracts from Elephantine do not mention a death penalty. They simply say that adultery is grounds for divorce. Also Proverbs 6:32–35 assumes that the penalty for divorce was vengeance on the part of the wronged husband, who had the option of accepting or refusing monetary compensation. The contracts do not prohibit extramarital intercourse by the husband, but some specify that he must not take a second wife. The Elephantine contracts are exceptional in that the wife may initiate divorce as well as the husband. Usually, in Jewish tradition, that right is reserved to the husband. The contracts do not, however, envisage no-fault divorce. If the husband initiated the proceedings, he normally had to pay "divorce money" or at least forfeit the *mohar* and return any dowry the wife had brought with her. If the wife were deemed to be at fault, she could take what she had brought with her, but she would forfeit the *mohar* and any other compensation. In any case, she would have to leave the home, which was the property of the husband. The idea that a guilty wife could be divorced without compensation is found already in the Code of Hammurabi in the eighteenth century B.C.E.

The debate about justification for divorce in the Jewish tradition has focused on the phrase "something objectionable" in Deuteronomy 24. The Hebrew phrase *'erwat dabar* might be translated more accurately as "something indecent," and it most probably implies sexual misconduct. In later tradition, however, the range of the phrase was expanded. There was a debate on the subject in the first century B.C.E. between the followers of Hillel and those of Shammai. The Shammaites argued that divorce was justified only in the case of adultery. (Compare the saying of Jesus in Matt. 19:9.) The Hillelites, however, argued that divorce was justified "even if she spoiled a dish for him" (*m. Git.* 9–10). Rabbi Akiba went further: "Even if he found another fairer than her," pointing to the phrase, "she does not please him." The Mishnah allows that "a wife that transgresses the Law of Moses and Jewish custom" may be put away without her *ketubah* (the *mohar* and dowry). Violating Jewish custom is interpreted as "if she goes out with her hair unbound, or spins in the street, or speaks with any man" (*m. Ketub.* 7:6).

A Prophetic Critique of Divorce

Ancient Israelite society was patriarchal. The word for husband (*ba' al*) also means "lord" (and is also the name of a Canaanite god). It is generally accepted that a husband has a right to have extramarital sex. (See, for example, the story of the patriarch Judah in Gen. 38.) The right to divorce was also heavily weighted in the husband's interest. Only rarely in the Old Testament is a voice raised in protest against these cultural assumptions.

The first protest is found in the prophet Hosea, in the eighth century B.C.E. Hosea uses the metaphor of marriage between Yahweh and Israel to depict the covenantal relationship. (The Hebrew word *berith* can mean either covenant or contract.) Israel is the adulterous wife. Hosea's depiction of how she should be treated is chilling: "I will strip her naked and make her as in the day she was born, and make her like a wilderness, and turn her into a parched land and kill her with thirst" (Hos. 2:3). He is speaking of how God would treat Israel when the Assyrians invaded. The passage should not be taken as prescriptive, although it builds on cultural assumptions about how an adulterous woman should be treated (but there is no other evidence that unfaithful wives were ever stripped naked). While Hosea, in chapter 2, portrays Yahweh as a jealous husband, he casts a different light on sexual politics in chapter 4: "I will not punish your daughters when they play the whore, nor your daughters-in-law when they commit adultery; for the men themselves go aside with whores, and sacrifice with temple prostitutes." Hosea does not address the right of men to divorce their wives, but he does object to the double standard that was pervasive in patriarchal societies. If it is wrong for women to be adulterous, it is also wrong for men.

The only figure in the Old Testament who protests against the idea of divorce is the prophet we know as Malachi. "Malachi" refers to the last four chapters (three in Hebrew) in the Minor Prophets. "Malachi" means "my messenger" and is used in that sense in Malachi 3:1. It was not a proper name, but was used as the heading for the words of an anonymous prophet.

"Malachi" addresses the subject of divorce in Malachi 2:13–16. The passage is translated as follows in the NRSV:

> And this you do as well: You cover the Lord's altar with tears, with weeping and groaning because he no longer regards the offering or accepts it with favor at your hand. You ask, "Why does he not?" Because the Lord was a witness between you and the wife of your youth, to whom you have been faithless, though she is your companion and your wife by covenant. Did not one God make her? [or: has he not made one?] Both flesh and spirit are his. And what does the one God desire? Godly offspring. So look to yourselves, and do not let anyone be faithless to the wife of his youth. For I hate divorce, says the Lord, the God of Israel, and covering one's garment with violence, says the Lord of hosts. So take heed to yourselves and do not be faithless.

This passage bristles with problems, and we cannot attempt a full discussion here.[10] It follows on another passage where the prophet complains that Judah has been faithless and "married the daughter of a foreign god." This is probably a reference to marrying foreign women, who worshiped other gods, a problem highlighted in the book of Ezra. The passage that immediately concerns us relates to the divorce of "the wife of your youth."

In Proverbs 2:17 it is the "strange woman" who "forsakes the partner of her youth and forgets the covenant of her god." Malachi breaks with tradition by putting the blame on the man rather than on the woman and by questioning the justification of divorce.

In view of the reference to "the daughter of a foreign god" in the preceding passage, it is often argued that the prophet was condemning people for divorcing their Jewish wives and marrying foreign women. There is no evidence that this is the case. If it were, we should expect the prophet to mention divorce first, before the marriage to the daughter of a foreign god, since the divorces would have to precede the idolatrous marriages. Malachi does not call for the divorce of the daughter of the foreign god. Idolatry and divorce are two instances of faithless behavior, but they are not one and the same.

The ringing phrase "I hate divorce" is also problematic. The word "hate" (Hebrew *sane'*) is the word that is normally used in divorce formulae in the sense of "repudiate." The form of the word that appears in Malachi is not the first-person singular, as the NRSV would suggest, but is a participle. The verse should be translated "for one hates (= repudiates), sends away, and covers his garment with violence." This does not actually change the sense of the passage all that much. Malachi is still condemning divorce as unjust and violent.

A key to the passage is found in Malachi 2:15. The preferable translation is the alternative offered by the NRSV: "has he [God] not made one?" The reference is to Genesis 2:24, which says that man and wife become "one flesh." The remainder of the verse, "and what does one seek? Godly offspring," can also be read in light of Genesis. In Genesis 1:28, the only mission given to the primal couple is to "be fruitful and multiply and fill the earth." On this reading, Malachi protests that the purpose of marriage is to have godly children. Divorce does not contribute to that goal, any more than does idolatry (marrying the daughter of a foreign god). Fidelity to "the wife of one's youth" is the corollary of fidelity to Yahweh. Here for the first time in the biblical tradition, marriage seems to take on a sacred character, insofar as Yahweh is the witness to the wedding. The contract becomes a covenant, because it involves the Lord. This text is a milestone in the development of the biblical understanding of marriage. It is the first biblical text that implies that "what God has joined together, no man should put asunder."

So radically did Malachi break with tradition that some scribes found the text impossible to accept. Some Greek manuscripts read instead "but if you hate and send away...." Others read an imperative: "but if you hate, send away..."—in effect, encouraging divorce.[11] This reading is difficult to reconcile with the rest of the verse ("covering one's garment with violence"), but the right to divorce was so deeply ingrained in Judean tradition that the scribes felt that the text could not condemn it.

Jesus in Context

Malachi is obviously important as background for the teaching of Jesus. It is not the only relevant background, however. Malachi was written sometime in the Persian period, probably in the fifth century B.C.E. Later in the Second Temple period, in the second and first centuries B.C.E., there arose a movement toward stricter interpretation of the scriptures, especially in matters of purity. A major witness to this trend is found in the Dead Sea Scrolls. A sectarian rulebook from the first century B.C.E., known as the Damascus Document, or CD, accuses people of fornication for "taking two wives in their lifetime, whereas the principle of creation is, male and female he created them" (CD 4:20–21). Scholars dispute the exact meaning of this text. It certainly forbids polygamy, and it apparently also forbids a second marriage while the first wife is alive. It does not explicitly address the question of divorce, but the attraction of divorce would be diminished if remarriage were not permitted. This text from the Dead Sea Scrolls shows that traditional views of marriage were being disputed around the turn of the era.

The teaching of Jesus in Mark 10, then, went very much against Jewish tradition, even if it was not entirely without precedent. As in the case of Malachi, some scribes found such a break with tradition incredible. In the parallel passage in Matthew 19:3–9, the statement that whoever divorces his wife and marries another is qualified: "except for unchastity." The unconditional prohibition of divorce recorded by Mark was too hard a saying to accept, even in a word of the Lord.

Questions for Discussion

1. What were the typical steps in the constitution of a marriage in ancient Israel?

2. What was the *mohar,* or bride price?

3. In what circumstances was divorce justified?

4. What objections can be raised against polygamy and divorce on the basis of the biblical record?

Chapter 2

Marriage and Gender
in the Old Testament

Ronald A. Simkins

Introduction

Marriage in the Old Testament is the expression of the gender relationship between men and women in ancient Israel. What it meant to be a man and a woman was realized by being a husband and wife. What ties marriage and gender together in ancient Israel is procreation. Gender refers to the socially recognized behavior of men and women as defined by the role of each in procreation, whereas marriage is the socially recognized arena in which procreation should take place. Because the relationship between the husband and the wife, and between Israelite men and women in general, is characterized by a gender asymmetry in which the husband dominates his wife, Israelite marriage and gender are usually labeled as patriarchal. But this designation begs a number of significant questions:[1] Given that most societies manifest some form of male domination, in what ways was the practice of Israelite marriage patriarchal? Or, in what ways and under what circumstances did an Israelite husband dominate his wife? At the core of understanding Israelite patriarchy and the Israelites' subordination of women, however, is the fundamental question: How did the Israelites' understanding of procreation shape their understanding of gender and their practice of marriage?

The Bible unfortunately gives little attention to the Israelites' understanding of procreation. Moreover, the Bible presents only a fragmentary, and sometimes even a contradictory, view of marriage and the family in ancient Israel. Nevertheless, a late Hellenistic text that places procreation in the context of marriage provides a suggestive model for interpreting gender and marriage in the Old Testament:

> My child, keep sound the bloom of your youth,
>   and do not give your strength to strangers.
> Seek a fertile field within the whole plain,
>   and sow it with your own seed, trusting in your fine stock.
> So your offspring will prosper,
>   and, having confidence in their good descent, will grow great.

> (Sir. 26:19–21)

This text uses agriculture as a metaphor for procreation to define the roles of the husband and the wife in marriage. The husband is like a farmer who sows seed in a field; the wife is like a fertile field that receives and nurtures seed so that it sprouts and matures.

Is this view of procreation also found in the earlier texts of the Old Testament? Although not stated so explicitly, this view is reflected in the common Hebrew usage of *zera'*, which is usually translated "seed," but when used in reference to a male it may refer to either semen or the offspring produced from semen. Moreover, the biblical writers' frequent use of creation metaphors drawn from their experiences with agriculture and the birth process (see, for example, Ps. 139:13–15; Job 10:8–11; Isa. 45:8; Amos 9:15) suggests that they perceived a metaphorical connection between agriculture and procreation.[2] In this essay I will argue that the Israelites understood the process of procreation in terms of agriculture, and that this metaphor shaped their understanding of gender and their practice of marriage.

Procreation and Agriculture in the Yahwist Creation Myth

The relationship between marriage and gender in the Old Testament is expressed most fully in the Yahwist creation myth in Genesis 2:4b–3:24. The narrative begins with God's acts of creation that culminate with the institution of marriage; the gendered roles of the husband and the wife are defined in the denouement of the story. Through the four-part structure of the myth and the development of two gendered word-pairs, the Yahwist creation myth defines marriage and gender in terms of the relationship between procreation and agriculture: the man (*'adam*) is born from the arable land (*'adamah*) (2:4b–17); the man is transformed into a husband (*'ish*) and his wife (*'ishshah*) is made from him (2:18–24); the married couple gain sexual awareness through eating the fruit of knowledge (2:25–3:7); as a result of their sexual awareness, the wife (*'ishshah*) will bear children[3] and the man (*'adam*) will work the arable land (*'adamah*) (3:8–23).

The myth begins with the creation of man. In order to provide someone to work the land and thereby bring vegetation to the dry, barren earth, Yahweh God formed man (*'adam*) from the arable land (*'adamah*). This wordplay — presented as male and female forms of the same word — attests to the man's relationship to the land. The man is dependent upon the arable land from which he was taken, and in the end he will return to the land. Yet the land is dependent upon the man if it is to be anything more than a barren desert. The land needs the man to till it and sow seed in it to produce vegetation. For this reason the man was created.

The creation of humans from dirt or clay is a common ancient Near Eastern creation metaphor, but the cultural understanding of this metaphor is not readily apparent to modern readers. Whereas we might think in terms of modeling clay figures, the various contexts in which this metaphor is used indicate that it is a vehicle for understanding the birth process. In the Mesopotamian myth of Atrahasis, for example, Enki's treading of clay and Belet-ili's pinching off of fourteen pieces in order to create humans are juxtaposed to a description of the process and rites of childbirth. In this context the fashioning of clay served as a metaphor for gestation during pregnancy: the first humans were shaped in the earth-womb from which they were born just as Enki and Belet-ili continue to work in the wombs of women to produce children.

Most scholars have compared Yahweh's creation of the man not to Enki and Belet-ili's creation in Atrahasis, but rather to Khnum's fashioning of humans on his potter's wheel. Indeed, this comparison with the Egyptian creator god is appropriate; Yahweh's creation of the man from dirt does evoke the image of a potter who forms a vessel on his wheel. But as several hymns to Khnum make clear,[4] the ancient Egyptians also attributed to Khnum the necessary and critical task of forming human fetuses during gestation. His role during the birth process is illustrated on a series of wall reliefs in the mortuary temple Hatshepsut at Deir el Bahari. In the first relevant scene, the chief god, Amun, who assumes the form of the king, is tastefully depicted having intercourse with the queen, Hatshepsut's mother. After the intercourse, the next scene portrays Khnum fashioning Hatshepsut on his potter's wheel. Then in the following scenes, Khnum and his spouse Heket, a birth-goddess, lead the pregnant queen to the birth chamber where she delivers Hatshepsut. According to these reliefs, Khnum is clearly the one who forms and shapes the fetus during gestation. His work and skill as a potter serve as a metaphor for the god's activity in the birth process.[5]

Returning to the Yahwist creation myth, Yahweh's forming the man from the arable land should be interpreted as a metaphor for man's birth from the earth. Yahweh acts as a potter in the manner of Khnum by forming the human fetus in the earth-womb, and then Yahweh acts as a midwife by delivering the man out of the earth, breathing into his nostrils the breath of life. The relationship of the man (*'adam*) to the arable land (*'adamah*) is thus both agricultural and natal.

In the second part of the myth, the man's primary relationship to the arable land gives way to a new relationship: the relationship between husband (*'ish*) and wife (*'ishshah*). Faced with the problem of the man's loneliness, Yahweh creates new creatures from the arable land (presumably in the same way that the man was created) with the purpose of finding an appropriate helper for the man. Unable to create such a creature, Yahweh then takes a new approach to the problem. Yahweh takes one of the man's ribs and from it makes a wife (*'ishshah*) for the man. The man in turn is transformed into a husband (*'ish*).

The relationship between the husband and the wife in this part of the myth is complex. Some scholars have argued that because both the husband and the wife have their origin in the original *'adam*, the *'adam* should be interpreted as a nongendered human creature. The husband and the wife would thus represent complementary gendered parts of the human creature.[6] However, the husband (*'ish*) is identified with the *'adam* throughout the rest of the myth. Moreover, the text emphasizes that the wife is created "from the husband" (*'ish*), just as the rib is taken "from the man" (*'adam*), suggesting that the wife has her origin in the husband and thus is dependent upon him. In relation to the arable land (*'adamah*) and other creatures the man is *'adam*, but in relation to his wife (*'ishshah*) he is *'ish*.

The wordplay between *'ish* and *'ishshah* suggests a complementary relationship between the husband and the wife that corresponds to the relationship between *'adam* and *'adamah*. In both cases, for example, the wordplay represents a unity of substance between the two members of the pair: the *'ish* and *'ishshah* share bone and flesh, just as the *'adam* and *'adamah* share dirt. The shared substance between the husband and the wife also implies a mutually dependent relationship between them, but unlike the relationship between the man and the arable land, the dependencies of this relationship are not yet defined. The correspondence between the two relationships is suggestive, but it is important also to note how the two relationships differ. First, the gender sequence of the pairs is different: the male *'adam* comes from the female *'adamah*, but the female *'ishshah* comes from the male *'ish*. Second, whereas the *'adam* is born from the *'adamah*, the *'ishshah* is simply brought to the *'ish*. These two relationships are not strictly parallel. The man's relationship to the arable land is agricultural and natal, but his relationship to his wife will, in the third episode, be conjugal and procreative. The *'ishshah* does not simply replace the *'adamah* in her relationship to the man. She forms a new kind of relationship with him, as indicated by his transformation from *'adam* to *'ish*. But the man also remains *'adam* and his relationship to the *'adamah* persists, just as a man continues to be the son of his parents even after he leaves them to marry a wife (see 3:24). Although not identical, the relationship between *'adam* and *'adamah* functions in the narrative to define the relationship between *'ish* and *'ishshah*. The character of this latter relationship is developed in the second half of the myth.

The pivotal third episode of the myth focuses on the wife's dialogue with the serpent and her and her husband's subsequent eating of the forbidden fruit of knowledge. By eating the fruit, the man and woman become like God, knowing good and evil. The knowledge of good and evil — probably a merism[7] for universal or cultural knowledge[8] — is what distinguishes the married couple from all the other creatures that Yahweh created from the arable land. Through knowledge the man and woman gain the potential for culture; the married couple become creators like God.

The specific way in which the married couple's newly acquired knowledge makes them like God is indicated by the context. The episode frames the man and woman's acquisition of knowledge with references to their nakedness.

Before they eat the fruit, the married couple is naked and not ashamed. The implication is that they are sexually unaware. Without knowledge they are like children unacquainted with the significance of their bodies, and so their nakedness means nothing to them. After they eat the fruit, however, the man and woman know that they are naked and they appropriately cover themselves. The married couple is now aware of their sexuality; their nakedness has significance and therefore they cover their genitals. The fruit of knowledge has made the married couple like God, and their similarity to God is symbolized by their knowledge of sexuality. The ramifications of this knowledge, of the married couple being like God, are spelled out in the remainder of the narrative.

In the final episode the Yahwist creation myth presents the particular gender roles of the man and his wife as the consequence of the married couple's new status of being like God. Scholars have traditionally interpreted the consequences outlined in this episode to be Yahweh's punishments imposed upon the married couple for disregarding Yahweh's prohibition against eating the fruit of knowledge. As a result, the married couple's gender roles are interpreted as the consequence of their "fallen" state — that is, their roles have been corrupted by sin. But this interpretation is inadequate. First, the woman and the man are not cursed for their actions. Second, in only one case does Yahweh impose what could be interpreted as a punishment on the couple — Yahweh curses the arable land on account of the man's actions, leaving it unproductive for agriculture. However, even in this case Yahweh does not alter the condition of the land. Yahweh just withholds temporarily the rain needed for agriculture, a condition that is alleviated with the flood. And third, the structure of the myth suggests that the gender roles ascribed to the husband and to the wife are the inherent consequences of their acquisition of knowledge. The description of the married couple's gender roles in this episode gives content to the relationship between *'ish* and *'ishshah* and defines how this relationship corresponds to the relationship between *'adam* and *'adamah*. Yahweh's narrative role serves primarily to institute the married couple's gender roles and to explain the implications of their knowledge and sexual awareness.

Yahweh inaugurates the wife's gender role by declaring that he will increase her toils and pregnancies. Because the woman now has knowledge and an awareness of her sexuality, childbirth is possible. She will bear children, but such births will be painful. Her life will be filled with the labors that are characteristic of a mother and wife in ancient Israel. Yet the woman's status as mother will be dependent upon her husband, for her husband will rule over her — that is, he will have control over her pregnancies. The woman's relationship to her husband is analogous to the arable land's relationship to the man. The land is dependent upon the man to bring forth vegetation. It will remain a barren desert without the man to till it and sow seed in it. Similarly, the woman's ability to bear children is dependent upon her husband, who must first impregnate her. The woman is like the arable land in that the fecundity of both is linked to the man's sowing of seed, but whereas the land's fecundity is expressed in terms of agriculture, the woman's fecundity is expressed in terms of procreation. The arable land also gave birth to the first man, but as the result of Yahweh's activity. Now all future generations will be born from the woman as a result of her husband's activity. The woman will replace the arable land as the mother of all living.

Although the Yahwist myth describes the woman's gender role (*'ishshah*) in relation to her husband (*'ish*), the man's gender role (*'adam*) is described in relation to the arable land (*'adamah*). The man's newly acquired knowledge and awareness of sexuality is expressed, not in terms of procreation, but in terms of agriculture. The man now has the knowledge to work the land, which is the purpose for which he was created. No longer will the man live off the fruit of God's garden. Through his toil and sweat the man will provide for his own subsistence — a task that is made more arduous until the advent of rain. The man will be like Yahweh in his gender role of working the soil. Just as Yahweh planted a garden and caused trees to sprout up from the earth, the man will also bring forth life from the barren land.

According to the Yahwist creation myth, the Israelites' understanding of procreation is expressed in terms of agriculture, and this understanding shaped their understanding of marriage and gender. The man's role in procreation is metaphorically compared to the role of a farmer and the woman's role is compared to the arable land. Just as a man sows seeds into the land and thereby causes the earth to produce vegetation, a man can sow his seed — his semen — into a woman causing her to give birth to a child. This view of procreation, of course, is not the view shared by most people in the Western world.[9] According to the current scientific understanding of procreation, the birth of a child is dependent upon the joining of a man's sperm and a woman's egg in conception and the development of the fetus within the woman's uterus until parturition. Both the man and the woman contribute equally to the genetic makeup of the child, each contributing twenty-three chromosomes. This understanding of procreation, however, is the result of relatively recent discoveries — about a century old — that were not evident to the ancient Israelites. The Israelites instead understood procreation in terms of the natural processes with which they were familiar. The similarities between agriculture and the process of childbirth were well known to the people of the ancient Near East and are widely attested in their literature. The references in the Yahwist myth to the man's birth from the arable land, the wife's creation from and dependence upon her husband, the association of the fruit of knowledge with sexual awareness, the wife's identification with the arable land, and the corresponding relationships between *'adam* and *'adamah* and between *'ish* and *'ishshah* all indicate that the Israelites shared this view of procreation.

Gender and the Practice of Marriage

The Israelites' view of procreation had significant implications for their understanding of gender and the practice of marriage. Unlike our understanding of procreation in which the man and woman contribute equally to the birth of a child, the Israelite understanding assigns the primary and essential role in procreation to the man. Only the man possesses the seed that will produce new life. The man's semen, like the seed that is planted in the soil, determines the character or quality of what will be produced; it contains all the essential characteristics of the child that will be born. A fertile woman is necessary for procreation — a barren woman, like barren soil, prevents the male seed from developing — but she contributes nothing essential to the makeup of the newborn child. Her role is to carry and nurture the man's seed until the child is born. Only after the child is born does the mother contribute to the character of the child through training and education. The woman's complete dependence upon the man's seed in order to fulfill her role in procreation thus results in her husband ruling over her (3:16).

Because the role of the woman in procreation is similar to that of arable land, she is treated in some cases as a man's property: by her father as a daughter, by her husband as a wife. In many cases regarding a woman's person, the Israelites treated her similarly to a man. For example, if a woman is injured by another or is murdered, her assailant is treated in the same way as if he had injured or murdered a man. However, in cases involving a woman's sexuality or procreative potential, she is treated like a man's property. The betrothal of a woman in marriage, for example, is arranged as an economic exchange. Because the groom's family will gain a potentially productive "field" in the bride, they compensate the family of the bride through the gift of a bride price. In the story in which Abraham's servant seeks a wife for Isaac, the servant compensates Rebekah's family with gold and silver jewelry, garments, and costly ornaments (Gen. 24:22, 53). A marriageable daughter is thus an economic asset to her father. If another man damages this asset — if a man seduces and has sexual relations with his virgin daughter — then the father is entitled to compensation. The man who seduces his daughter must pay a fine equal to the expected bride price (Exod. 22:16–17). A wife or daughter's procreative potential has an economic value like arable land, and thus in this regard she is treated like property.

Because the man possesses the seed in the process of procreation, the children who are the product of his seed belong especially to the father. We have already noted that the descendants of a man are referred to as his seed; they are *his* descendants. Little attention is given to the contribution of the mother. Whereas children, especially sons, are important to a mother for her to fulfill her marital obligation to her husband and to provide for her in her old age, they are important to the father to carry on his name. Ancient Israel is thus a patrilineal society, and biblical genealogies are traced from father to

son. Because a man's seed is equated with his posterity, several laws emphasize the importance of preserving (i.e., not wasting) his seed. For example, a
man should not have sexual relations with a woman in menstruation (Lev.
18:19), for during this period she cannot become pregnant and the use of
his seed would be a waste. Similarly, a man should not have sexual relations
with another man or with an animal (Lev. 18:22–23) — his seed would likewise be wasted. Sexual relations with a kinsman's wife are also prohibited
in this context (Lev. 18:20), but for a different reason. Although the man's
seed would produce a child, the paternity of the child would be in question.
In other words, because the land (the kinsmen's wife) does not belong to the
man, his seed would be indistinguishable from the seed of the man to whom
the land belongs. Finally, in the case when a pregnant woman is injured so
that she has a miscarriage, those responsible for the injury must compensate
the woman's husband for his loss of seed (Exod. 21:22–25).

Marriage and gender in ancient Israel were indeed patriarchal; the
husband dominated his wife. This gender asymmetry that is attested to
in the Old Testament is rooted in the ancient Israelites' understanding
of procreation. Although procreation is a natural process, knowledge of
procreation is socially constructed. Whereas we employ microscopes and
sonograms to understand the process of procreation, the ancient Israelites
who lived in a primarily agrarian society drew upon metaphors from agriculture. A husband's role in procreation was like that of a farmer because he
planted seed in his wife, and his wife's role was like that of the arable land
because she received the seed and nurtured it until the child was born from
her. This view of procreation shaped the Israelites' understanding of gender
and practice of marriage in two significant ways: the husband was responsible through his seed for the birth of his children, and the wife's sexuality
and procreative potential were treated as the property of her husband.

Questions for Discussion

1. The ancestor stories in Genesis provide us with the most information
   regarding the Israelite family. Try to explain features of the stories in
   terms of the Israelite understanding of marriage and gender. For example, why is there a preference for marrying kin? Why is Abraham
   reluctant to favor Isaac over Ishmael? Why does Sarai give her maid-
   servant Hagar to Abram? How does this fulfill her marital obligation?
   Why must Jacob work seven years before he can marry one of the
   daughters of Laban?

2. Read the story of Zelophehad's daughters in Numbers 27:1–11; 36:1–
   12. Why do you think that daughters did not inherit property from
   their fathers? Why are daughters allowed to inherit? How do they
   substitute for sons? Why must the daughters marry kinsmen?

3. Read the story of David's adultery with Bathsheba in 2 Samuel 11–12. According to the prophet Nathan's indictment of David, what was his crime? Why is Bathsheba compared to Uriah's lamb? Why does God punish David by killing the child that resulted from David's adultery?

Chapter 3

The Meaning(s) of Purposeful Non-Marriage in the New Testament

Bruce J. Malina

Introduction

All human societies have a social structure consisting of some set of norms defining and directing human biological mating relationships, interactions, and their outcomes.[1] These norms are directly based upon the experiences of human birth and the birth cycle, from the womb, through developmental stages, to death. The social structure in question is called kinship, a social structure that has taken many structural and symbolic forms in the worldwide human community.[2] At bottom, kinship norms are rooted in the social perception that human relationships can be and actually are established among persons by their being born of certain parents and/or by the possibility of births resulting from the sexual union of two (or more in cases of polygamy or polygyny) human beings. Marriage refers to such a union of two (or more) human beings insofar as it relates to kinship. Marriage is a subset of kinship norms.

Obviously, all adult people in the whole world can be divided into two groups, the married and the non-married. The non-married in turn can be divided into two groups: those who are unmarried by their own choice and those who are unmarried without their consent. The unmarried by choice are of two types, those who choose to be unmarried for centripetal, self-oriented reasons (egocentric), and those who choose to be unmarried for centrifugal reasons (allocentric). The unmarried without their consent are prohibited from being married by some external obstacle (law, custom, circumstances both physical and social). Since kinship is an integral part of some social systems, every marriage realizes prevailing kinship norms and is an affirmation of the extant social system. Consequently, a person's choosing to remain unmarried requires some explanation since such a status involves non-participation in the extant social system and implies a criticism of that social system.

In this essay I will deal with the range of meanings ascribed to non-marriage of both the egocentric and allocentric forms in the first-century Eastern Mediterranean world. Among modern authors, the status of persons refraining from marriage in the first-century Eastern Mediterranean world is rarely called non-marriage. Rather, following the fundamental gender division of patriarchal societies, these modern authors refer to the non-married status as celibacy (for males) and virginity (for females). There is also the status of widows (for previously married females) and widowers (for previously married males). The labels appended to non-married persons are usually of little value in discerning the significance of that state since those labels are often mixed or matched or applied without consistency. To use anachronistic terminology, I would ask whether there is a difference among bachelorhood, celibacy, virginity, widowhood, the widower status, or the status of those remaining unmarried simply because they have no partners.

My focus will be on the New Testament, and my task will be to determine and define the *meaning* of non-marriage in the New Testament writings. Hence the goal of this brief essay is to describe and define the purposes of non-marriage in first-century Israel. These purposes are necessarily bound up with the meanings ascribed to non-marriage behavior, and these meanings, like all meanings, derive from the prevailing social system, with its institutions, values, and person types. Furthermore, non-marriage is a significant type of behavior in the first-century Mediterranean world in general if only because of the two prevailing social institutions (politics and kinship); kinship was the focal institution for all, and marriage and non-marriage relate directly to this social institution.

A Model

All would agree that in the first-century Mediterranean world, all adult persons were either married or not married. Those not married were in that state either because as adults they were prohibited from marrying or because they chose to be unmarried. Those prohibited from marrying included those forbidden either by law or custom (slaves, who could not marry; soldiers, who could not marry until their period of service was over), or by circumstance (divorced females, widows, condemned prisoners).

Those unmarried by their own adult choice made this decision either for some functional or practical reason (occupations, such as a merchant, that meant being away from home, or for some philosophical reason) or for some symbolic reason (to "say" something to the members of their society).

For non-elites in the ancient Mediterranean world, marriage involved the fusion of honor of two kin groups by means of the marriage of a member from each family for economic and religious reasons.[3] In this historical period, economics and religion were embedded in kinship. The kin group was the religious unit just as the kin group was the producing and consuming unit.

Individuals who are given in marriage (females) and who marry, i.e., take as wife (males), are not expected to be friends, to fall in love, or to be psychologically intimate with each other. Rather, those given in marriage have the sole purpose of having offspring (period!). Offspring were for parental social security and kin-group support and nurture. Popular Stoic philosophers taught the following: "Sexual intercourse is justified only when it occurs in marriage and is indulged in for the purpose of begetting children."[4] It was no different in Israel, with its first Torah injunction being: "Increase and multiply and fill the land" (Gen. 1:28). In this context, Paul's phrase "to touch one's wife" (1 Cor. 7:1) meant to have a child.

Marriage within a Societal Context

What does non-marriage mean? Since human beings are social beings, they must necessarily interact with other humans in order to realize their basic human capabilities. To have effect on others, people in complex societies generally ply each other with symbols. We might lawfully threaten another with physical harm to get effect, either because we hold public office and can sanction our decisions, or we wear a badge and have a gun. Having effect by threat of force is called *power*. Similarly, we might give a person some specially printed paper and get a meal, a car, or a house in return. The paper, of course, is money, and the way we have effect is called *inducement*. Further, people mutually have effect on each other because they know and feel themselves bonded to each other by ties of solidarity and loyalty, that is kinship and kin-like ties. Children comply with requests of parents, just as good friends comply with requests made by their friends, because of existing ties of solidarity, commitment, and loyalty. A request activates internalized commitment, and non-compliance would produce feelings of shame. Having effect on another because of some implied threat of shame is called *commitment activation*. Finally, we might submit to a surgical procedure and have a lung removed because some certified person gives us good reasons for doing so at this time. The person in question whose good reasons we accept might be called a "physician," and the physician has effect because of the reasons given, an interaction called *influence*. In sum we have effect on others, and they on us, because we ply each other with power, inducement, commitment activation, and influence. These are the symbolic media that people use in social interaction to produce effects on others.[5] From the perspective of social institutions, politics favors power, economics favors inducement, kinship interactions favor commitment, while ultimate and proximate meaning institutions such as religion favor influence.

Just as people comply with the wishes of another because of the generalized symbolic medium of social interaction put to them, there are interactions where people are led to comply because the interacting partner *does not* interact with a generalized symbolic medium. People wish to have effect on another by purposefully withholding the appropriate generalized symbolic medium. These I will call negative generalized symbolic media. Such negative generalized symbolic media include, for example, pacifism, fasting, celibacy, and silence. It seems everyone knows about the silent treatment: a significant interacting partner speaks volumes by purposefully saying nothing at all. Such willful silence is an instance of such a negative generalized symbolic medium. Pacifism, fasting, and celibacy fall within the same category as silence. Each within its own institutional framework communicates by withholding the appropriate generalized symbolic medium. Pacifism speaks by purposeful non-use of available force; fasting by purposefully non-ingesting food and drink; celibacy by purposeful non-marriage. Each is, thus, intended to say something to others within one's society. As a rule, the message of these negative generalized symbolic media is unfavorable, a message of disapproval, of disfavor. They are forms of protesting the presence of some perceived evil within a given society.

However, as previously noted, not every form of refraining from social interaction is intended to communicate to others. There are forms of non-interaction that are focused on the concerns and ego-focused goals of the person in question. For example, nonviolence chosen to avoid bad karma, dieting chosen to lose weight, bachelorhood (and the female equivalent) chosen to avoid difficulties involved in raising a family, or silence motivated by lack of interest are all forms of non-interaction chosen because of a person's own ego-focused concerns. They have nothing to do with attempting to have an effect on another. Hence they do not qualify as media of social interaction since they are not concerned about social interaction at all.

Finally, there are generalized symbolic media used in a deviant way. These are positive generalized symbolic media used for negative ends, for example, for securing unfair advantage over others. These are self-serving, positive media employed in negative reciprocity relations better labeled counterfeit generalized symbolic media. They function much like counterfeit money. Such behavior is called hustling. It includes the use of power in order to extort, commitment activation for favoritism or nepotism, inducement in bribery and influence in lying, information control or information leakage.

The table on the following page presents a schematic view of the information presented here. Within this framework, non-marriage functions as an unwillingness to reciprocate with others in terms of the symbolic medium described here as commitment activity (solidarity, loyalty, belonging). It may be chosen either to have effect on others, serving as a negative generalized symbolic medium of social interaction, or without concern for others, solely with a view to one's own interests. Consider now, instances of this behavior in the Bible.

Biblical Passages

There are instances of persons choosing non-marriage both in the Old Testament and the New. The parade example in the Old Testament is that of the prophet Jeremiah. The passage runs as follows:

> 16:1The word of the LORD came to me: 2You shall not take a wife, nor shall you have sons or daughters in this place. 3For thus says the LORD concerning the sons and daughters who are born in this place, and concerning the mothers who bore them and the fathers who begot

Negative (and Negatively Used) Generalized Symbolic Media
of Social Interaction

	POWER	COMMITMENT	INFLUENCE	INDUCEMENT
Mediating materials	Force	Sexual relations and nurturance	Utterance, Discourse	Goods, Food/drink
(a) Freely chosen GSM: Effect on SELF	Nonviolence	Self-focused non-marriage	Non-speaking	Non-eating/drinking Abstinence, Dieting
(b) Freely chosen GSM: Intended effect on OTHERS	Pacifism	Other-focused non-marriage	Silence	Fasting
(c) Not freely chosen	Physical weakness	Social/personal incapacity to marry	Inability to speak	Starvation due to lack of food
(d) Socially constrained non-use	Legally prohibited use of force	Forbidden degrees or age limitations for marriage	Social times/places when/where non-speaking enforced	Prohibited/avoided food and drink
GSM used in negative reciprocity	Extortion	Favoritism, Nepotism	Lying, Information control, Leakage	Bribery
	POWER	COMMITMENT	INFLUENCE	INDUCEMENT

them in this land: [4]They shall die of deadly diseases. They shall not be lamented, nor shall they be buried; they shall be as dung on the surface of the ground. They shall perish by the sword and by famine, and their dead bodies shall be food for the birds of the air and for the beasts of the earth. [5]For thus says the LORD: Do not enter the house of mourning, or go to lament, or bemoan them; for I have taken away my peace from this people, says the LORD, my steadfast love and mercy. [6]Both great and small shall die in this land; they shall not be buried, and no one shall lament for them or cut himself or make himself bald for them. [7]No one shall break bread for the mourner, to comfort him for the dead; nor shall any one give him the cup of consolation to drink for his father or his mother. [8]You shall not go into the house of feasting to sit with them, to eat and drink. [9]For thus says the LORD of hosts, the God of Israel: Behold, I will make to cease from this place, before your eyes and in your days, the voice of mirth and the voice of gladness, the voice of the bridegroom and the voice of the bride. [10]And when you tell this people all these words, and they say to you, "Why has the LORD pronounced all this great evil against us? What is our iniquity? What is the sin that we have committed against the LORD our God?" [11]Then

you shall say to them: Because your fathers have forsaken me, says the LORD, and have gone after other gods and have served and worshiped them, and have forsaken me and have not kept my law, [12]and because you have done worse than your fathers, for behold, every one of you follows his stubborn evil will, refusing to listen to me; [13]therefore I will hurl you out of this land into a land which neither you nor your fathers have known, and there you shall serve other gods day and night, for I will show you no favor. [14]*Therefore, behold, the days are coming, says the Lord, when it shall no longer be said, "As the Lord lives who brought up the people of Israel out of the land of Egypt,"* [15]*but "As the Lord lives who brought up the people of Israel out of the north country and out of all the countries where he had driven them." For I will bring them back to their own land which I gave to their fathers.* [16]"Behold, I am sending for many fishers, says the Lord, and they shall catch them; and afterwards I will send for many hunters, and they shall hunt them from every mountain and every hill, and out of the clefts of the rocks. [17]For my eyes are upon all their ways; they are not hid from me, nor is their iniquity concealed from my eyes. [18]And I will doubly recompense their iniquity and their sin, because they have polluted my land with the carcasses of their detestable idols, and have filled my inheritance with their abominations." [19]*O Lord, my strength and my stronghold, my refuge in the day of trouble, to thee shall the nations come from the ends of the earth and say: "Our fathers have inherited nought but lies, worthless things in which there is no profit.* [20]*Can man make for himself gods? Such are no gods!"* [21]*"Therefore, behold, I will make them know, this once I will make them know my power and my might, and they shall know that my name is the Lord."*
(The italicized statements are considered later additions to the text.)

The literary form of this passage is that of a prophetic symbolic action.[6] A prophetic symbolic action is an action undertaken by a prophet at God's command in order to say something to the Israelites to whom the prophet's message is directed. The form has the following pattern: (1) command by God to a prophet to perform some action; (2) fulfillment of command by the prophet; (3) a statement from God (through the prophet) explaining the meaning of the action; (4) consequences for the people. This pattern is found throughout Ezekiel and Jeremiah as well as in the Synoptic story of Jesus (the baptism of Jesus; the Eucharist institution at the Last Supper).

Here, Jeremiah the prophet is commanded by God not to marry, that is not to have children (these go hand in hand in antiquity). The reason behind the command is the horrendous social situation about to befall evil Israel. The prophet's non-marriage effectively symbolizes and communicates word of this horrendous social situation. Jeremiah's celibacy proclaims forthcoming, overwhelming evil.

St. Paul

In the New Testament period, too, marriage and childbearing go hand in hand. Romantic love and the expression of mutual love through sexual relations are things of the future. The common view of elites (and perhaps most non-elites) in antiquity was that of popular Stoicism, here articulated by Musonius Rufus, a contemporary of St. Paul:

> Only those venereal actions are just which take place in marriage and for the purpose of procreating children, because they take place lawfully; but those venereal actions which are directed at sheer pleasure are unjust and unlawful, even if they take place within marriage. Sexual relations that are adulterous are most unlawful, nor are sexual relations between males any more decent because it is a crime against nature.[7]

Not all would agree with Musonius. Plutarch held:

> If therefore a man in private life, who is incontinent and dissolute in regard to his pleasures, commits some peccadillo with a paramour or a maid-servant, his wedded wife ought not to be indignant or angry, but she should reason that it is respect for her which leads him to share his debauchery, licentiousness and wantonness with another woman.[8]

Many more witnesses might be cited here. However, our question is non-marriage, and there are several passages in the New Testament dealing with the topic. Perhaps the earliest datable statements come from St. Paul in 1 Corinthians 7. In this section of his letter, Paul opens his responses to questions put by the Corinthian Jesus group members with a positive assessment of marriage/procreation. "To touch a woman" (1 Cor. 7:1) means "to have a child with one's wife," as Paul's explanation presumes. The Corinthian problem was whether Jesus group members should continue to have children, given the fact that the kingdom of God (Israelite theocracy) would be ushered in soon. While Paul says it is fine to have offspring now, yet "I wish that all were as I myself am" (1 Cor. 7:7). His reasoning is based "in view of the present distress" (1 Cor. 7:26). In other words, Paul, who was either married or a widower at this time, says he will not have any children or have no more children. Considering that in the reproductive theories of antiquity, the male was considered to deposit a fully formed miniature human being (homunculus) in the female to hold for nine months, Paul is saying he will abstain. He adopts the same perspective relative to Levitical marriages. It is better for young women (virgins) with the right to have a child by a deceased husband's brother to refrain, but they need not[9] (1 Cor. 7:36–37). The same is true of widows wishing to remarry (1 Cor. 7:39).

Paul states his reason for urging men and women to refrain from marriage:

> I want you to be free from anxieties. The unmarried man is anxious about the affairs of the Lord, how to please the Lord; but the married man is anxious about worldly affairs, how to please his wife, and his interests are divided. And the unmarried woman or girl is anxious about the affairs of the Lord, how to be holy in body and spirit; but the married woman is anxious about worldly affairs, how to please her husband. I say this for your own benefit, not to lay any restraint upon you, but to promote good order and to secure your undivided devotion to the Lord. (1 Cor. 7:32–35)

The point is that regardless of the various nuances Paul presents regarding marriage, non-marriage, and offspring, his urging of non-marriage is based on problems the married might have, given the present situation. The focus of their chosen non-marriage behavior is on themselves, not on communicating some message to others. In terms of the foregoing chart, Paul urges self-focused, ego-centered, non-marriage in view of the coming Israelite theocracy.

Paul's practical advice has a parallel in the advice of Epictetus, a Stoic philosopher who lives a generation after Paul:

> But in such an order of things as the present, which is like that of a state of war [a philosopher should not marry so as] to be free from distraction, wholly devoted to the service of God, free to go about among men, not tied down by the private duties of men, nor involved in relationships which such a person cannot violate and still maintain his role as a good and excellent man.... For see [if he got married] he must show certain service to his in-laws, to the rest of his wife's relatives and to his wife herself. Finally he is driven from his profession to act as a nurse in his own family and to provide for them. To make a long story short, he must get a kettle to heat water for the baby, for washing it in a bath-tub; wool for his wife when she has had a child, oil, a cot, a cup (the vessels get more and more numerous); to speak of the rest of his business and his distractions.[10]

Such functional reasons for non-marriage are self-oriented, with little concern for sending a message or witness to others.

The Gospel Tradition

The other well-known passage, presumably about non-marriage, is found in the Gospel of Matthew 19:3–12. The pattern of this passage is public teaching (challenge and riposte with opponents) followed by private explanation (to disciples). This structure is noted in Mark by place changes (see Mark 10:2–12; also 4:2–20; 7:14–23; and see Matt. 13:3–23; 15:10–20).

The specific articulation of the argument here in Matthew 19 is:

v. 3:   hostile question (challenge)

vv. 4–6:   riposte with another question from Genesis

v. 7:   hostile reply (another question) to riposte of vv. 4–5 based on Deuteronomy

v. 8:   riposte ad hominem with another reference from Genesis

v. 9:   riposte with final *half* answer (to shame opponents: men cannot commit adultery against their wives)

v. 10:   in private with disciples: question about the half answer

vv. 11–12: true teaching meant for Jesus group members. This true teaching is given in the form of an implied numbered parable:

> For there are eunuchs who have been so from birth,
> and there are eunuchs who have been made eunuchs by other people,
> and there are eunuchs who have made themselves eunuchs for the sake of the kingdom of heaven. (Matt. 19:12)

Parables are literary forms that express and refer to something other than what the speaker states. In other words, this parable of the eunuchs (castrated males, males who cannot have offspring) is not about eunuchs.[11] Numbered and implied numbered parables consist of a first set of elements (two or more) that are concrete and imaginable, and a final statement that is moral, abstract, not concrete at all. For example: "For pressing milk produces curds, pressing the nose produces blood, and pressing anger produces strife" (Prov. 30:33); "Three things are too wonderful for me; four I do not understand: the way of an eagle in the sky, the way of a serpent on a rock, the way of a ship on the high seas, and the way of a man with a maiden" (Prov. 30:18–19); or "Foxes have holes, and birds of the air have nests; but the Son of man has nowhere to lay his head" (Matt. 8:20); "He who receives a prophet because he is a prophet shall receive a prophet's reward, and he who receives a righteous man because he is a righteous man shall receive a righteous man's reward. And whoever gives to one of these little ones even a cup of cold water because he is a disciple, truly, I say to you, he shall not lose his reward" (Matt. 10:41–42); "What did you go out into the wilderness to behold? A reed shaken by the wind? Why then did you go out? To see a man clothed in soft raiment? . . . Why then did you go out? To see a prophet? Yes, I tell you, and more than a prophet" (Matt. 11:7–9).

Thus the literary pattern of the eunuch passage is that of a numbered parable in which the first two (or more) elements offer concrete pictures that set the stage for understanding the final element, which is the main point. The point to what? The discussion in Matthew 19 is about divorce, concluding with Jesus' prohibition of divorce. The disciples' response is that if the dissolution of a marriage is not permitted, then it is not expedient to marry! (Matt. 19:10). Jesus' response to this objection to marriage is this parable. In context, the parable is to solve the dilemma of a married male who should divorce his wife for reasons of *porneia.* According to Matthew (and his church) a Jesus group member may/must divorce his wife if she be guilty of *porneia* (translated "unchastity" here). *Porneia* means sexual misconduct as listed in the Torah, specifically Leviticus 18:6–23:

vv. 6–18:   forbidden degrees, i.e., incest laws

v. 19:   sexual relations during the menstrual period

v. 20:   adultery, which defiles the male adulterer (a fortiori the female)

v. 21:   infant sacrifices — interpreted in the first century of mixed marriages between Israelites and non-Israelites

v. 22:   same-gender genital relations for the male

v. 23:   cross-species genital relations for male and female.

It is important to remember that adultery in the first-century Mediterranean world meant dishonoring a male (the husband) by having sexual relations with his wife. Adultery is a crime against the husband. (Husbands who have sexual relations with unmarried, unattached females do not commit adultery.) In Israelite practice, a wife guilty of adultery must be divorced; perhaps Matthew is indicating the same for Jesus group members in his community. The parable urges a male with an adulterous wife to make himself a eunuch for the kingdom of Heaven. As Bernabé has noted:

> In the cultural context of the period, male honor depended, among other things, on the type of relations they might have with their wives, something which was defined by the general code for masculinity: dominance, aggressiveness, and demandingness. Deviations from the male role would lead to doubts about an individual's "manliness" and even to his "symbolic castration," and thus dishonor. In my opinion, this is what is depicted in Jesus' final paradoxical words (vv. 10–12).[12]

In other words, the purpose of the parable on eunuchs in Matthew 19:12 is to indicate that the divorce prohibition, even for males with adulterous wives, is for Jesus group members — an authentic evangelical "counsel." Jesus group members who marry are forbidden to divorce since marriage makes two persons "one flesh." This means that husbands will have to forego resolving honor difficulties in favor of their spouses. They will have to "lump it."

As for Jesus group members who are married to non–Jesus group members, which is the problem Paul faces at Corinth, he urges divorce if the married Jesus group members cannot live in peace with a non-member spouse (see 1 Cor. 7:12 ff.). And Paul certainly knew Jesus' teaching on divorce (see 1 Cor. 7:10–11).

To see how the Matthew tradition was applied in the early church, consider the following excerpt from *The Shepherd of Hermas* (written ca. 145 c.e.):

"I command you," he said, "to guard purity. Let it not enter your heart to think of another man's wife, nor about fornication [*porneia*], nor any such thing. If you do, you will commit a serious sin. Keep your wife in mind always and you will never fall into sin. For if this desire comes into your heart, you will make a slip and you will commit sin, if any other wicked thought enters your heart. For a desire of this kind is a serious sin for the servant of God and if anyone puts into execution such a wicked thought he draws death upon himself. Be on your guard then: Keep this desire from you. Where holiness dwells, there, in the heart of a just man, lawlessness should not enter."

I said to him: "Sir, allow me to ask you a few questions." "Ask them," he said. "Sir," I said, "if a man has a wife who believes in the Lord and surprises her in adultery, does he commit sin if he lives with her?"

"Before he finds out," he said, "he does not. But if her husband knows the sin, and she does not repent, but persists in her fornication [*porneia*], he becomes guilty of her sin as long as he lives with her, and an accomplice in her adultery" [he is like a pimp]. "Sir," I said, "what then is he to do, if the wife continues in this passion?" "Let him divorce her," he said, "and remain single. But, if he divorces her and marries another woman, he himself commits adultery." "But if sir," I said, "after the divorce the wife repents and wishes to return to her husband will he refuse to receive her?" "No indeed," he said; "if the husband does not receive her, he sins. He incurs a great sin. The sinner who has repented must be received. However, not often, for there is only one repentance for the servants of God. To bring about her repentance, then, the husband should not marry. This is the course of action required for husband and wife. Not only is it adultery," he said, "for one to pollute one's flesh [by adulterous sexual intercourse], but it is likewise adultery for anyone to act in imitation of the Gentiles [by acting like a Gentile]. So if anyone persists in acts of this kind and does not repent, keep away from him, do not live with him; otherwise you also have a part in his sin. This is the reason why you were commanded to live by yourselves, whether husband or wife be guilty. For under the circumstances, repentance is possible."[13]

Further, we might note here that one of the fundamental problems in this area in first-century culture was remarriage. The question was whether or not remarriage was permissible.[14] *The Shepherd of Hermas* clearly expresses the problem:

> Once more I spoke and asked him: "Sir, since you have borne with me once, make this also clear to me." "What is it?" he said. "Sir," I said, "if a wife or husband is deceased and either one of the survivors marries again, does he or she sin by marrying?" "There is no sin," he said, "but anyone who remains single after marriage achieves greater honor for himself and great glory before the Lord. But even in remarriage, there is no sin. Keep a watchful eye, then, on purity and modesty and live for God." [This is advice to the once married and the married.][15]

In sum, both in the parable from Matthew and in its practical application in the *Shepherd of Hermas*, non-marriage for the sake of the kingdom had to do with married people now bereft of a spouse. The purpose of the non-marriage was not to communicate something negative about society or God's judgment, but for one's own sake, i.e., self-oriented non-marriage.

There remain two other instances of significant non-marriage in the New Testament story. These are the examples of John the Baptist and Jesus. In the documents that describe their careers, there is no indication at all that they were married. Given the way their story is told, what would their non-marriage mean? Both are described as Israelite prophets, and perhaps non-marriage was part of their social function. Yet even so, what was the message of their non-marriage?

The case of John verges toward that of Jeremiah: non-marriage to communicate the fact that society was evil, not worthy of maintenance in its present condition, a condition to be remedied by the forthcoming theocracy that John proclaimed. Indication of John's viewpoint is provided by the tradition that John considered his generation to be evil ("brood of vipers" Matt. 3:7; Luke 3:7), and that he and his disciples fasted. Fasting was a generalized symbol of social interaction that was part and parcel of mourning behavior. Mourning meant proclaiming the presence of overwhelming evil. Since John fasted, his non-marriage would be like that of Jeremiah, part and parcel of his mourning stance toward Israelite society — a society marked by overwhelming evil.

Jesus, on the other hand, did not fast. This is totally remarkable in this first-century Israelite context; because later Jesus groups did fast, most scholars hold the tradition of Jesus not-fasting to be authentic. However, Jesus was assessed by some to be a prophet, "like Jeremiah" (Matt. 16:14 only; the other prophets mentioned, John the Baptist and Elijah, likewise had unmarried careers [Mark 8:28; Matt. 16:14; Luke 9:19]). This feature implies non-marriage, and this non-marriage as a sign of social protest. Yet Jesus did not protest the presence of evil in Israelite society. Instead he took on persons and groups whom he judged to be "an evil and adulterous generation," notably Israelite elites (Matt. 12:29; 16:4; Mark 8:38; see Matt. 12:34; 23:33). Yet given the obstacles to his proclamation thrown up by kinship groups, it would seem that Jesus distanced himself from family bonds (i.e., commitment activation). Such is the reported case of his own family.

> And his mother and his brothers came; and standing outside they sent to him and called him. And a crowd was sitting about him; and they said to him, "Your mother and your brothers are outside, asking for you." And he replied, "Who are my mother and my brothers?" And looking around on those who sat about him, he said, "Here are my mother and my brothers! Whoever does the will of God is my brother, and sister, and mother." (Mark 3:31–35, parallels Matt. 12:49–50; Luke 8:21)

Yet there is no mention of a wife or of non-marriage.

Further, when the tradition reports that Jesus insisted that his disciples must detach themselves from their families, there is a curious discrepancy. Mark 10:29–30 reports, "Jesus said, 'Truly, I say to you, there is no one who has left house or brothers or sisters or mother or father or children or lands, for my sake and for the gospel, who will not receive a hundredfold now in this time, houses and brothers and sisters and mothers and children and lands, with persecutions, and in the age to come eternal life.'" The parallel in Matthew 19:29 has the same cast of characters, while Luke 18:29 reads: "there is no man who has left house or wife or brothers or parents or children for the sake of the kingdom of God...." Luke has disciples leaving their wives. The same is true of the Q passage 14:26: "If anyone comes to me and does not hate his own father and mother and wife and children and brothers and sisters, yes, and even his own life, he cannot be my disciple" (Luke 14:26). Matthew in turn states: "He who loves father or mother more than me is not worthy of me; and he who loves son or daughter more than me is not worthy of me" (Matt. 10:37). The point is that in both instances, Luke includes separation from one's wife, while Mark and Matthew do not. Perhaps Luke mirrors the behavior of Paul and his companions, while Mark and Matthew refer to the behavior of other Jesus group apostles: "Do we not have the right to be accompanied by a sister as wife, as the other apostles and the brothers of the Lord and Cephas?" (1 Cor. 9:5). However, in all these instances, the point is that non-marriage in any case is self-oriented, not undertaken for the sake of communication with others, of witness, or of some other attesting behavior. It is functional.

Finally, for completeness' sake, I should mention the followers of the celestial Lamb in the book of Revelation. In context, these celestial followers of the Lamb, "undefiled by women for they are virgins" (Rev. 14:4), are the heavenly counterparts of those evil "sons of God who came in to the daughters of men, and bore children to them" (Gen. 6:4). What was evil about those prehistoric celestial, angelic beings is that they crossed the angel/human boundary. They crossed species and did not stay pure and unmixed in their angelic being. As Genesis mentions, their offspring were mutant giants.[16] Of course in human sexual relations, male humans are not defiled by female humans. They are of the same species. Yet as Jesus notes, at the resurrection humans will no longer have children; "they will be like angels in the sky" (Mark 12:25; Matt. 22:30; or as Luke 20:36 explains: "for they cannot die anymore, because they are equal to angels and are sons of God, being sons of the resurrection").

Conclusion

The biblical documents do in fact attest to non-marriage with a view to saying something social. The case of Jeremiah the prophet is clearly one of a negative symbolic medium of social interaction. As a form of communication, non-marriage means a negation of the reciprocities that make up social interaction. As a refusal to reciprocate, non-marriage places the one not marrying "out of social bounds," outside of the normal limits that define social interaction. Generally speaking, then, non-marriage denotes the refusal to reciprocate in the area of kinship, i.e., meaningful interpersonal bonding in terms of solidarity and commitment. The reasons for this refusal in Jeremiah are the woefully evil situation of society and the fate awaiting one's marriage partner and their offspring. Perhaps this message comes through in the non-marriage of John the Baptist and in the assessment of his contemporaries, perhaps of Jesus as well. This non-marriage is allocentric, intended to communicate something to others.

However, the non-marriage taken up by Paul and urged upon Jesus group members in the rest of the New Testament has to do with a self-oriented decision. It does not look to communicating something about the present state of affairs, nor is it bound up with any prophetic message. This non-marriage is egocentric (like dieting or nonviolence).

The question of labeling these non-marriage behaviors is rather difficult. If Jeremiah's behavior (and that of John and Jesus) is celibacy, it is part of their judgmental prophetic message to their generation. Is such celibacy worth imitating in another generation, another culture, without a prophetic call? While even Paul, who did in fact have a prophetic call, took up non-marriage (non-remarriage?), his decision had to do with personal problems raised by the forthcoming kingdom rather than by any prophetic message. Should his behavior be called celibacy, or simply bachelorhood or widowerhood? If this study demonstrates anything, it is that "celibacy for the kingdom" is not of a piece, with a single range of meanings. The other-oriented non-marriage of Jeremiah (and John and Jesus) is one thing; the self-oriented non-marriage urged by St. Paul is quite another. And when hope for a forthcoming Israelite theocracy eventually vanishes, so does the motivation based on "the present distress."

Questions for Discussion

1. What new insight do you have into the role of celibacy in the early church?

2. Analyze the contemporary Catholic requirement that priests be celibate. What are the reasons for this practice? What biblical model does it follow?

3. If one were to follow the example of Paul in the modern context, how would one best do this?

Chapter 4

"And the Greatest of These Is Love"

Raymond F. Collins

When searching for a scriptural passage to be read during the celebration of their marriage, many couples come upon a reading from Paul's First Letter to the Corinthians that speaks of love. The passage, 1 Corinthians 12:31–13:13, culminates in the magnificent affirmation that "the greatest of these is love" (1 Cor. 13:13). For couples, young and old, this passage appears to be an ideal choice for their wedding. Ultimately, a wedding is a celebration and public proclamation of a man and woman's love for one another. First Corinthians 12:31–13:13 really is an ideal passage to accompany the liturgical celebration of Christian marriage, but it is so for reasons quite different from those that readily come to the minds of couples about to be married. Why this is so may need some explanation.

Why Did Paul Write?

Paul's First Letter to the Corinthians was written sometime in the mid-fifties of the first century, not quite twenty-five years after the death and resurrection of Jesus. Several months before writing to these Christians, Paul had preached the gospel in their city, a relatively large metropolitan, commercial, and political center in the Roman province of Achaia. The city was located at the juncture of an overland trade route from north to south and sea routes from east to west.

Paul's preaching of the good news about Jesus Christ in the Achaian capital was so successful that within a short span of time after his initial visit several different house churches were established in Corinth. These different communities occasionally came together, in the fashion of other Greco-Roman associations, as one large church to celebrate a eucharistic meal (1 Cor. 11:17–34). All, however, was not well in Corinth. When the different house churches came together (1 Cor. 11:17), it became apparent that they were a troubled group and were not really united with one another.

Several different sources provided Paul with information about the situation. News of disagreements were brought to him by Chloe's people (1 Cor. 1:11). These people may have been a delegation sent to Paul to tell him what was happening at Corinth. Alternatively, they may have been a group of slaves sent to Ephesus on some business venture on behalf of Chloe who then took advantage of Paul's presence in Ephesus (1 Cor. 16:8–9) to meet

45

with him and tell him about the church of God at Corinth. Stephanas, Fortunatus, and Achaicus were another group of visitors from Corinth who came to see Paul (1 Cor. 16:17). This trio may have delivered the letter to which Paul began to respond in 1 Corinthians 7:1. Even if they were not the ones who brought the letter to Paul, Paul seems to have been relatively well informed about the situation in Corinth, with at least one letter and two sets of visitors.

Knowing as much as he did about the situation in Corinth, Paul was deeply disturbed by the reports of quarrels and disagreements among his beloved Corinthians (1 Cor. 1:11). This concern led him to write his "First Letter to the Corinthians."[1] Its stated purpose was the plea "that all of you be in agreement and that there be no divisions among you, but that you be united in the same mind and the same purpose" (1 Cor. 1:10).

Among the divisive issues faced by the community was that of "spiritual gifts" (1 Cor. 12:1). It was in dealing with this issue that Paul wrote his words on love in 1 Corinthians 13.

Paul's Use of Chiasms

Paul was a gifted and rather skillful writer. One of the techniques that he used to good advantage in 1 Corinthians was a literary device called "chiasm." In its simplest and perhaps most obvious form the device is a kind of literary sandwich. Paul began the discussion of an issue (element A in the chiastic structure). Then he turned his attention to what was seemingly another matter, a rhetorical digression that constitutes the chiasm's element B. Finally, Paul would again return to the topic at hand, treating it in some detail (element A' in the structure). The rhetorical digression is at the center of the A-B-A' structure.[2]

The reader of 1 Corinthians can easily see the chiastic structure in Paul's reflections on spiritual gifts in 1 Corinthians 12–14. In chapter 12 (the A unit), Paul puts the issue of spiritual gifts on the table, as it were; he tells the Corinthians that he does not want them to be uninformed about the matter (1 Cor. 12:1). Before his discussion gets very far along, before he has even identified any of the many gifts given to members of the community,[3] Paul pulled a semantic switch. Rather than writing about *pneumatika,* "spiritual gifts" (1 Cor. 12:1), a term that would emphasize the extraordinary and truly wondrous nature of some of the gifts that the Corinthians had received, Paul chose to write about *charismata,* "gifts" (1 Cor. 12:4). Doing so, Paul appears to have coined a new word, *charisma.*[4] This new word reminded the Corinthians that it is the *gift* that matters; it is not the extraordinary nature of some gifts that is important. The Corinthians could hardly miss his point: what matters most of all is the gifts that God gives to us.

In chapter 14 of the letter, the A' unit of his chiastic structure, Paul returns to the discussion of spiritual gifts. He develops a multifaceted comparison of the gift of prophecy and the gift of speaking in tongues, repeatedly showing that the gift of prophecy is far more useful for building up the church than is the gift of speaking in tongues. Paul's pointed discussion makes it clear that the way that some people used and took advantage of the gift of tongues was the real problem, one that Paul had to confront directly. The fact that he himself possessed both the gift of speaking in tongues (1 Cor. 13:1; 14:6, 11, 13, 18) and the gift of prophecy (1 Cor. 13:2; 14:19) made his discussion of these two gifts all the more authoritative and convincing.

Between chapters 12 and 14 of his letter, respectively the A and A' units of his chiastic arrangement, Paul embarks upon a reflection on love. This lengthy rhetorical digression encompasses the whole of chapter 13, from 1 Corinthians 12:31 to 1 Corinthians 14:1.[5] Chapter 13 is the B unit within his long reflection on the nature and use of spiritual gifts. In rhetorical terms it is possible to speak of chapter 13 as a rhetorical digression, but it is far from being off the point. Throughout this First Letter to the Corinthians the B elements in Paul's chiasms represent a kind of stepping back from the issue at hand in order to put the matter into the big picture, into a larger focus. Only when he has done so does Paul go back to the matter at hand, offering his detailed response to the issue in the light of the principles that he has developed in the rhetorical "digression," the B element in his chiastic argument.

Far from being an extraneous element in the letter, Paul's reflection on love in chapter 13 is an integral part of his discussion of spiritual gifts. What he writes about love provides the context and basis for the argument that he will develop in chapter 14 as he tries to restore order to a community that is divided over the issue of spiritual gifts, especially the gift of tongues, whose undue use was causing considerable disarray in the community as it came together for worship.[6]

Speaking of Love

The phrases "Strive for the greater gifts. And I will show you a still more excellent way" (1 Cor. 12:31) and "Pursue love and strive for the spiritual gifts" (1 Cor. 14:1)[7] are the encompassing elements that create a ring construction and set off Paul's reflections on love as a discrete unit within 1 Corinthians. The inside edges of these encompassing parentheses are "the more excellent way" and "love." From the very outset of his reflections, Paul wants the reader to know that he is about to write about the more excellent way, which is, in fact, the love that he describes in chapter 13. When we read what Paul writes between his literary parentheses, we immediately notice that Paul has expressed his thoughts in the form of another chiastic structure.

In 1 Corinthians 13:1–3, Paul writes about himself and the gifts that he has received, telling his readers that no matter how great his gifts might be, his gifts count for nothing unless he has love.

The "I" of this section of Paul's letter is not a hypothetical "I." Paul does not mean "if anyone has these gifts"; no, he is writing autobiographically. His "I" is Paul himself. Paul is the person who can speak in tongues (1 Cor.

14:6, 14, 18), who can prophesy (1 Cor. 14:19), who can speak of mysteries (1 Cor. 15:51), who has knowledge (1 Cor. 14:6), and who has the God-given ability to work miracles (2 Cor. 12:12). In 1 Corinthians 13:1–3 Paul offers himself as an example to the Corinthians in order to show the comparable value of the various gifts — beginning with the gift of tongues that they valued so highly and that he himself had in a greater measure than any of them — and the value of love, the more excellent way.

At the end of the chapter (1 Cor. 13:8–13) Paul again writes in autobiographical fashion, using the first person.[8] Once again he writes about the gifts, specifically naming prophecy, tongues,[9] and knowledge. In this passage, Paul also writes about love, speaking of it as an enduring gift (v. 8), the greatest of the gifts (v. 13). Paul has created a contrast between the absence of love, about which he wrote in verses 1–3, and the greatness and enduring character of love, about which he writes in verses 8–13. Three motifs appear in 1 Corinthians 13:1–3 and again in 1 Corinthians 13:8–13: the autobiographical "I," the gifts (tongues, prophecy, and knowledge), and love. These three identify the two passages as comparable literary units encompassing 1 Corinthians 13:3–7. Paul has thus created another chiastic structure, whose A and A′ elements are 1 Corinthians 13:1–3 and 1 Corinthians 13:8–13, respectively, and whose B element is 1 Corinthians 13:4–7.

This B element (1 Cor. 13:4–7) provides the reason that Paul writes about love as he does in 1 Corinthians 13:8–13, the A′ element of his exposition. These central verses of chapter 13 provide the basis for what Paul will write about the abiding character and greatness of love in verses 8–13. First Corinthians 13:4–7 is the heart of the matter, the center of what Paul writes about love in the entire chapter.

In fact, these verses constitute the core of Paul's entire discourse on spiritual gifts, chapters 12–14 of his First Letter to the Corinthians. Were one to arrange these three chapters in a macro-chiasm, their schematic structure would be this: A-B-C-D-C′-B′-A′. At the very center of the three chapters is 1 Corinthians 13:4–7 [D], encompassed by autobiographical reflections (1 Cor. 13:1–3 [C] and 8–13 [C′]), encompassed by short exhortations (1 Cor. 12:31 [B] and 14:1 [B′]), encompassed by a discussion of the problem at hand, the spiritual gifts (1 Cor. 12:1–30 [A] and 14:1b–40 [A′]).

What Paul writes about love in 1 Corinthians 13:4–7 is the centerpiece of what he has to say about charisms. These verses are the very heart of what he has to say about love.

In Praise of Love

Those who read these verses (1 Cor. 13:4–7) in English translation are generally unaware that the entire text is built around fifteen verbs in the third person[10] singular whose common subject is *agape*, "love." With a translation such as that found in the NRSV before the eyes, the reader of 1 Corinthians 13:4–5 might think that Paul employed a series of Greek adjectives meaning "patient," "kind," "envious," "boastful," "arrogant," "rude," "irritable," and "resentful." Paul does not use any of these adjectives.

Had Paul used adjectives in his description of love, he would have provided his readers with a list of the qualities of love, but he does not. Rather than using adjectives, Paul has used a series of verbs. The result is that rather than giving a static description of the qualities of love, Paul personifies love. Doing so, he shows love at work as it were.

He was not the first author in the ancient world to have done so. That distinction apparently has to be attributed to Plato, the great Greek philosopher. In a work called "Banquet" Plato praises love personified (*Symposium* 197A–E). This paean of praise takes the form of a series of short sentences that have love as their subject, underscoring the various qualities of love. In this encomium of love Plato sometimes emphasizes what love is; at other times he emphasizes what love is not, using the well-known rhetorical device of "comparison."[11] Comparison and contrast highlight the nature of love.[12]

A few centuries after Plato launched the symposium genre of Greek literature, Plutarch, one of Paul's contemporaries and one of the greatest of the Hellenistic philosophic moralists, wrote his own *Symposium*. In English it is known as "Table Talk." In this book, Plutarch gave a long and varied response to the question, "Why it is said that love teaches the poet?" Love is personified throughout the entire answer given by Plutarch.[13] As love teaches the poet, so love is skillful in supplying boldness and creating initiative.[14] Love makes the silent man talkative and softens the miser.[15]

The personification of virtues in the Greek literary world entered into the tradition of the Greek Bible. For example, the First Book of Esdras, written no later than the middle of the first century B.C.E., contains a paean in praise of personified truth spoken by one of the bodyguards of King Darius (1 Esdr. 4:33–41). Just as the traits of personified love in the writings of Plato and Plutarch are emphasized by means of rhetorical comparison and contrast, so the portrait of personified truth in 1 Esdras is sharpened through the use of rhetorical comparison. The righteousness of truth is compared with the lack of righteousness in wine, the king, women, and all human beings.

Several motifs in 1 Esdras's eulogy of praise are echoed in Paul's praise of love in 1 Corinthians 13. In the First Book of Esdras we read: "Truth endures and is strong forever, and lives and prevails forever and ever. With it there is no partiality or preference, but it does what is righteous instead of anything that is unrighteous or wicked" (1 Esdr. 4:38–39). In 1 Corinthians 13 Paul writes about the righteousness of love in verse 6. Then in 1 Corinthians 13:8–10 he writes about love's enduring quality.

The Heart of Love

Personifying love as they did, Plato and Plutarch wrote about *eros*. Like these great masters of Greek literature, Paul personified love, but he wrote about *agape*, the subject of 1 Corinthians 12:31–14:1.

The personification of love in 1 Corinthians 13:4–7 is almost a poem.[16] Paul begins on a high note, singing the praises of love as patient and kind. Then he speaks about the things that love is not. Love does not envy nor boast, does not get puffed up nor be rude, is neither self-seeking nor irritable, does not resent nor does it rejoice in misdeeds. To capture the joy that characterizes love, Paul tells his readers that whereas love does not rejoice in wrongdoing, it rejoices in the truth, fidelity. The contrast between these two activities of love is beautifully phrased in Paul's Greek text; it consists of two delicately balanced and parallel phrases. Paul brings his words of praise of love personified to a close with a series of two-word phrases, in which the adjective *panta,* "all things," precedes the noun. The reverse sequence of verb and its object in Paul's Greek text reveals what personified love really does.

What is this love about which Paul writes in 1 Corinthians? The first words of his fifteen-part paean in praise of personified love provide a clue. Paul's "hymn" in praise of love first proclaims: "Love is patient; love is kind" (1 Cor. 13:4). In the Letter to the Romans, Paul writes of patience and kindness as qualities of God himself (Rom. 12:4). Patience and kindness are, in effect, divine attributes.

Another clue as to the real meaning of love is found elsewhere in Romans. Paul writes: "God's love has been poured into our hearts through the Holy Spirit that has been given to us" (Rom. 5:5). According to Paul the Holy Spirit is God's gift to us; through the Holy Spirit the love of God has been poured into our hearts. In Romans 5:5 "love of God" is not the love of human beings for God; it is rather God's love for us. For Paul, "the heart" is a way to describe the human person to the very depths of his or her being. The heart is not a physical organ nor is it merely the source of human emotion. The heart is the core reality of the human person; it is at that level that God touches the human person through the empowering gift of the Spirit of God that pours God's love into the heart of the human being. The love of God is the power of God at work in human beings.

The love of God is the greatest of God's gifts to a human being because it is the fundamental, all-encompassing gift. The love of God is the one gift of God that endures forever. It is the gift that is the source of our faith and our hope (1 Cor. 13:7). God's love is the gift that is manifest in the manifold ways described in 1 Corinthians 13:4–7. It is the gift that is expressed in the various charisms that Paul mentions in 1 Corinthians 12. Each one of these charisms is a manifestation of the Spirit, God's power at work, for the common good (1 Cor. 12:7). Each charism is a means by which God acts (1 Cor. 12:6) among human beings, indeed, by means of human beings. Through the different charisms, empowered by the Spirit, God acts among us and within the church.

It is no wonder that Paul can write that even if he can speak in tongues, or prophesy, or have knowledge, or work miracles, or give away all his possessions,[17] but does not have love, he is nothing. Without the basic gift of God's love (*agape*), all of these things — prophecy and all the rest — are merely wondrous phenomena, *pneumatika*, the kind of spiritual phenomena that even a devotee of idols might enjoy (1 Cor. 12:1–2). Without the fundamental gift of God's love, none of these wonderful realities are charisms, the *charismata*, the gifts through which by the power of the Holy Spirit God acts among us and within his church, the Body of Christ.

The Gift of God's Love

It is most appropriate that married couples, young and not so young, choose 1 Corinthians 12:31–14:1 as a reading for their wedding ceremony. The reading speaks to the sacredness and sacramentality of Christian marriage. Ultimately marriage is a Christian sacrament insofar as in marriage God designates and empowers a man to be the expression and instrument of his love for a woman; in marriage God designates and empowers a woman to be the expression and instrument of her love for a man. In the union of husband and wife, God seeks to satisfy the human need for companionship, family, compassion, understanding, sex, tenderness, care during times of sickness, support when times are difficult, and all of the other many dimensions of wedded life.

That God has appointed and empowered a woman and a man to be the instrument of God's real love in ordinary circumstances is the awesome reality of Christian marriage. Should a married woman or man ever wonder whether she or he is loved by God, the answer should come easily. He or she should be able to respond, I know that I am loved by God because my spouse loves me. My spouse is the sign and instrument of God's love for me.

To speak of a sign and instrument of God's love is, in the traditional jargon of Western theology, to speak of a sacrament, an efficacious sign of grace. The Christian husband or wife is just that. He or she is the effective means by which God, through the power of the Spirit, manifests God's love for a woman and a man in the complex breadth of their being and the ordinary circumstances of daily life. A sacramental marriage is an expression of the intensity, physicality, and totality of God's love for a human being.

In the root sense of the term, the love celebrated in sacramental marriage is truly charismatic. In marriage, husband and wife are consecrated[18] — which means to belong to God in a special way, to be made holy — and empowered. Each has a charism that is properly and uniquely his or her own.[19] As the charisms of which Paul writes in 1 Corinthians 12 and 14 are so many expressions of God's love and the means by which the church is built up as the body of Christ,[20] so Christian marriage is another means by which the church is built up as the body of Christ. Herein lies the ecclesial dimension of the sacrament of marriage.

Marriage is a Christian sacrament not because its ritual celebration takes place in a church building; rather, it is a sacrament because the union of husband and wife builds up the church as Christ's body. Through marriage a new Christian family comes into existence. This family is, in the words of the old expression reprised again during the Second Vatican Council, the "domestic church."[21] The family, founded on the God-given love of man and woman for one another, is the cell on which the church is built up as the body of Christ. It is, as it were, the genetic material of the church itself.

The Challenge of Love

The charismatic character of Christian marriage is awesome. The sad reality is that prophets, teachers, leaders, and helpers in the church do not fully live up to the charism with which they have been endowed any more than do husbands and wives fully live up to the charism with which they have been gifted. Each of them is but one limited — and sometimes sinful — expression of God's love. Paul provides husbands and wives with a portrait of what their love for one other should be in order that it be a truly expressive sign and effective instrument of God's love.

Their love for one another should be patient, kind, neither envious nor boastful, neither arrogant nor rude, not insisting on its own way, nor irritable or boastful, not rejoice in misdeeds but rejoice in the truth, bearing all things and being ever trustful, constantly hoping and enduring what is necessary. To have a love such as this is the vocation of every Christian husband and wife.

Questions for Discussion

1. Many couples choose 1 Corinthians 13 as a reading at their wedding. In the light of this essay, why is this a good choice? How would you have answered this question before reading this essay?

2. What is lost in translating the work of love adjectivally instead of verbally?

3. How does the chiastic structure of Paul's discourse enhance the message?

Chapter 5

The Radicalism of Jesus the Prophet

Implications for Christian Family

Susan A. Calef

It is no secret that the family in America is in crisis. Social scientific studies document the decline of the well-being of American families, and daily news stories report the growing incidence of abuse and neglect of children and so, too, the increasing violence and behavioral problems of the nation's troubled youth. Christians, disturbed by the deterioration of the social and moral fabric of American society and its families, have voiced their concern and expressed their understanding of its causes and its solutions in what has become known as "family values" discourse.

In seeking to bring the wisdom of their faith tradition to bear upon the contemporary problems of the family, many Christians, both Protestant and Catholic, turn to the Bible for guidance. The particular way in which Christians read the Bible for guidance in the midst of the current crisis, however, is deeply problematic. Many, for example, search the Bible for but one thing: evidence that the patriarchal family and the "family values" embedded in it — male authority, female submission, and obedience on the part of children — are divinely ordained, hence, eternally normative.[1] This exclusive focus on the issue of family structure results in a highly selective and partial reading of biblical tradition, one that privileges the second creation account in Genesis 2 and the Deutero-Pauline "household codes" (Col. 3:18–4:1; Eph. 5:21–6:9; 1 Tim. 2:8–15; 5:1–2; 6:1–2; Titus 2:1–10; 3:1–7), texts construed as establishing the normative status of the patriarchal family, while ignoring or overlooking gospel traditions regarding the teaching and practice of Jesus.

Biblical tradition can indeed speak to the current crisis of family and the larger cultural crisis of which it is a part. I take issue, however, with the operative assumption in much family values discourse, namely, that only those biblical texts that explicitly speak of family have any relevance to how Christians should "be family." It is my contention that contemporary Christian reflection on family, surely an urgent task, ought to be informed by far more than the comparatively few biblical texts that explicitly treat marriage and family.[2] It ought to be informed, above all, by gospel tradition, the very tradition that, despite being the core of Christian faith, is conspicuously absent from far too many discussions of family in Christian circles. That tradition suggests that Christians are "discipled" to one whom it remembers as, among other things, prophet. Furthermore, that tradition calls the Christian family to prophetic witness in the contemporary world.

Jesus, a "Prophet Mighty in Deed and Word" (Luke 24:19)

Before turning to the gospel evidence of the prophetic status of Jesus, it is necessary to clarify what we mean by the term "prophet." In popular usage prophecy is synonymous with prediction; hence, prophets are regarded as clairvoyants who foresee and foretell future events, often of a foreboding nature. That this is an oversimplification of the biblical understanding of prophet has been established by critical scholarship, which regards biblical prophecy as a complex phenomenon.[3] In biblical tradition, a prophet is one who proclaims God's message to the people in word and deed. The prophet's authority to do so is based on the claim to have received a vision or "call" such as that experienced by Amos (Amos 7:14–15), Isaiah (Isa. 6:1–13), Jeremiah (Jer. 1:4–10), and Ezekiel (Ezek. 1–2); and in the writings of postexilic prophets, the Spirit of God is regarded as the driving force behind prophetic utterances.[4]

Although some prophets are said to have experienced subsequent visions, these were not prognostications of a clairvoyant type; for it was with an eye to the contemporary conditions of life in ancient Israel that the prophet delivered God's word, be it of judgment, as was often the case in preexilic Israel, or of hope and salvation, as in the exilic and postexilic eras. Thus, prophetic visions and utterances were not concerned with the future in and of itself but rather with the future as a divine response to contemporary human conduct. Often, particularly in the preexilic context, the message included a critique of social, political, and economic realities that were perceived as contrary to the right relations that God willed for the community, hence, the call for justice that is prominent in the preexilic prophets.[5] The prophet's mode of delivery included, at times, dramatic actions that were symbolic of the future consequences of present sin. To symbolize the coming humiliation of the nations that would be taken captive by Assyria, Isaiah walked around naked (Isa. 20:1–6); and Jeremiah smashed a potter's flask in public, pointing to the coming destruction of Jerusalem (Jer. 19).

Critical analysis of the Gospels indicates that in his historical and cultural context and in the early theological reflection of the church, both of which are reflected in the Gospels, Jesus was understood in terms of the biblical traditions of prophecy sketched above.[6] Although the four evangelists think of Jesus as far more than a prophet, all preserve traces of the early tradition that Jesus and his contemporaries understood him to be an eschatological prophet.[7] Due to constraints of space, this essay will focus on the Gospel of Luke, which not only preserves but also develops this tradition into a major element of its interpretation of the meaning and significance of Jesus, portraying Jesus as God's Spirit-filled prophet whose coming fulfills the ancient promise that God would raise up a prophet like Moses (Deut. 18:15, 18).

That the Spirit was the driving force behind Jesus' mission is established early in the Lukan narrative. Immediately after his baptism, Jesus experiences a vision corresponding to the inaugural vision of the prophets of old and receives the Spirit: "Heaven was opened and the holy Spirit descended upon him in bodily form like a dove. And a voice came from heaven, 'You are my beloved Son; with you I am well pleased' " (Luke 3:21–22).[8] Henceforth, the narrative emphasizes that Jesus, like prophets before him, is "full of the holy Spirit" (4:1) and acts "in the power of the Spirit" (4:14).

The prophetic status of Jesus is patently evident in Luke 4:16–30, a pericope regarded as programmatic for Luke's Gospel. Through his comments on the portion of scripture from which he reads (Isa. 61:1–2), Jesus claims, "The Spirit of the Lord is upon me ... " (4:18).[9] Shortly thereafter, in one of the few sayings preserved in all four Gospels (Matt. 13:57; Mark 6:4; Luke 4:24; John 4:44), Jesus applies to himself the proverb "no prophet is accepted in his own native place" (4:24). The emphasis on Jesus' prophetic status is reinforced by the references to Elijah and Elisha that immediately follow (4:25–27), a section that Luke has appended to his Markan source (cf. Mark 6:4). Jesus' self-understanding as a rejected prophet is further suggested by his later remark, "Yet I must proceed on my way today, tomorrow, and the following day, for it is impossible that a prophet die outside of Jerusalem" (13:33).[10]

That his contemporaries likewise considered him a prophet is also evident throughout the Gospel. Jesus' ability to raise the son of the widow of Nain leads the crowd to declare, "A great prophet has arisen in our midst" (7:16), an obvious allusion to Elijah's resuscitation of the only son of the widow of Zarephath (1 Kings 17:8–24). Elsewhere, Simon the Pharisee views him as a prophet, albeit a false one in his estimation (7:39). Later, in the post-resurrection appearance on the road to Emmaus, two of his disciples refer to "Jesus of Nazareth, who was a prophet mighty in deed and word before God and all the people" (24:19), an estimation echoed in Acts of the Apostles, the Lukan sequel. There, Peter implicitly applies to Jesus the Lord's promise to raise up a prophet like Moses (Deut. 18:18; Acts 3:22).[11]

Jesus and the Reign of God

The Gospels further indicate that the coming kingdom or reign of God was the raison d'être of Jesus' mission and of those he called to share it.[12] In Luke, kingdom language features prominently in his commissioning of the Twelve and the Seventy-Two. Summoning the Twelve, "he sent them to proclaim the reign of God" (9:2); and later, seventy-two others whom he appointed and sent ahead of him, are instructed to say, "The kingdom of God is at hand for you" when they enter a town (10:9, 11).[13] Reference to the kingdom ("the kingdom of God is like...," 13:18–21) features in many of the parables,[14] widely acknowledged as Jesus' most distinctive method of teaching. When a crowd attempts to prevent his departure Jesus declares, "I must proclaim the gospel of the kingdom of God to the other towns, too, because that is what I was sent to do" (4:43). Elsewhere Jesus urges his disciples, "seek his kingdom" (12:31), assuring them "your Father is pleased to give you the kingdom" (12:32), and later counsels, "Whoever does not receive the kingdom of God like a child will not enter it" (18:17). He also anticipates eating with his disciples in the kingdom of God at an unspecified time in the future (22:16, 18; 22:29–30).[15]

This prophetic eschatological vision of the coming reign of God bore radical implications for Jesus' own life and practice and for that of would-be disciples. According to the Gospels, Jesus did not marry; he did not conceive children; he did not assume the headship of a patriarchal household. Remarkably, he did not heed the ancient command, "Be fruitful and multiply" (Gen. 1:28). Rather, in order to pursue an itinerant ministry on behalf of the reign of God, Jesus abandoned his household and its work and called others to do the same. In the cultural context, such conduct represented a serious breach of filial duty on the part of an eldest son; consequently, he was, as the proverb that he cites self-referentially suggests, "a prophet without honor among his kin" (Mark 6:4), unwelcome in his hometown (Luke 4:24).[16] Moreover, in the Gospels, Jesus has, in fact, very little to say about family ties, and what little he does say was undoubtedly disturbing, even scandalous, to many of his contemporaries.

In one of the "hard" sayings on discipleship, for example, Jesus in effect pits discipleship against family loyalty, admonishing the crowds that follow him, "If anyone comes to me without hating his father and mother, wife and children, brothers and sisters, and even his own life, he cannot be my disciple" (14:26–27). Elsewhere Jesus' reply to two persons whom he calls to follow him (9:57–62) highlights the urgency of response to the kingdom of God and insists on the absolute priority of discipleship over blood kin obligations. The first responds to Jesus' invitation with a request to perform a sacred duty, "Let me go first to bury my father" (9:59). Shockingly, Jesus dismisses the priority of the duty to kin, commanding, "Let the dead bury their dead. But you, go and proclaim the kingdom of God" (9:60). Likewise, in an exchange reminiscent of the prophet Elijah's call of Elisha (1 Kings 19:19–21), a second would-be disciple requests, "First let me bid farewell to my family at home" (9:61). In striking contrast to Elijah, however, who permitted Elisha to provide for his family before departing to follow the prophet, Jesus' response is curt and uncompromising, "No one who puts a hand to the plow and looks to the things left behind is fit for the kingdom of God" (9:62).

Elsewhere Jesus declares, without apology or hint of regret, that the purpose, not just the consequence, of his mission is to set the members of a family against one another (12:51–53). Such enmity between family members is understood to be a foretaste of the eschatological tribulations soon to come. Thus, elsewhere Jesus warns of persecution by political and religious authorities (21:12) and of the betrayal by family members that such persecution will precipitate: "You will even be handed over by parents, brothers, relatives, and friends, and they will put some of you to death" (21:16). The divisive effect of Jesus' mission on families that is evident in the preceding quotes is the consequence of the transfer of allegiance to which Jesus called his contemporaries in view of the eschatological events that were now unfolding.

In his own person, then, Jesus stood in an unconventional, even iconoclastic, relation to the institutions of family and household of his time and culture. This does not mean, however, that the Jesus of the Gospels is "anti-familial," as some have concluded. To claim such is to overlook the traditions in which Jesus offers teachings that support families or takes action on behalf of family members, thereby affirming the continuing validity of family life and ties.[17] Rather, rhetorically his "hard" sayings on discipleship, which insist on the priority of the reign of God, compel a radical reprioritization on the part of his contemporaries, with Jesus and his cause, the reign of God, displacing blood kin as the ultimate and defining priority of one's identity and way of life.[18]

Family life is not thereby rejected or negated, however; for, significantly, the reprioritization to which disciples are called in view of the nearness of the kingdom involves incorporation into a new family. When Jesus is informed that his mother and brothers are standing outside and wish to see him, Jesus replies, "My mother and my brothers are those who hear the word of God and act on it" (8:21). That the radical reprioritization to which Jesus called his contemporaries is followed by redefinition of family strongly affirms that family, be it "real" (i.e., based on biological or marital bonds) or "fictive," remains absolutely fundamental and necessary in the life of Christian disciples.[19]

Jesus and the Reign of God:
A Radical Witness Concern for Justice

What prophetic witness to the reign of God entails for the eschatological family of his disciples is modeled by the Lukan Jesus in word and deed. A few of the prominent elements of that witness may be cited here: concern for justice, sharing of possessions, prayer, acts of mercy, and inclusive table fellowship. First, reminiscent of the preexilic prophets, Jesus voices a concern for justice — right relation — that is reflected in attention to the plight of the poor.[20] This emphasis is immediately apparent in Jesus' programmatic announcement of the mission for which the Spirit has anointed him: "to bring good news to the poor ... to proclaim liberty to captives and recovery of sight to the blind, to let the oppressed go free, and to proclaim a year acceptable to the Lord" (4:18–19).[21] This understanding of the mission is reaffirmed in his response to the query of the Baptist's disciples, "Are you the one who is to come, or are we to wait for another?" to which Jesus replies, "Go and tell John what you have seen and heard: the blind receive their sight, the lame walk, the lepers are cleansed, the deaf hear, the dead are raised, the poor have good news proclaimed to them" (7:22–23).

In his pursuit of that mission, Jesus issues a stern critique of the greed that contributes to the plight of the poor in ancient agrarian cultures.[22] When two brothers call upon Jesus to adjudicate in their squabble over the division of their inheritance (12:13), Jesus admonishes, "Take care, and be on your guard against all greed; for one's life does not consist in the abundance of one's possessions" (12:15). His admonition begs the question, "If not in an abundance of possessions, then in what does life consist?" to which the material that immediately follows (12:16–34) provides answer. First, to the crowd, which presumably includes the disgruntled brothers, Jesus tells a parable about a rich man whose good fortune (a bountiful harvest) creates an enviable problem (inadequate storage space for the fruits of the harvest), which he proposes to solve by tearing down the barns and building bigger ones (12:16–18). Storage of the surplus in bigger barns, so he thinks, will allow him to secure for himself not only a future — he will be able to eat "for many years" (12:19) — but also a present in which he can indulge himself ("rest, eat, drink, be merry!" 12:19).[23] The wisdom of his solution, however, is exposed as sheer folly when God declares, "Fool, this night your life will be demanded of you, and the things you have prepared, to whom will they belong?" The rich man has, as Jesus observes, stored up "treasure for himself" (12:21);[24] but at death, he will be separated from that earthly "treasure"; hence, the need to be "rich in what matters to God" (12:21).

It is worth noting that in telling the parable Jesus makes no mention of the man's obligation to share the surplus with the less fortunate, although in the context of Luke's Gospel, that obligation may be assumed. Rather, the parable addresses the root of the problem, which is the rich man's motivation in hoarding foodstuffs — a concern to secure his life "for many years," and the two foolish assumptions on which it is based: (1) that "life" is, above all, the physical, bodily life that can be sustained by food; and (2) that he can indeed secure it by his own efforts.[25] The point of the parable — that the rich man's greedy conduct is rooted in a "worry" (12:22, 25, 29) that betrays a fundamental lack of faith in God, the true and trustworthy source of one's well-being and life — is indicated by the thrust of Jesus' subsequent remarks to his disciples (12:22–34), which serve as commentary upon the rich man's conduct and assumptions.

Unlike the rich man, whose hoarding of a surplus suggests anxious pre-occupation with his own physical bodily life, disciples ought not worry about what they will eat or wear, and for two reasons: because "life is more than food and the body more than clothing" (12:22–23), and because the

Father, whose providential care is writ large in nature (12:24–28), "knows you need them" and can be trusted to provide (12:30). Disciples, then, ought set their hearts on the kingdom, trusting their other needs will be satisfied (12:31). In effect, this instruction on greed (12:13–34) presents a pointed contrast: the rich man, anxious to secure the good life for himself, foolishly stores up "treasure for himself" all for naught; the disciples, trusting in the providence of God, sell their belongings and give alms and, in so doing, wisely provide for themselves "an inexhaustible treasure in heaven that no thief can reach nor moth destroy" (12:33).

With an eye to the unjust disparities between rich and poor that greed creates, Jesus, like his prophetic predecessors, announces that God is about to intervene to set things right. In this case, the lack of justice that results in poverty and oppression will be redressed in a startling reversal of fortunes. Beginning his sermon on the plain as he began his sermon in the synagogue, with a reference to the poor, Jesus declares, "Blessed are you who are poor, for yours is the kingdom of God. Blessed are you who are hungry now, for you will be filled" (6:20–21). A sobering admonition to the rich follows, "But woe to you who are rich, for you have received your consolation. Woe to you who are full now, for you will be hungry" (6:24–25). Later in the narrative, the parable of the rich man and Lazarus (16:19–31) depicts the reversal in startlingly graphic terms. In the present life, the rich man is dressed in purple and fine linen and dining sumptuously each day (16:19), while the poor man Lazarus, lying at the door, helpless, sick, and starving, longs to eat the scraps that fall from the rich man's table (16:20–21). At death, their conditions are dramatically reversed: Lazarus is carried away to "the bosom of Abraham" (16:22), an image that evokes a banquet at which Lazarus reclines in a place of honor next to Abraham, while the rich man finds himself in the netherworld, longing for a drop of water (16:22–24). When the rich man, lamenting his plight, pleads for deliverance from his misery, he receives from his father Abraham not consolation but a sobering reminder, "My child, remember that you received what was good during your lifetime while Lazarus likewise received what was bad; but now he is comforted here, whereas you are tormented" (16:25).

Sharing of Possessions

The Lukan Jesus has much more to say about wealth and possessions than can be discussed here.[26] As previously noted, the parable of the rich fool suggests that one's use and disposition of possessions reveals in whom or what one places one's trust, one's faith. That the state of one's heart and what it treasures are revealed by one's use and disposition of possessions is further indicated by Jesus' encounter with two figures later in the Gospel.[27] In the first (18:18–23), an official asks Jesus, "What must I do to inherit eternal life?" to which Jesus responds by urging him to obey the commandments. Upon hearing that the man has observed all the commandments since his youth, Jesus issues a radical challenge: "There is still one thing lacking for you: sell all that you have and distribute it to the poor, and you will have treasure in heaven. Then come, follow me" (18:22). The official, however, is unable to respond; rather, "he became quite sad, for he was very rich" (18:23). His inability to respond to Jesus' call to discipleship suggests that, sadly, his worldly riches mean far more to him than the "treasure in heaven" that Jesus promises to disciples. The results of the encounter elicit from Jesus yet another sobering observation regarding the dangers of wealth, "How hard it is for those who have wealth to enter the kingdom of God. For it is easier for a camel to pass through the eye of a needle than for a rich person to enter the kingdom of God" (18:24–25).

In striking contrast to the sadness of the rich official and his story is the joyful story of another rich man, Zaccheus, whose heart is revealed by what he does with his possessions. Zaccheus is a chief tax collector, and so a very wealthy man, due to the opportunities for fraud and extortion that his occupation afforded. That he is, despite the advantage of wealth, a social outcast is indicated by the bystanders' complaint that Jesus is staying "at the house of a sinner" (19:7). Zaccheus, however, like many tax collectors and sinners, wants to see Jesus and so climbs a tree to see over the crowd that accompanies him. When Jesus invites himself to Zaccheus's house, Zaccheus responds with joy, declaring, "Behold, Lord, half of my goods I give to the poor; and if I have defrauded anyone of anything, I restore it fourfold" (19:8). Thus, Jesus' saving initiative affects in him a change of heart that is embodied in his disposition of possessions in relation to others. Significantly, he does not give away all his wealth, nor does Jesus command him to do so; rather, Zaccheus gives half to the poor and from the remainder will make restitution for any unjust acquisitions. Having experienced the grace of Jesus' mercy, Zaccheus seeks to make things right, to act justly.

Prayer

That Luke emphasizes the role of the Spirit in Jesus' mission was noted above. In addition, throughout the Gospel, Jesus' responsiveness to the Spirit is closely linked to his practice of prayer. In fact, in Luke, Jesus is praying at the time of the descent of the Spirit, and in the subsequent course of his mission, Jesus prays frequently, especially at pivotal moments: at his baptism (3:21), before choosing the Twelve (6:12), before his first prediction of the passion (9:18), and during his agony on the Mount of Olives (22:39–46). After the return of the seventy-two disciples he prays in thanksgiving for his Father's revelation to be childlike (10:21–22). His own prayer practice leads the disciples to ask him to teach them to pray (11:1), which he does (11:2–4), urging them to persistence in prayer to the Father for what they need (11:5–13; 18:1–8); and later, during his agony in Gethsemane, he exhorts them, "Pray that you may not undergo the test" (22:40; cf. 46). Thus, Jesus' mission on behalf of the reign of God is pursued in a spirit of filial trust in and dependence on the one whom he calls "Father," a trust and dependence expressed in prayer.

Although his mission is firmly rooted in a life of prayer, Jesus echoes the prophetic perspective that prayer and cultic praxis do not please God in the absence of justice, right relation with one's neighbor.[28] This perspective is evident in Jesus' warning to the disciples, "Beware of the scribes, who ... devour widows' houses and for the sake of appearance say long prayers. They will receive the greater condemnation" (20:46–47). Elsewhere, using the woe-formula of prophetic speech, Jesus criticizes the religious leaders, "Woe to you Pharisees! For you tithe mint and rue and herbs of all kinds, but neglect justice and the love of God; these you ought to practice, without neglecting the others" (11:42).[29]

Acts of Mercy

The Lukan Jesus not only speaks like a prophet, pronouncing "weal and woe" upon his contemporaries and sounding prophetic themes; he also acts like one. Throughout the Gospel, like Elijah and Elisha to whom he implicitly likens himself in the inaugural sermon in the synagogue (4:25–27), Jesus offers God's mercy — acts of compassion — in response to the bodily and spiritual needs of those beyond the boundaries of Israel. He heals a centurion's servant (7:1–10), a Gerasene demoniac (8:26–39), even a member of the party that arrests him (22:50–51); cleanses lepers (5:12–16; 17:11–19), one of whom, a Samaritan, he recognizes as a "foreigner" (17:18); and offers forgiveness to sinners (7:36–50), including those who crucify him (23:34a).[30] He calls Levi, a tax collector, and so a man despised by his contemporaries, to be his disciple (5:27–28), and frequently eats with tax collectors and sinners, to the chagrin of religious leaders (5:29–32; 7:34–50; 15:1–3). When his dining with tax collectors at Levi's home draws complaint from those leaders, he declares, "I have not come to call the righteous to repentance but sinners" (5:32), later advancing that mission by inviting himself to the home of the chief tax collector, Zaccheus (19:1–10), who is moved to conversion. Even at his crucifixion, in the company of society's quintessential outcasts, criminals condemned to death, Jesus offers mercy to one whom he perceives as not "beyond the pale," assuring him, "Today you will be with me in paradise" (23:43). Thus, in Luke, Jesus, like prophets of old, takes the side of the widow, the stranger in the land, and those on the margin of society.

In the course of his mission Jesus also challenges his contemporaries to practice mercy in an outreach beyond conventional expectations. Disciples, who share in his kingdom mission, are instructed "be merciful as your heavenly Father is merciful" (6:36). To a scholar of the law seeking to justify himself, Jesus holds up the conduct of an outsider — a hated Samaritan — as a model of the merciful neighborliness that reaches across cultural barriers to tend to the bodily needs of others (10:29–37). So, too, the parable of

the lost son (15:11–32) challenges the religious authorities, grumbling about
Jesus' table fellowship with tax collectors and sinners (15:2), to reckon with
the extravagant, even prodigal, mercy of God who aims to bring righteous
and sinner to the same table.

Inclusive Table Fellowship

Jesus also behaves like a prophet in performing dramatic actions that are,
like Isaiah's nakedness and Jeremiah's pot-smashing, symbolic of some future reality willed by God. Precisely which acts depicted in the Gospels ought
to be regarded as prophetic symbolic acts is the subject of debate.[31] In the
Lukan narrative, Jesus' table fellowship has a symbolic function. That this
is the case is indicated by the parable of the great feast (14:15–24), which
serves to interpret the many scenes of Jesus' radically inclusive table fellowship that precede it. Although in the course of his kingdom mission Jesus eats
and drinks with various parties — the Twelve, crowds, Mary and Martha,
Pharisees and scribes — it is above all his table fellowship with tax collectors
and sinners that is noteworthy and characteristic. This pattern of fellowship
earns him the scorn of the religious leaders (see above), thereby contributing to his eventual demise as a rejected prophet. What his opponents fail to
recognize, however, is that Jesus' table fellowship anticipates the eschatological, messianic banquet to be celebrated in the kingdom of God (Isa. 25:1–8)
and about which the prophet Jesus also speaks in the parable of the great
feast (14:15–24).[32] That the parable concerns the invitation to the eschatological feast in the kingdom of God is clear from the immediate context.
Just prior to the telling of the parable, Jesus' advice to his host ends on an
unmistakable eschatological note with Jesus referring to "the resurrection of
the just" (14:14). The eschatological note is sounded again in the exclama-
tion that occasions the telling of the parable: "Happy the one who will eat
bread in the kingdom of God" (14:15). The parable that follows envisions
a messianic community composed of "the poor and the crippled, the blind
and the lame" (14:21), the very sorts of people that Jesus has informed his
host ought to be invited to his table in the future (14:13), the very people
for whom Jesus has been anointed to bring good news (4:18–19).[33]

The Prophetic Discipleship of the Christian Family:
The Call to a "Radical" Witness

In an effort to redress the neglect of gospel tradition that is apparent in
much popular Christian discourse on family, this essay has attended to the
prophetic witness of Jesus in the Gospel of Luke. The gospel tradition, however, does not offer concrete directives or solutions to today's complex social
problems, including the problems of family. Rather, it offers a vision of life

that includes priorities, values, and virtues to be embraced and cultivated in Christian life.

What does the Lukan portrait of the prophetic Jesus offer for a vision of Christian family? A few preliminary suggestions may be offered based on the preceding examination.

1. The root (Latin, *radix*) of Jesus' mission, and so the source of his "radicalism," is his conviction of the absolute priority of the kingdom, the rulership of God. In word and deed Jesus provides witness to that kingdom and to kingdom values and priorities and calls disciples to share in that radical witness, thereby forming a family that is based not on blood kinship or marital ties but on "hearing the word of God and doing it."

Therefore, every Christian family participates in the larger "eschatological" family of disciples that is "church." By its participation within the extended family that has been the "keeper of the story" and bearer of the familial wisdom for two millennia, the individual Christian family both learns the tradition of the extended family and contributes to it in a mutual service that builds up both the individual family and the extended family. As members of the eschatological family of Jesus, the Christian family is called to share in his prophetic witness to the reign of the covenant God who, according to biblical testimony, is merciful, gracious, slow to anger, rich in kindness and fidelity (Exod. 34:6). Toward that end, amid the cacophony of voices and diverse messages to which Americans are exposed by mass media, the Christian family seeks to "hear the word of God and act on it."

2. The Christian family is a Spirited community. Conscious of the Spirit given in the baptism of each of its members, like Jesus it strives to respond to the promptings of the Spirit as it seeks to live its common life in faith, hope, and love and to witness to these gifts in relationships beyond the family.[34] As was the case in the life of Jesus, responsiveness to the Spirit requires the practice of prayer that reflects trust in and dependence on God as the true source of well-being and life. Prayer, of course, requires time and attention as well as quiet. In the midst of a culture that encourages compulsive "busyness" and competition to "get ahead" materially, the faithful practice of prayer and worship and the development of a spiritual centeredness may well be the most essential and urgent elements of the Christian family's prophetic witness to the world.

3. The Christian family, in its discipleship, is called to seek in its own life and in the world beyond its door the justice that the reign of God requires. Sharing Jesus' concern for the plight of the poor, it will commit itself both to acts of charity that provide relief to immediate needs of others and to acts of justice, by which unjust arrangements and relations — social, economic, racial, political, and ecclesial — are identified and rectified.

4. Having "heard the word of God" in scripture, including Jesus' teachings on greed and the dangers of wealth and possessions, in a culture of conspicuous consumption that proclaims "you are what you own," the Christian family will engage in critical reflection on its use and disposition

of possessions, asking: How much do I/we own? What are my/our needs as opposed to my/our wants? How do my wants impact the needs of others in the family, and how do our wants impact the needs of those outside the family? What does our attitude toward possessions reveal about the state of our hearts, what we treasure, and in whom or what we place our trust?

5. In its discipleship, the Christian family is called to practice what is traditionally referred to as the "corporal and spiritual works of mercy" in its common life and in its outreach beyond the family and to cultivate an attitude of active neighborliness.[35] As an expression of mercy, the Christian family will strive to practice a hospitality that is attentive to the marginalized, the outcast, the lonely.

6. Finally, gospel tradition suggests that in its discipleship of the prophet Jesus the Christian family will experience at times controversy, misunderstanding, even rejection, hence, a call to enter more deeply into the paschal mystery.

The current crisis of family, crisis though it surely is, also presents an opportunity. It can be an opportunity to reexamine our attitudes, values, and priorities, to reenvision the ideals toward which we wish to live, to refocus our attention and redirect our energies, to reassess who or what is at the root, the *radix,* of our lives as families. Indeed, it is a *kairos* of sorts, an "opportune or decisive time" such as that to which Jesus refers in the programmatic announcement of his mission, "This is the time [*kairos*] of fulfillment. The kingdom of God is at hand. Repent and believe in the gospel" (Mark 1:14–15).

In a recent discussion of the biblical narratives of the prophets Elijah and Elisha, biblical scholar Walter Brueggemann observes, "These characters are...a narrative embodiment of hope, asserting in quite concrete ways that 'it could be otherwise.' "[36] Jesus, like prophets before him, embodied that same hope and continues to do so; for every Christian family, in its discipleship of the prophet Jesus, is called and empowered to do likewise. In the midst of the extreme individualism and materialism that are taking a toll on our ability to live faithfully in community with one another, the Christian family, rooted in the covenant-love that finds its source in God and cherishing the kingdom values and covenant virtues that are the true source of well-being (shalom), is called to bear prophetic witness to the world and to the larger church that it can indeed be otherwise.

Questions for Discussion

1. What is your understanding of the word "radical" or "radicalism"? In what ways do you think it is appropriate or inappropriate in application to Jesus?

2. How important do you think it is for Christians to understand Jesus as "prophet"? Or are the other titles applied to him (Son of God, Christ, Lord, etc.) more important to Christian faith?

3. In what ways do you think the Christian family could provide prophetic witness to the world and to the larger church?

4. What do you think are potential obstacles to the prophetic witness of the Christian family?

Chapter 6

Equality in Marriage

The Biblical Challenge

Lisa Sowle Cahill

Roles in Marriage Today

Over the last generation or so, most Western societies have witnessed huge changes in the roles expected of women and men. Today's college graduates, male or female, expect to have the opportunity to marry and raise a family, while pursuing the career or vocation for which their education has prepared them. Women are no longer satisfied to see domesticity as their only option. Men want to enjoy a greater role in family life, spending time with children. Though both women and men realize that to combine family and work goals may at times be difficult, and will require sacrifice, they hope that, if they marry, they will find a partner with whom they can share the responsibilities and joys of multiple vocations. Supporting each other in this "balancing act" is, of course, even more important when stresses arise on the job or in family life, and when two incomes are necessary to make ends meet.

Fifty years ago, it was expected that women would give up "work" when they married, and certainly if they became mothers. Meanwhile, to be a "good father" or "good husband" was the virtual equivalent of being a "good provider" — of holding down a well-paying job while leaving the children at home in the care of their mother. Moreover, it was expected that the father and husband would be the primary center of family authority. While women's resourcefulness and the respect women earned was often acknowledged and praised, such praise was frequently set in the context of anecdotes about how the family's "strong women" controlled the men through indirect tactics. Women got what they wanted or thought was best for the children by persuading the men that they had come up with the women's plan of action first, or by acting "behind the scenes," utilizing female networks that did not directly confront or threaten male control. The popular 2002 romantic film comedy *My Big Fat Greek Wedding* derived much of its humor from playing on how quaint such models of feminine power have really become.

Catholic Teaching on Equality in Marriage

The Catholic Church has not been left behind in this swiftly turning tide toward women's and men's equality in marriage, and their corresponding equality in roles outside the home. In 1930, Pope Pius XI wrote an encyclical that provides a window onto the attitudes current in the generation in which the grandparents of today's college students came of age. Pius XI refers to marital love as having a certain characteristic order that also orders the home. It "implies the primacy of the husband over his wife and children, and the ready submission and willing obedience of the wife" (citing St. Paul's Letter to the Ephesians 5:22–23).[1] Women were supposed to be under the authority of men not only "regarding the government of the home," but also "regarding the administration of property." Pius XI was against any variety of what he regarded as an "unnatural equality" between wives and husbands. That included the "economic emancipation" of women, "which would authorize the wife, without the knowledge of her husband and even against his will, to conduct and administer her own affairs." It also ruled out women's "social emancipation," which would dangerously "free the wife from the domestic cares" and enable her "to follow her own bent, and engage in business and even in public affairs."[2]

By 1995, times had certainly changed. John Paul II, writing in anticipation of a United Nations Conference on the status of women to be held in Beijing, declared, "Thank you women who work!" He called the contributions of women to culture indispensable and praised "the great process of women's liberation," even while acknowledging that the work of liberating women from unfair social norms is still unfinished.[3] Several years earlier, he had already affirmed "the equal dignity and responsibility of women with men," concluding that this "fully justifies women's access to public functions."[4]

Nonetheless, some advocates for women wonder whether these changes, while certainly to be applauded, have gone far enough. John Paul II calls women and men equal in family and society but still defines their personalities, and to an extent their roles, in terms of a model of "complementary" male and female natures. This model reflects to some extent Pius XI's portrayal of gender roles (that is, social roles assigned by sex). For example, women are said to have an inherently maternal personality and a "special genius" that enables them to be compassionate and to nurture other persons more than men.[5] When women take up roles outside of the family, it should not be at the expense of "their true feminine humanity."[6] Meanwhile, men are called to relive on earth "the very fatherhood of God" and bear responsibility for overseeing "the harmonious and united development of all the members of the family."[7] The pope obviously does not intend complementarity to mean that men should dominate over women, nor that women should be confined exclusively to maternal and domestic roles in the home. Still, it is at least debatable whether the full equality of women with men in marriage, family, and society is compatible with seeing women primarily as compassionate nurturers and men as representing God to other family members. Moreover, men are shortchanged when their ability to represent in their own lives the compassionate, sacrificial love of Jesus is defined as inherently inferior to that of women.[8]

Today it can no longer be taken for granted that there are clear differences between men and women, in terms of behavior and personality. Both sexes exhibit a spectrum of traits, and personality differences within each sex are often much greater than the differences between any particular man and woman. It may be true that male and female humans, resembling other species of mammals, have some sex-based tendencies, related to reproductive behavior and reflecting differences in the brain, hormones, or prenatal environment. However, it is equally true that all women and men are raised in cultures that already have certain patterns of expected or acceptable female and male behavior. Socialization or "nurture" plays at least as great a part as "nature" in creating women's and men's personalities. The exact contributions and interplay of innate tendencies and social expectations may never be sorted out clearly. Yet we can at least say that the equality of the sexes demands that neither sex be strictly assigned to only certain kinds of roles and excluded from others.[9] Neither one should be assigned to roles that carry less social value and bring less freedom, respect, or opportunity for personal fulfillment and social contribution. Hence, in marriage as a basic human and Christian calling, equal respect, partnership, reciprocity, and shared authority should be the rule. This contemporary Catholic view of marriage is well represented throughout the works of Michael Lawler. In a recent work, he calls the sacramental marriage of Christians "an equal and loving partnership to be lived for the whole of life," and "an equal partnership to discover together the very depths of life."[10] This idea of marriage as an equal communion of loving partnership in which each seeks the good of the other and both share in serving family and community is the hallmark of Christian marriage today.

The Biblical Challenge

Equality of spouses in marriage is now a widespread social expectation in some cultures and has even been accepted by the Catholic Church theologically. Yet the earlier tradition about the inequality of women and men had a biblical basis. Cultural and theological changes notwithstanding, texts saying wives should be "submissive" to husbands still appear in the Christian Bible. What does this mean for the Catholic, Christian theology and practice of marriage? Is there a direct contradiction between biblical teachings and current theology? If not, how should those biblical texts be interpreted? Or are the texts no longer relevant or revelatory for today's Christians?

First, let us take a look at what is seemingly clear and incontrovertible evidence for the inequality of women and men in marriage. In several of the letters to the early churches attributed to St. Paul, there are instructions for the relationships of various family members (Col. 3:18–4:1; Eph. 5:21–6:9; 1 Pet. 2:18–3:7; 1 Tim. 2:8–15; 5:1–2; 6:1–2; Titus 2:1–10; 3:1). In all of these, the husband, father, and master (assumed to be the same person) is presented as having authority over subordinate family members: wives, children (including adult children), and slaves. While the latter two pairs (father/child and master/slave) are problematic in their own right, our focus here will be the marriage relation. Much of what we discover in looking at this relation in more depth will also apply to the other two relationships.

The two most developed versions are found in Colossians and Ephesians. Paul probably did not write either of these letters himself; they were written in his name by followers or disciples who are building on images and themes used by Paul himself, trying to communicate faithfully and expand on Paul's views of Christian faith and life. It is likely that Colossians was written first, and Ephesians modeled on it. After reminding believers that they even now are sharing in Christ's resurrection, the author of Ephesians tells them that forgiveness, love, and peace must rule their hearts (3:13–15). He then continues,

> Wives, be subject to your husbands, as is fitting in the Lord. Husbands, love your wives and never treat them harshly. Children, obey your parents in everything, for this is your acceptable duty in the Lord. Fathers, do not provoke your children, or they may lose heart. Slaves, obey your earthly masters in everything.... Masters, treat your slaves justly and fairly, for you know that you also have a Master in heaven. (Col. 3:18–22; 4:1)

The Letter to the Ephesians goes further. It develops these relationships at greater length and especially expands on the nature of marriage by comparing it to the union of Christ and the church. In fact, the comparison of the love of husband for wife to the love of Christ for the church that appears in Ephesians 5 has traditionally been used as a biblical basis for the Catholic view that marriage is a sacrament.[11] Our focus here, however, will not be on sacramentality as such, but on the relationship of women and men in marriage that this text presents or implies. The author begins with a general instruction to believers to "Be subject to one another out of reverence for Christ" (5:21). He then continues in part, "Wives, be subject to your husbands as you are to the Lord. For the husband is the head of the wife just as Christ is the head of the church, the body of which he is the Savior. Just as the church is subject to Christ, so also wives ought to be, in everything, to their husbands. Husbands, love your wives, just as Christ loved the church and gave himself up for her.... Each of you ... should love his wife as himself, and a wife should respect her husband" (Eph. 5:22–25, 33). The simile linking spouses to the Christ-church union seems to give even greater weight or value to the hierarchical structure of the relation between spouses described by the author of Colossians.

The implied message does not sit easily with many modern women — or men. We may well wonder why the Roman Catholic Church continues to include this reading on one Sunday and one weekday during the liturgical year and to offer different excerpts from it as possible readings for weddings, when there are so many other biblical texts available. One New Testament scholar wryly comments that, according to her parish priest, "almost no couples choose either the long or the short version of that reading, though a prospective groom will occasionally joke about it (e.g., 'I'd like to choose it, but I value my life')."[12] An undergraduate biology major who was a student in a "feminist theology" class I taught in 2003 shared a similar reaction in a weekly class paper:

> When I think about the main messages of the Bible, particularly the New Testament, what comes into my mind are the ideas of compassion, forgiveness, and love exemplified by Jesus. As a young girl attending church with my family I loved listening to the readings each week. I wanted to help the poor and the sick and do all of the things that were part of being a compassionate person. Perhaps this is why by the time I was in seventh grade I became a lector at my parish's youth mass, an activity I continued throughout high school, concluding with my final reading the Sunday I left home to attend Boston College.
>
> Each year however there was always something that bothered me about Paul's letter to the Ephesians. "Wives should be subordinate to their husbands as to the Lord" (Eph. 5:22). "Husbands, love your wives, even as Christ loved the church ... " (Eph. 5:25). Every time I heard these words read or read them myself they bothered me. After all it seemed rather unfair that as a woman I should subordinate myself to my husband when all he would have to do was love me in return. Before I knew anything at all about feminist theology and interpretation of the canonized Bible, I felt strangled by these words and others like them that can be found throughout the New Testament. For me as a woman of faith, it is hard to disbelieve the Bible, but it is harder to accept the words condemning me to a quiet and subordinate existence cleaning the home and caring for the children. My solution until now was to ignore these passages. Most Sundays I would go to church and enjoy the readings and homilies and when these passages were read I would refuse to think about them.[13]

In a way, young Catholic women in the United States today are fortunate to be in a position where such texts can be safely "ignored." For many generations, and even now in many cultures, these texts helped create very restrictive patterns in which women were forced to live, and even submit to male abuse. The U.S. Catholic bishops have taken a clear stand against domestic abuse, but they note that "one of the most worrying aspects of the abuse practiced against women is the use of biblical texts, taken out of context, to support abusive behavior.... Abused women say, 'I can't leave this relationship. The Bible says it would be wrong.' Abusive men say, 'The Bible says my wife should be submissive to me.' " The bishops rightly identify this kind of thinking as a distortion of the Bible's message. They condemn it, urging that the church and its pastors and teachers support and offer refuge to women trying to leave harmful and violent marriages.[14]

Nevertheless, the biblical passages commanding the submission of women still have a lingering cultural effect, and they are taken as the rule in some conservative Protestant Christian denominations today.[15] Even when they do not result in outright abuse, they leave women little defense against domineering, selfish, or irresponsible husbands. Ephesians 5 may command men to love their wives, but compliance is voluntary. The submission of women, on the other hand, seems to be enforced by a predetermined family and marriage structure that puts social and ecclesial approval on the side of male authority and leaves women little or no room to protest or take action if that authority is wrongly exercised.

Interpretations

Acknowledging such problems, biblical scholars, theologians, and Christian teachers have sought for ways to reconcile these texts with gender equality by placing them in context or exploring various layers of meaning. One of the more traditional methods is to interpret the texts as calling for "mutual submission." Instead of viewing only the wife's role as subordinate, the texts can be interpreted in the context of a call for all members of the Christian community to love, forgive, and seek peace with one another. Therefore, since husbands are to love their wives, they too in a way are "subordinating" their own interests to those of their wives. Just as Christ sacrificed himself for the church, so husbands submit to the welfare of their wives in marriage and family. As one Christian scholar argues, "Subordination to God-ordered authority undergirds Christian social ethics. This is not the foundation on which a tyrannical patriarchy rests: it is the nurturing environment for reciprocity within the legitimate structures of healthy families and a healthy society." He argues that the Bible also teaches "mutual submission," and "reciprocity in all our relationships." "Our Father calls all members of his household, not to misuse and abuse others, but to submit ourselves to one another...." Christian women should therefore not seek "empowerment."[16]

Catholic scholars and teachers are less wedded to the exact words of the biblical texts in trying to portray the relationship of marriage today. They are more sensitive to the unequal and even exploitative consequences an uncritical reading can have. In a "Letter to Families," Pope John Paul II includes a long discussion of Ephesians 5 without quoting either the metaphor of husband as head of the wife or commands to subordinate household members to be submissive to the husband, father, and "master." Instead the pope prefers the term "respect," and emphasizes mutual love.[17] However, the Catholic bishops do use the term "mutual submission," though refraining from further remarks indicating that women should not seek to become more empowered or escape sexist norms of the past. Instead, they combine the language of mutual submission with endorsement of women's shared authority with men in marriage, and role flexibility for both. According to the bishops, "marriage is a vowed covenant" and "partnership," in which "mutual submission — not dominance by either partner — is the key to genuine joy." "Mutuality is really about sharing power and exercising responsibility for a purpose larger than ourselves." This means "each family (couple) must decide what is best for them in a spirit of respect and mutuality. Especially when both spouses are employed, household duties need to be shared."[18] Certainly, official Catholic interpretations do not read biblical texts as giving men power over women in marriage, as assigning women and men to strict domestic and public roles, or as discouraging women's struggles for dignity and equality.

As Michael Lawler sees it, what is really meant in Ephesians is "an attitude of mutual giving way," which for spouses means "the total availability and responsiveness to one another required of best friends and lovers."[19] This is a beautiful ideal, inspiring to many as they enter the marriage relationship, and one to be affirmed. Yet "mutual submission" or "headship" language as a way of communicating it is dangerous. Such terms evoke and tacitly reinforce women's traditional inequality and often assume structures of marriage that guarantee women's submission to men but leave men's "mutual" submission up to their own choice.

Modern biblical interpretation has made important contributions to our understanding of the meaning of biblical texts about "submission." We know more about their original historical context, and we are more aware that other texts in the Bible present equal gender roles. Although this is not the place for an extensive discussion of women in the New Testament, scholarly consensus today is that women are certainly not depicted as uniformly "submissive." The Gospel of John has received special attention in recent years as a text in which women's leadership is prominently displayed and valued. Biblical scholar Sandra Schneiders believes that John presents women "in stark contrast to men, with the women appearing in the more positive light. The Samaritan woman contrasts favorably with Nicodemus; Martha with the Jewish leaders; Mary of Bethany with Judas; Mary Magdalene with Simon Peter."[20] In particular, Mary Magdalene, whom Christian tradition has erroneously and demeaningly handed down as a prostitute, appears in all four Gospels as the first witness to the resurrection of Jesus. In John's Gospel she is sent by the risen Jesus to announce the resurrection to the others (John 20:14–17), the mark of an apostle, according to the example of Paul.

Of more direct relevance to the interpretation of Colossians and Ephesians, there were obviously women fulfilling leadership positions in the churches Paul himself founded. This includes women, some married, who were leading churches that met in their houses (1 Cor. 16:19; Rom. 16:3, 5; Philem. 2; Col. 4:15). Often cited in support of transformed gender roles in the early Christian communities is a baptismal formula found in another Pauline letter: "As many of you as were baptized into Christ have clothed yourselves with Christ. There is no longer Jew or Greek, there is no longer slave or free, there is no longer male or female; for all of you are one in Christ Jesus" (Gal. 3:27–28). On the one hand, it is improbable that this verse should be read as meaning that all such social distinctions were immediately abolished in the community as a result of baptism. But it is quite likely that strong social demarcations requiring "exclusion" (Jew and Greek) or "submission" (women and slaves) were significantly altered. At the very least we can say there is a tension between the texts commanding women's submission to men in marriage and other texts proclaiming a new inclusive community of the baptized.

Historical Context

Then why were the passages on "submission" created and repeated by Christians in the first century after Christ, and why were they finally included in the collection of authoritative texts that we know today as "the Bible"? Some scholars, preeminently the Catholic, feminist New Testament scholar Elisabeth Schüssler Fiorenza, have made the case that the early Christian churches were regarded as dangerous "sects" by the Greco-Roman culture in which they emerged. Others feared that the very fact that Christians preached radical unity and equality in the "body of Christ" would be subversive to the family and the well-ordered state. Therefore, in order to avoid persecution and to enhance their chances of converting others to their movement, Christians "accommodated" what was originally a "discipleship of equals" to conform to prevailing social norms.[21]

Ever since the time of Aristotle in ancient Greece, philosophers had promulgated so-called "household codes" or instructions for household management, which prescribed the same ordering of relationships that we find in Ephesians and Colossians: subordination of wives, children, and slaves to the *paterfamilias*.[22] In fact, the Christian versions soften or transform these codes by prescribing mutual love, rather than one-way obedience from the inferior party. Especially striking is the fact that in the more ancient, non-Christian versions, slaves are never addressed as persons in their own right. Moreover, in the Christian codes, slaves (and implicitly, the other "lesser" parties) are held as ultimately subject to God, along with their masters, so that God is finally the authority and father over all, relativizing the power of the earthly male authority. It may well be the case that members of the Christian community were aware that the face they presented to outsiders did not entirely represent the ideals to which they aspired within their own circle. This is especially plausible given "clues" in the epistles that the household codes are not ultimately determinative of Christian relationships. For instance, in Colossians, even though slaves are told to be submissive, all Christians are repeatedly characterized as "fellow servants" together under Christ as Lord (1:17; 4:7, 12).[23]

The "Household Codes" Today

These kinds of explanations do not let the early Christians' probable choice to accommodate cultural norms entirely off the hook, of course. Whatever their original situation and intention, the household codes have undeniably had oppressive effects for women and have underwritten a hierarchy of power in Christian churches and families for centuries. As Carolyn Osiek notes, the association of men with Christ and women with the church (as bridegroom and bride) in Ephesians 5 has taken on a life of its own in Christian history, enabling the belief that women are inherently less than men and that their inferiority should define the way they relate to husbands in marriage.[24] Moreover, we could well argue, whatever the threats from society, followers of Jesus should have remained true to the type of community Jesus had formed in the first place. Therefore, Elisabeth Schüssler Fiorenza has concluded that patriarchal texts like the Christianized household codes are simply not revelatory of God's will for believers, even though they may have survived in the Bible.[25]

While one can appreciate the frustration, even outrage, of scholars and believers who are all too aware of the damaging effects of such texts, a slightly different perspective may be possible, one that would allow us to reinstate these texts as communicating a valuable "lesson" for marriage and for the Christian life in general. The message is not, however, about proper gender relations. It is about forming a Christian life and Christian marriage through trial and error, always keeping one's sights on the example of Jesus and never giving in to despair. Realistically speaking, the early Christian communities were never completely egalitarian transformations of the communities and families in which converts to the movement around Jesus already lived. This is especially obvious when we consider that the early church spread through the conversion of people in households, or even of entire households. The "new family" of Christ developed within or around already existing structures that were hardly egalitarian. Conversion reshaped family and social relationships in the light of new possibilities, but the process would inevitably have been partial, incremental, and to some degree experimental.[26] What would work, and what would not? What would illuminate the living memory of Jesus, and what would dim it?

The Pauline household codes represent the attempt of early Christians to embody their faith within the practical social circumstances that were the reality for them at the time. They challenged their culture but in the process compromised with it. Sometimes the compromise was too great. Their record of the results, now our "Bible," is a lasting lesson that Christians cannot flee their own historical period, that dealing with it successfully will be difficult, and that erroneous decisions — or at least faulty ones — will sometimes be made. This does not mean that a faithful Christian life is not possible. What it does mean is that self-criticism, openness to change, repentance, forgiveness, and reform will always be necessary.

While texts instructing "submission" in marriage and family need to be criticized and changed because they enforce patriarchy and undermine the truly equal love that is the goal of Christian marriage, these texts still have value. They cause modern-day Christians to think deeply and critically about the genuine meanings of love, sacrifice, and mutuality in marriage. They teach us that even when a wrong turn is taken in defining what is required of Christians, the motivation may be understood and if necessary forgiven. Whether in the church or in a marriage, past mistakes can be recognized and corrected. The household codes preserve a biblical record that perfection is not necessary to Christian identity nor to Christian marriage — in fact, it is impossible. Yet they teach us also that love and faith, though imperfect and stumbling, can lead us on to God through the everyday relationships and commitments we make with those around us.

Questions for Discussion

1. Under what circumstances would you recommend that Ephesians 5 be read during Sunday liturgy or used for a wedding ceremony?

2. What are some of the elements that go into interpreting a biblical text and defining its meaning "for today"?

3. What do you see as appropriate roles for men and women in Christian marriage and family?

Chapter 7

Marriage Is Good, but Celibacy Is Better

The Mixed Legacy of the Early Christian Understanding of Marriage

John J. O'Keefe

If early Christianity has bequeathed to posterity any united message about the value of marriage, it would be this: marriage is good, but celibacy is better. Such a declaration will surprise no one who has spent time studying the question. Even those who possess only a passing familiarity with the age of the church fathers (roughly 100–600 C.E.) will likely know this much. Indeed, most studies of marriage and family, at least in a Roman Catholic context, begin with a ritual consideration of the patristic position. Since Vatican II, the old claim that "marriage is good, but celibacy is better" has been largely abandoned by theologians (and many church officials) in favor of a theology that treats marriage as a vocation possessing nobility equal to that of celibacy.[1] The church fathers usually come off badly in these assessments; they are the bad guys who devalued human sexuality and rejected one of God's great gifts to men and women. St. Augustine, one of the greatest Christian thinkers ever to have lived, is often dismissed as the source of all that is wrong and twisted in traditional Christian perspectives on marriage.[2] Like most sweeping generalizations, this one too is a distortion. While ancient Christian ideas about marriage may be inappropriate for the modern world, they need not be reduced to mere foils for contemporary sensibility.

The most common narrative description of patristic teaching about marriage begins with, or at least includes as a salient feature, a critique of St. Augustine. Born in Roman North Africa in 354 to a Christian mother and a pagan father, Augustine received a classical education in Carthage, where he quickly demonstrated his brilliance. While infant baptism was not unknown at this time, it was not uncommon for people to wait until middle age or later to seek initiation into the church. Augustine remained unbaptized until after age thirty. Although unbaptized, Augustine was a born theologian. In his most famous work, *The Confessions*, he details the religious turmoil of his youth and the false steps he took along the road leading to his conversion. One of those self-described false steps was his involvement with Manichaeism.

Ancient Manichaeans were dualists. In their view, the world divided neatly into the forces of good and the forces of evil. Since the evil God controlled the material universe — that is, the place of bodies, sex, and all things earthly — spiritual seekers were obliged to renounce these things and gain freedom in a spiritual domain far from the dirty carnality of the world. Naturally, those who subscribed to the Manichaean system were ascetics — they practiced strict forms of physical self-denial, including renunciation of sex. The young Augustine found himself drawn into this vision of the world. On this, all would agree. The question is, was Augustine ever able to fully shed the influence of this sect? According to his own account in *The Confessions,* Augustine eventually realized that the Manichean position was intellectually bankrupt and fundamentally false. He, therefore, rejected it. In spite of Augustine's claims to the contrary, many contemporary critics claim that he never escaped. Manichaean dualism, they say, filtered into his teaching about marriage and sexuality and, ultimately, via Augustine, into the Christian tradition's teaching about marriage and sexuality.

An often-cited example of Augustine's imprisonment in this worldview is his theology of original sin. While contemporary theologians understand original sin as the common condition of estrangement from God that all humans experience, Augustine, and many of his generation, interpreted Adam's sin more literally. Adam was not a mythological figure symbolizing humanity; he and Eve were real individuals. They were literally the first man and the first woman. Likewise, their sin was also a literal sin. Somehow this sin resulted in the collective condemnation of subsequent generations of human beings. As Paul writes in his letter to the Romans, "no one is righteous, no not one.... " Unlike his contemporaries, however, Augustine sought to understand how the sin of Adam was transmitted from generation to generation. He concluded that the transmission took place by means of Adam's seed, his sperm.[3] Sex, it would appear, carries the burden of human alienation from God, but such a conclusion would be misleading. Augustine believed human sexuality was damaged by the fall but not ruined by it. His insistence on the physiological transmission of sinfulness is more, to use modern language, an affirmation of the genetic unity of humanity. We have, one might say, inherited a tragic gene that leads all to sin. Human rebellion, not sexuality, caused this tragedy.

While Augustine may receive the bulk of the blame for the traditional affirmation of the superiority of celibacy, other early Christian authors do not fair much better. Few, for example, would attempt to defend the teachings of St. Jerome.[4] Another son of the fourth century, Jerome led a complicated life, mostly far from his native Italy, in Roman Palestine. A true genius, Jerome was perhaps the only ancient Christian writer who could read Hebrew. He put this skill to use producing the Vulgate translation of the Bible, which is still the official Bible of the Roman Catholic Church. Jerome was also heavily involved in the ascetical movement of the fourth century and wrote extensively on the value of virginity and celibacy. Jerome wrote particularly unflattering things about marriage. In a famous letter extolling the virtues of virginity Jerome wrote, "I praise wedlock, I praise marriage; but it is because they produce me virgins. I gather the rose from the thorn, the gold from the earth, the pearl from the oyster."[5] When these and many other examples are assembled, the record of early Christian teaching about marriage seems very poor indeed. Augustine, because of his massive influence, is an easy target for those looking to blame someone for the failure of the tradition to honor a vocation by which so many of us find our way to sanctity.

Yet for all the attractive simplicity of this view, it is profoundly lacking in historical nuance. Vilification of the past is an easy way to overcelebrate the achievements of the present, but it is a poor way to reach understanding. The past, properly understood, can, and often does, help to illuminate the present. Patristic teaching about marriage is really the result of the complex interaction of three things: first, the witness of Jesus and the New Testament, second, the reality of marriage in the ancient world, and third, the emergence in the fourth century of something that we might call an "ascetical revolution." Each of these requires some explanation.

The Biblical Witness and the Ancient World

Even those who love marriage and wish to defend it must acknowledge that the New Testament sends mixed signals about married life. Jesus himself was not married. This is a powerful example. Likewise, when the apostles go off on the missionary journeys, we hear nothing about their wives. What happened to the wife of Peter? The text is completely uninterested in the question. Indeed, there are a number of texts that seem to recommend avoiding marriage altogether. Consider the following examples:

> Matthew 22:30: For in the resurrection they neither marry nor are given in marriage, but are like angels in heaven.

> Luke 20:34–35: And Jesus said to them, "The sons of this age marry and are given in marriage, but those who are accounted worthy to attain to that age and to the resurrection from the dead neither marry nor are given in marriage."

> 1 Corinthians 7:27: Are you bound to a wife? Do not seek to be free. Are you free from a wife? Do not seek marriage.

> 1 Corinthians 7:38: So that he who marries his betrothed does well; and he who refrains from marriage will do better.

Admittedly, these texts are taken out of context. Recognizing that many people in Paul's day expected a speedy return of the Lord helps to explain why Paul might recommend refraining from changing one's state in life. The passages from Matthew and Luke, however, do suggest that part of Jesus' teaching included a vision of the kingdom of God that was so new and radical that there would be no place for human institutions such as marriage. We may also soften the impact of these passages by recognizing, as Bruce Malina has done in an earlier essay, the very specific contexts in which these texts occur, but by the time of Augustine, the original contexts of these passages were long forgotten.

Clearly, the New Testament has many positive things to say about marriage, and these more positive texts are those that contemporary scholars use to construct a theology of marriage that defends the value and the good of marriage against the traditional hegemony of celibacy. Biblical interpretation, of course, is just that, interpretation, and the outcome of any act of interpretation depends, to a great extent, on the starting place of the interpreter. Contemporary theologians begin with an experience of marriage that is largely positive and rooted in the Western tradition of voluntary association in mutual friendship and romantic love. This does not imply that the Bible can mean whatever we want it to mean, but it does mean that the emphasis of the Bible will shift depending on the perspective of the reader.[6] Christian teaching about marriage, then, can be said to change as the culture in which the teaching is promulgated changes. If, as we have suggested, contemporary theologies of marriage, and the related biblical emphases, are rooted in the cultural experience of the modern West, then we can be certain that the theology of marriage that developed in the age of the fathers was rooted in the cultural experience of the ancient world.

Although friendship and love developed between men and women in the ancient world, this was not seen as a primary reason to marry. In the upper classes especially, marriage was an economic decision since it involved the transfer of wealth in the form of property and the continuity of family power. It was not uncommon for much older men to marry much younger women. As a result men frequently took concubines of lower social status, but closer in age. The Christian church gradually rejected this practice. Hence, although Augustine himself had a concubine for many years whom, at least according to his own report in *The Confessions*, he loved, he felt compelled to leave her when he became engaged to a girl half his age.

Marriage was also seen as a positive social good because it provided a context for procreation. In a culture where infant mortality was high, issues of birth rate and survival were taken far less for granted than they are today. According to historian Peter Brown,

[Ancient society] was more helplessly exposed to death than is even the most afflicted underdeveloped country in the modern world. Citizens of the Roman Empire at its height, in the second century A.D., were born into the world with an average life expectancy of less than twenty-five years. Death fell savagely on the young. Those who survived childhood remained at risk. Only four out of every hundred men, and fewer women, lived beyond the age of fifty.[7]

Marriage in this culture was a good thing, but it was not good for the reasons we think it is good. Setting ancient Christian views of marriage in the context of the ancient world helps us understand that ancient people were not motivated to marry primarily because of starry-eyed attraction, romantic infatuation, and a desire for intimate friendship. It also helps to explain why the church came to locate the primary good of marriage in procreation and social stability. However, the ancient context alone does not explain the church's fascination with celibacy.

Asceticism

If we were to locate one movement in the history of Christianity upon which we could pin the label "responsible for the idea that marriage is good, but celibacy is better," it would be ancient asceticism. On the one hand, the word "asceticism" is fairly innocuous. The term derives from the Greek word for "training" but in the tradition has come primarily to mean "self-denial." Sexual relations, food, and money were three primary pleasures that ancient ascetics sought to avoid through acts of self-denial. These self-denying ascetical practices became institutionalized in Christian monasticism, and we can say, at the risk of oversimplification, eventually came to dominate the Christian imagination with respect to what was and was not holy. To the extent that marriage did not embrace these ideals, it came to be seen as a lesser good. But we are moving too quickly. The ascetical revolution of the fourth century can be explained, and this explanation can help to soften the traditional teaching.[8]

As many scholars of the early church have noted, in the years before the conversion of the emperor Constantine to Christianity in 313, Christians lived under the threat of persecution for their faith. This does not mean that all Christians during this entire period of three hundred years were faced with the imminent threat of persecution — as I tell my students, most Christians died in bed. It does mean that persecutions could pop up at any time and terrorize the affected Christian community.[9] The worst of these persecutions happened in the middle of the third century and at the beginning of the fourth. Those Christians who were killed as a result of persecution were called martyrs, and the Christian community honored them as heroes by marking the anniversary of their deaths with special celebrations. The legacy of their witness can be seen in the frequent appearance of memorials commemorating martyr saints on the pages of the official church calendar. These celebrations were, in a way, the original holy days.

Beyond the annual commemoration, however, the existence of the martyrs communicated to Christians a message about their identity. The martyrs, like Jesus himself, risked everything for the gospel. To use a modern truism, they not only "talked the talk, they walked the walk." To the extent that all who accepted baptism in these early centuries put themselves in harm's way, the church came to see itself as the martyr church in some ways. In accord with the literal meaning of martyr, they were the people who gave witness to the truth of Christ and his church. The conversion of the emperor and the legalization of Christianity brought all of this to an end.

Although the end of persecution was universally hailed as welcome news, there was a cost. Constantine's conversion opened the door for risk-free Christianity. For the first time in the church's history, it was possible to be a Christian without taking any chances. Indeed, many conversions were politically motivated. Ancient people were no less prone than their modern counterparts to following the direction of the politically victorious. For the religiously serious, the existence of this new kind of Christian was troubling and left many asking questions about how to be a serious Christian in the midst of so much mediocrity. This is the context for the birth of Christian asceticism, which many called the bloodless martyrdom. It was an effort to preserve and advance the conviction that the Christian life must necessarily be heroic, self-sacrificing, and risky as opposed to pedestrian, self-promoting, and safe.

It would not be unfair to say that this sense of disappointment in the mediocrity of the church after Constantine caused the creation of a cultural revolution in the Christian world. The question was for them, as it continues to be for many people today, how do I imitate Christ more perfectly? When this desire for a true Christian life merged with those passages from the New Testament suggesting that remaining single was a more perfect way to imitate the Lord, ancient Christian asceticism was born. Following the example of Jesus and the recommendation of Paul, those who embraced this movement renounced marriage and family. They also adopted a rigorous interpretation of gospel passages cataloguing the dangers of wealth and power. Hence, Christian ascetics also accepted voluntary poverty. Many of the most celebrated ascetics of the fourth century were individuals who had forsaken wealth and privilege for the sake of the kingdom of God. Typifying these sentiments, the great monastic leader John Cassian once famously remarked to a young ascetic, "flee women and bishops,"[10] which might be alternatively read as "forsake sex and power."

In order to sustain these lives of rigorous commitment, ancient ascetics usually lived in communities and followed a regulated way of life. Hence, the impulse toward ascetical renunciation found its primary outlet in monasticism. Eventually the ascetic values of monasticism came to dominate the church. Their rigor became the Christian ideal, while marriage and family life was presented as a second tier, a less heroic form of following Jesus.

The story of the hegemony of monastic culture in Christian history has been told many times by those seeking to recover the dignity of marriage. However, in our eagerness to locate the source of the Christian suspicion of marriage, it is tempting to write off those who came before as mean-spirited clerical elitists. The original ancient impulse toward asceticism must be understood as stemming from a profoundly Christian desire to live up to the example of Jesus. As noted above, at least some passages in the New Testament suggested that renunciation of marriage was the best way to do this. Yet the example of Jesus and the recommendation of Paul, by themselves, cannot account for the success of this movement. After all, those same passages are still in the Bible and there is little evidence that Christian culture will soon experience a new domination by the ascetic spirit of antiquity.

Part of the success of this movement may also be attributed to the shape of family and married life in antiquity. As we have already seen, the forces that prompt most modern couples to marry were not the driving factors in ancient unions. Some scholars suggest that a desire to escape strictures of the ancient system can help to explain why so many found the allure of ascetic and monastic renunciation difficult to resist. While it may seem counterintuitive, many who embraced this difficult way of life did so precisely because they found in it a kind of liberation. Like the young person today who is drawn to a life of service to the poor as a sign of a more radical commitment, young people in the age of asceticism found themselves challenged by this radical reading of the gospel.

Finally, if we are to grasp fully the allure of this ancient practice, we must set it in the context of Christian eschatology. Eschatology is the branch of theology concerned with final things and fulfillments. What is it that we hope for? What is the final goal of the human person before God? Ancient ascetics believed that through their practices of physical renunciation they could begin to live now in anticipation of the way we will live after the resurrection. Ascetic renunciation does not, by definition, reduce to a hatred of body — although it sometimes did. It was much more a project aimed at transforming the body. Consider the modern exercise junkie. Such a person does not exercise for the sake of the pain but for the sake of the anticipated bodily transformation. We look better when we work out and we are usually healthier. Similarly, ancient ascetical practice was a spiritual exercise designed to sculpt the body and the spirit into a shape similar to the shape of the glorified body of the resurrection. To the extent the Bible suggested that marital and familial relationships would not be present in resurrected life, those who attempted to anticipate that life here and now elected not to marry. From the point of view of early Christian eschatological vision, celibacy was better than marriage because it more accurately modeled the future character of resurrected life.

Mixed Messages

While it is certainly true that early Christianity accepted the superiority of celibacy, it is also true that it affirmed marriage as a positive good. Cyril of

Alexandria links defending marriage to the truth of the incarnation of the Son in Christ:

> For the very reason that the holy Virgin gave fleshly birth to God substantially united with flesh we declare her to be "Mother of God," not because the Word's nature somehow derived its origin from flesh . . . but because . . . he substantially united humanity with himself, and underwent fleshly birth from her womb. He had no need of temporal birth, in the last days of the world, for his own nature. No, he meant to bless the very origin of our existence. . . . This is our reason for affirming of him that he personally blessed marriage by his incarnation.[11]

Indeed, many early Christian authors, including St. Augustine, vigorously defend the good of marriage. Augustine's treatise *On the Good of Marriage* was written explicitly to refute the radical anti-marriage message of Jerome. Jerome, as noted above, once declared that marriage was good because it was the only way to produce more celibates. Augustine vigorously rejected this idea. For him marriage possessed at least three intrinsic goods. According to historian David Hunter, "Augustine lays the foundation for what will become the classic Catholic teaching on the three 'goods' of marriage: offspring, fidelity, and the sacramental bond."[12] Augustine embraced the ascetical ideal, but he also understood that something so fundamental to the human community as marriage was a positive good intended by God.

Augustine's teaching on original sin, therefore, should not be misread as a fundamental rejection of sex and marriage. Yes, he believed that human sexuality was perverse and disordered after the fall and that disordered human desires can endure even into the married relationship, but this in no way constitutes a wholesale rejection of marriage. The ideal that original sin is transmitted through Adam's bad seed may seem to be an odd idea, but in a world not far removed from the ancient Israelite society described in Ronald Simkins's essay in this book, the idea is not surprising.

Still, although it is possible to look somewhat sympathetically at the ancient teaching that the good of celibacy is superior to the good of marriage, it is also possible to note the limitations of this vision. Like any religious movement, ancient asceticism was prone to abuse. Many individuals close to the movement were tempted to see this way of life as the only way of life. We have already mentioned Jerome. For all his brilliance, Jerome still found it necessary to reject marriage in order to affirm celibacy. Likewise another ascetic leader named Pelagius claimed that all Christians who were serious, not just monks, should embrace lives of radical renunciation if they wanted to be saved.[13] Augustine rejected Pelagius as he had rejected Jerome; he believed that asceticism was good, but not if it was used as a weapon to beat those who were unable to fully live into that ideal.[14] For Augustine, just as God intended marriage, God also had compassion on the weak who were not able to live lives of radical ascetic renunciation. However, because Augustine still affirmed the superiority of celibacy, the moderate character of his views can be difficult to see. Although Pelagianism is officially a heresy (one need not be an ascetic hero to enter the kingdom of God), Jerome is a saint, and the legacy of patristic teaching on marriage is more negative than it ought to be. The church's leadership came to be dominated by celibate clerics, and, in the tradition, Jerome's voice has often called louder than Augustine's even if the latter was mistaken for the former.

On the one hand, then, we may wish to affirm the eschatological and profoundly Christian context that produced the celibate ideal. We may even appreciate Augustine's caution about the tendency of those engaged in this life to fall into the trap of self-righteousness. Yet we may still believe that the tradition, in the end, does not value marriage precisely because it lists it as, at best, a contingent good alongside the superior good of celibacy. Contemporary scholarship reports that concern about the increasing dominance of the ascetical vision was not unknown even in antiquity. A roman monk named Jovinian argued for the essential equality of married and celibate Christians. Similarly, Julian of Eclanum, himself a married man, attacked Augustine's teaching as essentially Manichean.[15] Even John Chrysostom, both a celibate and a bishop, came to realize that the active life could advance the gospel more effectively than ascetic withdrawal. In his homilies he encourages husbands to love their wives and rather than challenge couples about their sexuality, he challenges them to live the gospel more radically through the renunciation of wealth.[16]

We can thus tease out of the ancient church examples that support the current consensus in Catholic theology of marriage; it is an unambiguously positive good, and it possesses a dignity equal to that of celibacy. We may even wish to incorporate into our contemporary reflection the economic themes found in the witness of Chrysostom: in a consumer culture, a marriage that witnesses to the contingency of life through the voluntary renunciation of wealth may be what the gospel requires if this generation is to imitate the radical impulses of the fourth century and promote a vision of the Christian life that escapes from debilitating mediocrity.

On the other hand, even as we work to recover and to correct, we should not be too quick to attack our ancestors in the faith. In our zeal to challenge the patristic legacy that claimed, "marriage is good, but celibacy is better," we ought not attempt to impose a new legacy that claims, "celibacy is good, but marriage is better." The ascetical movement of the ancient church witnesses faithfully to important Christian themes. Those who lived these lives of renunciation, if they did so faithfully, pointed to the fragility and contingency of human life and human relationships. In this way they can still serve as models for those attempting to follow a similar path as husband and wife.

Questions for Discussion

1. Why was the transition from the martyr church to the established church of Constantine so difficult for many people?

2. How do you explain the attraction of ancient asceticism?

3. What are some of the ways that modern Christians challenge mediocrity? How are they like and unlike their ancient counterparts?

4. How can married couples serve as a radical witness to the truth of the gospel?

Part Two

MARRIAGE AND TRADITION

Chapter 8

The Bond of Marriage

Timothy J. Buckley, C.S.S.R.

Why Focus on the Bond?

In its efforts to bring consolation and support to those who suffer the trauma of marital breakdown within its community, the Catholic Church struggles with a complex set of laws that limit its pastoral options. Apart from the fact that many of these laws were introduced to resolve historical problems that are no longer pressing, there is an underlying theology of marriage that I believe also limits the church's pastoral effectiveness. This theology is centered on the way the church has defined the bond of marriage, or at least the way that definition has influenced canon law as it stands and as it is applied.

It is with special pleasure that I write this chapter on the bond of marriage, for it was Michael Lawler who helped me to see the immense importance of the bond in any discussion of the Catholic theology of marriage. The context was a research project for the Bishops' Conference of England and Wales on the pastoral care of those separated, divorced, and remarried, which I began in 1990. By what I can only explain as the benign blessing of Providence I had become a friend of Michael's through Creighton University, where I had been taking part in the Christian Spirituality Program. I was grateful that he took an enthusiastic interest in my work.

My brief was to undertake a major piece of social research in the Catholic community of England and Wales and examine the theological and pastoral options. In the early days of the project Michael and I engaged in one of those fruitful brainstorming sessions, which finally alighted upon the bond as the heart of the theological question.

Bond or Bonds?

After twenty years of priestly ministry, all my pastoral instincts had told me that there was something seriously amiss in the pastoral application of the theology of marriage, especially in the face of the increasing incidence of marital breakdown. To start with, marriage is unique in that it is understood to have been raised to the dignity of a sacrament, having already existed as a state in God's created order from the very beginning. And of course therein lies the heart of the difficulty in defining the bond. Theologians are faced with the complex problem that there is not just a bond of marriage, but bonds of marriage, some sacramental and some not sacramental. When Jesus is invited to comment on the question in the context of the rabbinical argument over what grounds make divorce permissible in the Mosaic Law, he refuses to be trapped by the niceties of their arguments and takes the discussion onto another plane. By taking them back to Genesis he situates the discussion in the "ordinary" created order of things. While Moses had permitted divorce because of their hardness of heart, this was not what the Father had originally intended. Bearing that in mind, it takes some unraveling of Christian history to explain how, at a much later date, Catholic theology would situate the indissolubility of marriage, not in the Father's plan, but in marriage that has been constituted as a sacrament of the church. But that is not all: this only obtains if the sacrament has been consummated by a truly human act of sexual intercourse.

For those who wish to explore the reasons as to how and why we have arrived at this situation, I can only recommend that you read the second chapter of my book *What Binds Marriage?*[1] If you were ignorant of these facts before, trust me: the situation is as stated above. Of course, Michael Lawler has himself written about the bond of marriage, and in his recently published *Marriage and the Catholic Church: Disputed Questions,*[2] he brings to bear on the subject all his considerable skill as one who has a thorough grounding in and understanding of Thomistic/Scholastic theology.

The Importance of Scholasticism

I ask you to note at the outset the importance of Scholasticism in this whole discussion. It is only when you have understood the mindset and the worldview that permeated the thinking of the Scholastics that you will be able to unravel the extremely complex set of concepts that govern the theology of the bond.

First, let us look at this question more broadly. If this were simply a matter of theological theory like the notion of transubstantiation in relation to the eucharistic species, the study of these issues could be calmly pursued as part of that ongoing search for a language that best expresses the truth and thereby enriches our Christian lives. I do not introduce this comparison flippantly. The Scholastic notion of "transubstantiation" has enabled generations of Catholics to enter into the mystery of the Eucharist in a way that has truly transformed their lives. However, that transformation can be achieved with equal effect today among those for whom the philosophy of *matter and form / substance and accidents,* is a less than convincing way of trying to define the action of the Spirit making Christ present at Mass. The bread and wine still become the Body and Blood of Christ. Truly Christ is present in these sacred species so that we bow before the Blessed Sacrament with special reverence both during the action of the Mass and afterward when the host is reserved in the tabernacle. That said, we should never forget that Christ is truly present in the Eucharist above all so that he may be present to us and in us. Thus we become the Body of Christ, united with him and each other, heirs to the kingdom of God. No matter what philosophy we employ in trying to understand these mysteries, faith takes us beyond reason. Because of the Eucharist, we, like our brothers and sisters in every age including all those who lived before St. Thomas Aquinas applied the Aristotelian categories to this theological question, continue to be formed into the Body of Christ.

However, when we come to apply the worldview of the Scholastics to the marriage question there is a peculiar urgency to our concern. No longer can we comfortably acknowledge a development of philosophical and theological thinking that allows us an expansive acceptance of everything that may be helpful in unfolding the truth to us. Now we must ask: Has our application of medieval philosophical categories led us to definitions that at best reveal to us only part of the truth, but at worst can lead us into error?

What Kind of Existence Do the Scholastics Attribute to the Bond?

We will do well to focus sharply on the critical factor in this whole discussion: namely, the type of being the bond of marriage is thought to have. And more significantly still we need to examine how this understanding has been enshrined in the law of the church and how in practice that law is interpreted.

Let me take you back to Michael Lawler and his thoughtful writings on the subject. He understands well the notion of "being" in Thomistic philosophy and writes coherently and persuasively about it in a chapter of his aforementioned book, entitled "On the Bonds of Marriage." Thus we read:

> The bond arising from marriage is referred to constantly, but is defined or described only infrequently. Doyle, citing Urban Navarette, gives the now common theological and, therefore, canonical interpretation. "The bond is the unique relationship between a man and a woman by which they are constituted husband and wife."[3] The Second Vatican Council spoke of this bond in more personal language. "The intimate partnership (or relationship) of married life and love ... is rooted in the conjugal covenant of irrevocable personal consent."[4] A philosophical delay over relationship will enable us to clarify the nature of the bond arising from a valid marriage.
>
> The bond is a relationship, a category explained in, though in no way limited to, the philosophy of Aristotle and Aquinas. For our purposes here, we need focus only on one central teaching of that philosophy, the *praedicamenta*, or modes of being, specifically substance and accident. The essence of substance is to be in itself, *esse in se*; the essence of accidents is to be in another in which it inheres, *esse in alio tamquam in subiecto inhaesionis*.[5] Relation is not a substance, an

esse in se, neither a physical nor a spiritual substance and, therefore, it does not have autonomous existence. Relation is an accident, an *esse in alio;* it is a being in another, a being related to another. As an accident, it requires a subject in which to inhere, or else it would have no existence. Since the bond arising from a valid marriage is a relation, it is an accident, requiring for its very existence a subject in which to inhere. Its subject is the two spouses, fashioned by marriage into one coupled-We or one biblical body-person.[6]

The bond arising from a marriage, therefore, is correctly called an ontological reality. It is not correctly called "a separate reality,"[7] since no accident, existing as it does only in its proper subject, ever exists as a separate reality.[8] The bond arising from marriage comes into being from the loving relationship between a man and a woman, expressed in their lawfully manifested consent to "mutually give and accept one another for the purpose of establishing a marriage" (Canon 1057.2). Their consent transforms a man and a woman into a husband and a wife, related, bonded, or obligated one to the other as spouses in an intimate consortium of the whole of life.[9]

In a determined piece of writing Ladislas Örsy comes to much the same conclusion as Lawler when commenting on the *Code of Canon Law.* It will serve our purpose well also to quote him in detail:

> It [the bond] is not any kind of substance, or *esse in se;* it is an accident that belongs to a substance; the substance in question being that of a human person. The bond is the specific marital relationship of a man to a woman and vice versa, an *esse ad;* that is, a general orientation in the world of their intentionality; an orientation that permeates and dominates their judgments and decisions. Quite appropriately it could be called "conversion" (turning to in a radical sense) to another person. In the case of a sacramental marriage God himself grants a special grace-filled dimension to this bond.
>
> We use this scholastic terminology to convey a point: no new physical or spiritual substance is created either in a natural or a sacramental marriage. If it were so, it should follow that whenever the church dispenses from a natural or a sacramental marriage, this physical substance is "annihilated" — a patently absurd proposition.
>
> Marriage is not one of those sacraments that have for their effect what traditionally has been described as "character," an indelible sign on the soul; baptism is the obvious example. Precisely, because such sacraments bring about a permanent transformation in the person, they cannot be repeated. Although some theologians tried to apply the same doctrine to marriage (e.g., Hugh of St Victor, d. 1141), their opinion never gained acceptance (see *DTC* 9.2:2144–47).[10]

Thomas Doyle in COM-USA[11] uses the following expressions to describe the nature of the bond: an "ontological reality" (766), "an integral and not partial reality," "a separate reality" (808). A way of testing the meaning and correctness of these expressions is to try to locate the bond within the categories of being as they are referred to in nearly every work of Aquinas. Can the bond be substance? Certainly not, it has no autonomous existence. So it must be an accident. Among the accidents, a rapid survey of the categories shows that the only one that can accommodate it is relation, *esse ad*.

Now a relation can most certainly be an ontological reality, as long as it remains attached to a substance. No relation can, however, have a separate existence from the substance, not even in the Trinity — if we may go that far.

It follows that the bond is a relationship of obligation. But, due to the sacrament such a relationship is sealed by God's grace and his commitment to the spouses. Therefore, it should not be described in terms of merely natural obligations; it is a grace-filled obligation in the Kingdom.

When the church terminates such a grace-filled obligation through dispensing from the bond of a sacramental non-consummated marriage, it simply frees the person *in the name of God*, on the strength of a power of divine origin, from a *vinculum,* "chain," that is binding him or her.

Although we used the categories of scholastic philosophy and theology to explain the nature of the bond with some clarity and precision, the essential validity of our explanation does not depend on that system. It could be expressed in other ways.

Be that as it may, in this matter one should aim for the greatest precision obtainable — for the sake of those who eventually will have to carry in real life the burden of our theoretical conclusions.[12]

So both Lawler and Örsy argue that a sound interpretation of the Scholastic tradition would suggest that the ontological reality of the bond is not a separate reality. It does not have existence in its own right. It cannot, as it were, live independently of the relationship of the couple in question. They both explicitly refute the position taken by Thomas Doyle in his comments on the relevant canons, where he argues that the bond does have a separate reality. The difficulty is that in spite of the efforts and arguments of theologians like Lawler and canonists like Örsy, it seems to me that the position that holds sway, when it comes to interpreting the canon law of the church, remains that of Doyle. In practice, the philosophy that underpins the annulment process in the Catholic Church presumes that we adhere to Doyle's position. It is based on the conviction that once such a ratified and consummated sacramental bond has been established it remains in existence no matter what the subsequent circumstances of the couple concerned. To put it slightly crudely but to make the point, it does not matter if both husband and wife have been with new partners for forty years and live on the other side of the world to each other; still the bond reaches out across the world to bind them together. After all, it is this position that is used to safeguard the sanctity and permanence of marriage. It is the place in the sand where the line is drawn. But of course, the problem with lines in the sand is that they can eventually be blown or washed away, and it has long been my contention that this has happened. And I contend that it has happened because although we still religiously invoke the annulment process in thousands of cases every year, too many anomalies and injustices arise in this pastoral process for it to retain its credibility.

In Search of Precision

At the end of the quotation from Örsy he called for precision. His reason is that these are not just theological or canonical niceties but issues that directly affect people's lives and their relationships with God. Precision is of paramount importance if we are to unravel the problems that continue to beset us as we try to find pastoral solutions in the Catholic Church for those whose marriages have irretrievably broken down. These same people often find themselves at odds with the church authorities unless it can be established that the bond of marriage never actually existed in what would then become their putative marriages.

Örsy and Lawler argue their case persuasively on the nature of the ontological bond, and clearly they do so to try and unlock the impasse that still bedevils the pastoral care of the divorced and remarried in the Catholic Church. If they are right, and I am convinced they are, then they offer a way forward in that it does not make sound philosophical or theological sense to talk about the existence of something that no longer exists.

Indeed it is clear that Lawler is trying to press home the point even further in the chapter on the bonds of marriage in his recently published book, already referred to. He notes the age-old distinction between marriage as a world reality and a religious, sacramental reality, but then develops his analysis to embrace three distinct ways in which we might understand the bond. He reminds us of the teaching of Vatican II, which sees marriage as a *consortium* of the whole of life, and by translating *consortium* as "communion" he opens up the discussion and infuses it with a philosophy that also embraces the insights of modern psychology.

> Their mutual love binds them together in an interpersonal relationship, which is a bond and obligation of love. Their wedding binds them together in a civil relationship, which is a bond and obligation of law. Their marriage as sacrament binds them together in a religious relationship, which is a bond and obligation of divine grace.[13]

Such distinctions help us to reflect on the unfolding nature of any marital relationship, recognizing that it is not something that can be established in any given moment, but that is characterized by growth and development. Kevin T. Kelly, in his book *Divorce and Second Marriage,* argues in a similar vein, pointing out that indissolubility makes sense when we understand that "it is a commitment to undertake and achieve something...not the achievement itself."[14]

Now it seems to me that the theologians and canonists we have quoted are simply part of that consistent tradition that seeks instinctively to find a way forward when confronted with seemingly intractable pastoral problems. Putting it very simply the church has never satisfactorily managed to resolve the tension between a fundamental belief that God intended marriage (all marriage) to be monogamous and for life, and the lived experience of so many in every generation who fail to achieve this ideal. Literally from apostolic times when Paul tried to deal with the problem in the early church in Corinth (1 Cor. 7:10–16), there has never been precision. It took centuries before the criteria, which now govern the so-called Pauline Privilege, were established, and so it has continued until the present day. Many theologians and canonists, including those we have quoted in this chapter, continue to seek a solution to today's crisis, whereby so many find themselves excluded from the sacramental life of the church because of their marital circumstances. After the Second Vatican Council, "lack of due discretion" and "the inability to assume the obligations of marriage" were accepted as psychological grounds for the granting of annulments. However, this has served only to make for even greater imprecision, and there is a strong body of opinion that considers the legal process of the tribunal a quite inappropriate forum for the application of such principles. I think this is well illustrated in the book *Shattered Faith*[15] by Sheila Rauch Kennedy, an Episcopalian who complied with all the Catholic Church required of her to marry Joseph Kennedy, eldest son of Robert F. Kennedy. After many years and two sons she could accept that the marriage had broken down, but not that there had never been a marriage in the first place. Indeed she battled with the church's processes every inch of the way, writing very movingly:

> I realized that even though my reasons for opposing the annulment had remained constant during the two years that I had been defending my marriage, the factors influencing my thinking had broadened. I was still, as I had told Joe, concerned for the boys, but not for their legitimacy. I had always known the boys' legitimacy was protected by American law. I was still concerned that the children know that their birth was the result of great love, commitment, true happiness, and a Christian marriage rather than a non-existent union. They should never have to question that their lives brought immeasurable joy to both of their parents, and neither their father nor his church would ever be able to convince me otherwise.[16]

Is it not ironic that the very process the church employs to defend the sanctity of marriage was understood to be undermining it? Indeed Sheila regarded herself as "the defender of her marriage": so much for the officially appointed defender of the bond in this instance! I have much sympathy with her position and I heard it echoed, maybe not always so eloquently, by countless priests and people in the course of my research.

But I believe there is another irony and it is this: the very situation that has evolved is the result of a genuine attempt by the church to respond compassionately to the growing pastoral problem of marital breakdown, especially in the developed world. Indeed my own contention is that compassionate responses to pastoral problems have been the norm down through the centuries and explain much of the legislation that is now enshrined in the *Code of Canon Law* on subjects like consummation and canonical form.[17] As each new pastoral problem arose the church sought for a pastoral solution, but the result is a complex mass of legislation, much of which bears little relevance to the questions that confront us today. The Magisterium at every level needs to hear this from the theologians. It is not a battle between traditionalists and modernists, between conservatives and liberals. It is a genuine desire to seek clarity and precision.

A Way Forward

To begin with we must revisit the very fundamental question: When the Magisterium speaks of the bond, what is it referring to? If one thing is clear it is that there has been a consistent lack of clarity in this matter down through the centuries, and it is compounded even in our own time in official statements and most notably in *The Catechism of the Catholic Church*. We have only to compare articles 1614 and 1640 to illustrate the point. In article 1614 we are told that "the matrimonial union of man and woman is indissoluble." The text and context tell us that this is speaking of all marriages of all time. Yet article 1640 goes on to explain that *"the marriage bond* has been established by God himself in such a way that a marriage concluded and consummated between baptized persons can never be dissolved." Now which is it? Article 1640 is much more precise in defining the bond when using the word "bond" because the church has found ways of accepting the dissolution of all the other bonds of marriage that do not fall into that very precise definition. And here we are confronted with another paradox, for it is the very precision of this definition in article 1640 that creates the pastoral confusion in practice. People like Sheila Rauch Kennedy can accept the principle that God intends us to be married for life (article 1614); just as they would accept that God does not want us to kill. What they cannot understand is how, just as killing *can* be justified in certain circumstances (e.g., self-defense), when the marriage has clearly died, it can be argued that it is still in existence. And of course the only way in which that can be argued is by applying the Scholastic notion of the bond, which says that it is a substance, having a separate reality. Now if Lawler and Örsy are correct, this is patently absurd and we have a theological escape route.

Looking to the East

But there is another route we can pursue and it is the route of dialogue with other Christian traditions, not hamstrung by the theological categories that dictate to us in the Western church. In this I have been heavily influenced by my confrère, the late Bernard Häring, C.S.S.R., who intuitively looked to the East for a solution. This is not some simplistic idea that the Western church should adopt the concept of *oikonomia* and apply it in some new legal forum to rescue the annulment process. It is the recognition that as we stand in awe before the majesty of God, there is much that we will never know about human relations and relationships, that on many occasions all we can do is acknowledge our weakness and beg God's forgiveness and saving presence.

Discussing all these questions some years ago with Gregorios, the Greek Orthodox archbishop of Thyateira and Great Britain, I was granted one of those rare providential moments of enlightenment. "Timothy" he said, "Jesus came to redeem the world. Do you believe this?" "I do," said I. "Is there any situation which is beyond the saving presence of Jesus?" "There is not," I replied. And then he countered: "So what is your problem?"

In the Orthodox tradition the bishop is the *oikonomos,* the housekeeper, the one entrusted to keep good order. The bishop can exercise or delegate this responsibility in a variety of ways. Resolving the problems of divorce and remarriage is one area where he exercises this salvific ministry. The Orthodox would be the first to admit that their processes are not perfect, but the point I am making is that they are founded on a totally different philosophy and spirituality, one that is not bound by the logic that has to determine the existence or nonexistence of the bond.

It is my hope and prayer that we are gradually moving nearer to such an understanding. Maybe it will be one of the fruits of a future reunion of the Catholic and Orthodox traditions. Meanwhile, on the ground I see signs that many Catholics are discovering a newfound peace, which enables them to cope even when they are unable to find an official solution to their problems. For some this is the result of spiritual direction in the internal forum, for others it is the dawning realization that we are caught up in a mystery much greater than ourselves and in which we can never have absolute precision. In that setting they can confidently leave themselves in the hands of the Lord, believing that he can redeem every situation, something very akin to the *oikonomia* of the East.

And Finally

I hope it is clear from the tenor and argumentation of this chapter that I firmly believe in the sanctity and permanence of marriage. Unlike Michael Lawler I cannot claim the personal experience of a happy and fruitful married life, but as a Redemptorist priest I can lay claim to a wealth of experience both in the pastoral setting of parishes and as a preacher of missions and retreats. It was that experience that I was able to bring to my research. I was grateful for the opportunity to study the subject in depth both theoretically and at that deep level of human experience. I am convinced that the church is right to proclaim its firm belief in the sanctity and indissolubility of marriage and that when this is lived out among the faithful it is a sign of the kingdom of God. At the same time I recognize in the gospel of Jesus a message of hope and love and forgiveness that can reach into every broken human situation, including broken marriages of whatever kind. I do not believe that these two visions of hope are incompatible, and I do believe the community of the Catholic Church is challenged to resolve the problems we face in this field as a matter of urgency. This, too, will be a sign of the kingdom.

Questions for Discussion

1. Traditionally the church has spoken definitively about the bond of marriage. Do you think it would be more helpful to speak about the bonds of marriage? And if so why?

2. Scholastic philosophy has greatly influenced the way the bond of marriage is defined in the canon law of the church. Bearing this in mind, do you think the forum of the annulment process is adequately equipped to accommodate the insights of modern psychology in helping to determine the existence of the bond?

3. The salvation of the world is the only thing that can give meaning to theology and law. In the field of marriage do you think that the theology of the Eastern Orthodox Churches has anything to offer the Western Catholic Church?

Chapter 9

Christian Marriage

A Divine Calling

William P. Roberts

Introduction

When I was a high school student in the late 1940s, the prevailing theology of vocation communicated to us was simple and clear. Sufficient intelligence, adequate health, and sound moral standards were signs that one was called to priesthood or religious life. These two vocations were identified with the pursuit of holiness. If one was not generous enough to answer this call, one took the "easier" way out and got married. In doing so one would save one's soul by keeping the commandments. While this brief summary might run the risk of sounding like a caricature, I believe it reflects quite accurately the impression widely held at that time, especially in catechetical instructions and vocation talks to Catholic school eighth graders and high school seniors.

On an official and theoretical level the bishops at the Second Vatican Council reversed this kind of thinking. All the baptized, they proclaim, in whatever state or walk of life, are called to the fullness of holiness, the perfection of love (*Lumen Gentium*, chap. 5). No longer do most theologians and religious educators explicitly claim that priesthood, celibacy, and religious life are higher states of holiness. Indeed, many post–Vatican II church documents exalt the sacramentality and spirituality of marital life.

Deep-seated attitudes, however, are revealed more accurately in actions and policies than in verbal acclamations. There are two ways in which the church's bias against marriage as a divine vocation to the fullness of holiness and participation in the mission of Christ immediately come to mind. The principal argumentation officially given in the Latin rite of the Catholic Church prohibiting married persons from priestly ordination is that the priest ought to love God with an undivided heart, be fully dedicated to the kingdom of God, and be available for service to the church. One can only ask what such arguments imply about marriage as a divine call. Don't such arguments run contrary to the stance of Vatican II about the universal call to holiness and its claim that all the baptized are called to share in the kingly mission of Christ and that the married couple creates a church of the home?

A second way in which marriage is ignored as a divine vocation is in the Prayers of the Faithful. One regularly hears petitions at Mass that God will send more dedicated and generous persons to priesthood and religious life. But how often does one hear prayers for more vocations to the sacramental life of marriage?

The purpose of this essay is to reflect on Christian marriage as an authentic divine vocation that is neither superior nor inferior to the complementary states of life of the single person, the celibate, or the member of a religious community. To achieve this goal we present three theological considerations. First, we look at marriage in the context of the meaning of divine vocation in general and in brief comparison to the single and celibate states. Second, we reflect on Christian marriage as a unique way of fulfilling one's baptismal vocation. Third, we consider marriage as a particular response to the call that all Christians have to live the evangelical counsels.

Marriage and Divine Vocation

In this section we will address the following three issues: the meaning of divine vocation, the vocation of marriage in relation to the call to other states of life, and the discernment of a specific vocation.

The very term "divine vocation" is rooted in the belief that God is our ultimate creator who loves and cares for each one of us in our unrepeatable individuality. Each of us is called to image this loving God as fully as possible in terms of our unique personality, gifts, and limitations. We are called to accept who we are in the basic structure of our being and within that context and that of our environment to become all we can be as authentic loving human beings. We are called to love the Lord our God with all our heart, with all our soul, with all our mind, with all our strength, and our neighbor as ourself (Mark 12:29–31). We are called to share in God's life-giving energy on behalf of other humans, of planet Earth, and of the cosmos itself.

This call from God to become all we are in the deepest identity of our being is not lived out in the abstract, but in the concrete circumstances of our life. Two of the basic ways in which we achieve our destiny are through a particular state of life (married, single, celibate) and a certain type of occupation (professional, artisan, laborer, etc.). The former is the concern of this essay. One note, however, is important here. These are two separate lines of vocation concerning which every person eventually faces a decision.[1] Each must be freely chosen on its own set of merits in regard to what is best suited to the individual in her or his pursuit of the fullness of holiness. Hence, no state of life ought to be institutionally required as a condition for pursuing a certain type of occupation or ministry.

Marriage is a call to live in an exclusive, permanent, intimate partnership of life and love with one's spouse (see *Gaudium et Spes*, n. 48). A celibate lifestyle involves a permanent commitment to abstain from marriage and from sexual intimacy. This state can be lived either in the context of a religious community or in an association with other celibates, or on one's own. The single state can be lifelong but without a permanent commitment to remain unmarried, or it may be temporary, as can be the case of the premarried, the divorced, or the widowed.

How can persons discern which of these states of life is the one to which God is calling them? In the not too distant past, as mentioned earlier, the answer was found by comparing the states of life in the abstract. Considered in itself, celibacy was seen by official Catholicism as the more perfect state and clearly superior to marriage. The problem with this approach is that states of life in themselves do not exist. What exists are persons who are celibate, single, or married.

Discerning which state of life God is calling one to requires an honest intuition into who one is as this particular person. In light of one's spiritual, psychological, and temperamental makeup, one's gifts and virtues, limitations and flaws, one can prayerfully discern which state of life will bring one closer to God, empower one to be the most loving person possible, and make the greatest possible contribution to the human community.

Christian Marriage Rooted in the Baptismal Call

My basic premise is that Christian marriage is a special vocation that is rooted in and flows from one's baptismal life. For our purposes here I select five aspects of what it means to be a baptized Christian and how a married couple is called to live in a unique way each of these meanings in the very context of their marital relationship.

In baptism the person is sacramentally (that is, visibly, explicitly, and ritually) called and empowered: (1) to be incorporated into the life of the Trinity; (2) to participate in the death and resurrection of Jesus Christ (Rom. 6:1–6); (3) to become a member of Christ's church; (4) to be an integral part of a eucharistic community; and (5) to share in Christ's ongoing mission of proclaiming and advancing the kingdom (reign) of God.

1. In baptism we are baptized in the name of the Father, the Son, and the Holy Spirit. The distinguishing and central characteristic of the baptized Christian is belief in this Trinitarian God. As Christians we believe in a God who is the ultimate creator of all creation, who out of redemptive love for humans sends God's Son, God's Word to be one with us in our humanity, and who gives us God's very Spirit to enable us to share in this divine goodness and holiness. We believe that this God, Father, Son and Spirit, are so deeply united in being that they are, indeed, one God.

In marriage we live out this Trinitarian belief and commitment in many specific ways. We acknowledge that God, our Father/Mother, has created us as sexual beings, female and male. We accept our gender differences, our sexuality, and our sexual intimacy as gifts from God and as finite images of God's very life (Gen. 1:27). We image Trinitarian unity in our becoming one in marital partnership and fulfilling in this particular way the prayer of Jesus, "May they all be one, just as, Father, you are in me and I am in you, so that they may also be in us, so that the world may believe it was you who sent me" (John 17:21).

Our Trinitarian life is also manifested in our belief that Jesus, the enfleshed Word of God, is the human sacrament and manifestation of God's love for us, and that our marital love and intimacy are sacramental of Christ's intimate love for us. The faith experience of our spousal love provides us with a glimpse of the depth of Christ's love for all humans. In turn, the qualities of Christ's love inform and inspire the ways we show our love for each other.

In marriage we open ourselves to the Holy Spirit given us by God and Christ, the Spirit of Truth and Love. We believe we are temples of the Holy Spirit, and treat and respect each other as such. We rely on the presence and action of God's Spirit in our relationship to empower us to grow in the shared truth and love that are the cornerstones of our marital union.

2. Water is a sign of death and life. It causes both. In the baptismal ritual we are submerged in water as a sacramental symbol that through the gift of the Spirit we share in the death and resurrection of Jesus. We die to our sinfulness and live anew in the life of Christ. Thus begins a lifelong process of responding to the baptismal call of gradually dying to our dark side and increasingly living in the light of Christ. This baptismal process culminates in the faith experience of our ultimate death and resurrection.

In the meantime many diverse paths lead to this ultimate participation in Christ's death and resurrection, each with its own set of dyings and risings. Building an intimate marital partnership of life and love involves coming to grips in a unique way with our dark and light sides. What within us can prevent intimacy with our spouse are the same propensities that obstruct our growing union with God and our sharing of love with our neighbor: self-centeredness, pride, inability to admit fault and accept criticism, prejudices, impatience, intolerance, insensitivity, unforgiveness, fear of the truth, fear of the loss of independence, and fear of the change that intimacy demands. Growing in marital union daily challenges us to die to selfishness, to false images of ourselves, to sexism, to the harboring of grudges, and to all the fears that can prevent us from taking the risks involved in giving ourselves fully to another. All these baptismal dyings in marriage not only bring us to new life in our relationship with our spouse, but also to deeper union with God, to a closer following of Christ, and to greater empowerment to reach out to the broader human community. In this way we can truly become the people of the Light that baptism calls us to be (see, for example, Matt. 5:14–16).

3. Baptism is a sacramental initiation into membership of Christ's church. The crucified and risen Christ is invisible to mortal eyes. It is the church, the community of those who explicitly believe in Jesus Christ and who consciously strive to proclaim him and follow him, that makes Christ known to the world today.

The Christian married couple lives out this aspect of their baptism not merely by belonging to a local church community. More fundamentally, through their marriage they actually constitute their family as a domestic church, a "church in miniature," a church of the home (see, for example, *Lumen Gentium,* n. 11; *Familiaris Consortio,* n. 49). They do this by being a family that shares faith and prayer, by treating each other as Christ does, by sharing their gifts with the local parish community, and by reaching out beyond their walls to feed the hungry, to minister to the disadvantaged, to console the bereaved and the lonely, and to change some of the unjust structures that oppress so many of our fellow humans.

4. The center of the life of the community of the baptized, the church, is the Eucharist. We are a eucharistic community. Through baptism we are called to celebrate in memory of Christ what he did at the Last Supper and enacted on the cross. But we are called to do this not just in the liturgical celebration of the Eucharist. We are called to live Eucharist, indeed, to become Eucharist for one another. As Christ gave of himself (his body, his blood) at that Holy Thursday meal and on the cross on Good Friday, and continues to give of himself to us as the risen Lord, so we are challenged to give of ourselves (our bodies, our energies, our talents) in nurturing love to others.

There is no more personally and mutually intimate human way in which one can respond to the baptismal call to be Eucharist for another than in a faith-filled, loving, committed marriage. The couple's shared life with one another speaks out: this is my body given for you; this is the cup of my life, my blessings poured out for you. Every act of kindness and consideration, every service rendered, every communication of mind and heart participate in this self-gift. This ongoing eucharistic giving is celebrated in especially visible (sacramental) ways when the couple breaks bread together at the table, and when they give of themselves to one another in sexual intimacy. They experience in faith Christ's self-giving through their own self-giving. This, in turn, empowers and frees them to go beyond the confines of their own personal relationship and reach out eucharistically to their children, their extended family, and to the community of the underprivileged and the needy.

5. All the baptized are called to participate in Christ's ongoing mission of proclaiming and furthering the kingdom (the reign) of God in the world today (see *Lumen Gentium,* n. 13). Alone, and gathered together, we pray, time and time again in the Lord's Prayer, "thy kingdom come." But the kingdom of God can come into our lives now only to the degree to which we allow it. God and Christ can reign in our minds, our hearts, and our souls only to the extent to which we open ourselves to the Light and the Fire of their Spirit. Only then can the darkness of our minds be enlightened by God's truth and the stoniness of our hearts be melted by God's love. Only then can the age-old barriers that divide race against race, nation against nation, religion against religion, and gender against gender be shattered by

the grace of God, preserve us from mutual destruction, and bring us to the communion that God wills for all peoples.

An authentic and loving marriage provides in a unique way a daily and nightly opportunity to respond to the baptismal call of promoting God's kingdom, God's reign, in our lives and in the lives of others. In this intimate partnership of marriage we expose ourselves with all our vulnerabilities to each other. We strive to break down the barriers that can stand in the way of our relating to one another with greater honesty, humility, and empathy. In creating deeper communion with one another we are opening ourselves to greater communion with God. In permitting God to reign in our marital relationship and in our family, we are fortifying the institution of marriage and family, the foundations of human society. We are also becoming more empowered to go forth beyond the boundary of our family life and challenge the ignorance, injustices, and obstinacies that prevent God from reigning more deeply in our church, our nation, and human society at large. Finally, by achieving true intimacy in marriage we foreshadow in a finite way the total intimate communion of the heavenly kingdom that Jesus compares to a wedding feast (Matt. 22:1ff.).

To summarize, in this section of the essay we have reflected on Christian marriage as a true call from God to live out in a unique partnership of life and love one's baptismal call to participate in Trinitarian life, to share in Christ's death and resurrection, to participate in the life of the church, to be Eucharist, and to advance the kingdom (reign) of God proclaimed by Christ. We turn now to another dimension of the divine vocation of the baptized married person: responding to the mandates of Jesus' gospel.

Marriage and the Evangelical Counsels

The challenges posed by the gospel are beyond an easy count. They include many of the virtues already referred to in this essay. Of course, the ultimate and most significant evangelical counsel is love. Without love all the other virtues are stripped of their real significance (see, for example, 1 Cor. 13:1–3).

My interest in this section of the essay is to focus on the three evangelical counsels that have been traditionally associated with the life of members of religious communities: "poverty, chastity, and obedience." The most distinguishing characteristic of the vocation of persons called to this way of life is that they take public vows to live these three counsels in the context of their particular religious community. While the value of this type of vocation is beyond denial, two problems have emerged within the Catholic community. In much of the common thinking the notion of evangelical counsel has been limited to and identified with poverty, chastity, and obedience. This could lead to an ignoring or devaluing of the importance of so many of the other gospel counsels, some of which are more central to baptismal life than these three, and without which poverty, chastity, and obedience lose much of their Christian significance.

A second difficulty has been the identification of poverty, chastity, and obedience with the life of vowed religious. This obscures the fact that all the baptized are called, each in their particular state of life, to follow the gospel mandate to be poor, chaste, and obedient. In this part of the essay, then, I wish to reflect on Christian marriage as a divine baptismal vocation to pursue these three evangelical counsels in unique ways that differ from but complement how they are lived in religious communities.

Poverty

The Gospels present two versions of the first of the beatitudes. Matthew has Jesus tell us how blessed are the poor in spirit, for the kingdom of heaven is theirs (5:3). Luke goes further and has Jesus extend this beatitude to the poor (6:20). While not all of us are called to be actually poor, even the rich are called to be poor in spirit.

Members of religious communities strive to imitate this gospel ideal by contributing all they earn to their community. In turn, they receive from the community what they need for decent human living and for their own personal use and work. Christian married people, too, are called to live evangelical poverty. Let us explore six aspects of how pursuit of this counsel applies to marital life.

First, we are challenged to believe that God (not we) is the ultimate owner of all creation. We pass through this planet for a brief span of time. We come into this earthly life with nothing, and we leave it with nothing. During the interim what we "relatively own" is for our growth and development and for empowering us to achieve the goals God has for us. We are ultimately accountable to God for how responsibly or irresponsibly we have made use of the resources at our disposal. Have we cared for the earth and the environment as we have passed through? Or have we for selfish purposes raped the land, polluted the air, poisoned the waters, exploited the animal kingdom, and destroyed the ecological balance? In the home do we let the water and the electricity needlessly run? Do we carefully dispose of waste products? Do we preserve that small portion of the earth that is our domicile?

Second, the heart of gospel poverty is that people are more important than things. The first priority in marriage is the building of an intimate personal relationship with one's spouse. Where there are children they become the next highest priority. This is much easier said than done, especially in our contemporary economy. Where there is conflict between our jobs and the time and energy required to become best friends with our spouse and to be personally present to and with our children, which direction do we take? Are we willing to sacrifice the extra money, the promotion, the climbing the ladder to financial and career "success" when these stand in the way of building strong family communion?

Third, while religious give all they earn to their community and utilize its resources with appropriate permission, married persons give all they have to the building of the family community, the church of the home. In a true partnership, couples surrender personal financial independence, pool their resources, and make budgetary decisions and major expenditures through mutual agreement. During the child-raising years (and sometimes beyond) a substantial amount of their resources are dedicated to the nurturing and education of their children, and getting them started in their lifelong calling.

Fourth, a basic element of evangelical poverty, whether it is in the life of a religious community or in marriage, is simplicity of living. We strive for a lifestyle that is consonant with basic human dignity. We distinguish between needs and wants. We avoid the materialism and consumerism that leads to the hoarding of goods for their own sake.

Fifth, another significant aspect of evangelical poverty is trust (see Matt. 6:25–34). This is especially true in marriage where one's source of support relies on a job that could be lost without notice, or on a breadwinner who could be suddenly stricken or die. We live and act responsibly now, but we all face an indefinite future without any assurance that there will be adequate provision for our needs. But we trust that if we do our part the God who has always been for us and is now with us will be with us even if someday we must walk through a dark valley (see Ps. 23:4).

Sixth, the marital call to evangelical poverty also demands that we engage in almsgiving and share our blessings with the deprived. Indeed, the kingdom of heaven is for those who feed the hungry, give drink to the thirsty, welcome the stranger, clothe the naked, and visit the sick and the imprisoned (Matt. 25:31–46).

Chastity

We always hear of members of religious communities taking a vow of chastity, but rarely has there been word of the vow of chastity solemnly and publicly made in marriage. But both are vows of chastity. The religious takes a vow of celibate chastity in terms of dedication to the life and mission of one's religious community. The married couple vow themselves to a life of chastity in exclusive, permanent, committed relationship to one another. This notion deserves further exploration.

The entire baptized are called to a life of chastity. Chastity, however, cannot be identified with mere abstinence from genital activity. It is a virtue that involves the acceptance of our sexuality and the channeling of our sexual energies, needs, and desires toward becoming an authentically loving person and toward building genuine nurturing relationships with others.

In Christian marriage we choose to respond to the baptismal call to live chastely by entering into a unique communion of sexual intimacy with our spouse. We reject all other sexual activity apart from one another. We give of ourselves to each other in all the aspects of married life and celebrate our mutual self-gift in sexual intimacy. We commit ourselves to be faithful to the ongoing process of strengthening the marital bond that increasingly unites us to one another in Christ.

In expressions of sexual intimacy marital chastity is marked especially by three characteristics: true partnership, respect for personal dignity, and sensitivity. The couple are partners in bed as they are in the totality of their marriage. No one exercises control over the other. All decisions regarding frequency and ways of expression are by mutual agreement. There is mutual respect for the personhood of each. Neither is exploited or treated like a sex object. No one has more rights in the sexual area than the other. Finally, marital chastity involves being sensitive to the desires and comfort zone of one's spouse, and concerned about how he or she is affected physically, emotionally, and spiritually by our genital involvement.

Obedience

In baptism we commit ourselves to hear the Word of God and to follow it. This involves avoiding decisions that are based merely on self-centered desires. Rather, we are committed to make choices determined by what we believe God is asking of us within the framework of the gospel of Jesus Christ.

Within that framework, the member of a religious community discerns the will of God through the rules, constitutions, and mission of one's order and through the direction of one's "superiors." Within that same framework, in the partnership model of marriage one perceives the will of God in reference to what nurtures the Christlike union of the marriage, the communion of the family, and its responsibility to the broader community. Personal and household decisions are made in response to authentic family needs and wishes and with mindfulness of the effects one's decisions have on one's spouse and other family members.

Rather than say spouses "obey" each other, it is more accurate to say they mutually respond in love to the insights, instincts, and desires of each other. They resolve differences not by edict, but through prayerful negotiation and legitimate compromise.

The ultimate will of God for all of us is that we love. In a marriage one discovers God's will in discerning what nurtures the authentic love of the couple, their family, and their baptismal mission to extend their love to their fellow humans.

Conclusion

This essay has explored the meaning of Christian marriage as an authentic divine vocation, a calling from God to live out one's baptismal commitment by sacramentalizing the intimate love of God and Christ through a life of intimacy with one another. Acknowledging the reality that many Christians do not consciously look upon and approach marriage in this way, I conclude with several practical ways in which awareness of marriage as a true vocation and its connection with baptism may be heightened.

1. Homilies on marriage could point out the vocational and baptismal dimensions of this sacrament.

2. Marriage as a divine calling ought to be included in vocation talks along with discussions about the religious and single states of life.

3. Petitions in the Prayer of the Faithful should not be focused merely on religious and priestly vocations, but ought also to include prayers for an increase of persons capable of responding to the call to live their marriage as an intensification of their baptismal commitment and as a true and unique sacrament.

4. Premarital catechesis ought to concentrate heavily on the baptismal, vocational, and sacramental aspects of the day-to-day living of Christian married life.

5. Premarital inventories should include some introspection regarding how each of the couple views their future marriage as a true divine vocation that flows from their baptism, and how in practical ways they perceive the sacramental dimensions of Christian marriage. Are both of them on the same page in this regard?

6. Those involved in helping couples prepare their wedding liturgy could encourage them to include in their ceremony a renewal of their baptismal commitment. This could take place immediately preceding the proclamation of their marriage vows. Here I do not have in mind the terribly a-Christian formulas unfortunately used at baptisms and at the Easter Vigil. A person totally bereft of Christian faith could recite with us the promise to renounce Satan and all his works and empty promises, or, in the alternative formula, to reject sin, the glamour of evil, Satan, the father of sin and prince of darkness, to refuse to be mastered by sin and to live in the freedom of God's children. Such formulas are totally bereft of all the specifically Christian dimensions of baptism. I suggest that the renewal of baptismal commitment spoken of here include some of the positive aspects of baptismal life outlined in part two of this essay.

7. This leads to the last suggestion, the need to Christianize the marriage vows. As they stand, the traditional alternate formulas in the Catholic marriage ritual are completely lacking of any hint whatsoever of the uniqueness of *Christian* marriage.[2] These vows should explicitly include the intent to live one's marriage in the context of one's baptismal commitment, as a response to God's call, and as a sacrament of Christ's love.

Taking seriously Christian marriage as a true call from God will profoundly enhance the experience of married life and, in turn, contribute greatly to the strengthening of the very institution of marriage.

Questions for Discussion

1. What is your understanding of a divine vocation?

2. Do you truly perceive marriage as a call from God? Why or why not?

3. In your opinion do most married Christians look upon their marriage as a way of living out their baptismal commitment? If not, what can be done to help them make this connection?

4. What is your reaction to the way the author parallels married life to the evangelical counsels associated with religious communities?

Chapter 10

Casti Connubii to *Gaudium et Spes*

The Shifting Views of Christian Marriage

Bernard Cooke

In the midst of what appears to be a major shift today in human understanding and practice of marriage, it is instructive to compare papal teaching in *Casti Connubii* (On Christian Marriage)[1] from 1930 with the section on marriage in *Gaudium et Spes* (Pastoral Constitution on the Church in the Modern World) of the Vatican Council in 1965. In several ways the sequence of official teaching during the thirty-five years that separate these two church statements is a classic example of continuity and discontinuity, careful adoption of some more recent understandings and developments along with retention of the central core of traditional teaching.

The decades between the two documents, though marked by growing uncertainty about the precise binding force of the Roman Catholic Church's teaching on the purpose of marriage and the procreative responsibilities of parents, were not yet touched by the upheaval that followed Paul VI's encyclical *Humanae Vitae*. Unfortunately, in most circles that latter document was appraised almost exclusively with reference to its position on artificial contraception. Its broader teaching represented a continuation of the development contained in *Gaudium et Spes* that will be discussed below.

Casti Connubii (1930)

Quite clearly, Pius XI's encyclical *Casti Connubii* was written with the purpose of reiterating, amid threats to traditional views of Christian marriage, the teaching that had been passed down unchanged for decades and was considered basically unchangeable. The encyclical still reflects the church's conflict with the state over which set of laws should govern marriage — the laws of the state regulating marriage as a civil institution or the ecclesiastical laws that the papal teaching immediately equates with the law of God. The language and mentality of *Casti Connubii* is in large part legal and in some instances identical with the formulation of canon law. This is not to say that *Casti Connubii* does not take account of the personal dimension of Christian marriage; it continues the long-standing church teaching that the bond between the spouses is caused essentially by the free and deliberate consent of the two individuals. Without such agreement, there can be no true marriage.

This regard for the decision of each, however, does not mean that marriage is viewed as a union of two completely equal partners. The encyclical was promulgated at a time when the long-standing belief in the dominant role of the husband was generally taken for granted. For the most part the wedding promise of the bride was still to "love, honor, and *obey*." With few exceptions, the patriarchal structures and presuppositions of society in general and of the church in particular remained unrecognized and unchallenged. So, one finds in *Casti Connubii* explicit teaching such as "...the primacy of the husband with regard to the wife and children, the ready subjection of the wife and her willing obedience" (n. 52) that is somewhat jarring today.

Strange also to today's Catholics, accustomed as they have become (at least in much of the world) to women pursuing careers outside of the home, is Pius XI's stress on wife and mother as the only roles proper to women. The encyclical goes beyond recognizing the obvious difficulties that result from competing responsibilities of family life and pursuit of a career; it criticizes such involvement of a woman in public life as detracting from the dignity belonging to her as loving spouse and mother. "It is the debasing of womanly character and the dignity of motherhood" (n. 100).

Focus on motherhood as the distinguishing function of women is linked in *Casti Connubii* with the lengthy insistence on procreation as the primary goal of marriage and specifically of marital intercourse. Not only was the prohibition of contraception absolute, there was no allowance for family planning with limitation on the number of children. Each child is to be welcomed as a gift of God. At that point, not even the use of periodic continence to avoid conception was considered acceptable. Though the encyclical does recognize that the prohibition concerns marriage as an institution of nature, the argument is still strong and presumably irrefutable: the sexual intercourse of married couples has procreation as its primary purpose and no interference with conception is to be countenanced.

Despite the focus on contraception, the encyclical — which basically structures its exposition according to St. Augustine's famous threefold "good" of marriage: "offspring, fidelity, and sacrament" — recognizes that "fidelity" implies that Christian marriage has goals dealing with the couple as human persons and not just biological progenitors. While "fidelity" taken strictly pertains to observance of the matrimonial contract, the encyclical quickly moves the explanation to the role of genuine marital love. "True conjugal charity is not mere carnal desire nor limited to words of affection; it is a deep-seated devotion of the heart" (n. 34).

Love exhibited by the spouses in their home has a goal beyond that of the well-being of domestic life. It is meant to nurture the interior life of both husband and wife. "Their life-partnership must help them to increase daily in virtue, above all to grow in the true love of God and neighbor." In language that clearly moves church teaching in a more personal direction, *Casti Connubii* continues, "The mutual interior formation of husband and wife, this persevering endeavor to bring each other to the state of perfection may in a true sense be called . . . the primary cause and reason of matrimony so long as marriage is considered not in its stricter sense as the institution destined for the procreation and education of children but in the wider sense as a complete and intimate life partnership (n. 35). Such goals, e.g., fostering the love between the two, are nonetheless referred to as "secondary ends" (n. 84).

Pope Pius XII's "Breakthrough"

Though its importance has not always been recognized, the address of Pius XII to midwives in 1951 marked a definite step beyond *Casti Connubii* and a key turning point in the debate about sexual activity in marriage. In his address, though there was no change in the prohibition of artificial contraception, the pope recognized family planning in certain circumstances as acceptable, responsible, and even laudable. A married couple, however, could legitimately pursue this goal only by periodic continence, the so-called "rhythm method." This preserved the primacy of "nature" as the basic law dictating human morality, but it opened the door to the role of human choice in the exercise of marital intercourse and it shifted the ethical debate from "ends" to "means." Given that the choice of a couple to avoid conception was based on praiseworthy motivation, they were not free to decide on the means chosen to implement it. No "artificial" method of avoiding conception was permitted; the natural biological finality of marital intercourse was an ultimate law that allowed for no interruption. The positive morality of a couple's choice to limit the number of their children demanded, then, periodic denial of sexual activity as the only acceptable course of action.

Despite this and other papal statements, the years immediately before Vatican II were marked by widespread confusion regarding the Catholic Church's teaching on contraception. Introduction of the "birth control pill" seemed for a time to offer a solution to the discussion, but it, too, came to be regarded in official church circles as "artificial" and therefore unacceptable as a means of avoiding conception. Not only were Catholic couples uncertain about the exact meaning and the binding force of church teaching; confessors shared the uncertainty and often solved the dilemma by considering the prohibition of contraceptive means other than "rhythm" a *lex dubia* (doubtful law).

Questions being raised about marriage in the modern world, however, extended well beyond contraception. Economic and cultural changes were making the large extended family less common and the role of family members less determined. The post–World War II "sexual revolution" was challenging the restriction of sexual activity to married couples and the permanence of a lifelong marriage commitment. For a variety of reasons, families in countries like the United States were becoming more mobile; and as people became anonymous the power of neighborhood social judgment weakened. The world to which Vatican II's *Gaudium et Spes* was addressed was not the world of *Casti Connubii*. It would be a mistake, then, to see the teaching of Vatican II on marriage as addressed primarily to the issue of contraception. Beyond that one issue, it is a reassessment of Christian marriage with new emphasis on its personal dimensions, its unique role in people's sanctification, its sacramental function as a revelation of the divine.

Perhaps what most strikes one in comparing *Gaudium et Spes* to *Casti Connubii* is the change in tone and context. The church is no longer fighting the modern world and civil governments. Though it is obviously aware of the threats to Christian marriages, *Gaudium et Spes* breathes a different air; it sees married expression of human sexuality as a challenging ministry, as a sacrament revelatory of a gracious God, as a divinely given gift to enrich people's experience and personal growth.

In evaluating the teaching of *Gaudium et Spes* as a whole and specifically the section on Christian marriage it is good to remember the historical context in which it was produced and the role it played in the deliberations of Vatican II. The council took place only two decades after the disaster of World War II. All the European bishops and many others had personally experienced the war and the painful period that preceded it — the Spanish Civil War, the ascendancy of Nazism in Germany and Fascism in Italy.

As the nations recovered from the Great Depression and the havoc of the war years the culture of consumerism reemerged and gained strength in most of the world. Accelerating development of communications, particularly the advent of movies and television, meant that millions of people were being exposed to ideas and vicarious experiences that often were inimical to Christian understandings and values. Many patterns of external law and order were weakened or vanished with the collapse of the colonial system. Perhaps most importantly, the apparent failure of organized religion to confront the moral evils of the preceding decades meant that many people, particularly in Europe, no longer looked to the Christian churches for moral guidance and support. Cultural attitudes toward human behavior also changed noticeably, especially as they touched sexuality. Divorce that a short time before was looked upon as scandalous — families seldom referred to the divorced situation of family members — now was increasingly regarded as common and acceptable. Despite church strictures, more and more of the civilly divorced entered into second or third marriages, even though this meant abandoning membership in the church of their earlier years. Many people's values shifted as consumerism grew, and large families were no longer considered an unmitigated blessing.

It would be a mistake, as we said, to see the section on marriage in *Gaudium et Spes* (nn. 47–52) as dominated by the contraception debate. Its treatment is humanly broader and theologically deeper. Essentially the conciliar teaching reiterates the basic Catholic view of marriage as a God-given translation of faith into daily life and family life as the foundation for truly human society. While it exemplifies continuity in Catholic belief, it is not a static repetition of previous statements. Rather, it is a positive step in a more mature appreciation of human sexuality as a force for spiritual growth, as an agency of grace within marriage. It recognized Christian marriage as a freely chosen, lifelong bonding of equal partners. It placed love rather than law as the norm for the relationship and the growing spiritual life of the spouses as a goal at least as important as the biological life of offspring. While *Casti Connubii* did recognize and stress the role of love in marriage, *Gaudium et Spes* sees the spouse's love as the very essence of the relationship, "love which constitutes the married state," a love that is God-given, expressed in and securing its stability by the conjugal act of mutual self-giving. This is a far cry from the earlier stress on obligation that referred to the act of making love as a *debitum*. It is the very nature of marital intercourse that it demands complete fidelity. Fidelity is not basically the observance of a law; the love of the couple is itself the law.

At its roots, the statement in *Gaudium et Spes* is a rejection of the patriarchal vision of the family. It not only accepts but advocates the equality of the spouses, as persons, as Christians in the marital relationship. This is, of course, an aspect of its view that marriage is a unique form of friendship, a covenant that bonds persons and not basically a contract with permanent binding force. While honoring the role of women as mothers, it treats parenting as a responsibility shared by the couple, with the input of each providing an essential contribution to the healthy development of children.

Like *Casti Connubii*, Vatican II expresses concern about attacks on the indissolubility of marriage and on its procreative finality, but it is more realistic in recognizing the economic pressures on so many couples and the broader issue of overpopulation. Its outlook in general is more optimistic and positive, especially about human sexuality. The earlier encyclical had, of course, seen the love of the spouses as critical to their relationship, but *Gaudium et Spes* places it at the very heart of its treatment of marriage and appeals to it to interpret marital sexuality. No longer viewed as a concession to human frailty and a means of avoiding sin, sexual intercourse in the context of marriage is described as a source of maturity and sanctification.

Conclusion

It is in its understanding of human sexuality and its positive estimation of it that *Gaudium et Spes* is most discontinuous with previous church teaching. Again, it is important in evaluating this shift to remember the social and intellectual developments that separated the Second Vatican Council from *Casti Connubii*. The decades immediately before and after World War II had witnessed in Europe the philosophical school of "personalism" that had a marked effect on the council. Along with this, in both Europe and

North America, there had been an influential development of psychological research and widespread dissemination of psychological interpretation of human experience. More directly, there had been associations like the Christian Family Movement that had brought about, in Catholic circles, an important reorientation in people's attitudes and insights regarding sexual behavior in marriage. Quite healthily, this "revolution" had incorporated many of the better elements of psychological research and reflection, had developed a more open and straightforward approach to sexuality, and at the same time had avoided most of the immaturity and voyeurism that marked much of the so-called "sexual revolution." Very influential in this shift in Catholic moral judgments about married sexuality was the increasing availability of education for lay Catholics, both women and men, that marked the twentieth century.

The "innovations" in *Gaudium et Spes*'s treatment of sexuality are subtle but significant. While it certainly preserved the fundamental ethical judgments that characterized earlier Catholic teaching, Vatican II moved beyond the church-state conflicts that had marked nineteenth- and early twentieth-century papal statements about marriage and moved beyond viewing modernity as basically a threat. Aware of the challenges facing Catholic families in modern cultures, *Gaudium et Spes* still is optimistic about the possibility that Christian marriage can be a catalyst in the emergence of a more truly human world. Its message to Catholic couples is more encouragement than moral exhortation.

Gaudium et Spes was not the final word, but it remains a most important word about Christian marriage. It deserves to be much better known by Catholic couples than is now the case.

Discussion Questions

1. In what way can sexual expression of their love be seen as a source of "grace" for married couples?

2. Nurture of the relation between husband and wife is viewed by *Casti Connubii* as a secondary end of marital intercourse. How does the view of Vatican II differ? What are the theological implications of this shift for our own understanding of marriage?

3. What do the two documents see as the root of the indissolubility of Christian marriage?

Chapter 11

Friendship, Sacrament, and Marriage

The Distinction between Christian Marital Friendship and Non-Christian Marital Friendship

Todd A. Salzman

Introduction

In much recent theological literature, there has been a focus on the relationship between friendship and Christian love, and the role and function of friendship in the Christian life. Perhaps there is no more appropriate context for this discussion than the Christian sacramental marital relationship, where a Christian man and a Christian woman commit themselves to each other in a lifelong bonded friendship in Christ. In his essay "Friendship and Marriage," Michael Lawler has done a magnificent job of explaining the relationship between *agape* and *philia*, and demonstrating how friendship love functions as a model for the marital relationship.[1] In this essay, I will draw from Lawler's work on marriage, friendship, and sacrament to further explore the role and function of friendship in the marital relationship. I will briefly explore, first, the philosophical and theological perspectives on friendship or *philia*; second, the relationship between *philia* and sacrament; third, the sacrament of marriage as the greatest friendship; and finally, the implications of *philia* for Christian marriage in comparison to non-Christian marriage. In so doing, I hope to demonstrate that friendship, as it is understood in the Christian tradition, is an appropriate theological model describing the nature of a Christian sacramental marriage.

Philia: Philosophical and Theological Perspectives

Friendship has been a central theme historically in both philosophical and theological literature. Philosophically, Aristotle begins his two chapters on friendship in the *Nicomachean Ethics* with the following statement: "For without friends no one would choose to live, though he had all the other goods." In this statement, Aristotle reveals how fundamental and necessary friendship is to human beings. According to Aristotle, there are three types of friendship: pleasure, usefulness, and virtue or character. The difference between these three types of friendship is what bonds two people together. In friendships of pleasure and usefulness, the bond of friendship is the good that one gets out of the relationship. Once either the pleasure or usefulness ends, so too, does the friendship. Character or virtue friendship is grounded in the good of virtue. As Aristotle notes, "The perfect form of friendship is that between good men who are alike in excellence or virtue. For these friends wish alike for one another's good because they are good men, and they are good...." Such perfect friendships, then, are grounded in and bonded by the good, and seek the good which is a virtuous life.

According to Aristotle, friendship is possible only among equals. And while there is a sense in which, for example, a husband and wife can obtain equality, humans can never be friends with the gods because there is a fundamental inequality of nature that prevents it. As we shall see, Aquinas disagrees fundamentally with Aristotle on this latter claim. It is this fundamental difference that distinguishes Christian marital friendship from non-Christian marital friendship.

Marcus Tullius Cicero's *De amicitia* is one of the classic texts on the meaning, nature, and laws of friendship in ancient literature.[2] Cicero follows Aristotle's division of friendships, and defines true friendship as "a complete accord on all subjects human and divine, joined with mutual good will and affection."[3] True friendship is possible only among the virtuous, those who pursue the good, i.e., "those whose actions and lives leave no question as to their honour, purity, equity, and liberality; who are free from greed, lust, and violence; and who have the courage of their convictions."[4] Both Aristotle's and Cicero's work on friendship are crucial to the Christian tradition since their writings, along with scripture, had a profound impact on the Christian tradition's understanding of friendship.

Theological Perspectives: Scripture and *Philia*

Before investigating the relationship between friendship and sacrament, it is essential to determine the nature of Christian love since it is at the very foundation of the Christian life and sacramental theology. While Christian love throughout tradition has frequently been posited as *agape* — universal, unconditional, impartial, non-preferential love — there is an increasing amount of theological literature, drawing from both scripture and tradition, that posits the primary love of the gospel as *philia* — particular, conditional, partial, preferential love. If one looks to scripture, both *agape* and *philia* can be defended as reflecting the gospel imperative depicting God's love for humans as manifested through Jesus and the love that humans should have for each other. For example, these two passages — "may our lord Jesus Christ himself, and God our Father, who loved us..." (2 Thess. 2:16), and, "He who has my commandments and keeps them, he it is who loves me; and he who loves me will be loved by my Father, and I will love him and manifest myself to him" (John 14:21) — depict God's love for human beings as *agape*. (Although it is interesting to note that in John's citation, even though he uses the term *agape*, we see a hint of conditionality, mutuality, and reciprocity that reflects *philia*. Something is required from human beings — having and keeping God's commandments — in order for Jesus and God to love them.) In addition, the second of Jesus' two great commandments, "You shall love your neighbor as yourself" (Mark 12:31) and "love your enemies" (Matt. 5:44) posit *agape* as the love commanded between human beings. However, Jesus also calls us friends (John 15:15), and proclaims, "There is no greater love than this: to lay down one's life for one's friends" (John 15:13). If both *agape* and *philia* depict God's love for human beings and define how human beings are to love one another, the question then becomes, which is the primary love of the gospel, *agape* or *philia*?

There have been various theories on the nature of Christian love in the theological literature. Strict agapists such as Søren Kierkegaard[5] and Anders Nygren[6] maintain that Christian love is *agape*, unconditional, self-renouncing love, and that preferential loves, such as those manifested in particular friendships, are only another form of self-love, translated as ego-centric love. More moderate perspectives such as that proposed by Gene Outka[7] allow for special relationships within *agape*. That is, he does not see an intrinsic contradiction between *agape* and *philia*, though *agape* still maintains its preeminence as Christian love. Edward Vacek, S.J., is even bolder, claiming that while there is an intrinsic link between *agape* and *philia*, *philia* is "the most complete Christian love."[8]

Friendship is the most complete love in both the God-human relationship and the human-human relationship. In the God-human relationship, the particularity of Yahweh's covenant with Abraham, a "friend of God" (James 2:23, citing Isa. 41:8) and the Israelites is a preferential, friendship love. And while this covenant is universalized in the New Testament, the particularity of friendship love is reflected in the Incarnation, God choosing Jesus as his son, "the scandal of particularity."[9] In addition, even though Jesus loves all people (*agape*), he chooses twelve disciples to share a particular friendship with and, among the twelve, John is Jesus' favorite (though there may be some bias in this claim since it is made by the beloved disciple himself). In the human-human relationship, "There is no greater love than this: to lay down one's life for one's friends" (John 15:13). For Vacek, it is out of this particularity or preferentiality that we are able to learn to love universally. This statement reflects Aelred of Rievaulx's assertion in his classic treatise, *Spiritual Friendship:* "There can be love without friendship, but friendship without love is impossible."[10] *Philia* incorporates, and goes beyond, *agape* in that it is mutual and reciprocal. We learn how to love universally through our particular friendships. This mutuality or reciprocity is what distinguishes *philia* from *agape* and, more specifically, is at the core of a theological understanding of sacrament and is the primary love within marriage. As we shall see, marriage as sacrament can be defined in terms of a friendship bond (*philia*) shared as a lifelong commitment between husband and wife in union with Christ, which is universally shared (*agape*). It is *agape* which can strengthen the friendship bond, sustain that bond through difficult times, and extend it to all human relationships.

Tradition and *Philia*

St. Augustine draws upon the philosophical writings on friendship and Christianizes them. According to McNamara, there are four distinctive marks to Augustine's friendship.[11] First, God is the author and giver of friendship. Essentially, Augustine claims that we do not choose our friends, God does. This is a very profound assertion because it highlights the very sacred nature of friendship in which, not only does God sanction friendships between people, but also Augustine sees friendship at the very core of human identity and relationships. Second, along the lines of Aristotle and Cicero, friendship must be rooted in and seek the good. According to Augustine, only God is good. Therefore, friendship is necessarily directed toward, and seeks, God. In fact, the Trinity serves as the supreme model for friendship. Third, Christian friendship is transformed by grace. In and through friendship, we grow closer to the other person and to God. In every friendship, there is, in a sense, a Trinitarian relationship between two people bonded together by God's love and grace. Paul Wadell notes that, for Augustine, friendships "are not peripheral to the Christian life, but are relationships of conversion, in which Christians move to God by being transfigured in their love for God."[12] Thus, whereas Cicero's version of friendship was grounded in natural virtue, Augustine's is grounded in supernatural virtue. Finally, while we can never attain perfect friendships in this life, our friendships will reach perfection in the hereafter. Commenting on Augustine, Gilbert Meilaender notes, these "particular friendships are to school us in love; they are a sign and a call by which God draws us toward a love more universal in scope."[13]

Aelred of Rievaulx's treatise *Spiritual Friendship* combines both the philosophical — nearly a third of the treatise is quoted directly from Cicero's *De amicitia* — and theological sources, primarily scripture and Augustine, and is one of the most influential texts on friendship in the Christian tradition. In his treatise, he points out four stages in developing friendship: selection, probation, admission, and perfect harmony. In probation, or the testing period, of friendships, Aelred notes the virtues to be sought in another: love, affection, security, and happiness. However, these four virtuous qualities do not yet reflect the Christian nature of Aelred's friendship, for they are evident in Cicero's concept of character friendship as well. What distinguishes Aelred's perspective is that the foundation for these virtues, and indeed spiritual friendship, is the love of God.[14] In fact, the first sentence of Book One clearly states the essence of friendship: "Here we are, you and I, and I hope a third, Christ in our midst."[15] Through the Holy Spirit, God unites and binds two people in and through Christ in a sacred union of spiritual friendship. Because God is the basis and foundation of this friendship, according to Aelred, true friendship is eternal; it can never end.[16] Not only does Aelred define spiritual friendship as two people bonded in Christ, but he also projects the sacred notion of friendship on the essence of God's nature, and proposes that John 4:16, "God is love," might better read "God is friendship." Although Aelred recognizes that scripture does not clearly sanction such an alteration, he argues, "what is true of charity, I surely do not hesitate to grant to friendship, since 'he that abides in friendship, abides in God, and God in him.' "[17]

Thomas Aquinas certainly draws upon the traditional philosophical and theological sources to develop his understanding of friendship. For our purposes, there are two key aspects of Aquinas's discussion of friendship that will shape the remainder of this essay. First, while Aquinas agrees in large part with Aristotle's treatment of friendship, he disagrees fundamentally with Aristotle's assertion that we cannot be friends with God. As Aquinas writes, "charity signifies not only love of God but also a certain friendship with God." This friendship "consists in a certain familiar colloquy with God begun here in this life by grace, but will be perfected in the future life by glory."[18] Furthermore, Aquinas claims, Christ is our best and wisest friend.[19] In and through grace, we can attain a certain equality with God that allows us to claim friendship with God in and through Christ. The role and function of grace that creates a mutual, friendship love with God is at the heart of Catholic sacramental theology. Second, Aquinas claims that marriage between husband and wife is the greatest friendship possible for two human beings. And while non-Christians can share this friendship, it is the nature of spousal love, united in Christ through grace, that distinguishes Christian marital friendship from non-Christian marital friendship. Aquinas's insights require further explanation. To this we shall now turn.

Philia and Sacrament: A Living Faith

Having argued for *philia* as the primary love of the gospel and used throughout Christian tradition to describe our relationship with God, what is the relationship between *philia* and sacrament? First, we must define the nature of a sacrament and then explain how *philia* adequately explains this definition in terms of divine-human love. Following this, we will then explore how this extends to the sacrament of matrimony.

Adrian Thatcher provides a succinct definition of a sacrament. It is "a means by which God is uniquely present in the material, human world. For Christians, Christ is the ultimate sacrament, for it is through Christ that God became and becomes present in the material, human world, and in bringing grace into our lives, the sacraments bring the grace *of Christ*."[20] As stated, however, this definition reflects God's initiative, i.e., God offers salvific grace through Christ, what was labeled in Scholastic terms as *opus operatum,* the "gracing action of God in Christ." Salvation or acceptance of God's grace, however, can never be imposed on human beings; rather, its reception is dependent upon a free act of the will. As Karl Rahner emphasized, "since grace is only the event of salvation as brought about when it is accepted in freedom, and since this free acceptance can precisely be withheld by [humans], the sacramental manifestation of grace remains radically indeterminate *precisely from the human aspect.*"[21] Again, in Scholastic terms, *opus operatum* must be complemented by *opus operantis,* "the free faith of the participant cooperating with grace in this ritual." Sacrament, then, is not something that Christians receive, but "a graced interaction in and through which they express both their acceptance of the gift of God and the gift of themselves in return through Christ in the Spirit to the Father."[22] Through the recognition and acceptance of God's gift of grace, humans' relationship with God becomes mutual, reciprocal, and *philia.* In terms of our distinction in scripture between *agape* and *philia* then, we can reasonably assert that it is *opus operantis,* the recognition and reception of God's grace, which transforms *agape* and *opus operatum* into *philia.* Without acceptance of God's gift, the offer remains *agape,* not *philia.* The deliberate and active reception of God's love is an expression of a living Christian faith. This faith is necessary for marriage to be a valid sacrament.

In summary, then, the efficacious and salvific nature of a sacrament is dependent upon mutuality. That is, God offers salvific love in and through Christ, and humans are free to either accept or reject that offer. The faith manifested in the acceptance of God's grace in and through sacrament creates a friendship between the individual and God transforming the very nature of the person, the relationships that the person enters into, and the acts that follow from those relationships. As sacrament, marriage is the most profound of these human relationships; to that we shall now turn.

Philia and the Sacrament of Matrimony: Faithful Consent

Aelred of Rievaulx begins his reflections on spiritual friendship with the following: "Here we are, you and I, and I hope a third, Christ in our midst."[23] Though the context for his reflections is within the monastery, this statement is quite apropos for the sacrament of marriage. What distinguishes Christian marital *philia* from non-Christian marital *philia* is the inclusion of the person of Christ bonding man and woman together in marriage. As we have seen, while faith, or the conscious, free, and deliberate choice, is necessary to establish friendship with God, so too, faithful consent is necessary to establish the bond of friendship between husband and wife united in and through Christ. While faith establishes mutuality and friendship in relation to God in terms of sacrament, faithful consent establishes mutuality and friendship between husband and wife united with Christ in the sacrament of matrimony. What, then, is the nature of Christian marriage, faithful consent, and how do they distinguish Christian marital *philia* from non-Christian marital *philia*? We will explore each of these questions in turn.

The Sacrament of Marriage: The Greatest Friendship

Canon 1055 explains the essential nature of Christian marriage: "The matrimonial covenant, by which a man and a woman establish between themselves a partnership of the whole of life, is by its nature ordered toward the good of the spouses and the procreation and education of offspring; this covenant between baptized persons has been raised by Christ the Lord to the dignity of a sacrament."[24] Though this is the Catholic Church's contemporary juridical definition of the sacrament of marriage, one finds the roots of this definition in tradition and Aquinas's writings that refer to marriage as the greatest friendship (*maxima amicitia*).

With the recognition of marriage as a sacrament equal to all the other sacraments in the twelfth century, Scholastic theologians were interested in exploring the sacramental nature of marriage and how it fit into the church's life as a whole. The most influential of the Scholastics was Thomas Aquinas, who asserts that, of all friendships, that between husband and wife is the greatest friendship.[25] What is the basis for Thomas's claim, and how is Christian marital friendship distinct from other types of marital friendship? First, sexual intimacy is Aquinas's starting point for claiming that marriage is the greatest friendship. For human beings, the pleasure of sexual intercourse is "the most intense." This notion of coitus as an essential component of marriage is a recurrent theme throughout Aquinas's works. However, coitus alone cannot distinguish Christian marital friendship from other types of marital friendship or non-marital friendship for that matter. One can engage in coitus for a variety of reasons (adultery, fornication, rape, incest, etc.), some of which are antithetical to friendship. Furthermore, one can still enjoy the pleasure of intercourse outside the context of marriage.

In addition to sexual intercourse, then, Aquinas adds the necessity of commitment and the choice to live life together, the second requirement for marriage. According to Aquinas, a criterion for determining marital friendship as maximal love is that "the greater it is the firmer and more lasting it is." In his reflections on Aquinas, John Noonan poses the challenge of such a definition of marital friendship: namely, what about the case of cohabitation where a couple is committed, living together, and having sexual intercourse? A further aspect of marital friendship, then, is that the married couple, from the beginning, desires to extend their love through procreation. It is procreation where *philia* extends to *agape*; the particular love between the couple becomes a universal love desiring to share that love in procreation. For Aquinas, then, sexual intimacy, ongoing commitment, and the love shared between two people directed toward regeneration distinguish marital friendship from other types of friendships.

A further question remains, however, for Aquinas's definition of marital friendship. Those who marry civilly, or outside of the Christian context, demonstrate this lifelong commitment to each other, to share sexual intimacy, and to have children. Do these marital friendships differ from Christian marital friendships? According to Aquinas, the specifically Christian dimension of marital friendship lies in its nature as a Christian sacrament. The sacrament is conforming to Christ's charity as manifested in the passion. This charity is reflected in John 15:13: "There is no greater love than this: to lay down one's life for one's friends." This is the essence of marital friendship: total, mutual, reciprocal, and unconditional love for the other whereby this love is an imitation of the living Christ, and a commitment to the other as an image of Christ. It is this spousal *philia* that defines Christian marriage as sacrament, and distinguishes it from all other types of marital and non-marital friendship. Husband and wife bond themselves in lifelong friendship in Christ. Because God is the basis and foundation of friendship, according to Aelred, true friendship is eternal; it can never end.[26] Just as faith is required for a sacrament to be efficacious and a sign of one's friendship with God, so too in marriage, faithful consent between man and woman united in Christ is necessary to make a marriage a sacrament.

Faithful Consent and the Sacrament of Marriage

To understand the nature of faithful consent, we again refer to canon law as our point of departure. Canon 1057 is prefaced with the title: "Marital Consent — the Beginning of the Covenant." Consent initiates the covenant and establishes a marriage (along with consummation). The canon itself reads: "Marriage is brought about through the consent of the parties, legitimately manifested.... Matrimonial consent is an act of the will by which a man and a woman, through an irrevocable covenant, mutually give and accept each other in order to establish a marriage."[27] While the juridical nature of this language known as "the moment of consent" is less than adequate as compared to a theological understanding of consent as an ongoing, lifelong relational process, there is an important dimension to this definition that highlights the *philial* and sacramental nature of Christian marriage. Gustave Martelet notes, "Only if the future spouses freely consent to enter into married life by passing through Christ into whom they were incorporated in baptism" is a covenant marriage sacramental.[28] What distinguishes marital friendship from Christian marital friendship is not consent alone, i.e., both require consent, mutuality, and reciprocity for a marriage to exist. Rather, it is faithful consent, a consent grounded in each of the spouse's living faith in Christ, whereby they commit to each other in lifelong friendship united in Christ.

Christian Marital *Philia* and
Non-Christian Marital *Philia*

If, as Aquinas maintains, we can be friends with God and if, as we have argued, *philia* can serve both as a model for sacrament and as a model for marriage as sacrament, what distinguishes Christian marital *philia* from non-Christian marital *philia*? In other words, within the marital life, how does Aquinas's definition of marital friendship as the greatest friendship bonded in friendship with Christ differ from Aristotle's friendship defined by virtue where one cannot be friends with the gods? Through the mutuality of our relationship with God through the gift of grace in sacrament and, further, through the gift of husband and wife to one another united in Christ, the individuals, their relationship, and the acts that follow from it are transformed by their very nature.

Through the sacrament of baptism we become friends with God through the power of grace. This grace is an efficacious and salvific love seeking healing, reconciliation, and holiness. Baptism formally initiates this journey in friendship with Christ, yet it is an ongoing journey that requires an ever-growing, deepening, and maturing commitment to the friendship.

It is this maturing commitment and realization that one spouse brings to another spouse, and vice versa, in the sacrament of marriage. In sacramental marriage, the faithful consent of man and woman bonds the two together creating a relationship of healing, reconciliation, and holiness. The marital relationship becomes a witness to the Incarnation and the hope which that brings. Lest we idealize this relationship, which is hard to do given the number of divorces among Christians, this relationship also reflects the brokenness and the constant need for God's grace, forgiveness, and redemption. In a word, then, the marital friendship is perhaps the clearest human witness of the Incarnation. It lives the brokenness, finitude, and weakness between humans in this most profound of relationships, but overcomes these through the ongoing commitment to fidelity, reconciliation, wholeness, and deepening the bond of friendship. The marital relationship is a witness to God's presence and creative love extended to others. Through their shared lives, the marital relationship witnesses to the friendship within the Trinity shared with humanity.

Conclusion

While Christian and non-Christian married couples do many of the same loving and caring actions, such as raising and educating children, loving each other, sacrificing for each other, giving of each other, and sharing that love with others, the sacramental nature of marriage provides a moral imperative for, as well as a unique meaning to, these actions. It is by no means peripheral to the sacrament of marriage that the family is referred to as the domestic church. According to the *Catechism of the Catholic Church*,

" 'The Christian family constitutes a specific revelation and realization of ecclesial communion, and for this reason it can and should be called a domestic church.' It is a community of faith, hope, and charity.... "[29] As domestic church, Christian marital friendship as *agape* is a moral imperative. In other words, whereas Aristotle's *philia* focuses on good or virtue as the bond between people, and this bond is directly related to creating and sustaining the *polis* or just society, the explicit nature of that friendship, which requires a constant, benevolent, active love of neighbor, even enemies, is not a moral imperative. For Christian friendship, however, *agape* — or that self-emptying love that extends beyond the family, informs it, and is also deepened and nourished by that extension — is an explicit moral requirement. This imperative is at the heart of what it means to be a Christian, spouse, and friend.

Furthermore, through baptism and the shared commitment of faith between the married couple in friendship with Christ, the meanings of the acts that flow from Christian marital friendship are transformed by God's grace. The acts are expressions of a shared, living faith seeking to imitate Christ through our commitment as Christians. What distinguish Christian marital acts from non-Christian marital acts are the presence, awareness, and active response to Christ's invitation to live a life of charity, of which such acts are a concrete manifestation. Married couples live out the gospel imperative and witness to this imperative to their children and the community, by feeding the hungry, clothing the naked, comforting the sick, etc., and, in so doing, imitate Jesus' commandment. As Karl Rahner notes, however, anyone who performs an *actum honestum* or act grounded in charity participates in this remembrance as well. The difference is in awareness, and how that awareness shapes the identity of the couple and what they are doing when they perform such actions. Within Christian marital *philia*, these actions are a committed response to God's offer of friendship, which strengthens the bond of friendship between the couple, their friendship with each other and Christ, and extends this to all relationships.

Questions for Discussion

1. Describe your understanding of friendship.
2. Explain the nature of Christian love.
3. What is the relationship between sacrament and *philia*?
4. Explain the differences between Christian marital friendship and non-Christian marital friendship.

Chapter 12

Toward a Eucharistic Spirituality of Family

Lives Blessed, Broken, and Shared

Joann Heaney-Hunter

Introduction

Andrew Greeley tells a story about a father who took his four children to an ice cream parlor. The children fought, whined, and complained about all sorts of things such as who got to order first and who got the preferred flavor. It was not a pleasant experience. Surprisingly, when the father got home, he told his wife how much fun they had. How did he have fun? According to Greeley, it was because he was with his children whom he loved, and he took delight in feeding them and being with them.[1]

The story reflects the ordinary chaos of family life and could be translated to reflect families in all cultures. Moving past the surface of the tale, one sees a father's love and care for his children. In the simple act of watching his children eat ice cream, he could see past their imperfections and rejoice in the time he shared with them. Such is the reality of family life. It is a study in contrasts: the sublime and the ridiculous, the joyful and tragic, the holy and the sinful all rolled into one. For Christians, family life carries deeper meaning as well, because we believe that in its midst, we find the presence of Christ. This has been described as the domestic church[2] and has become an important part of the theology of marriage and family in the last thirty years and in particular since Pope John Paul's 1981 document *Familiaris Consortio*, which states that the family embodies Christ.[3] Another word for this embodiment is "sacrament," or symbol of Christ in the church and world.

For Catholic Christians, the pinnacle of sacramental life is the Eucharist. It is so significant that the Second Vatican Council called it "fount and apex."[4] In addition to its importance as meal and sacrifice, the Eucharist — partaking *of* the body of Christ *within* the body of Christ — represents a call to a life of sharing and service. As such, it is an encounter with the loving Christ who asks us to pick up our crosses and follow him (Mark 8:34). In the celebration of the Eucharist, it is possible to see "the whole of reality, the whole of life,"[5] and be changed by its implications.

The vision of Eucharist as a sharing in the life of Christ for the good of the world is at the heart of Christian tradition. Biblically, it is perhaps best exemplified in Paul's challenge to celebrate the Eucharist as a meal of unity (1 Cor. 11:18–27) and in John's juxtaposition of the Last Supper meal and the foot washing (John 13:1–15). Approached from these vantage points, the Eucharist calls believers to nourish and serve each other in the midst of daily life. It is the thesis of this essay that family life, through its daily experiences and events, does the same — it makes the crucified and risen Christ present and calls families to lives of nurture and service. In *Sermon 272*, St. Augustine reminds Christians that they are called to *become* Eucharist, the body of Christ, in the world. It is my contention that Christian families, in the context of daily living, are called to do the same.

Eucharistic Theology

In order to better understand how families live the call to be Eucharist, it may be helpful to review some basic principles of its theology. First, recall the meaning of the word "Eucharist" — to give thanks. The center of eucharistic theology is its dynamic action of thanksgiving. For what do we express thanks in the Eucharist? A number of possibilities emerge:

1. We give thanks to God for Jesus Christ, sacrament of God in the world, the savior and the bread of life. At the heart of eucharistic theology is the belief that the crucified and risen Christ is really present in the eucharistic action.[6]

2. We give thanks to God for life, because we believe that all life comes from God. Ronald Rolheiser reminds us often that part of our call as believers is to live with the recognition and the challenge that all life is gift, and to make a response that is worthy of that recognition and challenge.[7]

3. We give thanks for the people who make Christ present for us. Eucharist is not a commemoration of abstract theological principles; it is a living celebration of the life of Christ in the midst of the community. People make Christ present to each other, and the quality of that interaction may be the most concrete manifestation of the Eucharist in the world, and the dimension that is most relevant for this discussion of family life.

Second, one must remember the essential elements of the eucharistic action — blessing, breaking, and sharing, which reveal many layers of meaning. For example, one of the greatest blessings of the Eucharist is that Christ fulfills his promise to be with the community until the end of time. In turn, the community shares in Christ's promise by bringing Christ to others through their lives. The second element, breaking, also is manifested in many ways. Just as the eucharistic bread is broken, people come to the celebration with their lives broken — looking for Christ's healing. Finally, eucharistic sharing is realized at the table and beyond it. The body and blood of Christ are shared, prayer is shared, and community life is shared. The Eucharist, blessed, broken and shared, therefore, becomes a paradigm for Christian life, which also is blessed, broken, and shared.

Spiritual writer Henri Nouwen takes these elements of the eucharistic action and relates them to a spirituality of contemporary life, reminding readers that all life is blessed, broken, and shared.[8] In the pages that follow, I apply Nouwen's insight that human life is eucharistic to families. Just as individuals are called to be eucharistic in their spirituality, so are families, the foundational units of church and society.[9]

Family Life Is Blessed

Family life can be filled with blessings. A few of the more obvious blessings are the visible joy of couples in love, the pride of parents for their children, and the affection of couples who have shared a long life together. One blessing that is not often mentioned, however, is the unconditional, loving commitment, also known as covenant, that can flourish in marriage and family life. In a covenant relationship, couples are challenged to move beyond selfishness, work at loving unconditionally, and consider the meaning of the marriage relationship in the context of a loving relationship with God. Christian couples also act with the awareness that Jesus' relationship with God is the clearest example of what it means to live in an unconditionally committed union. The covenant of marriage calls couples to establish themselves as part of an eschatological reality and to recognize that they are called to live as the embodiment of Christ's life — a life blessed by God.

Covenant is described beautifully throughout biblical tradition; it is highlighted in the descriptions of God's covenant with the Israelites, as shown, for example, in the book of the prophet Jeremiah. "This is the covenant which I will make with the house of Israel after those days, says the Lord. I will place my law within them, and write it upon their hearts; I will be their God, and they shall be my people" (Jer. 31:33). This and other texts of the Hebrew scripture demonstrate that covenant is an unconditional, permanent, and faithful relationship of love between God and God's people. Various writers of the early church also emphasized the unconditional nature of covenant love in marriage. John Chrysostom, a fourth-century bishop of Constantinople, considered the covenant of marriage to be so sacred that it extended beyond this life into eternity. A poetic example of this thinking can be found in his *Letter to a Young Widow,* chapter 3:

> For such is the power of love, it embraces, and unites, and fastens together not only those who are present, and near, and visible, but also those who are far distant; and neither length of time, nor separation in space, nor anything else of that kind can break up and sunder in pieces the affection of the soul.[10]

How do the blessings of covenant love manifest themselves in contemporary family life?[11] As already mentioned, covenant begins when couples make an unconditional commitment to each other. Creating and sustaining a covenant relationship is a step that can be taken because a faithful God has demonstrated its true meaning throughout history, and because we have experienced the fully realized expression of covenant in Jesus' relationship with God, and in his fidelity to God's call, even to death.

We continue to see the life blessed by covenant manifested in the opening story. Looking in on that scene from the outside, the fiasco at the ice cream parlor may seem to be light years away from the covenant relationships described by Jeremiah or John Chrysostom. Despite the imperfection of the family in that story, however, the father recognized the kernel of covenant in the time he spent with his children. While he may ultimately have scolded or even punished them for their behavior, he nonetheless recognized the good that was present through the action of the family gathered. In other words, despite their obvious flaws, the family described was blessed because the father was committed to his children, and the children, despite appearances to the contrary, were tied in love to him through a covenant relationship.

Not all people consider the bonds of a committed, covenant relationship to be blessings. All too often, people try to find ways to limit commitments and potential liabilities and to protect themselves from the unknown potential for failure or unhappiness.[12] A eucharistic life, however, does not imagine such limitations. Instead, it invites persons to be living, breathing embodiments of Christ, the exemplars of selfless love. Using the Eucharist as a paradigm for family life demands that we love in the same way. A eucharistic vision of marriage and family life begins with a permanent, loving covenant of persons who embody Jesus Christ's fidelity to God and to their call in day-to-day life and persist in this fidelity despite its many challenges.

Family Life Is Broken–Dying and Rising in Relationships

Recognizing the blessing of covenant is the first step on the path toward a eucharistic family life. A second step is acknowledging that families who lead eucharistic lives will experience brokenness in a variety of ways. In reality, all life is a continuing process of breaking and rebuilding, of dying and rising, and of coming to terms with brokenness so that we can heal and return stronger and more willing to move forward. Romans 6:3–6, for example, provides an explanation of how, by virtue of baptism, believers enter not only into the resurrection of Christ, but into the brokenness and death that precedes it.

> Are you unaware that we who were baptized into Christ Jesus were baptized into his death? We were indeed buried with him through baptism into death, so that, just as Christ was raised from the dead by the glory of the Father, we too might live in newness of life. For if

we have grown into union with him through a death like his, we shall also be united with him in the resurrection.

Just as Christ died, we are called to die, and just as resurrection, not death, was the final answer for Christ, so it will be for us.

Brokenness forms a significant element of contemporary family life. Even prior to an actual marriage ceremony, for example, individuals face the brokenness of their lives as they come together to build a relationship. Many persons entering into marriage bring to it unrealized dreams, shattered promises, and maybe even lives devastated by circumstances or actions. Many are faced with uncertainty and a world that frequently seems to be without clear direction. They may encounter unbridled individualism influenced by a culture that insists one cannot count on anyone but oneself. Some face an inability to trust, which reveals brokenness in many relationships. Some couples encounter economic uncertainty, venturing into a marketplace that may be harsh and unforgiving. Many have experienced divorce themselves, or in their immediate families. The net result for many couples is that while they may *hope* for a satisfying, permanent relationship, frequently, they do not expect that they will succeed. Their prior experiences reveal their brokenness as they enter relationships.

Brokenness, moreover, continues throughout the family life cycle. Over the years, they learn what it means to die and rise daily. For example, couples who have freely chosen a covenant relationship recognize that they are called to renounce some of their freedom for the good of the marriage. In many ways, couples die and rise as they develop a union that is greater than the sum of its parts — a relationship where both parties are free to grow and help each other grow. By accepting the reality that no freedom is absolute, couples experience death and resurrection, and have the opportunity to live in the freedom of covenant and commitment.

Families with children at any stage of life know what it means to share in brokenness. The joy that parents experience when they bring children into their homes often is tempered by the suffering associated with raising them. As they grow and develop, children engage in a daily struggle toward independence. From the time they are able to say "no" as one- or two-year-olds, they move forward constantly, pushing boundaries, dying to one stage of life and rising to the next in a cycle of death and resurrection. Throughout the stages of childhood and adolescence, children move between independence and dependence, between needing parents and moving away from them.

As children experience the death and resurrection that accompanies growth and maturity, their parents die and rise along with them. All parents know the heartbreak of letting children make their own mistakes when everything in them wants to step in and prevent the problems from happening. Sometimes parents are like the father in the story of the prodigal son (Luke 15:12–32). As he handed over a share of his property to his younger son, the father must have had a fairly good sense of the problems that could arise. Even after the son had squandered his money and made other self-destructive choices, however, the loving father gladly took him back when he returned home, ashamed and poverty stricken. How many parents open their arms wide to their adult children who have made serious mistakes, but have recognized them and taken the courageous step to come home? Conversely, parents sometimes feel like the father in that gospel story as he dealt with his older son. How many parents deal with the brokenness of a family where one child believes that an unworthy sibling has received more than his or her due? Parents' dying and rising sometimes includes healing a self-righteous child who can't understand the love that they shower on an irresponsible child.

Families with children experience death and resurrection in other ways as well. Families who have children with extraordinary needs understand brokenness in ways that no one else can. They may experience denial, the desperation of trying to diagnose a child's problem, the trials associated with trying to find ways to make a child's quality of life as normal as possible. Families who have tried to adopt a child or children face challenges that may stretch them to the breaking point as they work to navigate painfully complicated systems and deal with unforeseen difficulties as they try to raise their children. Some families experience the agony of a child's death and the ensuing struggle that results as they continue to hope in the resurrection.

On the other end of the spectrum, many families today live with broken-ness as they care for aging relatives. How do families cope with elderly parents and other relatives who have a longer life, but not necessarily one that reflects enhanced quality? Families often face the challenges of trying to decide whether care takes place at home or in another setting, of arranging care, of trying to balance the needs of the senior citizen with those of the rest of the family. Even when those issues are resolved, the daily hurdles faced by those who care for the elderly are numerous.

These are just a few ways in which families make real the eucharistic action of breaking. In our lives, as in the Eucharist, we experience bread and lives broken. We grow in awareness of who we are, where we have been, and how we share that awareness with others. In family life each day, we are called to come to terms with our own brokenness as we celebrate the death and resurrection of Christ in the Eucharist.

Marriage and Family Life: A Sharing of Persons

A third critical dimension of the eucharistic action is sharing the body of Christ within the body of Christ. The Eucharist is the most powerful Christian symbol of sharing food and life, and it is in its celebration that we come to know Christ. Joining together in the context of any meal is an intimate activity; for centuries, breaking bread with one another has been a symbol of the unity that people share. Gathering together around a table requires that people set aside their differences, work at conversing, and begin to build community. In *The Holy Longing*, Ronald Rolheiser describes a Christmas celebration that reveals the challenges inherent in sharing a meal:

> You are readying to celebrate but things are far from idyllic. Your family is not the holy family, nor a Hallmark card for that matter. Its hurts, pathologies, and Achilles' heels lie open not very far below the surface but you are celebrating... and, underneath it all, there is a joy present. A human version of the messianic banquet is taking place and a human family is meeting.[13]

One of the great tragedies of contemporary American society is that many people have lost sight of the significance of the family meal, even the imperfect family meal. It is sometimes difficult to use the image in working with groups today, because so many people have an impoverished sense of what it means to gather around a table for a meal. Often enough, the best that we can do is talk about occasional celebrations that may provide us with a semblance of intimacy, but fail to yield the consistent development that emerges in the day-to-day sharing of food, conversation, and time together.

When one looks at the Eucharist as an intimate sharing of food and life, it is possible to see its connections with the ordinary existence of families. The joining of lives, of which sharing food is a metaphor, is the point where Eucharist and family intersect. Developing an intimate relationship is at the heart of family life because it is in becoming close, sharing deeply, trusting and respecting each other that we can come to understand the depth of God's presence in our lives. Family life is established on and grounded in intimacy, the basis of all deep relationships. These characteristics also are constitutive elements in eucharistic sharing.

Some examples may clarify the connection. Marriage and family relationships, for example, imply trust and friendship. The foundation of a marriage is two people coming together to trust each other in a friendship that has developed over time. In all dimensions of family life, trust in and knowledge of each other form the heart of relationships. Family members who demonstrate openness and a willingness to share themselves often have greater success in relationships because they have the ability to know and be known.

At the Eucharist, people come together around the table of the Lord to share a meal in trust and friendship, keys for union in Christ. The intimacy that develops as people share their oneness in Christ helps them to grow as members of a faith community. In the story of the road to Emmaus (Luke 24:13–35) the disciples come to know Jesus through the sharing of a meal. Just as Jesus revealed himself to the disciples, and reveals himself to us in the Eucharist, so family members make themselves known in the daily events of family life. Intimacy in family life leads to growth in relationships and provides individuals with the support to reach out beyond themselves. Achieving intimacy does not happen overnight. It takes time, effort, and consistent communication, which involves the risk of revealing oneself to another.

In the spirit of Christ's radical gift of self to all in the Eucharist, families are called to create a culture of generosity in their homes. While we live in a society that emphasizes the importance of material things to the detriment of everything else, a eucharistic stance toward life demands that people look beyond the material to create a culture of sharing the love of Christ in the midst of their homes and beyond it. How many of us know good people who are outwardly religious, but are caught up in a web of obsession with material possessions? While they are believers, they may not be able to translate those beliefs into concrete action and lifestyle. Eucharistic families are asked to consider the ways that they make the generosity of Christ, who freely gave himself for us, alive in the midst of the world today.

A final element of the link between eucharistic sharing and family life is the awareness of God's loving presence in every encounter with others. As Richard Rohr has noted, we find God disguised in our lives.[14] In the ups and downs, trials and tribulations, and give and take of ordinary family life, God is present. God builds on the imperfection present in every family life, and makes it holy. Recognizing the holiness in the ordinary, and becoming what we are — the body of Christ — in the midst of our lives, is central for developing a eucharistic spirituality of family life.

Conclusion

This essay has explored some of the ways that marriage and family life embody the Eucharist, the sacrifice of thanksgiving that makes present Christ in bread, wine, and people. In celebrating the Eucharist, the church gives thanks for Christ in our midst, and for the people that make up the body of Christ. What better place to begin to give thanks than families? The challenge is for families to give thanks for God's gifts in a mindful way, on a daily basis. The first school where we learn the meaning of Eucharist, the paradigm of thankfulness, is the family.

Families live the Eucharist by embodying its actions of blessing, breaking, and sharing. In family life, the covenant demonstrated in daily life is an invaluable blessing. The simple action of faithful presence, which is at the heart of all family commitment, is a clear example of eucharistic blessing. Just as we can absolutely count on Christ's fidelity to his promise to be with us, families living a eucharistic reality work toward the goal of revealing Christ's faithfulness to each other. While we recognize that no one will ever do this perfectly, belief in Christ's presence in the Eucharist challenges families to work toward leading lives of covenant and commitment. Furthermore, all families understand the reality of being broken for others, a critical element of the eucharistic action. On a daily basis, families sacrifice and suffer, and as they work through the struggles of daily life, they become mirrors of the eucharistic sacrifice. In the brokenness of ordinary life, families reveal Christ, broken for us. Finally, as the bread and wine of the Eucharist are shared, families share themselves day after day. In truth, they are the laboratories where persons develop the ability to share themselves and build up the reign of God in the world. As families try to build a culture of intimacy, generosity, and spirituality, they demonstrate eucharistic life daily.

Let us return to the family in the ice cream parlor. Recall that the father was happy because he was with his children whom he loved, and loved feeding. In the blessing of that family, in the brokenness they experienced, and in the sharing of simple food, they all experienced Christ. All Christian families are called to do the same. Through the witness of family life, we embody the life of Christ, present in the Eucharist, and make it really present in our communities and in the wider world.

Questions for Discussion

1. What does it mean to say that families embody Christ?

2. How do you, in your family, experience the blessings of family life?

3. What are some ways that you experience "being broken" in your family life?

4. How do you share yourselves in your family life?

Chapter 13

Sacramental Marriage and Holy Orders

Toward an Ecclesial Ministry for Married People

Thomas Knieps-Port le Roi

For the longest time, the Catholic Church has defined its position on marriage by referring to what appeared to be a preferable alternative: celibacy. Jesus himself was not married, and Paul recommended that the Christians in Corinth remain unmarried in order to respond more adequately to their newly gained freedom in Christ (1 Cor. 7:25–38). Paul was realistic enough, however, to understand that celibacy is a charismatic gift that cannot be imposed on or lived by everyone. While he ultimately refused to regard marriage as inferior to celibacy, later Christian writers have more or less emphatically advocated the higher value of the unmarried state, seeing in it a way of bypassing the devastating effects of sexual concupiscence. It was only with the Second Vatican Council's recognition of the universal call to holiness for every baptized Christian that the church recovered marriage as an authentic form of Christian discipleship. Recent magisterial teaching emphasizes that marriage and celibacy are complementary ways of Christian living that are mutually enriching and that *both* are indispensable to the life of the church.[1] According to a common theological interpretation, celibacy can be said to symbolize the *universality* of God's love toward humanity as a whole, whereas married people live and exemplify in a particular way the *intensity* of the divine love for every single human being.

In this essay, I intend to modify this perspective by relating marriage not to celibacy but to the ordained ministry in the church. My interest is thus not so much in marriage as a model of discipleship but rather in its sacramental character and, subsequently, in its ecclesial status and function. Could it be that just as it took a long time to accept the married state as a full Christian vocation, current theology has not sufficiently fathomed *the ecclesiological implications* of the marital sacrament? When placed in comparison to ordination, which has always been considered a sacrament conferring a ministry closely related to the proper mission of the church, the ecclesiological contours of marriage begin to take shape. The thesis I will argue is that sacramental marriage confers on the spouses a proper and true ministry that is not part of or subject to, but juxtaposed and complementary to, the hierarchical ministry. As this conclusion strongly builds upon the renewed Catholic understanding of the church as sacrament of salvation, I

134

will first explain what this concept entails for the seven sacraments and then turn to ordination and marriage.

The Sacramentality of the Church

In stating that the church itself is a universal sacrament of holiness, the Second Vatican Council undeniably introduced a radical development in the Catholic conception of the church. With this, it did away with an image of the church that had held sway throughout the second millennium in the West. This was the idea that the earthly Jesus established the church with a given institutional structure in order to continue his work on earth. The church was thus understood to be a kind of extension of Christ's existence or his enduring incarnation in history. This identification of the church with Christ led above all to a mystification of its hierarchical structure, with the pope understood as the vicar of Christ, at the summit of the pyramid of ecclesial ministry. The theologians of the Reformation protested against the gross abuses of this divinization of the church, distinguishing between a visible and an invisible church. While the visible or exterior church is manifest in its institutional structure, the true, invisible church exists only in the faith of its members and is known only to God. The Reformers thus did not avoid the attempt to play off the visible church against the invisible and to assign the former a purely functional importance. In contrast, post-Tridentine Roman Catholic ecclesiology upheld the unity between the exterior, institutional structure and the interior, spiritual dimension of the church. Since the two aspects should not be separated, the church increasingly presented itself as a "perfect society" (*societas perfecta*), which Christ had provided with all the necessary means for her mission. With a hierarchical structure that stretched back to Jesus and a divinely ordained sacramental system, it was supposed to carry out all that it had received from Christ, namely, to distribute salvation to a world that appeared to it as corrupted and bereft of grace.

It was against this conception that Vatican II adopted the programmatic statement, in its Constitution on the Church, that the church itself is a sacrament of salvation. Drawing from the patristic writers as well as the *nouveau théologie*, the council applied the label "sacrament," which had been used only for the individual sacraments, to the church itself. The church "in Christ, is in the nature of *sacrament* — a sign and instrument, that is, of communion with God and unity among all."[2] With this statement, the council introduced a new understanding of the relationship between God's salvation in Christ and the church. The church henceforth is no longer seen as solely the continuation or extension of the salvific action of Christ. It is much more the "realization" and "actualization" of this salvation for humanity. It realizes salvation by being its effective sign in the world. The church, in its preaching and its worship, is not only an indicator of salvation, as if it could be divided or separated from it (such as in the case of an anonymously believing member of a true, but invisible church). Neither can the church respond on its own to those who seek salvation, as if it were strictly identical with salvation, with Christ himself, or with the kingdom itself. When the council called the church the sacrament of salvation or the sacramental sign of God's saving presence, it did so to counteract both an exaggerated triumphalism and a purely instrumental conception of the church.

In a still wider perspective, the discussion of the sacramentality of the church has led to a fundamentally new conception of the relationship between the church and the world. In pre–Vatican II ecclesiology, the church portrayed itself as a holy entity in a godless and profane world. Salvation came from above. The grace of Christ was uniquely transmitted to the church, which, like a depository, stored up this grace and distributed it to the world as the need arose, by means of its sacramental system. Outside of this system the world had no means of contact with salvation. The church now understands itself as sacrament and no longer as a dispenser of sacramental grace. It exists within a world in and for which it must be the effective sign of divine salvation. The council has introduced a critical addition to ecclesiology by saying that Christ, through his Spirit, established "the Church as the *universal* sacrament of salvation (*universale salutis sacramentum*)."[3] The adjective "universal," added to the term "sacrament," means that the church not only participates in a universal salvation given by God but is itself established as a universal, effective sign of the love of God in the world. This, however, means nothing less than that the reality of the church surpasses any boundaries determined by abstract or sociological deduction. We discover here again the dialectic between identity and difference that we encountered in the relationship of the church to salvation: In its particular, historical reality, the church is the sign of God's universal bestowal of salvation and the instrument of his desire for the salvation of all people. However, it opens itself to the universal breadth of those called to salvation only when it relativizes and exceeds the narrow and well-defined space of its historical existence.

The council highlighted this openness in calling the church the "People of God." From the beginning God desired to call together a holy people for himself and wanted to share his divine life with them. Creation itself should be understood as an expression of God's self-communication. It reaches its goal and its fulfilment only when all of humanity is drawn together in union with God and one another. From the beginning — before and outside of the historical ministry of Jesus and the founding of the church — "church" is the place in which the free grace of salvation is given and received. Likewise, the eschatological goal of the universal "church" will be attained only if it coincides with the whole of reconciled humanity. The church, living in history and in the world, thus has the mission of "proclaiming and establishing among all peoples the kingdom of Christ and of God,"[4] in other words, of being the sign and instrument of inner union with God and of the unity of all people. It is in one respect a symbol and foretaste of the kingdom of God and in another remains radically distinct from this kingdom in its humanly sinful limitations. It is thus always a pilgrim church on the way to completion, together with all those who let the saving and freeing love of God take hold of and transform them. This understanding of the church is impressively spelled out in Vatican II's Pastoral Constitution on the Church in the Modern World.

The Sacraments as the Realization of the Sacramentality of the Church

What does the sacramentality of the church mean in regard to the individual sacraments? Clearly, it was not the intention of Vatican II to add an eighth sacrament to the seven defined at the Council of Trent. On the contrary, it wanted to show the church's connection to each of the seven sacraments. Karl Rahner is, above all, the theologian who helped recover the idea of the church's sacramentality and spoke of the sacraments as specific realizations of this broader sacramentality throughout a person's life.[5] Rahner argued that the church is not a mere representational sign of God's *offer of salvation* to the whole of creation but an eschatological presence of the arrival and acceptance of what is already *victorious salvation.* Salvation history is no longer open but has been definitively determined because Jesus Christ, in his becoming human and through his resurrection, has brought about its irreversible victory. If Rahner correspondingly spoke of the church as the presence of the irreversible victory of grace, he did not at all contradict the affirmation of the council that this grace is also manifest beyond the historical reality of the church. On the contrary, from Rahner's perspective this is the victory of God's desire for the salvation of all; in other words, God's desire to communicate himself to all humanity has already reached its goal in Christ, despite and even through humanity's sinful refusal. Rahner could certainly affirm, from the way in which he understood the sacramentality of the church, that the church is every community in which this victorious salvation is available, whenever humans accept this salvation in their particular circumstances and let it shine forth in their lives. It is exactly at this point where one can gain insight into the function of the sacraments and their unbreakable connection to the sacramentality of the church. The salvation of humans can be truly victorious only if it is also accepted by them and allowed to operate in their lives: "Consequently the Church as historical sign of victorious grace only attains the highest actualization of her own nature when grace is victorious in this sense in the individual and also is tangibly expressed and really occurs for the individual's sanctification. This is exactly what happens in the sacraments."[6]

With this conception Rahner also shows a possibility to elucidate better the connection between the objective operation of the sacraments —

a favorite theme of classic sacramental theology — and its subjective ap-
propriation by the recipients. As a sign of irreversible victorious grace,
the sacraments communicate God's absolute and unconditioned promise of
salvation. They accordingly effect what they signify and are thus, as the
Scholastics formulated it, an *opus operatum*. However, insofar as God's objective promise of salvation can be victorious in humans only if this act of
God is accepted, the sacraments can operate only through the freedom of
the recipients in faith, hope, and love.

From this it is also clear that the enduring presence of divine love is not
communicated to people in the abstract but to people immersed in the particular circumstances of their lives. The seven sacraments sketch the various
contours of human existence in need of divine salvation and can transform
these aspects if the grace they communicate is accepted in freedom. There is
a truly anthropological basis for the sacraments in the critical phases of life:
birth and death, coming of age and sickness, meals and sexuality. People
of all times have seen these different phases as more than mere biological
processes. It is at these times that the success of life — human salvation,
theologically speaking — is determined. And yet, what appears from this
perspective as individual salvation has also an ecclesial and ecclesiological
dimension. In these life phases the church actualizes God's saving presence in
each individual circumstance, realizing in them, and for always, its being and
mission as the basic sacrament of salvation. This has important implications
for marriage and ordination.

The Function of Holy Orders and
Sacramental Marriage for the Ecclesial Community

The tradition depicts ordination and marriage as so-called "sacraments of
vocation," which are destined for a determined role in the church or human
community. The new *Catechism of the Catholic Church* treats them after
the sacraments of initiation (Baptism, Confirmation, and Eucharist) and the
sacraments of healing (Reconciliation and Anointing of the Sick) under the
same title: "Sacraments at the Service of Communion and the Mission of
the Faithful."[7] Both marriage and ordination would be seen from a purely
sociological perspective as acts through which elementary functions for the
preservation and the building up of the community are transmitted. This is
true for ordination, in which the church bestows the office of responsible
minister, as well as for marriage, in which the community not only gives
a commission to provide new members for the church but also affirms the
relationship as exhibiting the ideal form of human community. However,
such a reflection does not yet show how the act through which the church
bestows its ministry or through which two people enter into a bond of love
is an act which has as its goal the sanctification of the people who receive
orders or who promise themselves to one another.[8] In other words, it does

not yet show how these acts are understood as sacraments. Thus, we seek to know how these two acts participate in the sacramentality of the church: In what way do they accomplish and actualize God's salvation?

One way in which we must understand this sacramentality in regard to ministry was already articulated by the early church in its response to Donatism. Namely, the ministry keeps its validity and its bearer his authority and power even if as an individual he is a sinner and exercises his office unworthily. The priest primarily receives the sacrament of ordination not in regard to his personal qualification but as an office given for the service of the church. It is thus clear that in the case of ordination, the presence and appearance of eschatologically victorious salvation is surely offered and addressed to the individual minister but is essentially actualized in regard to the identity and integrity of the church's mission as such. The church entrusts its salvific mission to individual persons, but it does so by investing its responsibility fully and radically in this act. In other words, it can be said that the salvation and holiness of the person being ordained is realized in the acceptance of an ecclesial function in which, taken as a whole, the holiness of the church itself is expressed and fulfilled. Therefore the sacramental ministry, taken as a whole, cannot be performed in an unholy manner because the sacramentality of the church itself remains in play.

Could one analogically deduce that marriage is also endowed with an ecclesial function in which the church engages itself completely and that married life, taken as a whole, stands within the permanent promise of salvation so long as the spouses remain in a bond of love, which they are called to witness to and manifest? In order to clarify this, we must first look in more detail at Holy Orders.

Holy Orders — Representing Christ as the Source of Salvation

A traditional argument holds that the church can make Jesus Christ present in space and time and can be said to effect the salvation of its members only if it is continually transformed into the image of the Word made flesh and if it — in the logic of the Pauline image of the "Body of Christ" (see Rom. 12:5; 1 Cor. 12:12–27; Col. 1:18 and 2:19; Eph. 1:22f. and 4:1–16) — becomes this body by remaining faithful to its head. Its mission of bringing salvation to all is brought about through Christ's action within the church as its head. For this reason the church has been given a ministry in which this headship of Christ is represented: the ordained ministry or Holy Orders. The Catholic tradition has regularly implied a structural opposition between the ordained ministry and the community. It has taught that ordained ministry is not one charism among others and cannot be said to emerge from the charismatic community as a work of the Spirit. It is, in fact, set *over against* the individual charisms and the community as a whole because it operates *in persona Christi capitis*,[9] in the person of Christ as the head of the church.

One does well not to overemphasize this christological basis for the sacramental ministry. Vatican II taught that, along with this Christ-centered view, the ministerial representation of Christ for the community must be understood as having its basis in the *common* identity of all believers with Jesus Christ in the Spirit by virtue of their baptism. The minister should not be identified with Christ; he is no *alter Christus*. His role of standing before and for the community is grounded not in a position *above* the community but must be understood as at the service of the unity of the community. He represents Christ to other baptized persons, but he does so by taking part in the mission of the whole church. The ordained ministry is seen as distinct from the community, at the same time it arises out of the community and remains within it. St. Augustine summarized this well in describing his role to his own community, saying, "When I am frightened by what I am to you, then I am consoled by what I am with you. To you I am the bishop, with you I am a Christian. The first is an office, the second a grace; the first a danger, the second salvation."[10]

This brief look at the theology of ordination shows that through the sacrament of Holy Orders the church is constituted and prepared for its mission of salvation. Ordination brings about a position in the ecclesial community that the church cannot fill on its own. Through it, it is reminded that salvation does not come from the community and that its mission of bringing salvation does not mean that it, itself, is salvation. In other words, the ordained ministry, in representing Christ as both head and primary agent of salvation, shows the absolute preeminence of divine action and shows that the promised salvation comes only from God through Christ in the Spirit. In this sacrament the church is assured of the only ground and sole legitimation for its mission and worship. If the ordained minister is promised the salvation necessary for the task, if, in other words, the ministry is transmitted by means of a sacrament, this takes place in relation to the integrity of the church's mission, which depends upon this action and this minister for its fulfilment. This is the ecclesiological aspect, the individual dimension of it being that the minister is given the grace for carrying out his office. Given the immensity of the task of maintaining the place of Christ within the community, the minister, a person like any other and himself a member of the ecclesial community, may well approach the office with trepidation. In any case, it struck fear in Augustine.

Sacramental Marriage — Representing Christ's Unifying Love

The ordained ministry engages in particular acts in which the minister promises salvation to particular people. In a similar way, in married life there are particular moments in which the personal love of the spouses becomes salvation for one other. Just as the sacramentality of Holy Orders is not exhausted in such particular cases, so also does marriage have a broader grounding in the saving mission of the church. This is explicitly pointed out in the New Testament household code found in Ephesians 5:23–33 with its famous parallel between the bond between Christ and the church and the marriage bond. It is upon this resemblance that the tradition bases its understanding of the sacramentality of marriage.

Today it is undisputed that the wording of Ephesians 5:32 in itself ("This is a great mystery; I am referring here to Christ and the church") is no proof for the sacramentality of marriage. The "mystery" (*mysterion* in Greek, translated into Latin as *sacramentum*) refers to the gift of Christ to the church and does not refer to marriage. Here marriage appears solely as the image of this bond but henceforth becomes connected with Christ's salvation mystery. The resemblance is legitimized by the reference in verses 29–32 to the union of love "in one flesh." The citation from Genesis 2:24 ("Therefore a man leaves his father and his mother and cleaves to his wife, and they become one flesh") indicates that this bond between the first spouses is grounded in the act of creation but plays an important role also in the covenant between Christ and the church. Thus, between the unity of marriage and the unity of Christ and the church there is the same relationship as the one that exists between the order of creation and the order of redemption. The covenant is the reason for creation and its end insofar as it carries and embraces creation as its precondition in order to have a covenant partner. Creation occurred only because God willed the covenant; the covenant, however, is only possible insofar as the covenant partner is there, with and in creation. Applied to marriage, this means that, as the Ephesians account shows, the bond of love between two persons as a creational reality exists only because God in Christ willed to conclude the uniting covenant with humanity. Conversely, Christ can join himself to the church in a covenant of love only because God has given unifying human love a basis in creation. This means that there is not only an exterior resemblance between the unity of love between two people and the unity between Christ and the church; there is in fact a causal and participatory relationship. The unity of marriage is grounded in the unity of Christ and the church, and the union of Christ with his church is brought to fulfillment in the union of love between two people inasmuch as this human love is expressed in its created aspect.

Thus it can be said that in the sacrament of marriage one catches sight of a broader constitution of the foundational sacrament of the church. If the sacramental being of the church is to "show and realize the inner union with God and the unity of all of humanity," then the unifying love between two people in marriage is that act that expresses and realizes this sacramentality. To the degree to which the spouses definitively promise themselves to each other, they show that the church's mission of uniting humans with God and one another in the love of Christ can be fulfilled. Thus, when marriage is celebrated sacramentally, the individual salvation of the spouses is involved; they need and receive the grace of God for their marriage. This also means that something happens decisively in and for the church.

Sacramental Marriage and Holy Orders as Complementary Ecclesial Ministries

I have sought to show that the church effects the saving action of God in Christ in a sacramental way and can thus be called a foundational sacrament. Its being and mission as the universal sacrament of salvation is accomplished in each sacramental action in which the victorious salvation won in Christ is actualized in individual persons in the situations decisive for their salvation. Of the seven sacraments, I have been interested in the two that are specifically concerned with service to the ecclesial community. I argued that the sacramentality of marriage and ordination derive from their ecclesial role. In these two sacraments the church fulfills its constitution and authentically accomplishes its mission of salvation. In Holy Orders the church is assured of the *ground* and *legitimation* of its mission of actualizing a salvation that comes solely from God through Christ in the Spirit and that is beyond the church's power to control. In marriage, the church actualizes the *means of the accomplishment* of this mission in the unifying and saving love of God in Christ. In the church both functions have constitutive importance in bringing about salvation, making them *sacramental,* which means that the church's saving mission becomes effective in ordination as its ground and legitimation and in marriage as the mode of its accomplishment.

The promise of salvation in which both ordination and marriage exist brings with it an authentic accomplishment of the church's mission, that of becoming holy. Because the church places its mission and sacramentality entirely in the hands of individual persons, its holiness depends on the subjective holiness of those who are ordained ministers or who live a married life. The ministry of the church does not forfeit its holiness if on occasion the minister sinfully performs it, but the church would truly be no longer holy and could no longer sanctify its members if all of its ministers were unholy. This is also true in regard to marriage. The married life of the baptized exists within the permanent and effective promise of salvation if the spouses share a bond of love which, according to Ephesians 5, is the love with which Christ loves the church. If there were no longer any marriage that lived this unifying love, then the church would fail in its mission of salvation. It is thus the obligation of both the ordained minister and the married person to continually take up the objective sacramental promise of salvation into the progress of their lives so that their subjective salvation more and more conforms to it.

Thus marriage and ordination both participate in like manner in the saving mission entrusted to it by Jesus and diversely, in distinct ways, take part in the sacramentality of the church. They have complementary functions and competencies without which the church could not fulfill its task of making present salvation. This connection has not been well developed in post–Vatican II ecclesiology and sacramental theology. The idea still exists that the priestly ministry alone, in its vertical connection to Christ, is the conduit of salvation. The New Testament, however, leaves no doubt that there is also a horizontal connection to Christ, one that exists when people allow themselves to be taken up into God's movement of love and in turn love their brother and sister (see 1 John 4:11–12). Married life is a sacramental sign whose saving love is destined not only for the spouses but also for the church as a whole. Marriage thus has a ministerial character similar to that of the ordained ministry. I can conclude that sacramental marriage implies a marital ministry that is not ranked lower than the ordained ministry but has a similar, complementary role.

Translated from German by David Dawson Vasquez

Questions for Discussion

1. How do you understand the relationship between Christ and the church? What does it mean for the church to make Christ present to all humanity? How do you understand the idea that the church is a foundational sacrament?

2. What do you understand to be the meaning of the words "salvation" and "grace"? Do you think that God's love can be communicated through the various sacraments of the Catholic Church?

3. Do you believe that the priestly ministry represents Christ? When the priest is ordained by the bishop, what does that imply for himself and for the Christian community in which he will be serving?

4. Can you imagine that couples represent Christ in and through their marriages? In your judgment, do you think that marriage is simply a private arrangement between two persons or can you think of any meaning it could have for the church?

Chapter 14

Sacramentality and Social Mission

A New Way to Imagine Marriage

Thomas M. Kelly

If ever there was a place and time to reflect theologically on the sacrament of marriage, the contemporary culture would be ideal. Not since the early church has the Catholic laity enjoyed the recognition and responsibility that was retrieved for it at the Second Vatican Council. At the same time, new and interesting developments on what constitutes sacramentality are broadening in theological circles. A new and growing movement in Catholic theology has recognized that such reflection on marital sacramentality is necessary, in part, because the mission of the laity to the world cannot succeed apart from new and more dynamic understandings of the marital commitment. According to *Lumen Gentium* the laity has a unique mission to the world. "These faithful are by baptism made one body with Christ and are constituted among the People of God; they are in their own way made sharers in the priestly, prophetical, and kingly functions of Christ; and they carry out for their own part the mission of the whole Christian people in the Church and in the world."[1]

I will argue in this essay that in order to understand the mission of the laity in the context of church, one must understand it in terms of marriage — the primary vocation of the vast majority of laypeople. In order to understand that vocation, one must look carefully at the way marriage has been understood as a sacrament in traditional church teachings. What becomes evident is a serious contradiction between an active social mission for the family encouraged by the church and a passive or receptive idea of sacrament. I will suggest a new way of thinking about the sacrament of marriage that will enable laypeople to envision the family as a transforming force in our society today. With such an understanding, the sacrament of marriage and the reality of family can become the primary mode through which Catholic social thought encounters the world.

The laity in the Catholic Church is unique in that they are "secular" by nature and by their vocation they seek the kingdom of God through "engaging in temporal affairs and by ordering them according to the plan of God."[2] It would seem that if the vast majority of laypeople are married, and they are, and that one's primary relational commitment would affect how one approaches reality in general, and it does, then one's marital vocation is hardly superfluous to the mission of the laity. It must be central. The growing failure of marital relationships in our culture as well as the failure of traditional sacramentology to speak to the experience of married couples calls for new ways of envisioning the sacrament of marriage and integrating it into the social mission of the church.

Increasingly, theologians have come to recognize that marriage and the family life emerging from that commitment are life-giving forms of ministry, even discipleship, already being lived out in the church. Further, it is also the context through which lay Catholics "learn how to distinguish carefully between those rights and duties which are theirs as members of the Church, and those which they have as members of human society."[3] What has become a new focus in the theology of marriage is the meaning and consequences of such marital sacramentality, especially as the church engages and attempts to constructively transform the world.[4]

Traditional Marital Sacramentality

Many scholars look to John Paul II's *Familiaris Consortio* as a recent starting point for the church's discussion of marital spirituality, domestic church, and how both are connected to Catholic social thought.

According to John Paul II, "the Christian family, in fact, is the first community called to announce the Gospel to the human person during growth and to bring him or her, through progressive education and catechesis, to full human and Christian charity."[5] Further, "as an educating community, the family must help man to discern his own vocation and to accept responsibility in the search for greater justice, educating him from the beginning in interpersonal relationships, rich in justice and in love."[6] The notion of family early in the document is clearly one that is active, dynamic, and engaged with the world. This is further confirmed in the following:

> The Church, therefore, does not accomplish this discernment only through the Pastors, who teach in the name and with the power of Christ but also through the laity: Christ "made them His witnesses and gave them understanding of the faith and the grace of speech (cf. Acts 2:17–18; Rev. 19:10), so that the power of the Gospel might shine forth in their daily social and family life." The laity, moreover, by reason of their particular vocation have the specific role of interpreting the history of the world in the light of Christ, in as much as they are called to illuminate and organize temporal realities according to the plan of God, Creator and Redeemer.[7]

This "plan of God" is specified first by emphasizing that human beings are created to love. "Love is therefore the fundamental and innate vocation of every human being."[8]

An interesting understanding of the theological significance of marriage is then introduced. This understanding is communicated through an analogy external to the marital relationship itself, that is, the analogy employed is *abstracted* from married love and used to indicate and signify something else. "Their bond of love becomes the image and the symbol of the covenant which unites God and His people."[9] What precisely characterizes "covenantal love" is never specified in the document.

Various scriptural images of covenant, especially in Jeremiah and First Isaiah, reveal a relationship of sin and punishment that should not characterize married love or married infidelity. For example, early in the book of Jeremiah, Israel is depicted as a new bride in love with the Lord her husband — "I remember the devotion of your youth, your love as a bride, how you followed me in the wilderness, in a land not sown" (Jer. 2:1). This relationship drastically changes later when Israel, unfaithful to the covenant, is depicted as an unfaithful wife who pays for her infidelity by being publicly stripped and raped. "And if you say in your heart, 'Why have these things come upon me?' it is the greatness of your iniquity that your skirts are lifted up and you are violated" (Jer. 13:22, 26). There are, it seems, limits to the analogy of covenant fidelity between the people of Israel and their God when speaking of married love. The reason for the analogy of covenant love is explained when the roots of married sacramentality are examined.

> Receiving and meditating faithfully on the word of God, the Church has solemnly taught and continues to teach that the marriage of the baptized is one of the seven sacraments of the New Covenant. Indeed, *by means of baptism,* man and woman are definitively placed within the new and eternal covenant, in the spousal covenant of Christ with the Church.

And later:

> By virtue of the sacramentality of their marriage, spouses are bound to one another in the most profoundly indissoluble manner. Their belonging to each other is the real representation, by means of the sacramental sign, of the very relationship of Christ with the Church.[10]

The sacramentality of marriage, according to *Familiaris Consortio,* derives from the baptism of the spouses, not from the reality of their marriage. In other words, the sacramentality of marriage is extrinsic to marriage and is efficacious through previous baptism, not through a reality present in marriage in and of itself.[11] This leads, by necessity, to an understanding of marital spirituality as passive and to the analogy that the marital relationship between spouses parallels the biblical relationship between Israel and God. The marital relationship mirrors the relationship of the church to Christ. If the sacramentality of marriage is derived solely from the baptismal sacrament and is analogous to an idealized relationship between Christ and the church, there is nothing intrinsic to the marital relationship itself that signifies its sacramentality.

This approach to the sacramentality of marriage is, of course, deeply at odds with the *active* and *socially engaged* Christian family envisioned earlier in *Familiaris Consortio*. A key presupposition here is that the character of a family, its values, its direction, and its capacity for service, will emerge from the quality of the marital covenant. A passive sacramentality, that is, a sacramentality envisioned as a receptor of a prior sacrament, may be advantageous for the reception of certain "fixed" teachings on sexual morality.[12] But such a view misses the crucial connection and thus fails to communicate the relationship between the role of the family and the social transformation sought through Catholic social teaching. For example, where is "God's plan" when a family attempts to enter into solidarity with the poor or tries to live out the principle of subsidiarity? Where is "God's plan" when married couples and families discern how to adopt an option for the poor? Such an option could take many forms and must emerge out of the lived contextualized vocation and faith-commitment of a particular family. Further, such an option requires a dynamic notion of sacramentality — one that emerges from and develops within the nature of married love itself, informed and formed by the community we call church.

From Marriage to Family as Domestic Church

Familiaris Consortio follows its framing of marriage as a sacrament derivative of baptism by working out an understanding of how the family as a "domestic church" fulfills its mission "to guard, reveal and communicate love, [as] a living reflection of and a real sharing in God's love for humanity and the love of Christ the Lord for the Church his Bride."[13] Four concrete aspects of the family's mission as a domestic church are then developed: (1) forming a community of persons, (2) serving life, (3) participating in the development of society, and (4) sharing in the life and mission of the church.

The first two "missions" of the family are mainly internal. Forming a community of persons and serving life are concerned with qualitative relationships between spouses, procreation, and possibly raising and educating children. The third "mission" is mainly external as the family interacts with the society in which it lives. "Thus, far from being closed in on itself, the family is by nature and vocation open to other families and to society, and undertakes its social role."[14] First, the family engages society by simply being what it is, "an experience of communion and sharing."[15] Its social and political role consists in "manifold social service activities, especially in favor of the poor," "hospitality," and political participation in the process of how laws affect the rights and status of families.[16] This third section concludes with a very strong call for families to live out their faith in the context of the challenges in their particular societies.

The social role that belongs to every family pertains by a new and original right to the Christian family, which is based on the sacrament of marriage. By taking up the human reality of the love between husband and wife in all its implications, the sacrament gives to Christian couples and parents a power and a commitment to live their vocation as lay people and therefore, to "seek the kingdom of God by engaging in the temporal affairs and by ordering them according to the plan of God."[17]

The fourth "mission" for the family has to do specifically with the "life and mission of the church." This section of the document more so than any other has the strongest "extrinsicist" notion of sacramentality — one that is buttressed by a curious definition of "faith." For example, a family participates in holiness when "Christian spouses and parents offer the obedience of faith."[18] "Faith" is understood as the "Discovering and Admiring Awareness of God's Plan for the Family."[19] The family is properly family only when it obediently accepts "God's Plan." This seems to be a reference to church teaching on sexuality and reproduction. "God's plan" here refers again to the internal mission of the family — but in determining the family as mainly a *receptor* of "God's Plan," the possibility for *actualizing* the family as engaged in society's problems seems to be greatly diminished. Engaging society constructively requires an active, creative dynamism springing from the interior of marital life and love. Conversely, "God's plan," as the blueprint for the mission of the family, is a passive sacramentality of marriage that is dependent upon baptism for its meaning.

Repeatedly in *Familiaris Consortio* the ground for the sacramentality of marriage is affirmed to be baptism. This is stated clearly in the fourth section: "[Marriage] takes up again and makes specific the sanctifying grace of Baptism."[20] While a marriage which lacks baptism for either spouse is not sacramental (regardless of the nature of the love shared), the marriage of a baptized couple for "social reasons" — i.e., for motives other than the strictly religious — is *de facto* sacramental.

> Nevertheless, it must not be forgotten that these engaged couples, by virtue of their Baptism, are already sharers in Christ's marriage Covenant with the Church, and that, by their right intention, they have accepted *God's plan* regarding marriage and therefore are at least implicitly consent to what the Church intends to do when she celebrates marriage.[21]

In what can only be a direct response to this approach to sacramental theology in *Familiaris Consortio*, Michael Lawler comments:

> Baptism does not give faith nor make believers in any but a very passive sense, namely, it gives the know-how to faith and to being a believer. The Code's sweeping assumption that the Church is dealing with Chris-

tian believers from the moment of baptism, and that therefore every valid marriage between baptized persons is by that very fact a sacrament, is a rather simplistic, theologically naïve assumption, and one that is manifestly false in countless cases in our day.[22]

A critical problem thus emerges for the theology of marriage. If the abstract "marriage" is always sacramental, how does one understand its failure in so many cases? Is this a failure of God? The church? Baptism? The couple? And if this "sacrament" is based on the baptism of two people (usually as infants) who do not believe or do not participate in the life of the church, is such a notion externally imposed, even contrary to human will?[23] What form of sacramentality can answer these questions?

What does the common but insufficient understanding of sacramentality rely upon for its own justification? Partly it is a bifurcated understanding of reality as "nature" and "supernature," both of which require God to be absent from part of reality and fully present to the other part.

> The very spatial imagery of "elevation" bespeaks a two-tiered reality within which that which belongs to the lower, nature, is raised to the second level, supernature. This strong meaning of elevation is unacceptable in light of an authentic doctrine of grace flowing from and in harmony with the doctrines of the Trinity and creation.[24]

This "strong elevation" is a dualistic way of understanding sacrament, and it flows from philosophical movements prominent at the origins of Christianity.[25] These are problematic because their continued influence militates against new and meaningful understandings of sacramentality. Whether one speaks of the visible and invisible, the concrete and the abstract, the profane and the sacred — the message is the same. It seems that something can be deemed sacramental only as an instance of something greater than what it actually is.

With a world thus comprised, grace must encounter our world from outside of it — i.e., extrinsically — and transform mundane realities into truly significant events by obliterating its "natural" essence, so to speak. This oversimplified but nevertheless prominent understanding of sacramentality would be contrary to the notion that all space and time is sacred because it is created by God, and that sacraments remind us of those specific events that are central to our self-understanding as a people of God, i.e., as church. In part this is due to deficient understandings of the self, and the way in which God's grace is operative in the world.

What is needed is an understanding of sacramentality that can both understand the grace inherent in married love and allow for the human element within such a love to fail, even at times, to break completely. Only then can concrete married love become a form of discipleship — an active choice of mutual giving and receiving — and not a form of magic. This relationship can be a kind of ministry in and of itself, especially when it extends itself to others and eventually to society. It can serve the church by giving the vast majority of its members an adequate understanding of what they are and can be. This in turn leads not only to a deeper awareness of the community life of the church, but also to a better understanding of the sacraments.

An Intrinsic Sacramentality?

In language used throughout theological history, something is sacramental when it "effects what it signifies," i.e., by being what it is, it reveals what it wishes to communicate. John Paul II affirms this as true of the family when he declares in *Familiaris Consortio:*

> The role that God calls the family to perform in history derives from what the family is; its role represents the dynamic and existential development of what it is. Each family finds within itself a summons that cannot be ignored, and that specifies both its dignity and its responsibility: family, become what you are.[26]

But what does this actually mean? Anyone who teaches undergraduates is well aware of the fact that "sacrament" is usually, if not always, interpreted as another word for "magic." The fact is, the community of faith has done a poor job of effectively communicating a nonmagical understanding of sacramentality. In part, this is due to deficient understandings of God (Trinity) and grace. The following description of sacramentality is aware of this fact.

> A Sacrament makes grace (the self-communication of God outside the Trinity) effectively present for you by bringing it to your attention, by allowing you to see it, by manifesting it. Sacraments presuppose the omnipresence of grace, the fact that the self-gift of God is already there to be manifested. But because it is always present it frequently goes unnoticed.[27]

The rather broad understanding of sacramentality presupposed for this essay is one that understands "sacrament" *to cause the effective acceptance of grace,* wherever found.[28] This grace, this communication of God is agapic love, which in the context of married love always co-exists with friendship (*philia*) and sexual love (*eros*).[29] It is important not to sentimentalize or romanticize such love, for to effectively will the good of another may in fact mean to challenge not only one's self, but the subject of one's love, quite forcefully.[30] It is this deep and rich meaning of agape, always in conjunction with friendship and sexual love, which is most appropriate for understanding the intrinsic sacramentality of married love.

To say that "marriage is intrinsically sacramental" is to understand "sacramental" in a broad, as opposed to a narrow sense.[31] A narrow sacramentality confines such a designation to those who possess some knowledge or have participated in a particular ritual (whether at the age of conscious consent or not).[32] This limits the manner in which we understand God as present and efficacious in the world as well as our response to that presence. By extension, it also limits one's social ethics. A broader sacramental vision acknowledges that all of reality is imbued with grace, for God communicates self as gift to all creation. It must be possible that all creation, including those outside certain ecclesial and intellectual contexts, be able to experience and respond to God's grace. Such an experience and response may not be as refined or clear as it is within the faith community — but at the level of possibility it must exist. Within this total worldview, the church designates seven specific events — *Sacraments* — as critical to the church's self-realization.[33]

To say something is sacramental because it "effects what it signifies" is to say that it reveals what it wishes to communicate simply by being what it is.[34] This is quite different from the neo-platonic dualism mentioned earlier, for it is not an abstraction from the concrete that reveals something else; *it is in and through the concrete reality that more becomes known.* This recognition of the transcendental dynamism of created reality leads to the recognition that what we seek and desire is infinite. "Our hearts are restless till they rest in you, O God," is not an abstract heart, but a concrete one deeply imbedded in the chaos and confusion of this world. And the dynamism of this movement beyond — one that is intrinsic to human being and knowing — has its end in something much greater than the self.

Augustine's thought develops this insight by first confirming the function of a sign in *De Doctrina Christiana,* "A sign is something which besides the impression which it induces in the senses, of itself causes something else to come into thought."[35] This is ultimately verified by Aquinas when he confirms the "commonly used" expression that sacraments effect what they signify.[36] So what would it mean to say that marriage is intrinsically sacramental? Note, it is not being argued that only Catholic marriage or Christian marriage is sacramental, but marriages wherein there is a real presence and interplay of sexual love, friendship, and agape (as previously defined) are at least, potentially, sacramental.

From the very nature of married love as an integrative whole of sexual love, friendship, and agape, one can experience the love of God. For married people this could be the direct experience of a multifaceted love, given and received in equality and justice. For the children it could be the primal trust and love that one experiences first and then aspires to in one's own development in relationship to others. For the community it could be experienced in the presence of members whose concern for others is always a part of their family life and their civic engagement. What must first be demonstrated for this to be theologically possible is the deficiency of any notion of sacramentality coming from "outside" or "above" the relationship itself. Speaking out the grace of a comprehensive love, married love by its nature in the concrete reality of human life can effect what it signifies.

Conclusion

The most fruitful definition for the sacrament of marriage in the present inquiry is to define it *by what it does*. If the point of departure from Augustine and Thomas is that sacraments "effect what they signify," how might that be transposed into our contemporary culture in a way that is meaningful? If a sacrament effects what it signifies, then to signify God's grace must have specific content. This rather broad understanding of sacrament can now be more fully explored. In a world where God's grace undergirds all creation, where all creation came to be through God's grace, then to see anything in its depth and fullness is to see the manifestation of grace.

The following may be one way to discern whether a marriage can be considered intrinsically sacramental. The spouses effectively will the good of each other and their children through concrete choices aimed at the fullest realization of each other's humanity. A certain respect for the otherness and individuality of each person in the family as well as others in one's community will characterize the initial disposition to relationality. Forgiveness and understanding as well as patience and endurance characterize relationships that will bend and even sometimes break.

There will be a desire and willingness to focus on relationships over material things, status, or power. Family time and energy is emphasized over other competing realities. There will be a sincere explicit mission to one's community, especially to those weakest and most vulnerable. This may include direct service to the homeless in one's community through serving at soup kitchens and shelters. It may include awareness and pro-active involvement of municipal policies toward the homeless. It may include active fundraising and consciousness raising about the plight of homelessness.

There will be an active seeking of knowledge of one's context and the education of one's children on the consequences of societal action or inaction. There will be an awareness focused on the social impact of decisions both familial and societal, and how the poor are affected. The love and nurturing that characterize the marital relationship and by extension the familial relationship will, by definition, expand into one's community and society through active participation in civic and ecclesial institutions. Sacramental love never simply stays at home. In short, an intrinsically sacramental marriage will model and extend *self-gift* as a way of being, both inside and outside the family in a plethora of ways.

Insofar as this marriage takes place within an ecclesial community, it can both give and receive much. It can give an example of conditioned and conditional people intentionally making and maintaining an unconditional commitment to each other. The possibility for such a commitment, the unconditional love of God, can become a visible reality through the public witnessing of such love in everyday life. The church provides the marriage a supportive community that challenges contemporary trends in relationships. In so doing, the church fulfills its prophetic duty to put forth the Incarnation,

God's perfect self-gift, as the supreme example of love toward which Christians aspire. In a true community of love, challenged and inspired by the Incarnation of God, the church's mission of social transformation emerges from an understanding of faith and sacrament as an *existential* commitment to God *and* to each other through the concrete willing of the good of others. This could be the specific role and function of married laypeople and their families as they act as a leaven for the church's mission to the world.

Questions for Discussion

1. What is the traditional notion of sacramentality grounded upon according to Kelly?

2. What is Kelly's new theology of sacrament based upon? Does it make sense to you?

3. What is the connection between family and the role of the laity in the world?

4. Does the Catholic Church's vision of family life and the pursuit of justice, especially through the option for the poor, challenge contemporary and prominent notions of family?

5. How would you rethink the priorities of your family if you were to adopt Kelly's understanding of marriage and its consequences for family life?

Part Three

MARRIAGE AND EXPERIENCE

Chapter 15

Cohabitation

Integrating Ecclesial and Social Scientific Teaching

Gail Risch

Cohabitation, which now precedes the majority of marriages in the United States and a number of other countries, has been addressed by ecclesial documents and analyzed by the social sciences. Ecclesial teaching prohibits living together and sexual intimacy prior to marriage. A large body of social scientific research, most of which was conducted during the 1990s, shows a relationship between premarital cohabitation, subsequent marital instability, and higher rates of divorce. The relationship is discussed in ecclesial documents, by theologians writing about marriage, and in marriage education programs.[1] The most recent research shows evidence that the once relatively unquestionable connection between cohabitation and marital instability has dramatically diminished. There is also strong evidence that other factors, not cohabitation per se, can place couples at greater risk for divorce.

Michael Lawler argues convincingly that to recognize scientifically the church's actual situation and to perform the required theological reflection, practical theology requires sociology.[2] This is no truer than in the case of cohabitation. In this essay I argue for the integration of theological discussion and social scientific data about cohabitation, especially for a discriminating interpretation and application of the most recent data to sustain credible dialogue between theology and the social sciences. This approach, which points out a connection between sociological research, theological doctrine, and pastoral action, reflects the Second Vatican Council teaching in *Gaudium et Spes*, specifically, that "in pastoral care sufficient use should be made, not only of theological principles, but also of the findings of the secular sciences, especially psychology and sociology" (n. 62). I argue not for wholesale acceptance of premarital cohabitation, but for church teaching and pastoral practice that is informed by the most recent and credible empirical data, is reviewed and revised routinely, and is, therefore, relevant to current human experience and needs. The first part of this essay examines pertinent ecclesial documents, the second surveys the most recent social scientific research on cohabitation, and the last offers concluding remarks about the integration of theology and scientific data.

Ecclesial Documents

I intentionally use the term "ecclesial documents" to reflect the notion of "church" implied by the documents discussed here. In these documents the term "church" refers to the Magisterium, the official teaching body of the Catholic Church, which is only a part of, and should never be confused with, *Lumen Gentium*'s whole church, the People of God. The documents discussed in this section present teachings of the Magisterium. The intentional differentiation between "Magisterium" and "church" is appropriate when current realities, in this case the reality of cohabitation, indicate that reception of particular magisterial teachings has not occurred; that is, certain official magisterial teachings have not been accepted or embraced by the whole church, the People of God.[3]

Three ecclesial documents contribute most directly to this essay. The first is Pope John Paul II's 1981 apostolic exhortation, *Familiaris Consortio* (*On the Family*). Its opening sections declare that "since God's plan for marriage and the family touches men and women in the concreteness of their daily existence in specific social and cultural situations, the Church ought to apply herself to understanding the situations within which marriage and the family are lived today, in order to fulfill her task of serving" (n. 4). According to this document, the church is called to understand the variety and complexity of the social and cultural settings in which human relationships, especially marriage and family, exist. Furthermore, the document affirms the role of scientific research as a means of understanding and fulfilling the task of service. "The church values sociological and statistical research when it proves helpful in understanding the historical context in which pastoral action has to be developed and when it leads to a better understanding of the truth" (n. 5). Scientific research, in other words, can enrich our understanding of truth and inform developing approaches to pastoral action. John Paul's document first conveys a positive attitude toward the social sciences and, therefore, provides enormous support for a link between ecclesial and social scientific data. It seems clear that dialogue between the social sciences and ecclesial teaching, which is to undergird pastoral action, is not only encouraged but is also necessary for the ongoing development of effective pastoral responses to the changing realities of human life.

But a serious caveat emerges as the document further explains that "such research alone, however, is not to be considered in itself an expression of the sense of the faith" and that "it is the task of the apostolic ministry to ensure that the church remains in the truth of Christ" (n. 5). What "truth" is regarding relationships is determined exclusively by the Magisterium, and the faithful are to be educated in that truth. The document's attitude toward scientific data, which interprets social realities of the faithful, is cautious and calculated in order to maintain the priority of magisterial teaching. Such a posture establishes social science as a subordinate partner in the dialogue and inhibits rather than enhances the possibility of real dialogue.

Familiaris Consortio is a relatively comprehensive work that addresses numerous issues related to marriage and family, but it speaks explicitly about cohabitation or "*de facto* unions" in only one short section. It acknowledges there are various reasons that couples cohabit, each of which presents "arduous pastoral problems...and social consequences" (n. 81). It does not explore reasons that couples cohabit or describe pastoral problems, but names as social consequences "the destruction of the concept of family; the weakening of the sense of fidelity...possible psychological damage to the children; the strengthening of selfishness" (n. 81). It suggests that pastors should make "tactful and respectful contact with the couples concerned and enlighten them patiently, correct them charitably and show them the witness of Christian family life...to regularize their situation...above all there must be a campaign of prevention" (n. 81). The emphasis of this document is clear: pastors should take steps to understand the contexts and elements of cohabitation and resulting pastoral action should convey magisterial teaching regarding *de facto* unions. It dictates a position rather than engages in dialogue. It is important to note that in 1981, the year in which *Familiaris Consortio* was published, little social scientific data about cohabitation was available. Since then, a large body of data has accumulated, most of it in the past fifteen years.

The next ecclesial document to consider is *Family, Marriage, and "De Facto" Unions* from the Pontifical Council for the Family. This document, originally promulgated in 2000 and published in English a year later, elaborates upon the brief statements of and direction indicated by *Familiaris Consortio*. Opening remarks describe it as the product of meetings of "outstanding persons and well-known experts from different parts of the world" who analyzed "this delicate problem," the phenomenon of *de facto* unions.[4] It intends to present "a word of guidance" in light of the "international political juncture" of the institution of marriage, and "proposes to contribute in a positive way to a dialogue...and to take part in the socio-political debate."[5]

As is typical of ecclesial documents, specific authors, their areas of expertise, and their associations are not identified, nor does it provide the source of nonecclesial information incorporated into the text. Readers unfamiliar with the style of ecclesial documents may find the absence of such references both unusual and perplexing, especially if they are familiar with scholarly and scientific work, which cites numerous sources to establish credibility, verify findings, and provide supportive, collaborative, and even dissenting positions for the sake of clarification. To be sure, the primary purpose of an ecclesial document is to state official teaching, and the primary purpose of social scientific documents is to report research findings and to contribute to ongoing scholarly discussion of a particular subject. Ecclesial documents are not of the same genre as social scientific works and, therefore, are not well-suited for participation in ongoing scientific discussion. However, I suggest that an ecclesial document, such as *Family, Marriage, and*

"De Facto" Unions, that explicitly claims to contribute to a dialogue with other sciences and to take part in sociopolitical debate, could take steps to better facilitate and substantiate its intention toward dialogue. Clarity about authorship and authors' expertise could enhance the credibility of the document's statements. References and citations for nonecclesial, scientific information implied or explicitly mentioned could be included. Effective interdisciplinary dialogue is informed about and considerate of the partners' style, language, and procedures in order to establish mutual respect and the integrity of the dialogue.

Family, Marriage, and "De Facto" Unions states that *de facto* or cohabiting unions are a widespread phenomenon and defines them as "heterogeneous human realities...(of a sexual kind) that...ignore, postpone, or even reject the conjugal commitment" (n. 2). It notes that children are increasingly a part of cohabiting households and contends that while not all *de facto* unions have the same social status or the same motivations, they all have common elements (n. 4). It claims that *de facto* unions imply a sexual relationship with a relative tendency toward stability, as compared to sporadic or occasional cohabitation and marriage. The instability associated with *de facto* unions, it suggests, "comes from the possibility of terminating the cohabitation," a notion of "commitment" that includes the possibility of terminating the relationship, and a "strong assertion to not take on any ties" (n. 4). It says there is a "need to delve into the ideological and cultural background" (n. 7) of cohabitation. The document appears to be at least aware of social scientific data on cohabitation; the last point could be interpreted as an invitation for greater understanding of the social contexts of contemporary cohabitation and, therefore, further research.

A prominent concern woven throughout *Family, Marriage, and "De Facto" Unions* is the perceived elimination and "de-structuring of the institution of marriage" (n. 8). Because marriage is defined as the only acceptable context for sexual relations, cohabitation is seen as a violation of magisterial teaching. It argues that institutional or public recognition of *de facto* unions would result in "grave religious and moral consequences" (n. 39) on the role of marriage as the foundation of family and, therefore, the common good of society (nn. 16–17).

A social scientific reading of this document generates a number of responses. First, it is correct that cohabitation is an increasingly widespread phenomenon; cohabitation before first marriage has become the norm and attitudinal data support this inference. Only 7 percent of women born in the 1940s cohabited before the age of twenty-five, compared to 37 percent of those born in the 1960s.[6] By 1995 over half of all first marriages were preceded by cohabitation.[7] It is also correct that cohabiting unions increasingly involve families with children.[8] By the mid-1990s at least 50 percent of cohabiting unions included children, and the percentage of children born since the cohabitation began was at least 15 percent.[9] The document acknowledges correctly that persons cohabit for various reasons, but does not refer to or provide social scientific sources for this information, which have long been available. As the document generalizes further, it becomes increasingly difficult to verify what it calls "common elements" of cohabiting relationships. Claims it makes about the relative stability of cohabitation and the level of commitment of cohabitors are tenuous because they are made without supportive empirical evidence, which is demanded by social science. In this particular instance, generalizations about cohabitors' commitment to and the stability of their relationships are especially inappropriate because they are inconsistent with the far more nuanced and detailed findings of recent social scientific research, which will be discussed below.

Finally, what the document describes as the "de-structuring" of marriage presumably refers to social changes, or what might best be described as the *re-structuring* of the formation and composition of family and marriage. Social historians recognize that social institutions, marriage included, have evolved and continue to do so. Human institutions are not static entities. They develop, change, grow, adapt to, and are shaped by complex social and cultural situations. Neither indiscriminate acceptance of, nor absolute resistance to, change is reasonable and responsible. On the other hand, opposition to change may derive from fear of that which is unfamiliar and different or from the threat of loss of control and authority. Fears might be dispelled by replacing speculation and assumption with credible and accurate information and by entering into thoughtful discussion with scholarly authorities. A discerning theological and pastoral approach to cohabitation acknowledges the dynamic nature of human institutions, including the People of God, their families and marriages. It must also comprehensively consider the social context of this increasing and widely accepted social phenomenon, including all available and relevant information.

The last ecclesial document to consider is *Marriage Preparation and Cohabiting Couples: An Information Report on New Realities and Pastoral Practices*, published in 1999 by the National Conference of Catholic Bishops (now the United States Conference of Catholic Bishops) Committee on Marriage and Family. It is a resource whose purpose is "to impart information that is current and relevant" and "to offer a descriptive overview of common pastoral approaches" to situations and issues connected with cohabiting couples.[10] This document, which is not an official ecclesial statement, appears to be a response to *Familiaris Consortio*'s call to understand the variety and complexity of the particular social and cultural settings in which human relationships exist and to develop pastoral responses to these situations. By providing information based on empirical research and describing common pastoral approaches with cohabiting couples, it participates in a positive way to the ongoing dialogue to which *Family, Marriage, and "De Facto" Unions* purports to contribute.

The first part of *Marriage Preparation and Cohabiting Couples* summarizes selected empirical information about cohabitation and marriage, all of which is supported by social scientific research dated from 1988 to

1998, which supports the magisterial prohibition of cohabitation. It locates cohabitation "within a context of widespread sexual activity outside of marriage" and goes on to state that "Cohabitation is a pervasive and growing phenomenon" that has "a negative impact on the role of marriage as the foundation of family."[11] The remainder of this section, which lumps all cohabitors together and paints a very bleak view of cohabitation and its possible outcomes, includes statistics about the incidence of cohabitation, a profile of the cohabiting household, reasons for cohabitation, and factors that put cohabitors at risk for marital instability. The second part of the document, while maintaining that cohabitation violates magisterial teaching about sexual love and marriage, discusses pastoral approaches with cohabiting couples within the context of "the gospel values of love, understanding, and acceptance."[12]

The bishops' document is a significant and sorely needed development in terms of an ecclesial–social scientific exchange about cohabitation and pastoral approaches informed by empirical data. Compared to the first two documents discussed, it is far less ecclesial in style and tone and more pastoral in terms of its attitude and content. However, its use of empirical data is in need of serious updating. Although it was published in 1999, conclusions it makes are based upon empirical information that has since been expanded or superseded with more recent data. If the bishops understand that human realities, especially human relationships, are dynamic in nature, and that social scientific research that explores them is a dynamic enterprise, they should acknowledge the need for ongoing consideration of new data, which may confirm, elaborate upon, or replace former conclusions. They should acknowledge that the reality, experiences, and meanings of cohabitation in current social and cultural settings and cohabitation's relationship to marriage and family are areas that have and continue to undergo significant changes over a relatively short period of time. They would, hopefully, agree that the exchange between the sciences and religion must progress steadily and continually if pastoral action is to truly understand and serve human needs and that effective pastoral action should be undergirded by an understanding of the most recent empirical information about cohabitation.

As is typical of magisterial teaching, all three of the ecclesial documents discussed above exhibit a physicalist approach toward judgments about human action, especially judgments about sexual behavior. This approach focuses narrowly on the sexual dimension of cohabitation; largely ignores its intentions, situations, and meanings; and generally sees behavior apart from contexts. The physicalist perspective is radically different from the personalist perspective generally taken for granted by contemporary Christian ethics.[13] Any acceptable contemporary understanding of being human and human action agrees that persons and their actions are situated in particular contexts; persons are socially situated, politically situated, historically situated, physically situated, and interpersonally situated. Also taken for granted by contemporary theology is the ever-changing nature of our human contexts. Discussions of interpersonal and sexual relationships, informed by contemporary social science, have gone beyond the simplistic physicalist approach that formed earlier judgments about human action. Without adequately considering the full context, ecclesial teachings and their judgments about human behaviors lack sufficient ground and credibility.

Ecclesial teaching and pastoral action must be grounded in values, not upon judgments of particular acts or functions. To be relevant to the whole People of God, it must not absolutize one particular historical or social context. If the Magisterium is to be an agent of dialogue, it must take into account the contradictions between ecclesial teaching and the lived experience of people in modern cultures. It must respect and trust scientific evidence and admit that new historical circumstances require new or at least more nuanced responses and interpretations. In their present state, ecclesial teachings and their mode of communication attempt to dictate, not dialogue. The church is a changed people in a new historical and developing context; there are new issues, information, and situations, all of which call for new approaches and responses. The People of God is a community of conscience that presumes a combination of freedom, knowledge, collaboration, and obedience. Its sophisticated understanding of the person, especially of interpersonal and sexual relations, marriage, and family, encompasses far more than the procreative dimension.

Recent Social Scientific Research

As mentioned above, generalizations about cohabitation and cohabitors are credible only if they emerge from and are grounded in scientific data. It is absolutely necessary they be reexamined and revised periodically in light of new data. The most widely cited fact about cohabitation is that it has increased by over 1000 percent over the past four decades.[14] The percentage of first marriages preceded by cohabitation rose from about 10 percent for those marrying between 1965 and 1974 to over 50 percent for those marrying between 1990 and 1994; the percentage is even higher for remarriages.[15] Several other facts are widely known among researchers. Cohabitation is a relatively short-lived experience with most ending with either marriage or termination of the relationship. Recent estimates indicate that the probability of a first premarital cohabitation becoming a marriage is 58 percent after three years and 70 percent after five years.[16] Another fact is that cohabitation is not a childless state; the increase in nonmarital childbearing is largely due to cohabiting partners, not to births to women living alone. Approximately 40 percent of cohabiting couple households now contain children.[17]

Another generalization, supported by most *earlier* empirical data, about the effect of cohabitation on marital stability is that cohabitation is associated with increased risk of divorce for cohabitors who eventually marry. This generalization is often accompanied with the conclusion that cohabitors are less committed to each other than married couples. Simply, it is not accurate to lump all cohabitors together as if all cohabitations are the same. People cohabit for incredibly varied reasons, and their experiences of cohabitation are equally varied. It is, therefore, very risky and virtually meaningless to speak of "the average cohabitor" and to develop pastoral approaches based on generalizations.[18]

As indicated above, cohabitation prior to marriage has increased, especially since 1980, to the point that premarital cohabitation precedes the majority of marriages. The divorce rate, on the other hand, increased dramatically during the 1970s, peaked around 1980, then declined slightly, and has been relatively stable since then. While the rate of premarital cohabitation increased, the rate of divorce actually decreased.[19]

The evidence that indicates that those who live together before marriage are more likely to break up after marriage is controversial because it is difficult to distinguish the "selection effect" from the experience of cohabitation itself. There is no evidence that cohabitation *causes* divorce, but it has been demonstrated that cohabitation is more common among those of lower economical and educational levels, those who are less religious, those who have been divorced, and those who have experienced parental divorce, fatherlessness, or high levels of marital discord during childhood.[20] In other words, the characteristics of people who select cohabitation in the first place are also those factors that increase the risk of marital instability.[21] In fact, the same characteristics are related to relationship instability, whether the relationship is cohabitation or marriage.[22] It has also been shown that certain characteristics are associated with marital stability, such as older age at marriage, higher economic status, higher educational attainment, growing up in a two-parent family, religious affiliation, and the importance of religion.[23] The key point is that the particular characteristics of the partners are directly related to the stability or instability of the relationship, whether it is cohabitation or marriage.

There is some evidence, which has received less attention, that the experience of cohabitation itself makes cohabitors more prone to marital disruption because cohabitors may come to accept a temporary and less committed attitude toward relationships.[24] It is possible that certain characteristics of cohabitors could be compounded by the experience of cohabitation to make a couple more divorce-prone. Commitment is a slippery concept and hard to measure, but the fact is that relationships and commitment develop over time. Couple relationships typically move through stages of dating, possibly cohabiting, to marriage; commitment grows and deepens as a relationship grows and deepens. From this it follows that commitment would be lowest for dating couples and highest for those who are married.[25]

The most salient new information is that recent research shows a crucial difference between cohabiting couples who plan to marry and those who do not. Some of the most respected researchers conclude that cohabiting couples who plan to marry or are engaged have characteristics very similar to married couples. Linda Waite states that "couples who live together with no definite plans to marry are making a different bargain than couples who marry or than engaged cohabitors."[26] Steven Nock found that those who married after cohabiting appeared more similar to those who married without cohabiting than to those who were currently cohabiting.[27] Brown and Booth concluded that cohabitors with plans to marry are quite similar to married couples and that only cohabiting couples without plans to marry have significantly lower-quality relationships. They suggest that cohabitation is similar to marriage for the majority of cohabitors, approximately three-quarters of whom plan to marry.[28]

A recent article by Waite concludes that "compared to marriage, *uncommitted cohabitation — cohabitation by couples who are not engaged —* is an inferior social arrangement."[29] What is crucial here is the distinction between two social realities, uncommitted cohabitation and committed cohabitation by couples who are engaged. Men and women who choose uncommitted cohabitation do not have the same characteristics as those who cohabit while planning their wedding. Waite states explicitly that it is *uncommitted* cohabitation that is linked to higher chances of divorce and other social problems related to domestic violence, lack of commitment, lack of emotional well-being, finances, housework, and parenting. *Committed* cohabitors are dramatically different from those who are not planning their wedding. From the perspective of empirical research, commitment is one of the most distinctive determinants in relationship stability.

Lawler translates Waite's terminology into theological terms. He sees committed cohabitation as "*prenuptial* cohabitation, because marriage is consciously intended to follow it."[30] This term contrasts sharply with *nonnuptial* cohabitation, in which there is no intention to marry. Since the majority pattern is now cohabitation followed by marriage, the majority of cohabitors can, in fact, be described as prenuptial. Focusing on the relation between premarital cohabitation and marital instability obscures the fact that the majority of cohabitants not only expect to marry but do marry and often does not take into account the numerous other variables that are linked to relationship instability. Pastoral action and marriage preparation that is attentive and responsive to the contemporary situation will explore with cohabiting couples who seek Christian marriage each partner's personal characteristics as well as their intentions for, and understanding of, marriage. In relation to cohabitation, the Catholic Church could be a leader, rather than an adversary, in recognizing and nurturing prenuptial cohabiting relationships.

Another striking piece of new data about cohabitation is strong evidence that the relationship between cohabitation and marital instability is decreasing, especially among the most recent cohorts. Teachman found that premarital cohabitation that is limited to a woman's husband is not associated with increased risk of marital instability.[31] Schoen has reported that the risk of marital dissolution previously associated with cohabitation largely disappears for the most recent cohorts.[32] McRae found that younger generations do not show the same link between premarital cohabitation and marital dissolution, and suggested that as cohabitation becomes the majority pattern before marriage, as indeed it has, this link will become progressively weaker.[33] Another recent study, which controlled for parental divorce, age at union formation, educational attainment, importance of religion, having given birth before marriage, and country of birth, found that the difference between the stability of marriages preceded by cohabitation and those not preceded by cohabitation virtually disappeared for those married in the 1990s, thus supporting the selection theory.[34] While it is still true there is a connection between cohabitation and marital instability, these studies show that connection has already dramatically diminished and suggest it is likely to continue to do so. The increased selectivity of marriage preceded by cohabitation appears to explain in part the plateau in the divorce rate in the United States; the increase in cohabitation may be siphoning away some of the couples most likely to divorce.[35] Heaton suggests that cohabitation has an indirect effect promoting marital stability by delaying age at marriage.[36] In light of current research, the generalization that ties cohabitation to marital instability appears far too unnuanced and indiscriminate to be accepted at face value. Careful consideration on this information should precede pastoral action.

Ultimately, cohabitation in the United States and Europe is just one component of a constellation of longer-term social changes, a discussion of which is beyond the scope of this essay.[37] We know that family and marriage are dynamic and undergoing radical change, and there are strong indications that cohabitation is changing too. For many, perhaps most, cohabitation is a step on the road to marriage.[38] Early cohabitors tended to be people more willing to break social norms, but for recent cohorts cohabitation has become part of the normal courtship pattern. Recent research finds that cohabitors do not always exhibit characteristics linked to greater risk of divorce and that cohabitation does not always provide couples with experiences that lessen the stability of marriage.[39] How cohabitation fits into the marriage process is an important question for theological discussion and pastoral practice. How the church has understood the relationship between cohabitation, betrothal, and marriage throughout Christian history is extremely important and relevant to current reality.

People who are familiar with the history of Christianity and understand that church tradition, including tradition and teaching about marriage, has evolved over centuries, will be more likely to listen critically to the question that theologian Adrian Thatcher poses, "When does Christian marriage begin? Before or after the wedding?"[40] The conventional view is that marriage begins with a wedding, but an earlier Christian view is that marriage begins with betrothal, followed later by a wedding ceremony, which was compulsory for Catholics only after the Council of Trent in 1563. Couples began living together immediately after betrothal and before the wedding ceremony, and children were regularly conceived and born to betrothed couples. In fact, during the Middle Ages and up to the eighteenth century it was widely held that sexual cohabitation was permitted after the betrothal.[41] Betrothal was the legally binding and publicly recognized act that marked the beginning of the couple's life together. This arrangement, which was emphatically premised by the intention to marry and where the formation of marriage is a process rather than a clearly defined moment or rite of passage, is called "processual marriage."[42] The two-staged entry into marriage was lost due not to religious or theological reasons, but to an effort to eradicate clandestine marriage in the Catholic Church in the sixteenth century and politics and class distinctions in the Anglican Church during the eighteenth century. Both Thatcher and Lawler suggest that if cohabitors intend to marry they may already have begun their marriage and advocate the retrieval of the betrothal tradition, the recognition and celebration of the betrothal of prenuptial cohabitors by the community as it was in an earlier Christian tradition.[43] Revival of the betrothal tradition would highlight the crucial difference, which has been largely ignored by magisterial teaching, between prenuptial and non-nuptial cohabitation. The betrothal tradition is not only grounded in Christian tradition but can be supported by contemporary empirical data.

Christian marriage has undergone striking changes over the centuries and will certainly accommodate many more. Only the historically illiterate oppose additional changes to Christian marriage traditions on historical grounds or presume that Christian tradition has always equated prewedding sexual abstinence with moral behavior. The discerning Christian will consider the fact that cohabitation is nothing new in the Christian tradition and that contemporary cohabitation replicates some facets of an earlier church tradition. A pertinent question is what might be learned from the premodern processual notion of marriage that could be appropriated pastorally to the situations of many contemporary cohabitors. If the notions of consent and consummation, so central to the canonical question of when marriage begins, are broadened to more accurately reflect and appreciate the processual reality of contemporary Christian marriages,[44] we might better appreciate the notion of marriage as a lifelong process. The Second Vatican Council's *Gaudium et Spes* defines marriage as "an intimate partnership of married life and love" (n. 48). This understanding of marriage suggests, I think, a partnership over the course of married life, a relationship that is surely a dynamic, continuing process of formation that evolves over time. A marital relationship does not simply and suddenly come about with the public pronouncement of vows. It is a relationship that grows through various stages of friendship and intimacy, different levels of commitment, through trial and error of building a relationship that ultimately involves all the complexities of sharing the whole of life.

Ecclesial teaching is sometimes detached from the lives and experiences of people and, therefore, is often not seen as an inspiring source of authority and wisdom in the area of sexuality and intimate interpersonal relationships. It has been slow and often unwilling to respond to, or engage with, social changes and has been unable to sift through beneficial aspects of cultural advances. Its undue preoccupation with sexual morality tends to color sexuality largely in terms of problems, not potential, and as an abstraction rather than a contextual experience. This approach does not allow for the creative ambiguity and deep joys of sexual relations and widens the gap between human experience, ecclesial teaching, and pastoral practice.

Conclusion

Prenuptial or committed cohabitation does not appear to be a threat to the institution of marriage or to diminish its priority. If, however, the types of cohabitation are simply lumped together and the most recent scientific data is overlooked, then cohabitation may be viewed as a threat to marriage. Early studies provided clear empirical evidence that negative consequences, particularly those associated with some cohabitors' characteristics, are related to cohabitation, but *the most recent* studies show that it is inappropriate and misleading to generalize about all cohabiting relationships or all cohabitors. Recent studies provide more nuanced data and have the advantage of comparing earlier data with the most recent findings. The current widespread social acceptance of cohabitation has altered the composition of cohabiting couples and creates an opportunity to rearticulate the theology of marriage in new and compelling ways that reflect current reality and empirical data. A comprehensive understanding of the social reality of cohabitation does not advocate for cohabitation, but considers the entire context of the relationship, characteristics of the partners, and their intentions. Ecclesial discussion about cohabitation should be attentive to and informed by credible and recent empirical data. From such discussion could emerge ecclesial teaching that is grounded in tradition and the results of scientific research and formulated in a way that reflects current reality and enhances the theology of marriage. That enhanced theology of marriage would include the fundamental distinction between prenuptial and non-nuptial cohabitation, reinstate the betrothal tradition, and serve as a catalyst to guide pastoral attitudes toward and ministry with cohabiting couples.

Questions for Reflection

1. How do you understand the relationship between ecclesial teaching and the social sciences? Do you think ecclesial teaching and pastoral action can be informed by the social sciences? What examples come to mind?

2. What authority do you give to ecclesial teaching? To the experience of people in modern society? How should ecclesial teaching and human experience be integrated?

3. What is your view of cohabitation, that is, living together before marriage? What is the source of your view? Do you think cohabitation is a threat to the institution of marriage?

4. How do you understand the terms "premarital" and "prenuptial"? If marriage is a lifelong relationship, when is a couple truly married? Can a couple be more married after fifteen years than after five years?

Chapter 16

Engagement

A Time to Discern, a Time to Build

Gregory M. Faulhaber

Introduction

In many ways a person begins her or his preparation for marriage at birth. Basic personal and relational qualities and skills are formed early in a person's life and continue to develop over time. Traits and characteristics, such as communication skills, an ability to trust, feelings of self-worth, appreciation of the gift of sexuality, and others, are foundational to marriage, and they are developed and nourished in families and life experiences well before a couple becomes engaged. Pope John Paul II in his apostolic exhortation on the family recognized this fact, stating: "Marriage preparation has to be seen and put into practice as a gradual and continuous process. It includes three main states: remote, proximate and immediate preparation."[1] Remote preparation starts in childhood and is developed more thoroughly through adolescence. Proximate preparation begins near the time of puberty, leading one into adulthood, and immediate marriage preparation takes place within the months preceding a wedding. While recognizing the importance of remote and proximate preparation for marriage, this essay will concentrate on the stage of immediate preparation, and it concerns what most people would speak of as the time of engagement. It starts with a positively received proposal and two people publicly announcing their intention to be married. It ends at the marriage ceremony or if the couple at some point decides to stop the preparations and not get married. In either case it is a very important time for the couple, with many tensions and high expectations. It is a time to work on bringing together two lives and families into one, a time to build on the foundations already established, a time for a couple to examine their relationship more deeply, a time to question and to inquire, a time to discern the vocation of being married to this person "until death do us part."

I am a Roman Catholic priest, ordained twenty-four years, with a wide variety of ministerial experiences dealing with engaged and married couples. Over that time I have witnessed the vows of more than four hundred couples at their weddings and have been involved in the marriage preparation of hundreds of others through Engaged Encounter weekends, sponsor couple programs, and other prenuptial workshops. I have been a member of our marriage tribunal and have listened intently to the stories of a few hundred cases of other couples applying for annulments in the church because their marriages were not successful. I also have been teaching courses in human sexuality and marriage at Christ the King Seminary in East Aurora, New York, for the past ten years and am the director of formation for our seminarians who in many ways are like those engaged to be married. Both groups have declared their intentions to enter into a particular lifelong vocation in the church and are in the final phases of discernment of that vocation. Neither receives much support for that commitment from the world around them that seems to be in almost constant change and fluctuation.

Need for Openness

When a couple calls and asks me to witness their marriage vows, I usually congratulate them on their engagement and move very cautiously with them through the process of marriage preparation. I stress that they are engaged, not married, and the time of engagement is critical for planning to live out their marriage over a lifetime, not just the single day of their wedding. My job as a priest is to assist them in that preparation along with the rest of the church, but it is their responsibility to prepare themselves for marriage. I care very much what happens to them, but this is their life. What occurs during engagement and the marriage itself will affect them much more deeply than it does me. Pretending to be someone or something that they are not might allow them to be married in the church, but they will be living with the consequences. The church has been involved with preparing couples for marriage from the beginning of its existence and does have much wisdom to offer engaged couples. However, there will be little accomplished during the time of engagement if there is a lack of openness upon the part of those involved. Consequently, it is crucial for the engaged couple and all those involved in their marriage preparation on behalf of the church to listen carefully to each other and to express themselves sincerely and honestly in an understandable manner. Failure to do so is a recipe for almost certain disaster, and we have witnessed enough marital tragedies in recent years.

Need for Good Preparation in Challenging Times

In 1996 the National Center for Health Statistics did a survey of first marriages that had occurred in the United States fifteen years previously, and it discovered that 43 percent of those marriages had ended in divorce or separation. Although it is difficult to predict the future, current statistics from the U.S. Census Bureau estimate that close to 50 percent of first marriages entered into this year will end in divorce at some point in the future.[2] Faced with these bleak statistics many choose to delay marriage or avoid it altogether. Fear of marital failure is a legitimate concern in today's society. The median age at first marriage for women in the United States increased from 20.8 years in 1970 to 25.1 in 2000, while for men it went from 23.2 years to 26.8 over the same time period. In 1970 only 6 percent of women ages 30 to 34 had never married. In 2000 that number had more than tripled to 22 percent.[3] There are a number of factors that have helped to bring about these developments, some positive and others negative, and this essay does not have the space to deal with them adequately. Our purpose here, however, is to ask: how can the time of engagement be used better to avoid failed marriages? What concerns need to be addressed during this time of immediate marriage preparation to help couples be better prepared for the challenges that lie ahead? Which qualities in their relationship are viewed as being positive, and are there danger signs that tell them to postpone or cancel their wedding plans?

Certainly, one short chapter in a book is not able to address all of these concerns fully, and there is no foolproof method or test to predict any couple's future success and happiness in marriage. Each couple is unique and needs to be evaluated individually. Yet good immediate marriage preparation can assist them in their final decisions concerning this lifelong commitment, and it can be helpful in preparing them for a flourishing start to their marriage. Good preparation is carried out best as a team approach involving clergy, married and engaged couples, and other professionals such as counselors, liturgists, and musicians. Premarital assessment inventories can be helpful to facilitate discussion among engaged couples in concrete ways. They pose questions to the couple about themselves and their relationship and help to promote greater understanding. Some of the topics covered in these inventories address family, friends, interests, communications, marriage expectations, sexuality, finances, religion, and values, and as long as the strong and weak points of a couple's relationship become more evident the couple honestly answers the questions put forth. The three most commonly used marriage preparation inventories in the United States today are FOCCUS, PREPARE, and PMI.[4] Drs. David Olson and Barbara Markey, respective authors of PREPARE and FOCCUS, have indicated that between 10 and 20 percent of couples who take their inventories choose to delay or cancel their wedding, compared to 3 to 7 percent of couples from other premarital approaches. Dr. Olson also asserts that PREPARE scores from three months before marriage have been successful in predicting with 80 to 90 percent accuracy which couples were to be happily married and which would eventually separate and divorce.[5] I have used all three of the above inventories and have found each of them very helpful in my own work with the engaged. From my own personal experience the percentage of those couples choosing to delay or cancel their wedding plans has been even greater than what Drs. Olson and Markey indicate, somewhere between 20 and 30 percent. Going through such preparations is no guarantee of a couple's marital success, but it does provide much food for thought and discernment while also positively nurturing some foundational skills and values to build and deepen their relationship.

Qualities of True Love

One of the most popular scripture readings chosen for weddings is 1 Corinthians 12:31–13:8a.[6] This passage was written to the community at Corinth to stress the centrality of the gift of love for the community of believers. Without love we have nothing at all. This is a reality for the existence of any Christian community, and particularly for forming the community of persons that needs to exist between husband and wife in marriage. The passage goes on to describe some of the qualities of true love: "Love is patient; love is kind; love is not envious or boastful or arrogant or rude. It does not insist on its own way; it is not irritable or resentful, it does not rejoice in wrongdoing, but rejoices in the truth. It bears all things, believes all things, hopes all things, endures all things. Love never ends" (1 Cor. 13:4–8a).[7] Good marriage preparation helps the engaged couple and the church at large to evaluate whether true love exists between the couple or whether it is infatuation or some other impostor. Do the engaged exhibit the qualities of love expressed in the scripture or not? No one is perfect, but a person must be able to look beyond one's own desires and selfishness in order to love another. There needs to be honest communication of thoughts and feelings without fear of rejection or angry outbursts because one does not get his or her way, and this communication needs to be mutual. One person cannot support a marital relationship by himself or herself. It requires much patience and persistence on the part of both.

No matter how hard one tries to be sensitive to the other person's needs and to communicate well, there will be times that one person upsets the other by what is said or done. How a couple handles this situation is crucial. Are they able to admit that they were wrong or that they made a mistake, and what do they do to repair the damage? My grandfather was a carpenter, and he had a saying: "A good carpenter is not someone who never makes a mistake in his work. All people make mistakes. A good carpenter recognizes when he makes a mistake and knows how to fix it." The same can be said to be true about a good marriage. A couple in a good marriage acknowledges when they have a problem and learns how to handle it. The couple needs to know how to resolve conflicts and to be able to forgive one another. Running away from the problem or denying it only produces more difficulties. Pretending that a troublesome issue or characteristic will go away after marriage is a common fault of many engaged couples. I have witnessed this in many failed marriages with which I have dealt in annulment cases. People were aware of problems such as alcohol or other drug abuse, sexual deviances, abusive and demeaning behavior, and other serious issues during the engagement, but they went through with the marriage anyway, thinking that their spouse was going to be different after the wedding. This is not love. A person must be loved for the gift that he or she is, not for whom she or he might become. Serious problems do not go away with a wish or a promise that the person is going to change. They require much effort, and often professional help.

Families and Friends

One area of conflict that often comes up during engagement involves dealing with the couple's families of origin along with friends and other acquaintances. Engagement is very much a time of grace, but often it also involves much anxiety and stress. Everyone has high hopes and expectations, and all kinds of people seem to jump in to offer their views as to what should or should not be done down to minute details. Many an engaged couple have given serious thoughts to eloping in an attempt to escape the hassles of preparing for their "dream day" that seems to be evolving into a nightmare. It is important to put such preparations in proper perspective and to remember that the people involved are always more significant than the details of the celebration. The wedding and reception last only a few hours while relationships with families and friends encompass a lifetime. The couple is forming a new family in marriage, and that family does not exist in isolation. Each person brings her or his own family background and experiences of friendships into the relationship, and most often will continue to interact with these people throughout their marriage. Consequently, it is important for engaged couples to pay attention to their families and friends and how these involvements affect their relationship with each other. They are building a new family and should ask themselves how able they are to do this. The foundation of that new family has already been set by years of upbringing and experiences, which always need to be carefully examined. How does this history influence one's ability to be a good spouse and parent, and are the couple's backgrounds and visions of marriage and family life compatible with each other? Are they able to make decisions for themselves without undue interference of family or others? These are important questions not only for the wedding day but for the marriage as a whole. They need to listen to others and to be sensitive to their concerns, particularly to those who seem to have their sincere interest at heart. However, one cannot please everyone when it comes to every wedding detail or to living out their life as husband and wife. After listening to others, couples need to be able to make their own decisions about their wedding and married life together.

Sexuality and the Purpose of Marriage

Sexuality and appropriate sexual expression is another important area of concern during the time of engagement and throughout one's lifetime. Certainly, a person develops his or her sexual identity beginning already in infancy, and the majority of a couple's sexual attitudes and practices have been established well before they became engaged. However, consideration of the area of sexuality is crucial to immediate marriage preparation, no matter how old the couple may be. In many ways our society is saturated and obsessed with sex. Powerful sexual images assault us almost everywhere we turn in music, television, video games, movies, the Internet, magazines, and other mass media venues. Yet in many ways people today still find it difficult to speak about sexuality, and various difficulties may arise. Many are confused or ignorant about Roman Catholic teaching in regard to sexuality and fail to appreciate its wisdom.

From the first chapter of the first book of the Bible, sexuality is seen as something good, a gift from God, but it is often misused and may lead one into sin if not properly appreciated. The Catholic Church teaches that sexuality is ordered to the love of man and woman in marriage. God is seen to be the author of matrimony, endowing it with its benefits and purposes. "The acts in marriage by which the intimate and chaste union of the spouses takes place are noble and honorable; the truly human performance of these acts fosters the self-giving they signify and enriches the spouses in joy and gratitude." The sexual union of husband and wife has a twofold purpose: the good of the spouses themselves joined together in an intimate union of their persons and the good of the transmission of life.[8] "By their very nature, the institution of matrimony itself and conjugal love are ordained for the procreation and education of children, and find in them their ultimate crown."[9] John Paul II stresses that the family is the foundation of society, and that foundation is grounded in the love of husband and wife forming a community of persons together. This conjugal communion establishes the base upon which the broader communion of family may be built. It serves life, bringing children into the world in a responsible way, educating them, and promoting the dignity of the human person. The family participates in the development of society and shares in the life and mission of the church.[10] This instruction on marriage and human sexuality emphasizes that sexual intercourse is properly reserved for husband and wife in marriage, although many have become sexually intimate well before marriage. Various surveys today indicate that over half of U.S. high school students claim to have had sexual intercourse, and that figure is over three-quarters for college students.[11] One should not assume that none of the engaged is a virgin, but it is safe to say that a good percentage of them have experienced sexual intercourse with each other as well as with other partners. It is estimated that approximately half of the couples who come to the church seeking to be married currently are living together in a sexual relationship, and some would place this figure as high as 60 or even 80 percent.[12] These facts evoke a number of concerns.

Sexuality is only one part of an engaged couple's relationship, but it is a powerful force that at times might cloud good decision-making. Those who are sexually intimate before marriage need to be realistic about how influential their sexual involvement is upon their decision to marry. Becoming genitally intimate is rightly something very precious to many people and reserved for the one with whom they intend to spend the rest of their life. There is already a certain commitment present for them, and the natural bond of sexual intercourse makes that attachment even stronger. Such connections may cause one to overlook certain problems or uncertainties and restrict one's ability to make a truly free choice about marriage. Often, couples live together before marriage thinking that this is helpful to test their relationship before getting married and thereby helping to prevent a future divorce. However, studies in the early 1990s have displayed well that in the United States those who have cohabitated before marriage have a divorce rate that is 50 percent higher than couples who have never cohabitated. Those who have cohabitated more than once prior to marriage have an even higher divorce rate. Research has shown that those who choose to live together before marriage have certain attitudes, issues, and patterns of behavior that led them to the decision to cohabitate. "These same attitudes, issues, and patterns often become the predisposing factors to put them at high risk for divorce when they do choose to move from cohabitation to marriage."[13] Appropriate sexual expression during engagement helps to prepare the couple for a lifelong commitment of marriage. It displays affection, warmth, and caring, while waiting for that time when the couple is able to make the full commitment of marriage. It ultimately involves respect for oneself and the dignity of the other person. It requires authenticity, mutuality, discipline, patience, and sensitivity to one's own wants and needs as well as to those of one's partner. It is informed about that which brings life to a relationship and that which leads to its demise. It is expressive of true love as described in 1 Corinthians 13.

God, Faith, and Religion

One of the questions I ask of a couple during my first meeting of marriage preparation with them is: "Why do you want to get married in the church? Is this something that is important for you or are you here to please someone else?" As a Roman Catholic priest I am able to be the official witness of marriages where at least one of the parties is a practicing Catholic. Often, those who are engaged are at a point in their lives where they might have drifted away from more active participation in organized religion and go to church only occasionally or on special occasions. Busy schedules of school, work, social life, and other interests make it difficult to find time, and young adults are often searching to take ownership of their faith life. They also often receive little attention in the life of most parishes. In the midst of all this, they now come to the church to be married, and there are many questions. Do they or at least one of them have faith? Is there a desire to be involved in church beyond the wedding? Have they discussed their own practice of religion, passing faith onto children, and such issues? Engagement is an excellent opportunity for the partners to examine their own relationship with God and the church and to search more deeply into the role that faith, God, and religion play in their relationship with each other. Through such an examination the engaged couple is better able to answer questions about what kind of marriage ceremony is appropriate for them. It is hoped that the ceremony is expressive of their faith and love of each other, their God and church, and that their preparations for that day reflect the significance and dignity of married life.

The Roman Catholic Church teaches that a valid marriage between two Christians is a sacrament, and through it husbands and wives take on a new relationship with each other and their God. In marriage they encounter their God in a unique way, and the union of husband and wife is a symbol of the union of Christ and his church. Jesus Christ's self-giving and sacrificial love for his people is the model of love to be followed by all Christians in their concern for others, and it is also the standard for the love of woman and man in marriage. At their wedding the couple stands before God and the church, declaring their love and commitment to each other. It is a sign that they are not alone in their marriage, and they need this support to survive the many trials of today's world. If the couple truly loves each other, they are partaking in something that comes from God. God is present, for God is love (1 John 4:16). That presence needs to be renewed and strengthened continually throughout marriage, and that is why it is important that the couple comes before the community of the church, not only on their wedding day, but throughout their married life. I was raised with the saying that the family that prays together stays together, and my experiences with families throughout my priesthood have confirmed this.[14]

A Time to Discern, a Time to Build

It is not possible to deal fully with all the concerns of immediate marriage preparation in this one short essay. Some issues such as finances have not even been mentioned, and much more could be said about each of the topics that were discussed. Engagement is a crucial time in the life of a couple, and it really is just the beginning of married life. The attitudes and skills formed during this time are foundational, and they need to continue to be developed after the wedding day, particularly in the first few months and years of marriage. Continual enrichment is necessary for the success of any good relationship. It is hoped that what is put forth here has provided some thoughts to make engagement more fruitful. The institution of marriage is under assault in many ways today, and good preparation is needed in order for it to survive. At times that preparation might question the readiness of a couple for marriage, and they might decide to postpone the wedding or even call it off. It is a time to discern, and that could be the best decision. More often, that discernment leads the couple to stand before God and the church, declaring their marriage vows on their wedding day. In either case, it is a time to discern more fully one's calling in life. It is a time to build a future founded on and flourishing in love.

Questions for Reflection

1. Are most engaged couples open to marriage preparation? Do most churches and their ministers help or hinder that preparation?

2. What differences between an engaged couple would be most difficult to resolve: religious, race, culture, family, age, economic, or other? Explain why.

3. List ten qualities present in true love, and discuss which ones would be most important for marriage. Can you think of any couples that best model these qualities for you?

4. In your opinion what are the attitudes, issues, and patterns that lead couples to live together outside of marriage that would also harm their ability to live out a lifelong commitment of marriage?

Chapter 17

Vulnerable to the Holy

Meditating on Friendship, Sex, and Marriage

Enda McDonagh

For all the sexual liberation and license of the Western world in the last century, many even of the liberated are still ill at ease with their bodies and their sexuality. From the prudish to the promiscuous, from the flaunting to the repressed there may emanate a sense of dismay and sometimes of terror in face of bodily and sexual turbulence, one's own or another's. Without dwelling on the many abusive sexual practices of the day and their violent and commercial brutalities, it is important that more attention is paid by Christians, married and single, ordained and lay, to God-given bodily beauty and sexuality and their creative potential as well as destructive possibilities. For Catholic Christians at least this creative potential in its sacramental realization has a holy-making dimension which is indeed rooted in creation itself. "Male and female he created them. In the image of God he created them" (Gen. 1:27). I offer these reflections on marriage considered as friendship as well as sexual communion under the rubric of "Vulnerable to the Holy." I take for granted the more scholarly treatment of "Friendship and Marriage" in Professor Lawler's recent book *Marriage and the Catholic Church*.[1]

Basic to human bodiliness and its beauty is its vulnerability. In its contact with the world through the famous five senses, the human body and person is vulnerable to other bodily beings, including of course human beings. "Sensitive" to other bodily beings would be the more usual expression but "vulnerable" carries important overtones of the painful openness and the possibility of hurt that all such encounters involve. The eye can bear only so much light, the heart only so much love, and humankind only so much reality.

Friendship and Vulnerability

On the night that Jesus acclaimed his disciples as friends, no longer servants but friends, one of them betrayed him, their leader denied him and all the other disciples deserted him except John, the beloved disciple, his mother, and some of his other women disciples-friends. In calling his disciples friends, Jesus was revealing in some ways the climax of Creation-Incarnation. Of course humans were created out of love and for love, for love of the Creator, love of one another, and love of self, not in some self-regarding, selfish way but as cherishing and caring for that God-given (bodily) being. Yet that the Creator God should become human, a bodily creature, and should enter into the give and take of human friendship to the point of being betrayed and deserted and beyond that to laying down his life for these and all his potential human friends and betrayers, all of humanity, remains barely credible.

The personal bonding, spirit-infused and embodied, that constitutes friendship is one of the adornments of human community. Even if the claim that one would rather betray one's country than one's friends is cynical in intention, and the corruption of friendship in political and commercial cronyism has become a common disease, the loyalty and affection of friendship and the self-sacrifice that frequently accompanies them can be a beacon of light and a continuing source of hope for people threatened with darkness and despair.

Friendship at this level is not common and never easy. Even allowing for the human weakness of Jesus' disciples-friends, discerning the potential richness and potential destructiveness of any particular friendship or of human friendship in general is a daunting task. The experiences of living and broken friendships provide many immediate insights, although in the reflective theological mode of this essay more systematic analysis is called for. As the mode is theological the analysis will have to struggle with both the divine and human dimensions of friendship.

In the typical case, human friends form a unity or community while retaining their distinctiveness. The distinctiveness is more accurately described as difference between two people, the irreducibility of the one to the other. In sharper terms still they could be seen, despite their bonds of unity, as utterly other and indeed, as they were in the beginning, still to a large extent strangers to one another. The difference, the otherness, the strangeness is at once the basis for their bonding in friendship and the threat to its survival. All strangers who become friends — and only strangers can, like spouses at first meeting, parents and newborn children, all the friends acquired over a lifetime — are always at risk of fresh and hostile estrangement. Life is littered with broken marriages, broken families, broken friendships. The fragility of marriage, family, and friendship is notorious. Yet friendship endures sometimes heroically, although it may in many instances be in need of repair. The multiplicity of counseling services witnesses to this truth, but friendships succeed, when they do, only because of the resilient capacity and continuing need of people for friendship, love, and community.

Strangers in the Half-Light

Tracking personal relations from casual acquaintance to close friendship to marriage and parenthood may follow diverse routes. The historical development of any particular friendship or marriage can lead to fascinating questions and sometimes disquieting or elusive answers. When did we first meet? What did we see in each other? What kept us together or (nearly) drove us apart? Conversations of this kind are the privilege of all relationships. A different kind of approach is adopted here. We seek to understand some of the major underlying characteristics of how humans may relate to one another and eventually to God.

All begin as strangers. The newborn is stranger to her parents as they are to her. More radically, human beings were in that novel sense also strangers to their Creator-God as God was and is to them. The act of creation or better, in terms of the Genesis poetic narrative as well as in terms of evolution's scientific narrative, the process of creation is a story of emerging strangers. Creation, divine or human, as alienation or estrangement may not be the more usual description, yet it is essential to maintaining the individuality and distinctiveness of the created. For human creatures the alienation, the separation as an other, is crucial to human and divine autonomy, to the theism of the Jewish, Christian, and Islamic traditions. Only within that context of alienation, separation, and autonomy are the free relationships of friendship and love possible. The language of alienation itself seems foreign to that of love and friendship, suggesting rather their antithesis in enmity. However it is useful to stress the depth of difference (a softer term) critical to an eventual depth of unity as well as to attend to the fragility of all human love relations, constantly threatened by hostile alienation as in the crucial case of Jesus and his friends.

More significantly, the alienation or otherness of human persons and of human persons and their God reveals that all loving relations have, as it is said, to be worked at, to be built on. They are always in process like creation itself. And that process is always also a process of overcoming alienation, of reconciliation. In the great reconciliation story of God and God's creation, the divine creative energies continually reveal and integrate the developing otherness of every aspect of that creation. Alienation and reconciliation constitute a kind of dialectic of true creation. Without the simultaneous exercise of reconciliation, it would not be one creation or God's creation. And for all human creatures within that divine world, the sharing in God's work of creating and reconciling is their glory.

In images that parallel those of alienating and reconciling, friendship may be explored in terms of darkness and light, the darkness and light that interacted in the Genesis story and in the Passion and Resurrection stories. The dark stranger aptly describes every human being newly encountered. In a developing relationship the darkness is partially banished as the light of the other's life emerges. In even the closest friendship or marriage some darkness remains and may at times intensify. The other never becomes fully transparent for the very obvious reason that there is more to everybody than meets the eye, even the most familiar and practiced eye. That "more" could on occasion be a threat but it is also a promise and a potential of more light, of more to be loved. It is hardly necessary to belabor the analogy between human relations understood in these terms and divine-human relations as recorded at least in the Jewish and Christian scriptures. The light of divine self-revelation is the context for divine-human relations in the history of Israel as in the person of Christ, light of the world, the light shining in the darkness, the darkness that did not comprehend or eventually master it (John 1).

In certain circumstances darkness may prevail between friends. Reconciliation and creation are no longer operative. Trust is destroyed and love embittered. That is the dangerous world of human relationships as between persons and even classes of persons, ethnic groups, or whole nations. The grand social breakdown is called war. Yet the creative, reconciling Spirit, the Holy Spirit is still at work in the broken personal relationship as it is in the destructive enmities of war. The sheer hurt that comes with disappointed personal loving may open to the healing presence of the Holy where that Holy has been experienced and is recalled from the first now broken loving. In the dramatic falling in love as well as in the steady growth of friendship, the primacy of the other transcends in theological terms to the primacy of the Ultimate Other. That "other" in its very linguistic development (Hebrew *qadosh*, Greek *hagios*, Latin *sanctus*) refers to the Holy One of Israel and of Jesus Christ. Loving the other, the neighbor, in whatever relationship and with whatever intensity hurts one into the awesome encounter with the Creating-Reconciling God. Genuine human loving in friendship as in marriage — in what Pope John Paul II has called a civilization of love as opposed to a civilization of hatred and war — involves exposure to God, makes one vulnerable to the creating and reconciling work of the Holy and, at times of serious breakdown, to the process of repentance and forgiveness in social as well as personal terms. A world largely at peace with itself will be a world in which friendship prevails between persons and peoples, between races and religions.

Friendship, Sexuality, and Marriage

Sexuality plays a role in all friendship, and in all human relationships. Only embodied sexual beings encounter one another and can be vulnerable to one another. Indeed human sexuality in its spiritual-embodiedness is a key element in the human attraction and gradual bonding characteristic of friendship. For most friendships this may be a largely subconscious element although it may readily come to consciousness in certain circumstances without changing the simple friendship character of the relationship. One has only to attend to the distinctive tone of one's friendships with men and women, if one is lucky enough to have both kinds, to realize how sexuality affects both casual and close friendship. Therein lie once more both the gift or promise and the threat. Unless the creative and reconciling energies of friendship are effectively working, the friends may easily drift apart or more painfully deteriorate in an exploitative shallow sexual intimacy.

All developed friendship includes an intimacy of mind and heart, of emotion and body with its own repertoire of expression. Its power lies in the focus on the other and so on its openness to that other and to her or his personal and ultimate mystery, the Holy. Without real openness and vulnerability to the human other in herself or himself with all their irreducibility, there cannot be openness to the ultimate other, the divine Holy. To use the human other as a stepping stone to the Ultimate is as much a betrayal as to use the other for one's own immediate satisfaction. In all this, the dynamic of sexuality is at work to nourish the friendship or to destabilize and ultimately destroy it. The very contours of the human sexual body with their spiritual, mental, and emotional companions express both the reaching out to and receiving of the other in the most intimate and inclusive way. When this loving communion is also life-giving in the procreative sense, the love that was friendship now becomes fully sexual and in permanent commitment transcends simple friendship into marriage. In that unique relationship, friendship is transformed but not erased. In the course of a developing marriage the friendship between the spouses must develop also. As with Jesus and his disciples, the final goal of marriage and family is fuller friendship — between husband and wife and between parents and children.

Only the experience of marriage itself can capture the highs and lows of its directly sexual expressions. Even the communion in one flesh may be variable in its loving significance and personal completion as it reflects the varying health and happiness of the spouses and of their relationship. In their daily living and loving they encounter, reveal, and cherish more of each other's distinctiveness, strangeness, and otherness. All this is heightened by their sexual otherness, that is, the desire it kindles and the fear it may provoke in its very strangeness. Poets and painters have attended to the wonder and excitement of newlyweds (or lovers) undressing for the first time. The revealing and concealing in their vulnerability move on delicately to touch and taste, to smell and sound. So through the five senses the couple prepare for the sexual intimacy of one flesh union, the closest and most profound giving and receiving of the other. In Christian understanding this is no longer a giving and receiving of just the human other. From Adam's brief love song in Genesis through the Song of Songs and onto the explicit connection between marital love and that of Yahweh/God for his people invoked by the prophets Hosea and Isaiah, as well as that of Christ for his church, marriage and married loving carry a divine surplus. In expressing their vulnerability to each other so fully and powerfully, married people also express their vulnerability to the Holy. As marriage is for Christians a sacrament, so the marital act of union is by the same token of sex (nature) and grace, holy-making.

Justice in Love

One of the persisting dangers of the recovery of the primacy of love in Christian living, including Christian marriage, and in its theological companion, moral theology, is the ignoring or even suppression of justice as essential to all human and divine-human relationships. St. Thomas Aquinas has several insights on justice relevant to this meditation. His definition of justice may be summarized as giving the other her due. The otherness of the other so central here demands the kind of respect, recognition, and response that the most exalted feeling of love may not ignore, still less suppress. In the more juridical presentation of marriage prior to Vatican II, legal considerations predominated to the extent that marriage's supreme expression of loving in sexual intercourse was described in terms of the *debitum,* that which was due in justice. Moving beyond that understanding was clearly necessary, but theological evolution had to proceed without permitting a sentimental view of love to eliminate the mutual respect due in justice. Of course the justice-in-love requirements of marriage extend far beyond the marital act, central as that is. In financial arrangement as in domestic duties and still more in parenting, justice should flourish. Too many marriages and friendships perish because of the injustice of one or both parties. Without the hard edge of justice, which Aquinas described as the form of all the virtues, love collapses into sentimentality, separation, and even hatred. Without that formative love, justice can easily become the harsh boundary of the separate.

In another teasing insight Aquinas describes the virtue of religion, by which human beings relate to God, as a subset of justice. Worship is due to God in justice. For Aquinas the Christian theologian, charity was still the primary virtue and the form of the virtue of justice in all its dimensions. He was, however, echoing the close connection in the scriptures, particularly the Hebrew scriptures, between divine justice and mercy, Yahweh's love and compassion for his people and his characteristic justice. Love of God and love of neighbor, already to the fore in the Hebrew scriptures and given utter primacy by Jesus, incorporate without ambiguity the justice due to God and neighbor. In practicing that justice to the neighbor, one is also reaching out to God and being vulnerable to the Holy. "As long as you did it to one of these least ones . . . " Justice in marriage love, beyond patriarchy or matriarchy, beyond sentimentality, neglect, or violence, provides a profound opening to the transcendent as each person encounters more fully the holy in the other.

Hurt, Healing, and the Holy

"No love, no marriage" became a kind of slogan in the sixties and seventies even if it did not convince many marriage tribunals at the time. "No hurt, no love" might sound a more forbidding note. Yet human experience and Christian revelation would seem to endorse it. It is not that either would glorify hurt or seek it as some badge of authentic loving, but it does seem to be the inevitable companion of human existence, including that exalted form of human existence, love. For bodily beings pain and mortality are inescapable. For embodied spirits the pain turns personal into a mental sense of hurt. In human relations, given that people remain at best half-strangers in the half-light, misunderstandings and worse are to be expected. Intimacy and estrangement are never far apart. The Jewish-Christian history of the intimacy-estrangement dialectic at a human and divine-human level hardly needs further rehearsing, and it opens up to a second strand of that history, the creating-reconciling strand. In marriage as in friendship, the dynamic of creating and reconciling is the source of growth through the shared joys and divisive hurts. In the shared celebration of the joys and in the mutual forgiveness of the hurts, the sacrament of marriage realizes the healing and holy-making presence of the Incarnate God.

Questions for Discussion

1. What is the role of struggle in the building of a successful marriage?

2. How does marriage contribute to the sanctification of the married couple?

3. What is the role of vulnerability in loving relationships and why is it necessary?

4. Discuss the nature of friendship within the marital relationship.

Chapter 18

The Christian Spiritual Life and the Family

Wendy M. Wright

In 1996 my mother threw away her sole remaining pair of high-heeled shoes. They were vivid red, pointy-toed and spiky, worthy of the most retro thrift store, and had not been on her feet for decades. The gesture was significant enough to have merited a public announcement to gathered family members, accompanied by a chagrined sigh. After her admission of the deed done, she paused, "I feel as though I've thrown away my youth." Now, I must tell you that at the time my mother was in her late eighties, spry and sharp as a tack, but nonetheless legally blind and, as she would say, "chronologically advantaged." The announcement came as a surprise only because none of us had any idea that such wondrous footwear might be ferreted away in the recesses of the bedroom closets where she and my father had long stored the sensible, flat-soled shoes befitting their retirement years. It was also something of a surprise that the gesture was accompanied by bemusement.

That was 1996. The image has come back to haunt me. Our youngest child, an eighteen-year-old college freshman, looms over me even while slouching at the breakfast bar shoveling in a last mouthful of cereal before rushing out the door to a Saturday morning pick-up football match. Our eldest, settled now as a graphic designer in Los Angeles, is a stylishly outfitted, bright and competent adult. When I visit, along with the delight of being together and pride at her achievements personal and professional, I feel bemused, even confused. At what point did her father and I cease to be the ones in the prime of life? It is not only the salt and pepper at the temples, it's the sense of being seen as slightly passé, as no longer part of the generation defining the present but as part of that cohort fading not so gently into history. I wonder how I fit in. I used to know, I think. Before I married my husband, I was like my eldest. Well, maybe not as stylish or quite as competent. But with the world and my life stretched out tantalizingly before me, part of a generation of social and political visionaries before whose dedication and commitment the world's ills were going to fall away. Before our three children were, my husband and I were a vibrant young couple, earnestly engaged in the important work of making the world a better place to live. We were the ones who, with some understandable impatience, had to endlessly explain the way things *are* to parents who couldn't quite seem to catch up. Our middle daughter has now taken over that family task of eye-rolling explanation. We have become the slow-learning recipients of her longsuffering attention.

"What in heaven's name," you might ask, "has any of this to do with the vaulted themes under consideration in this volume?" With Jesus Christ, serious Christian discipleship, Latin encyclicals, the hallowed institution of marriage, and solemn-sounding ideas like sanctity and sacramentality? And I will answer: "Everything."[1]

The Christian Story and Experience

I began with the story of my mother's shoes because that is what is foremost on my mind these days. Not the shoe episode itself but the theme that the shoe episode evokes, namely, the transitions of the life cycle experienced in the context of family life. And that is a very good place to begin theologizing: from experience. Theologian Karl Rahner said so and did so. As did any number of earlier theologians of the Christian humanist variety such as Ignatius of Loyola, Francis de Sales, and Bernard of Clairvaux. These latter even have the title Saint prefixed to their names. They did so because they believed that the created order itself, including the human capacity to reflect, could provide some glimpses of the divine order; that by analogy (not perfect mind you), one might know the Creator by way of that which has been created. Not that they just sat down with their paltry and limited personal experience and tried to deduce the mysteries of the universe from it. No, they really knew their stuff. Their catechism, for instance; those who lived at a time when there was a catechism. The point is they didn't just know the Christian tradition as something outside themselves, as a set of formulas or rules that they were supposed to recite or assent to. They *lived into* their tradition. They swam in it like an ocean or entered it like my son seems to enter the lyrics of the songs that sing to him through his headphones. The words are alive. They define, describe, speak to, and intertwine with experience. The words might explain experience or maybe personal experience will make the words come alive in a new way. In either case, religion was not something that happened on Sunday morning or something they turned to when crisis threatened to unhinge them. Religion was the language of their lives. It explained who they were and why they were, directed them to what was important, and helped them to realize it.

So let's begin like they did, with experience and the language of Christian tradition, and see how life in family might be illuminated. And maybe we'll also see what being part of a family has to contribute to the larger tradition. The specific piece of the tradition I'll turn to is the spiritual piece. Maybe this will surprise you. "What has religion to do with spirituality?" you may exclaim. It is a common modern misapprehension that the two terms are discrete. In fact, all the great religious traditions of the world contain vast spiritual visions that accord with their basic understandings of the way things work most authentically. So in religious traditions spirituality, ethics, rituals, symbols (both verbal, such as myths, scriptures, doctrines, and philosophies, and visual, such as art, architecture, and gestures), and social patterns all form part of a coherent way of looking at and approaching reality. Ideally, these ways should inform the way people live. That informing should also include family living.

Here is a simplified version of the vision that lies behind Christian spiritual teachings. First, human beings are created by and in the image and likeness of God. That's the basic answer to the "who-am-I?" question. This assertion has its source in the book of Genesis, which is the first book of the larger book that Christians call the Bible. The opening scenes of Genesis show God at work creating the universe: light and darkness, sun and moon, the birds of the air, the fish in the sea. Finally God creates humankind. They are male and female and are fashioned in God's own image and likeness (Gen. 1:27).

Generally, Christians have taken this narrative account to mean that there is something unique about human beings. Like the rest of creation, human existence is the result of the gracious activity of a divine Creator. Unlike the rest of creation, human beings are fashioned in a special way. They are *imago dei*: like God, as well as fitted to love and know God. (In passing I'll note that the gender issues encoded in this passage have been the source of centuries of arguments about the relationship of men to women, but that is the subject of another paper.)[2] To continue with the biblical narrative: the fact that human nature as we know it is anything but reflective of the divine is explained in Christian theology through an amplification in the Genesis story of the expulsion of the original man and woman from the paradisiacal Garden for which they were created. "We fell," we say. As a result, that divine image in us was wounded or tarnished (some theologians and spiritual traditions would say it was effaced). We thus find ourselves alienated from God and from our intended nature. Here the broad outline of the cosmic story shifts from the early books of the Bible to the later stories about Jesus. Jesus' birth, life, death, and resurrection, as understood by Christians since earliest times, tell the story of the restoration of that ruptured relationship between God and humankind. In Jesus, God comes to be with us. Immanuel, that appellation the Gospel of Matthew bestows on him (Immanuel means God-with-us). Through the Incarnation, human beings thus are made one with God again (the technical term here is "atonement" and it should be noted that there is not one but many theories about how and why that *at-one-ing* takes place. Be that as it may, the story doesn't stop there). Jesus not only was born, lived, and died for this rapprochement but later sent his own Spirit to continue the atoning work and in so doing created a community, the church, believed to be inspired by the breath of the divine Spirit. The spiritual life then, in the traditional theological understanding, is a life wafted on the wind of the Spirit, an inspired life that is not privatized but deeply communal, for the Spirit moves *among* the faithful and the gifts of the Spirit are given for the flourishing of the whole. In fact, the Christian Godhead itself is conceived in relational metaphors. The God, three-in-one, who creates, redeems, and sanctifies and is known as Father, Son, and Spirit, is conceived as a dynamic community of mutual and overflowing love.

The Domestic Church

So what difference does this make for family life? I'm going to suggest that, of the many implications that might be drawn from the arc of this central Christian narrative, two stand out. First, that the family *is* the domestic church. Second, that family life is sacramental and that the foundational practice of the Christian spiritual life for those who are familied is the art of being attentive to that fact.[3] To put it another way, spirituality in general, and spirituality in the Christian family in particular, is about the way we *see,* and what story informs our seeing.

Regarding the question of the domestic church, this is not a new phrase, although it has come back into currency recently and is used by a whole raft of theologians in numerous ways. Perhaps you might think that by domestic church I mean that the family borrows rituals or prayers from the repertoire of the gathered church community and incorporates them into its own practice; that spiritual families say the rosary together or attend a lot of functions that the parish sponsors. Or maybe you think that being the domestic church means that parents are the first teachers of faith for their children. Both of these answers have some merit to them, but I'm going to define the domestic church in the following manner. The domestic church is the smallest unit of church. It is not simply a derivative or recipient of the life of the gathered church. It is not church primarily because it adopts "churchy" rituals. Rather, a family is church precisely when it is a community that, knowing itself as originally created in the divine image, struggles together to live into the possibility of a transformed, Spirit-filled life. With the sacred canopy of the Christian story sheltering it, through mutual forgiveness and mutual feeding and being fed, family members form one another into the persons they were created to be: *imago dei,* persons who love God and neighbor. The very fact of consciously engaging in that swimming in the ocean of tradition (like Ignatius, Bernard, and Francis de Sales) *together* makes us church. We participate in the very life of God's own self, that dynamic community of mutual and overflowing love.

There is, of course, another connection between the gathered church community and the domestic church. They are both communities of storytelling. They help us know who we are. And the larger church, as the carrier of more than our own small stories, helps remind families that they are beloved children of God, creatures created for divine intimacy. To the extent that the story of the individual family story and the greater story celebrated by the gathered church are woven together — through sacramental participation, familiarity with scripture, ethical awareness, prayer, or other spiritual disciplines — the stronger the story will be internalized. But it is in the domestic church that the story is taught experientially. In part this is a matter of raising children in the faith. But the tender love of parents for their children, the mutual forbearance of spouses, the solidarity of siblings, the care given to the elder generation — these are all avenues through which families *live out* or *embody* the truth that all human beings are beloved children of God and deserve to be acknowledged as such. As I read to a daughter at bedtime or sit on the sidelines to cheer a son's soccer team or visit an ailing grandparent in the hospital or comfort a despondent spouse, as I practice loving, I *participate* in a small way in the self-giving activity of Love itself.

The domestic church is also the place where the *dynamics* of the Christian spiritual life are enfleshed. The Christian Spirit-filled life has a particular shape. That shape is revealed in the person of Jesus, the Christ. And while different Christian thinkers, eras, and denominations have stressed varied aspects of that revelation; there are some constants that abide. The Spirit-filled life is a life defined by relational love. Love of God, love of friend, love of neighbor, even love of enemy. The Christian life means treating others as one would like to be treated. It is also a life marked by the capacity for forgiveness. The dynamic pattern of that life is *kenotic,* or self-emptying, as was the life of Jesus. It thus consists of expanding beyond our present, limited capacities for love. As we grow, we become more spacious, more capable of genuinely loving each other and ourselves and we ride more surely on the breath of the Spirit. The ramifications of this expansion are enormous. But the process is not always easy. The classic language of the spiritual life describes it as "dying to self."

The domestic church is an intimate laboratory in which this *kenotic* pattern can play itself out, if we would but let it. Any parent knows that the advent of a child, even one welcomed with joy, is a stretching, sometimes painful process of growing beyond one's present capacity to love. Love grows as the heart is pried open to welcome a new life. This sort of love is neither generic nor intrinsically self-referential. Rather, parental love, in the majority of people, creates a capacity to care for another in a way that is radically generous, radically new. Sometimes the process feels like "dying to self" but, if genuinely realized, that dying is in fact a being born into a new, more spacious self, a self whose interest includes, even privileges, another self. And this is not a one-time event. As a child grows, so grows a parent's capacity to love, to embrace — often painfully — an entire lifetime's joys and sufferings of another as one's own. Patience, humility, flexibility, discernment: these are some of the capacities, virtues if you will, that the experience of parenting calls forth.[4]

The Sacramental Life

Catholic tradition designates seven formal Sacraments (Baptism, Eucharist, Confirmation, Reconciliation, Ordination, Marriage, and Anointing of the Sick), privileged channels through which divine grace is communicated to humankind. But all life is potentially sacramental in the "small s" sense of the term. A sacrament is simply a visible medium through which an invisible reality is manifested.[5] In the Catholic tradition the Seven are central and privileged, but there are potentially an infinite number of sacramental times, places, persons, and events that can reveal God's presence among and with us. It is especially the *relational* or *in between* experiences of God-with-us that are experienced in family life. This takes us to the question of how the sacramental nature of ordinary life might be perceived. It is true that much of family life seems made up of dreary duty or of interactions, as meaningful as they might be, that hardly conduce to experiencing God-with-us. We tend to identify our God-perception with peak moments: the intense love encounter, a glimpse of awe-inspiring beauty, a tragic loss cushioned by the compassion of friends.

But there is another way of seeing: an attentive awareness to the subtle movements of the Spirit in our hearts, interactions, and communal lives. This attentive awareness is one of the foundational practices of the Christian spiritual life. It might be characterized in this manner. Reality is not simply approached as a series of events to be analyzed, ciphers to be decoded, or problems to be solved. Rather, reality is approached as a sacrament through which glimpses of God's Spirit might be caught or intimations of the Spirit's movements intuited. By this I do not mean to suggest that everything that happens is the result of some divine puppet master pulling the strings of the universe and that God "wills" everything that happens. This sort of view of God seems to me to get humans off the hook. We need to take responsibility (to use the biblical phrase) to act justly, love mercy, and walk humbly with our God. Or, to put it another way, the Christian life is a life that takes seriously the admonitions sprinkled throughout the gospel: love your enemies, forgive seven times seven, do as I have done to you. Follow me. It means we must do more than just amble through life saying, God must mean this to be. We are called to live into our capacity to love and to reason in order to choose wisely and live well. Still, this following is not merely ethical or cultic. It is not exhausted by observing the rules and going to Sunday worship. It means cultivating a deep sensibility that God is indeed with us, that divine presence intertwines with our every daily activity, that, if we and all persons are created in God's image and likeness, then we have the challenge of truly *seeing* that, and of relating to one another with that fact foremost in heart and mind. We are invited to *live* love. That *kenotic* and spacious love is patterned in the life of Jesus. This does not ask us to be doormats or slaves to family members' whims. It does call us to become communities of genuine respect, tenderness, and care. We must be gentle with our own failings and the failings of each other. Attentive to the ways we are invited to grow in order to love more surely and graciously by the breath of the Spirit flowing between us.

I want here to return to my mother and her red high-heeled shoes. Perhaps it is an odd example of the way this attentiveness works but it's the one that is given to me at this moment in my life. And if I know anything about spiritual attentiveness, the truth is that God can't find me where I think I ought to be; God can find me only where I am. I might interpret my eighty-year-old mother's act of throwing away her shoes and of feeling that she'd given up her youth in a number of different ways. First, I might simply ignore it, thinking it had no intrinsic meaning beyond the fact of it. Alternatively, I might see her response through a psychological lens: this speaks of my mother's vanity or of her refusal to acknowledge the factual truth: that she really can't navigate in stiletto heels anymore. On the other hand, I might see it as charming evidence of her quirkiness, her eccentricity. Or I might find it to be an inspiring example of her remarkable capacity to remain feeling vibrant and youthful well into her twilight years.

I might let my probing lie there. But the fact that the image lingers with me, that it spoke to me deeply at the time, and that it continues to inhabit my thoughts is worth paying attention to. The point is not to find an "answer" to one's pondering but to live in the place in the self where the questions are being born. Not that there isn't a very real place for problem solving and definitive answers in our lives. There certainly is. But I'm suggesting (with back up from the masters of the Christian spiritual tradition) that the deeper reality that sustains our lives is not best apprehended in the problem-solving mode. Living attentively is different from having burning questions to which you have to find a definitive answer. It's more like allowing the partial answers to yield to new insights, which in turn yield to more questions. This attentiveness has to do with turning things over tenderly, with approaching life as a mystery to be plumbed, an astonishment etching itself on the heart.

So the fact that I linger with the image indicates that it may say something about me as well as my mother. It raises questions about my relationship to my own aging, about my vanity (not red high-heels perhaps but that salt and pepper at the temples) as well as invites me to a certain *joie de vivre* that refuses to surrender the juice of my life. Remembering it lo these many years later and seeing myself now in my mother's shoes, so to speak, also connects me to the mystery of the human life cycle. What does it mean to inhabit the differing ages of our lives well? Does our culture force us to mourn when we've reached the age when glamour fades? What do the aging have to offer us? What wisdom do we throw away as we shut the aging up in institutions and hold up for emulation only the physically beautiful, the strong, and the young?

The questions go deeper still. How are we all children of God together? Was my past and my daughter's present impatience based on a sense of honoring each other's gifts or is it shaped by the hurried restlessness of our society that resists thoughtful rumination? What does it mean that my mother is no longer a young woman, that her mortality is more and more lined on her features for all to see? Have I loved her well? Have I treasured her specific life? Have I loved my own young adult children well? What is it to love well? When and where and how do I guide, advise, or disapprove?

When am I called to simply be present, to support, to rejoice, and grieve with them? How has love touched me through my mother and through my children? How have I been brought to a place of awe and wonder by the miracle of the fact that we are alive and have been given each other to love? How is the love that I bestow connected to the way I have been loved? Both by my parents and by the God whose love sustains existence itself? What divine grace is manifest between us as we go about our ordinary lives, in our disagreements as well as our moments of intimacy? What does that great story have to say to my/our small story? Maybe the Bible doesn't always give us a formula or rule to follow but words and images to swim in like the ocean. Do we have the courage to take the plunge?

These questions are the stuff of attentive awareness. Not that we need brood obsessively over every detail of life. But the Christian revelation awakens us with the astonishing thought: God is with us. Can we be attentive enough to discover the ways that this is true in that most intimate of communities, the domestic church?

Questions for Discussion

1. Have you ever thought about family life and the spiritual life as connected, or have they seemed to be two discrete arenas of experience?

2. Do you think that a family has to be "perfect" to be seen as an arena for spiritual reflection, or is the Christian spiritual life something that is practiced in the midst of all sorts of contexts?

3. How do you see the relationship between the formal seven Sacraments recognized by Roman Catholicism and the "sacramental" perception of daily life suggested here?

4. From your own experience, supply a story about the way God has been present in your family. (This might be your family of origin, an extended family, or any of the many configurations of family encountered today.)

Chapter 19

Living the Dual Vocation
of Christian Parenthood

Julie Hanlon Rubio

Part of the genius of Michael's Lawler's well-known book *Marriage and Sacrament: A Theology of Christian Marriage* is his ability to make the rich sacramental theology of the Catholic Church understandable by applying it to a "not so fictionalized" couple, Will and Wilma.[1] Through the course of the book, Will and Wilma meet, fall in love, marry, grow together in Christian discipleship, share the gift of sexuality, and welcome children into their lives. Lawler rightly notes that just as Will and Wilma are called to be fruitful through procreation, they are also obligated to practice neighbor-love beyond the confines of their family.[2] He then sets out the following ideal:

> To be fully generative and fruitful, Will and Wilma will have to decide how they can enliven and nurture not only their mutual communion, not only their own children, but also the community in which they will pursue their communion and which they will leave to their children and their children's children. If their marriage is ever to become full sacrament, they will have to be fruitful in the third way as well as in the other two.[3]

Finding ways to realize this ideal is, I submit, one of the most difficult tasks facing contemporary Christian couples. How can commitments to marriage, children, and community be honored given the limits of human energy and the twenty-four-hour day? Can any family do it all? Should they even try? In this essay, I will examine some of the experiences of couples who try, and will argue that despite the difficulties, Christian couples ought to strive to balance commitments to both family and community, or to embrace what I call the dual vocation of Christian parenting.

Foundations

In my recent book, *A Christian Theology of Marriage and Family,* I argue that Christian parents have a dual vocation: to care for their children and to contribute to the humanizing of society.[4] In the Christian tradition, a vocation is a calling to serve God in a particular way. Earlier generations of Catholics may have viewed the religious vocations of priests and nuns as far holier than the ordinary lifestyles of married couples.[5] Today, however, most Catholics understand that a person can have a vocation to a religious, married, or single lifestyle, all of which can be paths to holiness. Those who marry and become parents have chosen the vocation of marriage and parenting. While that vocation is typically associated with caring for children, Christian faith obligates parents to serve others as well.

Most Christians consider sacrifice for children to be essential to the vocation of marriage. It seems almost unnecessary to argue for the special obligation parents have to care for children. Yet because the Christian tradition prioritizes love for neighbors and strangers, many Christian theologians have found it necessary to justify parents' particular commitment to children. Their central theological claim is that natural connections between parents and children are morally significant:

> If we really believe bodies matter, and are prepared to follow this insight where it takes us, we cannot help but acknowledge the fact that a child is produced by the bodily union of its mother and father, that the mother carries it in her body for nine months, that the child usually shares their genetic inheritance, is of enormous significance and provides a uniquely firm foundation for a relationship of love.[6]

The experience of Christian parents most often confirms the naturalness of the parental obligation to care for children. Mothers and fathers who spend hours holding colicky babies, wake during the night to feed crying infants and comfort fearful toddlers, or forgo luxuries so that their children will not have to, do so without considering the cost. In a multitude of ways, for no other reason than the fact that they are parents, parents give themselves in love to their children. The Christian tradition testifies to the profound experience of parental love in its recognition of the importance of parental obligations. Clearly, sacrificial love for one's family is a crucial part of the parental vocation.

However, this value does not provide an adequate basis for a full discussion of the Christian vocation of parenthood, because the Christian tradition also calls believers away from their families to the work of public discipleship. In the New Testament, Jesus locates his vocation outside of his family. This can be clearly seen when, in his response to his family's attempt to interfere with his preaching, he identifies those who do God's will as his true family (Mark 3:31–35). This passage can be misread as a denial of the moral value of family life or too easily explained away as a lesson about priorities.[7] A better reading, in my view, is that Jesus names the community of believers as his true family and finds his public vocation in and through this community. Here and in other "hard sayings," Jesus poses troubling questions about the compatibility of discipleship with family duties.

Yet Jesus also looks back to the Genesis creation narrative in order to uphold the sanctity of the marriage covenant (Mark 10:6). This indicates that his concern is not with marriage itself but rather with idolatry of family that can stand in the way of discipleship. Thus while affirming the goodness of marriage, he challenges his hearers by calling them to "hate" their families (Luke 14:2) and asks them to leave their families behind for his sake and the promise of a new family united in God (Mark 10:29–30). As Lisa Cahill notes, while these sayings may seem baffling to us, they become clear when viewed in the context of Jesus' public ministry to the marginalized, for "loyalty to one's own group and dedication to the status of that group over all others and at the expense of whoever stands in its way are incompatible with a life of mercy, service, and compassion for the neighbor in need or for the social outcasts and the poor."[8] Because Jesus preaches that devotion to family can be dangerous to the person who wants to live a holy life of compassion, the ethical priority of the kinship bond is called into question.[9] Thus it seems that those who would serve God may marry and become parents, but they must resist the temptation to make care for kin their only mission in life.[10]

The earliest Christians evidently tried to do just this, and they were sometimes called "homewreckers" by critics who questioned the willingness to let faith conflict with duty to family.[11] Both in Roman and Jewish contexts, Christians stunned others with their refusal to honor cultural norms prioritizing the family. On the other hand, the New Testament includes significant affirmations of marriage (Eph. 5:21–33), indications that some Christians tried to reconcile their faith with their high estimation of ordinary family life. This strain of Christian thinking developed over time into a strong theology of marriage as sacrament. Yet the dominant strain of early Christian thinking appears to have been suspicion of the value of family life when compared with the value of single-hearted discipleship.[12]

However, as anyone who has sat in the pews of a Catholic church in recent years knows, the more family-affirming strain of the tradition eventually triumphed. Still, echoes remain of the more radical early strain of the Christian tradition (which questions the possibility of harmoniously combining love for God with love for family). The contemporary Christian tradition celebrates both the public vocation of discipleship and the more private vocation of giving oneself in relationship. The respect for the radical family-questioning strain can be heard in the Catholic Church's continuing insistence that celibacy is a higher calling than marriage.[13] It can also be heard in the quiet lives of priests, monks, and women religious that say to married Christians, "There is more to life than family. God may be more deeply known and loved by those who are free from other passions." Every time the superiority of the celibate life is recognized, the sacredness of family life is implicitly questioned, even if marriage is also recognized as a tremendous gift. The higher valuing of the nonmarried life challenges the idea of marriage as a universal vocation. It recalls the life of Jesus and suggests that his sacrifice of family life for the sake of public mission should not be forgotten.

Contemporary Catholics must take seriously the central place of disciple-ship as a public vocation in the Christian tradition. This vocation is rooted in the New Testament teaching that family can stand in the way of one's com-mitment to God. Jesus asks his disciples to break out of traditional family roles in order to follow him. The Christian tradition, at least in its earliest stages, also associates discipleship with leaving one's family behind. Con-temporary Christians who want to be true to scripture and tradition have to consider what it might mean to practice discipleship today. For Catho-lics, who are blessed with a rich tradition of social teaching emphasizing the spiritual importance of work and the social mission of the family, the call to go into the world is especially strong.[14]

Yet the commitment to care for children, grounded in natural connections between parents and children and the rich experience of Christian parents, is also an important part of the Christian tradition. Thus, it is necessary to find a way to balance these two important aspects of Christian life.

Dual vocation is a term that seeks to uphold the primary importance of public discipleship testified to in the Gospels and the early Christian tradition *and* the deep valuing of family that is rooted in nature and the experience of the Christian parents. Dual vocation should serve as a norm for Christian mothers and fathers, reminding them that both work in the world and work in the home are crucially important. Work in the world may take many different forms. Dual career couples will be studied below because paid work outside the home is the most common way for men and women to contribute to the community. However, dual vocation differs from dual career in its emphasis on work as a calling to public discipleship. Spouses in a dual career marriage who work purely for financial reasons may not realize this calling, while families in which one spouse holds a paying job and the other does volunteer work may. Alternatively, one spouse may work full-time while the other works part-time and handles more parenting and community work. The key to the public side of the dual vocation is not pay but commitment to the good of both family and others.

Social Scientific Studies of
Dual Career–Dual Parenting Couples

Dual vocation/dual career may sound good in theory, but how does it look from the inside? Currently, there is a wealth of information of dual career couples. In 1990, three-fourths of mothers with preschool children worked. Dual career families are now the most common family form in America, constituting three-fifths of all families. The dual career lifestyle appears to have advantages (increased professional satisfaction for women, increased family time for men, more shared experiences and higher levels of intimacy for couples, higher self-esteem for both, stronger relationships between both parents and children, and more money) and disadvantages (too much to do for men and women, child care worries, fatigue, lack of personal time and couple time, less time for children, guilt, increased couple stress due to arguments about career paths and the division of labor in the home, and possibly, a higher risk of divorce).[15] Although the research on dual career couples is not conclusive, one can make some general statements with some confidence:

1. *Children receive some benefits.* For instance, employed mothers may be more sensitive to infants than nonemployed mothers. Maternal sensitivity is a key measure of healthy child development, because sensitive mothers respond to their infants and give them a secure base for future social growth.[16] Many studies have shown that nonemployed women experience greater levels of distress or depression than employed women. Generally, this would predict lower levels of maternal sensitivity. Children in dual career families are also more self-reliant, less likely to hold gender stereotypes, more likely to be internally motivated, and more likely to have strong relationships with both parents.[17]

2. *Children experience some difficulties.* Especially in high-power dual career marriages, in which both spouses work long hours and children spend long hours in daycare, parental relationships with children suffer and children's development can be negatively affected. When asked, children of working parents warn parents not to neglect their children; they especially want more time with fathers.[18] Some studies indicate that a sixty-hour work week, in which parents work a combined total of sixty hours outside the home and limit child care, diminishes these difficulties.[19]

3. *Couples experience stress.* Housework remains a major source of tension. Arlie Hochschild's oft-cited study of dual career households reveals a sizable difference between the number of hours working men and women contributed to household labor. Hochschild contends that women work an extra two hours a day, or two weeks a year.[20] Although some argue that Hochschild overstates the differences,[21] most recent studies affirm both the persistence of the gap and the link between perceived fairness of housework distribution and marital happiness.[22] Some studies linking dual career marriages and divorce give cause for concern, though defenders of the dual career model point out that housework imbalance (not dual career marriage itself) may be the root of the problem. Other key stressors are job-family role strain (when pressures from both arenas conflict) and psychological distress.[23] These stressors are clearly evident in the lives of most dual career couples.[24]

4. *Successful dual career couples adapt key coping strategies* in order to deal with the inevitable stress: Many how-to books for dual career

couples discuss strategies that make life easier for busy families, like maintaining good communication, being more efficient and organized, planning time for relaxation, hiring out services like house cleaning and yard work, and lowering standards for some tasks. In addition, as one important new study shows, many middle-class dual earner couples, less-studied than high-income couples, scale back their career expectations, adopt a one job/one career model, and/or take turns putting one career before the other.[25] This study reveals that many dual-earner couples make sacrifices at work in order to contribute professionally without compromising their family life. They resist cultural expectations of long work weeks and question the cultural valuing of work over family. When couples adopt strategies such as these, they are more likely to find satisfaction both at home and at work.

5. *Couples experience benefits.* Intimacy increases between couples when both experience the challenges of work inside and outside the home. They understand each other's struggles and share the work and joy of family life.[26] This increased intimacy is not all bliss. As one father puts it, "Shared parenting adds a level of discussion which wouldn't exist in a traditional marriage. I would have had no input.... On the other hand, there would be no room for conflicts in a traditional relationship. With shared parenting comes a new area of potential tension and conflict — differing opinions."[27] Still, despite the difficulties of intimacy, most couples seem to think it is worth it. The literature is replete with statements from couples affirming that life is crazy, but very full, and they are in it together.

Dual Vocation in My House

While I don't claim to have an ideal or representative dual career/vocation marriage, my own experience may put some flesh on the bare bones information gleaned from studies. My husband, Marty, and I fell into dual career–dual parenting almost by accident. We started dating in college, graduated in 1987, and took some time off for travel, volunteer work, and exploring different career options. Two years later, we both entered graduate school. A few months into my master's program, I knew that I had found my calling and would want to complete a Ph.D. and teach theology. Marty knew almost as quickly that he wanted something else. He tried different things for a year before finding his vocation as a high school history teacher. When we married in 1992, we were both teachers. As we looked around at families we knew, we were happy to have found jobs that would allow us significant time with each other and future children.

When our first child arrived in 1994, we agreed to share parenting and use some outside child care. For four years, I taught part-time during the school year and put in more hours with the kids, whereas in the summers,

Marty took over as primary parent while I wrote and taught summer school. In 1999, we moved to St. Louis, and I took a full-time teaching job, but we continued the same pattern, though as our children grew older, I worked more hours. In my quest to secure tenure, I was sometimes in the office on Saturdays or holidays to finish important writing projects. This year, as Marty works on a master's degree and seeks more administrative duties, I will scale back my work. I suspect that this pattern of give and take will continue throughout our careers.

The schedule we currently keep is complicated enough to require an hour by hour breakdown on our refrigerator. Often, we work from early in the morning until late at night. On a typical weekday, we both rise at 6:00 a.m. While I work out, Marty gets ready for work and shares some time with Thomas, our middle son. At 7:00 a.m., he leaves for work, and I combine getting ready with overseeing breakfast and dressing, making lunches, and leading ten minutes of Bible study. I walk two of our boys to elementary school at 8:00 a.m. and drop another off at a church preschool at 9:00 a.m. Two days a week, I am back around noon to pick up my youngest and spend the day playing and doing housework. Marty gets home around 5:00 p.m. (after his workout) and evenings are filled with homework, dinner, dishes, baths, stories, and bedtime rituals. By 8:30, we're often at the kitchen table grading papers or preparing for classes. Three days a week I stay at school until 5:00 p.m., and Marty picks up the kids (a babysitting co-op to fill in the gaps). On good days, we're in bed by 10:30, but often, I am up late grading or reading. The week also includes kids' activities, school events, taking care of neighbors' kids, shopping, cleaning, yard work, volunteering, church, and Sunday school. By Friday, when we almost always make pizza and watch a video with our kids, we are pretty exhausted. We look forward to catching up on sleep and downtime during the weekends, which have not yet become as frenzied as seems typical for families like ours.

The stresses in our dual vocation families come from many different sources. While we log far fewer hours at work than our friends in business or law, our days are sometimes just as long. Though we value the time we have with our kids when they come home from school, our late nights at the kitchen table result in a lack of sleep that can be detrimental to our well-being. The related lack of personal time for reading, conversation, and relaxing also takes its toll. Because we have to juggle whenever unplanned events (meetings, a sick child, school holidays, etc.) occur, ongoing change in our schedule is necessary. Sometimes we argue over who will need to bend or how to deal with household problems, and this adds to the stress in our lives.

Is it worth it? Most days, we think so. As teachers in Catholic institutions, we both love our work and feel that it contributes to the common good. We have the opportunity to form students in important ways. When I teach courses on marriage and family, I bring my perspective as a parent into the classroom. When Marty teaches economics, he uses examples from our home life, and when he leaves early two days a week, he models involved fathering for his impressionable female students. Neither of us can envision a life without this sort of contribution to the broader community.

On the other hand, we are committed to being around to parent our children, and we love having time to listen to them talk about their days, volunteer at their schools, play ball in the afternoons, and travel during our summers off. Our children have very close relationships with both of us. We both take care of them when they are sick, comfort them when they are afraid, discipline them when needed, push them to do their best in school, and listen when they have problems. From us they are learning that fathers and mothers can nurture and challenge. We would not trade the relationships we have with our kids for more time at work anymore than we would fail to answer the public callings both of us perceive to work outside the home.

Conclusion

The Christian tradition seems to call parents to embrace a dual vocation of commitment to family and society. Committing to a dual career marriage is one way to realize this vocation. Dual career families now constitute the majority of American families, and studies of these families reveal both costs and benefits. Potential disadvantages should not be denied, for the stresses of dual career life are real. Nevertheless, Christian couples who see their careers as vocations and make necessary sacrifices in order to spend time with family should find it possible to balance these two fundamentally important goods. Clearly, this is not the only way to maintain fidelity to both the gospel call to public discipleship and the special obligations of parents to children. Some couples may choose to split a dual vocation because the vocation of one cannot mesh with family care or because one feels called to work in the home. Still, dual vocation/dual career couples who pursue both public and private callings seem to have a unique opportunity to shape their family together even as they maintain commitments to the common good.

Questions for Discussion

1. Define the term "vocation." Explain why Christian tradition has frequently prioritized a religious vocation (e.g., priesthood or religious life) over a vocation to parenthood.

2. What is your definition of discipleship? Explain the relationship between parenthood and discipleship.

3. Explain the difference between a "dual vocation" and a "dual career."

4. List and explain four ways in which parents can live discipleship in their dual vocation.

Chapter 20

Married and Aging

A Value to Society

Aldegonde Brenninkmeijer-Werhahn

Introduction

The human being is a historically evolving subject. Each one of us continually redefines oneself in light of this ongoing lived journey. One's physiological, emotional, psychological, mental, and spiritual states change continuously. Nevertheless, these states relate always to the same person. There are four basic stages in the life cycle: childhood as the first stage; younger adulthood the second stage; a period of active independent life the third stage; and dependence and frailty the fourth stage. In between each of these stages one also finds critical transitional stages: between the first and the second stages are adolescents, who are undergoing puberty and are still on the way to maturity. Between the second and the third stages, young people eagerly await emancipation and independence, gaining experience in ways which can sometimes be difficult. Between the third and the fourth stages we come face to face with the boundaries that separate a mature from an aging *homo sapiens,* moving from independence to greater dependence.

In this latter transitional stage we begin to realize that we cannot retrieve our past. The overriding question we face at this point is: how do we, in our inner selves, manage the aging process? Unless we have integrated the lived experience of each stage, while our lived years might move us into the next stage, we may lack the maturity that is reflected in healthy human development. In other words, we have to embrace all phases of maturation, each with its own specific lessons, insights, and understanding, before we can begin to accept willingly the stages of aging. Each stage of transition has its specific turning points: in early ages this may be the move from kindergarten to primary school, or from high school to university, or from professional life to retirement, etc. All of these transitional periods entail not only a shift in physical and spatial locale, but more importantly, they challenge us to grow and mature emotionally, psychologically, relationally, and spiritually. This chapter is a reflection on the latter stages of aging, especially within the marital relationship, and the knowledge, wisdom, and insight we can gain from these couples in the aging process.

Facts of an Aging Society

To understand our current situation it is vital to be attentive to "the signs of the times." As each life cycle has its own specific destiny, so has each epoch its specific message, which gives us an opportunity as a community to grow toward a more just and loving world. What is new today is that the number of those who reach an advanced age is greater than ever. Sociological research speaks of an "age of the elderly."[1] At the beginning of the twentieth century, one in every twenty-five people in the United States was sixty-five or older. Today one in eight — a total of 33.2 million Americans — is sixty-five or older. A person who reaches sixty-five can expect to live for seventeen more years; many live well beyond that.[2] In Europe every fifth person today is over sixty, and it is expected that in twenty years it will be every fourth person. And of these, every fifth person will be over eighty. According to a recent report in *Signum*, in 1952 there were only 350 individuals who, following the courteous British custom, received the queen's telegram upon reaching their centenary, whereas it is projected that in 2031, there will be 35,000.[3] These statistics indicate that, especially in the West, adults are living considerably longer lives and, thus, have a greater opportunity to reflect upon, and integrate the insights of a life of experiences and lived relationships, and to share these insights with younger generations.

The Culture of Youth: Challenges to Teaching and Internalizing the Lessons of Aging

Younger generations, however, are not always open to these insights, especially in our "culture of youth" whereby society values everlasting youth over age. Rather than embracing the transformation from one life stage to another, society's message is that we must resist such transformations in order to preserve our identity and acceptance within a culture that does not tolerate aging. Posters, films, and magazines make it appear as though the value of life lies solely in being and staying young, regardless of one's age. But are the lessons of aging not realized rather through values such as self-esteem, satisfaction with one's life and its accomplishments, overcoming jealousy of the young, having no resentments against what is new but embracing it instead of taking malicious delight in seeing a new development fail? Internalizing the aging process and the insight, knowledge, and wisdom that it provides challenges our current cultural paradigm and reflects many Eastern cultures where the aging are respected and consulted for their insight and wisdom. There is, then, the constant need to confront, and challenge, society's obsession with preserving eternal youth. One way to do this is by educating the young in the value of aging.

The seeds for successful aging start in adolescence and are sown in the family by one's parents. This is the time when a person's character is rapidly changing, along the way to bodily, psychological, and spiritual maturity. It is the growth experienced during this time that builds foundational values for later life. These values will vary, evolve, and develop over the course of time. For instance, one's sense of commitment to a kindergarten playmate is largely transient, whereas commitment between a married couple celebrating their silver jubilee is solid and permanent. Unfortunately, the intergenerational transference of foundational values that guide young people throughout life is often missing. Instead, it is often the media (television, movies, MTV, the Internet, etc.) with its misguided, hedonistic values that is forming the character of a whole generation. Furthermore, the voices of the elderly, those who have moved through the aging stages and have integrated and built upon those foundational values, are frequently silenced by an overarching "culture of youth" supported, endorsed, and exploited by the media. In this way, the elderly are no longer always able to play a key role in helping to pass on values that are an important element in family life and in each family's history.

The Meaning of Aging

"Aging gracefully" is an aphorism that has taken on a whole new meaning in the culture of youth and extends to physical characteristics as well as the ability to contribute to the common good. Whereas, in times past, aging gracefully meant easing into retirement and having the opportunity to enjoy grandchildren and the leisure time that retirement affords to engage in volunteer work and pursue hobbies, now it has come to include a preoccupation with resisting the aging process. Today, the loss of beauty and physical attractiveness that accompanies this process is generally not always welcome. The physical charms of someone over seventy are clearly less attractive and exciting than those of younger persons. This preoccupation with maintaining youth fails to realize, however, that on the face of the elderly person life has written so many stories. If we look, for example, at the last self-portrait of Rembrandt we discover a depth that was not there before. We marvel, also, at the last works of Michelangelo and realize they are actually his best works. The challenge for contemporary culture is to regain an appreciation of, and respect for, the physical attributes of an aging population.

With regard to the aging population's ability to contribute to the common good, we observe two phenomena among society and the elderly. First, instead of keeping them actively engaged, there is age discrimination or ageism whereby society alienates the elderly and loses a significant number of persons from among the pool of talents and abilities when its members reach sixty-five. On the other hand, it also happens that this group chooses to drop out and let the younger generation take over, or focuses exclusively on pursuing hobbies and leisure. There are, however, opportunities to give something back to society and the church. To contribute something to the community enriches one's own life. Society should make a deliberate effort to promote lifelong service and learning for the older generation.[4] Churches, likewise, have a tremendous opportunity to incorporate the aging as a vital, active, and contributing population within the community. For example, they might do this by planning ongoing Christian education targeting people in the third and fourth stages of life, or by setting up a church community service center whereby capable aging members of the community provide services to other members of the community who may be incapacitated — for example, by offering a ride to the doctor or help with mowing the lawn or changing a light bulb. A lot more could be said, but let me just mention that in the Catholic Church one all too often hears a kind of apology for not having enough young worshipers in church. There are indeed serious issues to be addressed concerning the church's relationship with younger people.[5] But what would the church do if this faithful group of older worshipers were to withdraw from a liturgy that is all too frequently barren?

In a beautiful letter to the elderly, Pope John Paul II sums up well the positive and holy reality of the aged: "Old age can be seen as a truly 'favorable time' for bringing life and God's plan for each person to its fulfilment, a time when everything comes together and enables us to grasp the meaning of life better and attain to a true 'wisdom of the heart.' "[6] Coming to old age can mean a new beginning of life: the chance to intensify precious friendships, to cultivate hospitality and community life, to share one's gifts and professional competence for the benefit of society, and to help build up the future for the coming generation. It is a great preparation for later life if we have practiced this already in earlier life.

Marriage and the Aging: Two Marital Narratives

With this background on the aging process and the intergenerational tensions in mind, we can now reflect on the meaning and nature of marriage among the aging population. Two texts may be cited to illustrate the difference between the perspective of young persons who still have marriage and aging ahead of them, and that of older people for whom most of their life is behind them.

Recently in a newspaper my attention was drawn to a personal ad placed by a marriage mediation service, with the headline: "Do you want a first-class marriage? Enchanting beauty, 29/175, descended from a prominent international, well-to-do family based in Marbella, USA and Western Europe. She is what a demanding citizen of the world seeks but rarely finds — outstanding career, with her own capital, enthusiastic traveller and sportswoman. Her realistic plans for her future involve a stable and happy family life... a strong sense of responsibility — she is now available... for a 1st-class marriage."

By contrast, consider the story from Ovid's *Metamorphoses,* a well-known piece of literature: *Baucis and Philemon.*[7] The gods Jupiter and

Mercury descended to earth on a hillside of Phrygia disguised as human travelers. When they were wandering in the region where the aged Philemon and Baucis lived, they sought a place to rest, but no home would receive them; on the contrary, people took them for tramps. Then they knocked at the door of a tiny, reed-thatched cottage, Philemon and Baucis's humble home. This couple had married when they were little more than children, had lived in that lonely place for sixty years, and were still content in each other's company.

Their poverty did not hinder them from receiving the visitors as if they were long-lost relatives. They set out a place to rest, lit the fire, and prepared a meal for their unknown guests. In that household there were no servants and no masters: each of the two old people gave orders, and each obeyed.

While eating the meal and drinking the wine, the hosts realized that each time the wine-jar was emptied it filled up again of its own accord. The gods in this way revealed their divine identity to their hosts and announced that the whole area would be destroyed, but that the kindness of the elderly couple had moved them to spare their lives. They told Philemon and Baucis to leave the cottage and climb the hill with them. The old people struggled up the hill behind the gods. When they looked back they saw that the land and farms had disappeared. There was nothing left but marshland and their cottage alone on the hillside. They were in tears, but while they wept, the cottage walls were transformed into stone pillars, the floor turned to marble, and the thatch into yellow gold.

"Old man, old woman," said Jupiter, "tell us what you desire most in all the world." Baucis and Philemon murmured together for a moment, and then Philemon said, "Let us be your priests and look after your temple. And, since we have lived all our lives peacefully together, let me not live to bury Baucis, nor Baucis live to bury me. Let our lives end at the same moment."[8] Their prayer was answered and they lived for many years as priests of the temple. After many years had passed, they suddenly saw their skins simultaneously turn into bark. Baucis became a linden and Philemon an oak, and they just had time to kiss one another for the last time before the transformation was complete.

In the first example, we see the desire to start with a first-class marriage, whereas in the latter one, we see a couple ending their sixty-year journey, inseparable from each other. While the one relies on the international marriage market, with the allure of a well-to-do family, extraordinary career, capital, happy family, and a sense of responsibility, the old couple are poor but still content in each other's company, accustomed to giving each other orders and obeying one another, and praying to end their lives at the same moment. In these two stories, one sees clearly the contrast between a largely hedonistic perspective on the meaning and nature of marriage focused on many of the trappings of Western culture, and the trust in a relational perspective that has fully integrated the life stages and is grounded in love, trust, commitment, and fidelity, regardless of the external trappings such as wealth and success. The latter exemplifies well the art of growing old together.

Aging, Marriage, and Family

The longevity of marriages, due to radical improvements in science, technology, and medicine, is substantially changing the meaning and nature of marriage and the family. If the spouses are working together on a lifelong commitment and they stay together, then the average duration of a marriage is longer than it ever has been. Celebrating a golden anniversary has become quite normal for many couples. A series of great challenges for couples appears when children have left home, retirement has come after a long working life, and the spouses have not cultivated their togetherness. When health permits, the spouses may live another twenty-five or even thirty years together. For husbands and wives in their third and fourth stage of life this is indeed a new social reality. Since society as well as the churches has not yet fully responded to this new reality, the spouses do not yet have a tradition to turn to for well-established norms or examples of living a meaningful and happy marriage even after they have been married for sixty or more years. Consequently, this novel epoch provides a laboratory of lived experience to chart what heretofore have been uncharted waters.

In this new context, what in fact do we mean by marriage? Who defines the meaning of marriage today? Does the term not refer to a man and woman who, by their covenant, become spouses and through their marriage create a family precisely for the sake of nurturing and educating children in the art of aging? Through marriage, specific values find their particular meaning for the newly formed family: trustworthiness in what one has taken on; adhering to one's word; fidelity toward the person whose confidence one has accepted; the ability to distinguish between true and false in word, attitude, achievement and all matters, and to assist each other in doing so. This is the foundation for staying together even after twenty years, when the children have left home. Marriage creates the space in which spouses can discover over the course of time what continuity entails. It reveals elements of the experience of time that resemble eternity: to rely on and to trust God, to endure, to support each other, to carry on. It is when one marries that one begins to understand what it means to found and to establish a family, to build up one's own traditions and the marital relationship.

Growth and development through marriage and the various stages of aging is cumulative, and its transmission to children is cumulative as well. That is, the various stages of aging are not isolated in knowledge, perception, understanding, and growth; we further our knowledge and understanding of the values and insights that precede our current stage, and add new values to that understanding. This developmental project is both communicated to and handed on to our children, but our children also contribute to our own growth and development individually and within the marital relationship.

Unfortunately, as the high divorce rate indicates, there can be a breakdown in the transmission of values between parents and children.

The Impact of Later-Life Divorce[9]

Aging can be most difficult if people's fulfilment lies only in their professional lives and social activities. When the children have left home is when many divorces and second marriages occur. Between 1980 and 1985, the divorce rate among the elderly in the United States increased from 0.7 percent to 2.27 percent. However, studies in 1990 estimate that, as the baby boom generation enters old age (over sixty-five), more of them will be divorced than widowed.[10]

One should not underestimate the effect on aging and the integration of values of a second or even third marriage with a much younger partner. It is important to bear in mind that not only may a person be leaving behind an unhappy loved one, but starting again also creates a discontinuity in one's own life story and will bring another unpredictable future. In light of these options, new issues come to the fore, such as the visitation rights of grandparents, the reaction of the adult children to new marriages, questions of inheritance, and the adjustment to additional family members when previous emotional difficulties may still be unresolved. Divorce at any age involves a deep sense of loss; however, these feelings may have a greater personal impact for those in later life, triggering, for example, a decline in self-esteem. Many older women who are divorced suddenly find themselves without economic support and have to find employment.[11] We already face the phenomenon that, increasingly, the extended family is no longer just a collection of aunts, uncles, and cousins, but also of stepparents and half brothers and half sisters, or of stepbrothers and stepsisters with no blood relation at all.

The Aging: Further Considerations

This brief study has addressed some important issues surrounding the nature of aging and its impact on marriage and the family. There are, however, other issues that I will merely allude to that need to be addressed as our population continues to age. First, the significance of aging and the aged has not yet received adequate attention in theological research. To explore and develop a "theology of, and for, the aging" in light of the experiences of seniors would be a most valuable project for scholars to undertake.

Second, as we face an ever-aging society with apprehension, there remain other important questions that deserve equal attention. What significance, sociologically and culturally, do we ascribe to the elderly in general? Do we as a society embrace all ages in their various stages, or do we discriminate on the basis of age, and the ability to preserve eternal youthfulness? Do we recognize an aging population as a value that every healthy society requires in order to be complete? Or do we have a more fragmented attitude toward aging and see old age simply as a waste, a residue of the last third of a person's lifespan?

Finally, we must reexamine the relationship between aging couples and family life and take account of the aged as citizens who are worthy of the attention of the entire community. We must also address the self-images of the aging themselves. How do the aging look at themselves? Are they aware of their true human dignity and the significant contributions that they can continue to make to family, culture, and society as they journey through the latter stages of life? This question illustrates well that the aging individual needs to become aware of his or her personal high value and that the culture and community should facilitate them in the process of recognition and integration. Couples in general, and older couples in particular, should not lose their value as citizens but become more aware of it. Communities should seriously reassess the value of the family for their wholeness and well-being.

An Old Testament biblical passage well articulates the general challenges facing the cultural integration of the aging. "Before Elijah journeyed to the mount of Horeb he was afraid for Jezebel and fled to the desert, and sitting under a furze bush wished he were dead.... Then all of a sudden an angel touched him three times and said, 'Get up and eat to strengthen yourself to reach Horeb, God's mountain'" (1 Kings 19:4–8). This story illustrates the temptation facing aging people. Frequently one hears the phrase: "Well, my life no longer has any significance," or some say, "We have left our life behind us." But to reach Horeb, God's mountain, in a dignified way a thoughtful Christian would do better to say "we have brought our life before us." Gerontological studies show that faithful people have a higher quality of life and are better able to be hopeful and optimistic, to have greater self-esteem, and to control their lives.

Conclusion

To speak or to write about aging is in fact possible only when you have some knowledge of aging and have experienced the process. To write about the *ars moriendi* (the art of dying well) is not something to be overly spiritualized, which can give the impression of an innocent idealism. To do it reliably is therefore not easy.

It has become apparent that growing old does not simply mean having lived a certain number of years or that one's physical strength is in decline, but rather that there is both a proper and a false way to grow old. It depends entirely on how one feels about aging when one is still younger.

Each particular phase of life is there for the sake of the whole. Should a phase be harmed in some way, particularly in youth, one's entire life may suffer. For the youngster this will depend on whether he or she has experienced the right or the wrong way of living youth; in the young adult, on the zeal for life of the young person; in the adult, on the fullness of achievement and mature experience; in the aged, on the way of regarding the heritage of one's whole life. Each of us is accountable for our own development and how we integrate the meaning of each stage of the life cycle into the subsequent stages. While there is no clear and precise recipe for this process, we must continue to explore those dimensions that facilitate human wholeness and holiness in the aging population.[12]

Through the story about the old couple Philemon and Baucis, I tried to show how closely the beginning of the life journey is connected with the end of one's pilgrimage. The story teaches us that the old couple is able in a unique manner to change and grow until the very end, in a way that is gratifying for them and for others. From this tale we can also understand the profound secret of old people who always stay young. It is not through physical strength only, but principally through inner strength, wisdom, and the goodness of their hearts that Philemon and Baucis made themselves happy and became a delight to others. This is the supreme challenge of the aging process.

Questions for Discussion

1. Are there lessons in Christian discipleship that those who are younger can learn from those who have reached a later stage in life's journey?

2. Whoever was never young will never mature. How do we in our inner selves manage the aging process from early adulthood onward? What kind of person do we want to be in later life? How does our understanding of friendship (especially within marriage) change and develop as we progress through these stages?

3. Does modern society have an equal respect for all the stages of life? Does it recognize the diversity of these stages as a value that each healthy society needs in order to be complete? Or does society have a more fragmented view of aging and see old age as a waste, a residue of the last third of our lifespan?

4. How can faith be stimulated and nourished in old age? In other words, what can the churches do to facilitate a "theology of, and for, the aging" that both nurtures the aging and continues to challenge them to grow in their spiritual, personal, and communal lives?

Chapter 21

Marriage and Non-Practicing Catholics

Florence Caffrey Bourg

When people describe themselves as non-practicing or inactive Catholics, they usually mean they were baptized in the Catholic Church, but seldom attend Catholic worship services. Beyond this, it is hard to generalize. Perhaps in their youth, they regularly participated in worship and religious education, or perhaps their contact with the institutional church ended with infant baptism. Some have positive attitudes toward Catholicism, but rarely find time to attend Mass. Some are angry at the institutional church, but do not join another religious community because Catholicism is too ingrained in their identity. Some distance themselves from the church because a painful experience has left them angry with God. For others, Catholicism is a nearly irrelevant piece of family background that evokes no strong feelings.

I begin this essay with a profile of non-practicing Catholics and their beliefs, based on studies from the behavioral sciences. Special attention is given to young adults of marrying age. Next, I explore questions that arise when baptized but inactive Catholics request a Catholic wedding. For instance, does it make sense for Catholic clergy to officiate at weddings for people who do not seem to share, or even comprehend, Catholic beliefs and traditions concerning marriage? How can we reconcile (1) Catholicism's premise that all people have a natural right to marry, (2) the premise that sacramental marriage be celebrated only when a couple "intends what the church intends" by marriage, and (3) the premise of church law that "a valid marriage contract cannot exist between baptized persons without its being by that very fact a sacrament"? How intense does a person's faith need to be in order for that person to participate in a sacramental marriage?

In responding to these questions, I argue that the leap of faith entailed when today's young adults marry must be taken seriously; meanwhile, the church community's responsibility to nurture those with immature faith must also be taken seriously. I envision and propose a future Catholic Church that *maintains and enriches its sense of sacramental marriage, but reconsiders current emphasis on juridical structures* as a means to affirm its convictions about marriage as sacrament. The proposed strategies aim to resolve *theoretical* quandaries concerning baptized-but-inactive Catholics *and* serve as a *practical* means to bring inactive Catholics into a renewed relationship with the church community.

How Many Non-Practicing Catholics Are There?

It is difficult to ascertain an exact percentage, since the criteria of sociological surveys which determine religious affiliation differ[1] and involvement with institutional Catholicism often fluctuates over a lifetime. One typical pattern (mirrored in other religious communities) is for people to drift away from their church during adolescence and early adulthood, and then return when they wish to arrange a wedding. Some drop out again after the wedding, and then reaffiliate when they have children old enough for religious instruction.[2] Other common scenarios occur when civilly divorced Catholics are alienated by their church's annulment process,[3] or when marginal Catholics marry non-Catholics and then decrease their religious activity or become active in their spouse's religious community.[4]

A respected 1998 University of Chicago survey found 37 percent of American Catholics rated themselves "strong" Catholics, and 29 percent attended Mass weekly. A 1970s version of the survey found 48 percent attending Mass weekly and 46 percent rating themselves "strong" Catholics.[5] Recent studies reveal many self-identified Catholics think one can be a "good" Catholic without going to Mass.[6] Thus, while Mass attendance has declined in recent decades, the majority of those raised Catholic still consider themselves Catholic as adults, even if contact with the institutional church is limited. Mass attendance rates do not tell us everything about religious behavior; this will become evident as we further examine beliefs and practices of inactive Catholics.

Are Catholics of "marrying age" less active in the church community than the Catholic population overall? Typically, yes. In *Young Adult Catholics,* Dean Hoge and associates distill results of a 1997 survey of 848 persons who were raised Catholic and confirmed as teenagers.[7] In this sample, evenly divided between Latinos and non-Latinos and between those aged twenty to twenty-nine and thirty to thirty-nine, 59 percent of non-Latinos and 62 percent of Latinos had been inactive in church life (that is, attending Mass fewer than twelve times a year) at some point in their lives, beginning at an average age of twenty. At the time of the survey, 45 percent of previously inactive Latinos and 48 percent of non-Latinos had become active again, beginning at an average age of twenty-five.[8] Only 11 percent of non-Latinos and 9 percent of Latinos said they were no longer Catholic.[9] Seventeen percent of Latinos and 15 percent of non-Latinos were categorized as "non-attending Catholics," for they identified as Catholic but attended Mass less than six times per year (including holidays, weddings, and funerals). "Occasional attendees," those attending once monthly, or at least six times per year, represented 22 percent of non-Latinos and 24 percent of Latinos. Almost half of each group (49 percent of Latinos/48 percent of non-Latinos) reported attending Mass two or three times per month or more. However, only a small percentage of the total sample (9 percent of Latinos/8 percent of non-Latinos) were "parish-involved" Catholics, meaning that they attend Mass weekly *and* have been involved in activities such as a scripture study group, choir, or parish council in the past six months.[10] It appears the majority of younger Catholic adults, particularly in their early twenties, are not closely connected with parish life. Yet if we concentrate on Catholics of "marrying age," the picture looks somewhat brighter. Most who drop out return around age twenty-five — at or before the current age of first marriage in the U.S., which averages twenty-seven for men and twenty-five for women.[11] If 48–49 percent of Hoge's sample (including those under twenty-five) attend Mass twice a month or more, and 29 percent of the overall Catholic population are weekly attendees, then perhaps Catholics of marrying age are not drastically less religious than Catholics generally.[12]

It is reasonable to presume that the more frequently one attends Mass, the more likely one will be to seek a Catholic wedding. Of course, there will be exceptions — regular Catholic churchgoers who marry without canonical form,[13] and persons who almost never attend Mass but still want a Catholic wedding. How many Catholics have their marriages witnessed by the Catholic Church? Sociologist James Davidson reports that according to the 1960 U.S. *Official Catholic Directory,* there were 303,735 canonically valid marriages the prior year. The *OCD* reports 293,434 such marriages in 1995, despite an increase of about 17 million U.S. Catholics.[14] The overall U.S. marriage rate declined during this period, but the decline in officially sanctioned marriages among Catholics was disproportionately greater, indicating that many had bypassed their church's official procedures in conducting their weddings. What could their reasons be? Some people are so disconnected from their Catholic roots that they never seriously consider a Catholic wedding. Others opt out more deliberately, perhaps because their intended spouse is not Catholic,[15] or because a prior marriage precludes a Catholic wedding.[16]

What Do Non-Practicing Catholics Believe?

Surely there is such a thing as a baptized nonbeliever. However, it is important to clarify that many non-practicing Catholics attest to belief in God; indeed, their beliefs and practices may resemble those of more active Catholics. Those who are angry at the institutional church — for example, some divorcees who remarry without an annulment — may have a lively faith, perhaps deeper and more mature because it has been tested by painful experiences. Often they desire to be more active in Catholic worship or leadership roles, but do not feel welcome or comfortable participating.[17] Similar cases exist among Catholics who marry Christians of other denominations; some couples would rather worship together at a Protestant service (where

Catholics are usually welcome to take Communion) than at a Catholic Mass (where eucharistic sharing is generally discouraged).[18]

Hoge and associates found many young adults who could be called non-practicing believers:

> Cessation of church attendance was seldom due to doctrinal problems or religious doubts; more commonly it was a by-product of changes in these people's lives. . . . A common pattern was that when they left home for college or work, they also stopped churchgoing. . . . But the most frequent reasons given for stopping church attendance were vague and inarticulate, and we grouped them in the category "too busy, lack of interest, or lazy."[19]

Among Latinos, 70–73 percent (respectively) of those whose Mass attendance (fewer than twelve times a year) placed them in occasional and non-attending categories had high scores on a "traditional doctrine" scale measuring belief in Catholic teachings about Christ's divinity, the Eucharist, and life after death. This was *higher* than for parish-involved Latinos, of whom 69 percent had high traditional doctrine scores. Among non-Latinos, 65 percent of occasional churchgoers and 56 percent of non-attendees scored high on the traditional doctrine scale, compared to 79 percent of parish-involved Catholics.[20] Scripture reading among those with tenuous links to a parish was notable.[21] Almost everyone prayed: 99 percent of Latinos and 96 percent of non-Latinos.[22] How often do marginal Catholics pray? Among occasional churchgoers, 39 percent of non-Latinos and 52 percent of Latinos reported praying daily. For the non-attending category, 28 percent of each group prayed daily.[23]

What explains the phenomenon of Catholics who attend Mass less than once a month, but still read the Bible, pray regularly, and/or espouse (at least some) core doctrines? Part of the explanation is probably a combination of hectic schedules[24] and procrastination. Perhaps these Catholics figure God won't be upset at them for sleeping in on Sunday morning, so long as they pray regularly, affirm the faith they were taught as children, and try to live by the Golden Rule. Part of the explanation is also that an increasing number of Americans consider themselves "spiritual but not religious."[25] This approach to life seems to mean:

> I would like to have some kind of fulfilling experience in my life, but I do not want to be constricted by the demands of an institutional religion. Being spiritual is to be uplifted by the spectacular awe felt at watching a sunset over the Gulf of Mexico, while being religious is sitting on a pew listening to some dreary moralizer preaching about sin to a bored congregation. Spiritual means freedom and exaltation. Religion means rules, rote rituals, and, well, religion. Spiritual is large and religion is small. Being spiritual will make me feel fulfilled but

being religious will make me feel guilty. Being spiritual is good but being religious is, if not bad, at least second best.[26]

A solid majority in Hoge's survey considered themselves "spiritual" persons.[27] "Spiritual but marginally religious" Catholics may prefer spiritual expressions that are private and make minimal demands on them; nevertheless, they may seek a Catholic wedding ritual to accentuate the solemnity of a turning point in their lives. A recent review of Belgian marriage preparation programs tallied reasons that 571 individuals sought a Catholic wedding.[28] Recalling that church attendance rates among European Catholics are lower than among Americans, it is reasonable to presume motives cited for seeking a Catholic wedding would resemble those of inactive U.S. Catholics.[29] Respondents could list multiple motives; the most prevalent were:

- I married in the church because there is something special about a church wedding. (91 percent)
- By marrying in the church the people present see that you promise fidelity to one another. (86 percent)
- I married in the church so that God could witness my promise of fidelity. (81 percent)
- I married in the church because I want my children to grow up Christian. (81 percent)
- I married in the church to ask God's blessing on my marriage. (76 percent)
- I married in the church because it makes you feel more bound to each other. (74 percent)
- For me as a Christian, it goes without saying that one marries in the church. (71 percent)

Researchers proposed motives that more distinctively reflect contemporary Catholic theology of marriage as sacrament.[30] These were cited by about half the newlyweds:

- I married in the church because marriage is a symbol of the covenant between God and people. (59 percent)
- I married in the church to show that as a married person I am linked to the community of faith. (55 percent)
- I married in the church in order to experience the nearness of God when loving each other. (54 percent)
- By marrying in the church you show that the life of Jesus is important to your marriage. (51 percent)
- I married in the church because I experience that our feelings for each other have something to do with the divine. (47 percent)

Newlyweds were asked which topics they desired to discuss during marriage preparation. Most important were texts and music for the wedding, chosen by 93 percent. "Sacramental meaning of marriage" was cited by 75 percent and "Christian formation of children in the home" by 73 percent. Other topics pertaining to ongoing faith development in marriage were less enticing.[31]

This study reveals a pattern: "spiritual but not religious" Catholic newlyweds eagerly invite God to their weddings, but have a harder time envisioning God as part of their ongoing marriage, and an even harder time envisioning a relationship with a church community. We must give due respect to faith convictions that led these relatively inactive Catholics to seek a church wedding; peer and parental expectations were seldom cited as motives.[32] They could have skipped the Catholic ritual, or skipped marriage altogether, but didn't. They asked God to witness and bless their promises of fidelity, and feel "more bound" for having done so. They see communal dimensions in religious marriage; namely, public recognition of their vows of fidelity and expression of their desire to raise a future generation of Christians.[33] If we consider connections between concepts of "fidelity" and "faith," and between "God's blessing" and "grace," then these couples echo, albeit incompletely, key components of Catholic marriage theology. There is some disconnect between their understanding of marriage and current Catholic teaching on marriage as sacrament, but less than pessimists might expect.

Pieper's report illustrates typical differences between younger and older Catholics. "Catholics raised and catechized prior to Vatican II [1962–65] would have formed a discernibly 'Catholic' viewpoint on matters of sexuality and marriage, not necessarily because theological arguments for such doctrines were clearly apprehended, but because their souls had been soaked in a Church that dyed them a different color from their non-Catholic friends."[34] Older generations are likely to have become alienated by bad experiences with a priest or nun, or by Catholic policies and doctrines; in many cases, the experiences, policies, and doctrines concerned sex and marriage. Catholics of marrying age today are more culturally assimilated, and their religious education had far less distinctively Catholic/Christian content than that of their parents and grandparents.[35] Because Catholicism has far less emotional sway over them, and because of nondescript catechesis, many have only a vague sense of Catholic doctrine on sex and marriage and do not worry much whether their marital and sexual behavior will undermine relationships with their church or with God. This cohort can go their own way without a strong sense of rebellion, loss or guilt, or a sense of resentment toward the church.[36]

Standing in Another Person's Shoes

In my theology of marriage course, I ask students to imagine themselves as baptized/inactive Catholics who have arrived at a church office to ask about wedding arrangements, *or* as a Catholic priest who fields their request. The exercise allows everyone to "stand in another person's shoes" and examine the issue from multiple viewpoints.

The first students to talk are usually those playing the role of engaged couples. They desire welcoming and forgiving ministers who will "not judge" people whose romantic relationships and religiosity haven't conformed to ideal standards. From their perspective, the key Christian values at stake are hospitality toward strangers and, if the situation warrants it, mercy toward sinners. They may not know much about theology or the Bible, but they recall the biblical phrase "God is love" and Jesus' greatest commandment, to "love one another." This love is what engaged couples, whatever their level of church affiliation, want to celebrate and ask God to bless. Moreover, they insist, Jesus had a reputation for welcoming the outcast and forgiving sinners; a church claiming to follow Jesus' example shouldn't hassle or reject people who request a blessing on their wedding day.

To understand the priest's perspective, one must know basic Catholic teaching on marriage.[37] Catholicism presumes humans have a right to marry, for we are social creatures by God's design. Catholicism considers *Christian* marriage a *sacrament:* in its simplest description, a visible sign of God's invisible grace. Several Old Testament texts compare God's covenant with the Chosen People to marriage, Ephesians 5 compares marital love to Christ's relationship with the church, and the book of Revelation has similar imagery. Meanwhile, several New Testament texts convey Jesus' strong stance against divorce. Protestant, Orthodox, and Catholic scholars have long debated how to interpret these scripture passages. For now, official Catholic interpretation is that valid, consummated Christian marriage is a sacramental sign of God's grace and Christ's love for the church and cannot be dissolved except by death. What qualifies as a valid Christian marriage? If both spouses were baptized (in any Christian church) they are presumed Christians and their marriage is presumed sacramental. If vows were properly witnessed, the marriage is presumed valid; for Catholics, "properly witnessed" means according to canonical form. Church law states, "a valid marriage contract cannot exist between baptized persons without its being by that very fact a sacrament" (Canon 1055.2). Roman Catholicism considers spouses ministers of marriage through their consent. For valid administration of any sacrament, ministers must "intend what the church intends" by that sacrament; likewise those who aren't ministers ("recipients") must have "faith" and "intend what the church intends" to receive (or participate in) that sacrament.[38] When two baptized persons marry, Roman Catholicism considers each spouse a minister *and* recipient of a sacrament; their intention, expressed in their vows, must include fidelity (that is, unity, exclusivity), indissolubility, and openness to children. The key Christian values at stake are permanent unity in marriage and confidence that when we pray for God's grace through sacramental rituals, God enables us to live as signs of

God's own love. Church policies are also meant to provide orderliness in community life, so everyone knows who's married and who isn't.[39]

It isn't hard to appreciate the priest's quandary. People have a right to marry, but is "intending what the church intends" possible for this couple?[40] The priest suspects this couple, accustomed to a spiritual life that places few demands on them, is now requesting a marriage that will ask more from them than they're bargaining for. They may know Catholicism calls marriage a sacrament, but for them this means simply that weddings are religious rituals. If their religious education was especially good, they may have heard that the sacrament endures beyond the wedding, and that sacramental marriage reflects Jesus' self-giving love for the church. These seem like worthy goals (not metaphysical necessities) to them, for today's young adults often come from families scarred by divorce or abuse. Most think the primary purpose of marriage is to bond with a soul-mate.[41] They may not process their church's notion that their marriage will be indissoluble by any human power; it doesn't register with reality as they know it. Pleasantly surprised that they are considered ministers at their wedding (this coheres with their sense of religious freedom), they might be insulted to learn that if they opted for a beachfront wedding with a judge as the state's witness, the institutional church would say a sacramental, valid marriage couldn't result. They assume "validity" refers to civil law, not to church law and sacramental theory. They don't foresee that if they divorce and seek remarriage in a Catholic ritual, they will have to demonstrate to a church court that some necessary ingredient for validity was missing when vows were exchanged.

Students playing engaged couples will exclaim, shouldn't the church rejoice if non-practicing Catholics are interested in a Catholic wedding, or for that matter, in marrying at all — even in a civil service or another Christian church? When so many couples have sex, live together, and have children without any intention of a lifetime commitment, why quibble about abstract "validity"? If a marginal Catholic survives an abusive marriage and painful divorce without losing her faith, and God blesses her with a loving man who wishes to marry her, why not celebrate? Why risk alienating her by insisting on an intrusive process to test the validity of her failed marriage?

Bridging the Gap?

How do we honor an inactive Catholic's right to marry without "demeaning the dignity of the sacrament"?[42] Here are guidelines from Pope John Paul II:

- The Church can admit "improperly disposed" people to celebrate marriage, because when couples decide to commit their lives in indissoluble love and unconditional fidelity, this involves, even if not in a fully conscious way, an attitude of profound obedience to God's will, which cannot exist without God's grace. They have begun a journey toward salvation that can be nourished by preparing for and celebrating the sacrament. Given the uprightness of their intention, Christ's grace will not fail to support them.

- Engaged couples, by virtue of Baptism, share in Christ's marriage Covenant with the Church.... By their right intention, they accept God's plan for marriage and at least implicitly consent to what the Church intends when she celebrates marriage.

- Further criteria for admitting couples to ecclesial celebration of marriage based on their level of faith would involve grave risks: the risk of making unfounded and discriminatory judgments, the risk of causing doubts about validity of marriages already celebrated and about sacramentality of marriages among Christians separated from the Catholic Church, thus contradicting Catholic tradition.

- However, when in spite of all efforts, couples explicitly reject what the Church intends when marriage of baptized persons is celebrated, pastors cannot admit them to marriage.

- Evangelization and catechesis before and after marriage, affected by the whole Christian community, are urgently needed so that everyone who marries celebrates the sacrament validly *and* fruitfully.[43]

Some Catholic commentators insist that adults, in order to minister and participate in sacramental marriage, must have faith that is somehow explicit and connected with Christian tradition. Michael Lawler states,

> Those who marry without active Christian faith, be they ever so baptized, marry also without Christian sacrament.... Surely a valid Christian sacrament, something more than a "religious marriage," must have some explicit reference to that *more*.... The key that opens the door to such covenantal and sacramental meanings is not just the intention of the spouses to marry, their intention to "fidelity, indissolubility, and openness to children," but rather their intention informed by their Christian faith to be rooted in, to represent, and to pass their marriage through Christ and his Church.[44]

Similarly, Ladislas Örsy writes, "Just how intense does someone's faith need to be in order to bring him the capacity to give and receive the sacrament? Further, how far should his beliefs extend? As for intensity, a precise answer is virtually impossible.... Beliefs should certainly extend to the principal mysteries of the Christian tradition, such as the Trinity and the Incarnation, resurrection and eternal life, and so forth."[45] Lawler says people lacking active, explicit faith can marry validly, with or without canonical form (they aren't merely cohabiting) but their marriages aren't sacramental.[46] Official recognition of valid, non-sacramental marriage would require revision of church law; Lawler and Örsy think Canon 1055.2 should speak of "Christian believers" rather than "baptized persons."

Other Catholic commentators consider current guidelines sufficiently nuanced, if we distinguish between minimal validity and ideal fruitfulness of
sacramental marriage.[47] Citing Karl Rahner, Susan Wood says we must pay
due respect to "implicit" Christian faith. Consenting to indissolubility, fidelity, and openness to children requires open-ended faith. "This ultimate
kind of promise and love cannot be explained apart from a transcendence
that is oriented to God."[48] Implicit faith is different from lack of faith, expressed by *explicit denial* of what the church intends when marriage of
baptized persons is celebrated.[49] Rahner believes the fullness of sacramental
expression occurs when encounters with God in ordinary life (the "liturgy of
the world") are explicitly linked to revelation in Christ and brought into relationship with his church; the official sacraments serve this purpose. Yet the
entire continuum of implicit and explicit human encounter with God, in visible signs throughout our lives, has a sacramental nature.[50] Rahner's thought
relies on scripture, which says love of neighbor is our way to love God
(Matt. 25:31–46; 1 John 4:20–21). Christianity's name for this love, charity (Latin: *caritas*) is called the greatest virtue.[51] Robert Barry, a theologian
of the age cohort surveyed by Hoge and Pieper, writes,

> Even marriages entered into by Generation X couples who do not
> show evidence of strong faith life are sacramental, not merely due to
> a technicality, but due to actual, if perhaps weak, faith present at least
> implicitly in spouses who consent to marry. Even if the couple be-
> longs to a generation marked by a widespread deficit of well-formed
> explicit faith [due largely to weak religious education in decades fol-
> lowing Vatican II] the substance of that faith they were baptized into
> does take an explicit form in the act of marriage. The vows express
> the couple's explicit intention of mutual and unconditional love; they
> consciously and explicitly enter into a covenant that provides them the
> daily opportunity to perform acts of true *caritas*. The vows of the wed-
> ding are signs, not just of the seeds of some future possible sacrament,
> but rather of the tender sprout of a true and active sacrament, in fact a
> sacrament that serves as the best hope for "indifferent" Generation X
> Catholics growing in an active and living faith.[52]

The consolation prize offered by Lawler and Örsy — that baptized Catholics without explicit, active faith could be recognized as marrying validly —
arises from concerns Barry calls "noble" and "seemingly obvious." But does
it give due regard to the ancient Catholic premise that valid ministration of
the church's sacraments does not require holiness and perfection of each individual minister? Does it appreciate the enormous leap of faith entailed when
today's young adults marry? For a generation disproportionately raised in
broken homes, their souls soaked in the cultural message that sex and procreation without lifetime commitment are perfectly acceptable, marrying is
an act of transcendent faith. When spouses sincerely consent to faithful,
lifelong, procreative marriage, especially in a Catholic ritual, they uphold

a countercultural sign of the love Christ's church stands for — even if they, as individuals, cannot maintain that countercultural witness for a lifetime. Anyhow, says Barry, because "any notion of the Church as an overbearing presence, standing in judgment about validity or non-validity of one's marriage, is utterly absent from consciences of the vast majority of Generation X Catholic couples ... advocates for the Church's recognition of valid but non-sacramental marriage will have a very small audience among Generation X Catholics."[53]

Each of these authors has part of the answer to our quandary. Can we use their shared wisdom to envision a church wherein the sacramentality of marriage is attested to ritually, liturgically, publicly by married couples and by the ecclesial community, but *not* in a juridical fashion? Absent a juridical annulment system with the purpose of identifying particular marriages as invalid and non-sacramental, this discussion would have a different focus, and probably more consensus. All agree Christian marriage can serve as a visible sign of God's grace, a sacrament. All agree we need a system that accounts for those with immature faith, honors their right to marry, and supports them as they grow in faith. A sticking point is what to do when marriages fail. This concern is important, but it disproportionately steers Catholic thought and practice, draining resources that might be directed toward awakening a sense of sacramentality among marginal Catholics who marry and upholding exemplars of sacramental union for the benefit of the larger community. Yes, communities need some way to determine who is and isn't married. The church's structures of canonical form, dispensations, annulments, etc., were originally intended to meet that need. In practice, they don't do so today. Many Catholics disregard canonical form, and many more ignore the annulment process, which is confidential anyway. The annulment process itself has alienated countless people from the church.[54] If all Catholic divorcees who remarried sought annulments, church courts couldn't handle the caseload.

Raising concern that Catholicism's current juridical structures surrounding marriage have outlived their usefulness *doesn't* mean denying the tradition's rich sense of sacramental marriage (as Orthodox Christianity demonstrates). Vows for Catholic weddings should maintain their focus on fidelity, lifelong permanence, procreativity, and marriage as a sign of God's grace and Christ's love for the church. Remote, proximate, and immediate preparation for marriage and follow-up care for married couples should do likewise. Determinations of who is married to whom can safely be left to the jurisdiction of civil courts, as in the earliest centuries of Christianity. Still, for the sake of manifesting Christian ideals unambiguously, limits could be set on the number of weddings the church would witness for an individual (in Orthodox Christianity, the limit is three). Imagine if the attention and resources now devoted to identifying individuals or categories of people as invalidly married were redirected toward *positively* cultivating sacramental marriage and celebrating it wherever it is manifested. Couples could visit catechism classes to share how marriage has enriched their faith. Teens could create essays and videos profiling couples who are models of Christ's love. There could be better support for sponsor couples assisting engaged couples and newlyweds. Rituals could be developed for renewing marriage promises (like baptismal promises) during Mass, perhaps on Vocation Sunday. Any in the congregation who wished to renew the sacramentality of their marriage could do so — there would be no checking for documentation of validity. Liturgists might compile scriptures and hymns especially appropriate for people celebrating a second marriage after failure of their first marriage.[55] Tribunal staff could be reassigned to solicit testimonials about married couples who have been exemplars of Christ's love for their acquaintances and to devise strategies for celebrating these testimonials in parishes and surrounding communities.

My proposal that the church refrain from making juridical statements about "who is married to whom" would require revision of church law; this could be long in coming. In the meantime, aforementioned strategies for cultivating sacramental marriage can be initiated. If successful, such initiatives might lay the groundwork for a future church that no longer relies on juridical structures to affirm its convictions about Christian marriage as sacrament. Such a church might be a place inactive Catholics would like to call home.

Questions for Discussion

1. Try the role-play exercise mentioned above, or interview a Catholic minister and an inactive Catholic. Do concerns arise that are not mentioned in this chapter?

2. What risks are entailed in Catholicism's current teaching and practice concerning inactive Catholics and marriage? What risks might there be if Catholicism revised its teaching and practice?

3. Brainstorm for strategies that might help cultivate a sense of sacramental marriage among Catholics. Would these be meaningful for today's Catholics of marrying age?

4. Are the issues raised in this chapter relevant to people who aren't Catholic? Explain.

Chapter 22

Interchurch Marriages

Theological and Pastoral Reflections

Michael G. Lawler

For the past thirty years I have taught a course on the theology of marriage at a Catholic university.[1] As a result, I have been called upon regularly to give advice to young couples planning to marry, some 35 percent of them these days in the United States of two different Christian denominations. Like all young people in the culture of divorce in which Americans now live, they have questions about commitment, lifelong marriage, divorce, and children. If they are of two different denominations, they also have particular questions about the interchurch marriage they are planning, for they have heard that heterogamous marriages are less stable than homogamous marriages.[2] Two approached me last semester, I shall call them Sarah, who claimed to be a Catholic, and Philip, who was a Presbyterian. What follows is a brief resume of our conversations.

Theological Considerations

An important first item is how to talk about their marriage. At our first meeting Sarah and Philip used a traditional term, "mixed marriage." In 1917, the Catholic Church's *Code of Canon Law* proscribed mixed marriages. "The church everywhere most severely prohibits the marriage between two baptized persons, one of whom is a Catholic, the other of whom belongs to a heretical or schismatic sect" (Canon 1060). No one in 1917 could be in much doubt: in the eyes of the Catholic Church, and many other churches, a mixed marriage was something evil and to be avoided. In 1983, however, the *Code* was specifically revised in the matter of "mixed marriages." It now reads: "Without the express permission of the competent authority, marriage is prohibited between two baptized persons, one of whom was baptized in the Catholic Church . . . the other of whom belongs to a Church or ecclesial communion not in full communion with the Catholic church" (Canon 1124). The softening of the language was obvious to Sarah and Philip, especially the language referring to Philip. No longer is he described negatively as a heretic or schismatic; he is now described positively as a Christian of another church. This softening of the language furthers the matter of terminology.

Several terms are used to describe religiously heterogamous marriages. The broadest are "interreligious marriage," which emphasizes the different religions involved, and "interfaith marriage," which emphasizes the different belief systems involved. I believe that both terms are not specific enough to describe the marriage of a Christian married to another Christian of a different denomination and are best reserved for the marriage between a Christian and someone of another religion. The *Code*'s description of Philip as a Christian belonging to another church points toward a term that has become common, namely, "interchurch marriage." This term describes the marriage between spouses from two Christian denominations, in which each spouse participates in her or his own church and, to some degree, in the spouse's church, and in which both spouses take an active part in the religious education of their children.[3] This definition has the disadvantage that it embraces only a small percentage of interchurch couples, those at the high end of the religiosity spectrum,[4] but it has the advantage of being the term coming into common usage. "Interchurch marriage" is the term I will use throughout this essay. I will use it in its broadest sense, however, to embrace every marriage in which the spouses belong, however loosely, to two different Christian churches or denominations.

When I explained to Sarah and Philip the *Code*'s abandonment of the term "mixed marriage," they asked what caused such a sea change. The answer to this question is the answer also to another question: What do a Catholic woman and a Presbyterian man have in common that might provide a good basis for a Christian married life together? The answer to both questions is their Christian baptism. Baptism is no longer looked upon as an exclusively confessional matter in the divided Christian churches. No one is baptized exclusively into the Catholic Church or the Presbyterian Church; one is baptized into the one, holy, catholic (universal), and apostolic church of Jesus Christ. In spite of intense pressure to repeat the teaching of Pope Pius XII that this church of Christ is identical with the Roman Catholic Church, the Second Vatican Council in 1964 refused to accept that identity and taught instead that the church of Christ "*subsists* in the Catholic Church."[5] The church established by Christ, that is, is imperfectly embodied in but is not identical with the Catholic Church; it is also imperfectly embodied in but is not identical with the Presbyterian Church or any other Protestant Church. While each and every Christian is incorporated into and nurtured in the church of Christ through faith and baptism in a specific Christian denomination, baptism is never to be thought of as incorporating them into *only* that denomination. Though, in ecumenical theology, each local church or denomination is wholly church, none of them is the whole church.

Today all the major Christian denominations accept that those who believe in Christ and have been properly baptized are brought into a certain union with the Catholic Church, and with the Presbyterian Church, and so on. They accept baptism in one another's churches as incorporation into

the one, universal church of Christ, and hence they do not rebaptize anyone who changes religious affiliation from one Christian denomination to
another. The degree of communion between believers of different denominations may not be perfectly clear in any given case, any more than the degree
of communion within any given denomination is clear, but it is certain, and
has been recently reaffirmed by Pope John Paul II. "All those justified by
faith through baptism are incorporated into Christ. They therefore have a
right to be honored by the title of Christian, and are properly regarded as
brothers and sisters in the Lord by the sons and daughters of the Catholic Church."[6] No longer does the Catholic Church look on Presbyterian
Philip as a heretic or schismatic; he is a Christian and a brother. There
is a foundational Christian union in the Lord between Sarah and Philip
that results from their shared baptism and their shared Christian faith. This
foundational communion shared in the Christian churches through baptism
is one reason the Catholic Church has radically mitigated its language about
"mixed marriages." One mutual resolution Sarah and Philip should make is
not to permit their Christian, faith-filled, and baptismal unity to be obscured
by less foundational confessional divisions.

The union in Christ between Sarah and Philip through their shared faith
in and baptism into Christ, the Christian bond between them if you like,
is further solidified by three other bonds. Their mutual love unites them
in an interpersonal bond of friendship; their wedding unites them publicly
and legally in the bond of marriage; their celebration of their marriage in
the Lord unites them in a religious bond of sacrament. Their marriage in
very deed becomes, to paraphrase the Second Vatican Council, "an intimate
partnership of love, life, and religion,"[7] which establishes them in a union so
close that the Bible describes it as "two in one body" (Gen. 2:20). I choose to
describe their union as a *coupled-We,* to intimate the bonds that bind Sarah
and Philip together. So close is their communion of love, life, and religious
faith that the Catholic Church has established their marital communion as
the sacrament or symbol of the steadfast communion between Christ and his
church. The unity Sarah and Philip achieve in their church-blessed marriage
places them under the gospel injunction, "What God has joined together
let no one put asunder" (Matt. 19:6). It was reflection on their blessed
communion and on this gospel injunction that drove Presbyterian Philip to
raise a question. "If Sarah and I are united in baptism and marriage blessed
by both our churches," he asked, "how can those same churches separate
us for the Holy Communion of the Lord's table?"

Shared Communion

I let this section stand by itself because the question of shared communion
is *the* neuralgic question for many interchurch couples. They argue exactly
as Philip did. We are made one in Christ in faith and baptism; we are made
one body in Christ in marriage; we desire to celebrate and enhance our

unity and one-bodiness in Christ in the sacrament of communion, Holy Communion with the Lord and one another at the Lord's table; how can the churches who have celebrated our oneness turn around and say we are not and cannot be one in Holy Communion. For many interchurch couples, the inability to share communion is a serious challenge to their Christian life together and sometimes a challenge also to their marital life together. That creates a serious pastoral challenge for the churches.

There are two major Catholic documents relevant to the question, the *Code of Canon Law* (1983) and the *Directory for the Application of Principles and Norms on Ecumenism* (1993). No Christian, Protestant or Catholic, should expect any Catholic minister to go beyond the principles and norms embodied in these two foundational documents, for no Catholic minister can go beyond them and still claim to be giving a distinctively Catholic witness. Neither, however, should any Catholic, clerical or lay, impose restrictions beyond what is embodied in these two documents. The main text of canon law sounds not only prescriptive but also restrictive. "Catholic ministers may lawfully administer the sacraments to Catholic members of the Christian faithful only and, likewise, the latter may lawfully receive the sacraments only from Catholic ministers with due regard for 2, 3, and 4 of this canon" (Canon 844, 1). Due regard for Canon 844, 2, 3, and 4 requires understanding of the exceptions and conditions enunciated therein and serious interpretation of their possible application in any given case.

> Whenever necessity requires or a *genuine spiritual advantage commends* it . . . Christ's faithful for whom it is physically or morally impossible to approach a Catholic minister, may lawfully receive the sacraments of penance, Eucharist, and anointing of the sick from *non-Catholic ministers in whose churches these sacrament are valid.* (Canon 844, 2)

> Catholic ministers may lawfully administer the sacraments of penance, Eucharist, and anointing of the sick to members of the oriental churches which do not have full communion with the Catholic Church, if they *ask on their own* for the sacraments and are properly disposed. This holds also for members of other churches, which in the judgment of the Apostolic See are in the same condition as the oriental churches as far as these sacraments are concerned. (Canon 844, 3)

> If there is a danger of death or if, in the judgment of the diocesan Bishop or of the Episcopal Conference, there is *some other grave and pressing need,* Catholic ministers may lawfully administer those same sacraments to other Christians not in full communion with the Catholic Church, who cannot approach a minister of their own community and *who spontaneously ask for them,* provided that they *demonstrate the Catholic faith in respect of these sacraments* and are properly disposed. (Canon 844, 4)

The *Directory* is just as clear. "In certain circumstances, by way of exception, and under certain conditions, access to these sacraments [including
Holy Communion] may be permitted, or even *commended,* for Christians of
other churches and ecclesial communities" (n. 129). The *Directory* raises the
question of shared communion with non-Catholic Christians, thereby suggesting, *ipso facto,* that extraordinary shared communion is a possibility.
The conditions under which a Catholic minister may administer the Eucharist to a baptized, non-Catholic Christian are specified as fourfold: "the
person be unable to have recourse for the sacrament desired to a minister
of his or her own church or ecclesial community, ask for the sacrament of
his or her own initiative, manifest Catholic faith in this sacrament, and be
properly disposed" (n. 131). Catholics may ask for the sacrament of Eucharist "only from a minister in whose church these sacraments are valid
or from one who is known to be validly ordained according to the Catholic
teaching on ordination" (n. 132). All of these conditions are the ones I have
underscored at various points in the above discussion of Canon 844.

What is to be noted here is that exceptions and conditions, though carefully defined and delimited, are listed and never retracted. The problem is
that not all official Catholic interpreters interpret the exceptions and conditions in the same way. Some interpret them rigidly to the letter; others,
equally competent, interpret them more broadly. Predictably, this difference
of interpretation causes discontent, confusion, hurt, and frequently anger
among both Catholic and Protestant spouses. That anger, and the division
induced among interchurch families at the Lord's table, as the German bishops note in their document on Eucharistic Sharing (1997), can easily lead to
"serious risk to the faith life of one or both"; it can "endanger the integrity
of the bond that is created in life and faith through marriage"; it can lead
to "an indifference to the sacrament and a distancing from Sunday worship and so from the life of the Church."[8] These considerations highlight
shared communion as a specific example of what Pope John Paul II said
to interchurch couples gathered in York Cathedral in 1982: "You live in
your marriage the hopes and the difficulties of the path to Christian unity."
They highlight also the interchurch marriage as a situation requiring special
pastoral care.

Since I have introduced the German bishops' document on Eucharistic
Sharing, we can start there in our examination of how principles must be,
can be, and are interpreted. The document, as the title indicates, is focused
on the sharing of communion in interchurch marriages, and because of that
focus gets immediately to concretizing the principles of Canon 844 and the
Directory. "Families in interchurch marriages may experience '*serious (spiritual) need*' in certain situations . . . [and] in situations of pastoral need the
married partners living in interchurch marriages may be admitted to receive
communion in the Catholic Church under certain conditions."[9] Everyone
familiar with the *Code* and the *Directory* will know the provenance of that
statement.

The practical question is how is "spiritual need" to be assessed and who is to assess it? The bishops give a pastoral and obvious answer.

> Since pastorally the establishment of objective criteria for "serious (spiritual) need" is extremely difficult, ascertaining such a need can as a rule only be done by the *minister* concerned. Essentially, this must become clear in pastoral discussion. Does the couple concerned (and any children) experience being separated at the Lord's table as a pressure on their life together? Is it a hindrance to their shared belief? How does it affect them? Does it risk damaging the integrity of their communion in married life and faith?[10]

It is a good pastoral rule: a discussion between the couple and the minister on the spot, usually a priest, who might best understand their situation. There are many interchurch families who could establish their "serious (spiritual) need" in such an open pastoral discussion.

Two years earlier, in 1995, the Catholic archbishop of Brisbane issued a document entitled *Blessed and Broken: Pastoral Guidelines for Eucharistic Hospitality,* which contained a section on interchurch marriages. Noting that "the Directory of Ecumenism states that eucharistic sharing for a spouse in a mixed marriage can only be exceptional," the archbishop agrees with his German brothers that the verification of the required conditions and dispositions is best assessed in pastoral discussion. "It is sufficient for the presiding priest to establish, by means of a few simple questions, whether or not these conditions are met." Of great moment in the Brisbane document is the recognition that some interchurch couples "could well experience a serious spiritual need to receive communion each time he or she accompanies the family to a Catholic mass,"[11] and that this need can be met. Though the Roman *Directory* states that shared communion for interchurch spouses can only be exceptional, a spouse in an interchurch marriage could well experience exceptional ongoing need for shared communion. There is, in some though probably not all interchurch marriages, not only the exceptional one-time case but also the exceptional ongoing case. The ongoing spiritual need in this ongoing interchurch case, again, can be assessed in pastoral discussion between the local priest and the couple, but has to be referred to the archbishop for the authorization of exceptional, but ongoing, shared communion.

An example of a different interpretation of the foundational principles, exceptions, conditions, and circumstances is the document published jointly in 1998 by the Catholic bishops of Great Britain and Ireland under the title *One Bread One Body.* This document does not focus exclusively on interchurch marriages and the question of shared communion. As its subtitle asserts, it is a teaching document that sets forth, first, "the teaching of the Catholic Church on the mystery of the Eucharist" (n. 2) and, then, norms "to govern sharing of the sacraments between Catholics and other Christians in our countries" (n. 8).[12] I cannot deal with the first part here, since focus and space prohibit it, but it is a rich exposition of the contemporary Catholic theology of Eucharist in an ecumenical context. It should be read meditatively by everyone, Catholic and Protestant alike, who wishes to understand the Catholic approach to the Eucharist and why that approach mandates shared communion as an *exceptional,* rather than a *normal,* reality for the Catholic Church. The second part of the document, the norms on sacramental and eucharistic sharing, is of major interest to us. The bishops adopt two interesting strategies. While acknowledging the general norm that allows shared communion in exceptional circumstances "when strong desire is accompanied by shared faith, grave and pressing spiritual need, and at least an implicit desire for communion with the Catholic Church" (n. 77), they introduce a shift from the category of *need* to the category of *pain.* This enables them to point out, correctly, the brokenness of the Body of Christ, the pain that results from a broken body, and the fact that taking away the pain (in this case by the palliative of shared communion) does not necessarily achieve healing. Healing is achieved only by dealing with the underlying problem.

In the case of interchurch families, however, the *pain* of being unable to share communion is not the point. The point on which all the discussion of shared communion turns is the more radical *serious (spiritual) need* felt by interchurch spouses who already share communion in baptism, communion in marriage, and, above all, communion in the intimate partnership of life, love, and faith. Their shared communion in all these facets of life, inchoate and imperfect as it may sometimes be, creates the interspousal *need* for the shared communion of Eucharist. When unfulfilled, that need certainly causes pain, as unfulfilled hunger causes pain. But it is the need, not the pain, as it is the hunger, not the pain, that must be satisfied. It is not palliative but authentic pastoral care that is required.

The second strategy the bishops adopt is one found nowhere in the *Code,* the *Directory,* or any other Vatican document, the transposition of the exceptional *case* to the exceptional *unique occasion,* "an occasion which of its nature is unrepeatable, a 'one-off' situation which will not come again" (nn. 106, 109). Examples of such unique occasions are baptism, confirmation, first communion, ordination, and death. Though they have earlier employed the classical Catholic language about marriage, "a partnership of the whole of life (*consortium totius vitae*)," the bishops betray no understanding of what that might mean in practice in the case of committed married couples, interchurch or same-church. The Christian "partnership of the whole of life" is not about unique and occasional events; it is about the seamless whole of life.

The *consortium totius vitae* language derives from ancient Roman definitions of marriage, like the one found in Justinian's *Digesta* (23, 2, 1), which controlled every discussion of marriage in the West. "Marriage is a union of a man and a woman, and a communion of the whole of life, a participation in divine and human law." The phrase "communion of the whole of life" (*consortium totius vitae*) is ambiguous, open to two separate but not separable interpretations. It can mean as long as life lasts ("until death do us part"), and then implies that marriage is a lifelong covenant. It can mean everything that the spouses have ("all my worldly goods"), and then imply that nothing is left unshared between the spouses. Over the centuries in the West, the two meanings have been so interwoven that marriage is considered the union of a man and a woman embracing the sharing of all goods, material and spiritual, as long as life lasts.[13]

A marriage that lasts as long as life lasts is certainly a unique event in the modern world, but it is a diachronic unique event. Any couple journeying through life together can attest to the fact that marriage is an ongoing situation, much more than a one-off wedding, much, much more that a "one-off" baptism or ordination. A marriage is not a one-off wedding; it is, to repeat, a partnership of the whole of life. The "unique (one-off) occasion" confuses wedding and marriage, legal ceremony and diachronic, lifelong partnership. If married people allow it to stand unchallenged, there can be no exceptional but ongoing sharing of communion, though the German, Australian, and South African norms, which I have not yet mentioned,[14] all interpret such ongoing exception as possible because of ongoing "serious (spiritual) need." Again, discontent, confusion, hurt, and anger, can result and may possibly damage both marital and ecclesial communion.

To conclude this section, I wish to return to the four conditions under which a Catholic minister may administer communion to a baptized person: the person is unable to have recourse to a minister of his or her own church, must ask for communion on his or her own initiative, must manifest Catholic faith in the sacrament, and must be properly disposed. Since these conditions are required of all Catholics for the reception of Eucharist, it is not surprising to find them required also of all non-Catholics. The requirement of proper disposition, required of all who approach Holy Communion, needs no comment; the other three do.

The South African Directory explicates the inability to have recourse to a minister of one's own church. This inability "need not be one that exists over a period of time but could arise out of the nature of the situation in which the petitioner finds himself or herself." They offer as example "when spouses in a mixed marriage attend a eucharistic celebration together."[15] It is a good and obvious point. Again, it is not about a unique occasion, but about an exceptional but ongoing situation in which an interchurch wife and husband participate together in the Lord's Supper, have a serious need to share communion together, and cannot have recourse on that situation to his or her own minister. If all the other conditions are fulfilled, then on each and every situation, by authoritative interpretation of the norms, the non-Catholic spouse may share communion in the Catholic Church. It is worth noting that the first version of this South African Directory did not obtain Vatican approval and that Roman "suggestions" were incorporated into a revised version released in January 2000. The language of the second version is more precise, more accurately reflects the present discipline, but yields nothing on exceptional practice. What was in the original version explicitly continues to be in the new version implicitly.

This leads to the requirement that a person ask for communion on his or her own initiative. Why, we may ask, establish such a requirement? Such a requirement is necessary to respect individual conscience and, in these ecumenical times, to avoid all suspicion of proselytizing. In earlier times, it was common for some churches to *invite* all baptized Christians who shared their faith in Eucharist to share communion with them. Others suggested this approach could be taken as an invitation to the person to disobey the rules of his or her own church. When my mother, for instance, "invited" me to do the dishes, I always knew I was in trouble if I did not accept the "invitation." It is difficult to argue that I was completely free. It has become common, therefore, to replace "invite" with "welcome" to the Lord's table, as is done, for instance, in most Anglican churches worldwide today. "Welcome" does not invite anyone to go beyond the rules of his or her own church to share communion, but it does respect the consciences of those who believe they can and must go beyond those rules. The initiative is always with the person involved; there is no proselytism; all that is offered is Christian hospitality and welcome when a person has come to his or her own decision.

And what of the requirement to share Catholic faith in the sacrament? The German bishops summarize that faith briefly: "the crucified and risen Lord Jesus Christ gives himself to us in person in the eucharist as Giver and Gift in bread and wine and so builds up his Church" (n. 4). Three essential Catholic elements are contained in that summary: the connection between Eucharist and the paschal sacrifice of Christ, the real presence of Christ in Eucharist, and the connection between Eucharist and church. Any Christian who accepts those three realities in faith is manifesting Catholic faith. Christoph Cardinal Schonborn, archbishop of Vienna, has offered a short-form statement of the Catholic faith required for sharing communion in a Catholic church. "Everyone who can in good conscience say 'Amen' to the eucharistic prayer of the Catholic mass may take communion in a Catholic Church."[16] There are many Protestant Christians, and specifically many interchurch spouses, who can readily say "Amen" to that.

A final point is essential in this discussion. With respect to the require-ment of sharing Catholic faith, the South African Directory, citing without acknowledgment Pope John XXIII's instruction to the Fathers at the open-ing of the Second Vatican Council,[17] notes the "crucial distinction between the substance of the faith and the way in which it is expressed."[18] Believing in the substance of defined Catholic eucharistic *faith* is one thing; accepting the undefined Catholic *theology* which seeks to explain that faith is quite another. The British and Irish bishops employ this distinction in their own way by explaining Catholic faith in the eucharistic presence of Jesus with-out any reference to the word which was once the touchstone of Catholic explanation, "transubstantiation," a word they relegate to a footnote.

Contrary to popular unwisdom, this word was never part of Catholic *faith* about Eucharist. The Council of Trent, frequently cited as defining transubstantiation as Catholic faith, simply asserted that the change that takes place in bread and wine is "most aptly" (*aptissime*) called transubstantiation.[19] The bishops acknowledge the non-substantive nature of the word by relegating it to a brief footnote. The South African bishops insist that, when it comes to judging the substance of the faith that is present, "due cognizance must be taken of those ecumenical agreements that display the existence of a substantial agreement in faith." They offer as an example the agreement reached by the Anglican Roman Catholic International Commission (ARCIC) regarding the Eucharist and have no hesitation in stating that, "in the light of that agreement, members of the Anglican communion may be presumed to share the essentials of eucharistic faith with us [Catholics]" (n. 6.3.8).

We began this section with a quotation from the *Code of Canon Law,* noting that it "sounds prescriptive." After our journey through the *Code,* the Roman *Directory on Ecumenism,* and various authoritative interpretations of both, it now appears as much permissive as prescriptive. "The purpose of every law in the Church," asserts Father Ladislas Örsy, one of the church's most distinguished canon lawyers, "is to open the way for God's unbounded love." For that to happen, he notes, quoting Pope Paul VI, "we need not so much new legislation as a 'new attitude of mind.' "[20] That new attitude of mind, I suggest, needs to be ecumenical, it needs to realize that there are other Christians besides Catholics, that all of them are united to the Catholic Church through the bonds of baptism, and that some of them are further united to the Catholic Church through the bonds of sacramental, covenantal marriage to a Catholic.

The Catholic tradition about sacraments is that they not only signify grace but they also cause it instrumentally.[21] The aphorisms are well-known; sacraments "effect what they signify," "cause by signifying," are "efficacious signs of grace." The full and intimate communion achieved in marriage between a non-Catholic Christian and Catholic spouse, and the communion achieved directly and indirectly between them and the Catholic Church, can be signified in shared eucharistic communion. More importantly, those two interconnected communions can also be "caused," affected, enhanced, deepened, and broadened in shared communion. Sacraments, the Second Vatican Council taught, "not only presuppose faith, but by words and objects they also nourish, strengthen, and express it."[22] That they do this, and do the same with love and communion, is a frequently ignored factor in the debate over shared communion. The council taught with its usual care that "the expression [or signification] of unity generally forbids common worship. Grace to be obtained sometimes commends it."[23] The overall argument of this section, and of authentic episcopal teachers of the church, is that the serious spiritual need experienced by interchurch couples is an exceptional but ongoing "sometimes" that commends it.

Pastoral Considerations

When I explained to them that their growing communion in love had been long preceded by their baptismal communion in Christ, Sarah and Philip told me this was the first time they had ever heard that. This points to a serious problem that contemporary couples in interchurch marriages frequently have to face, namely, their ignorance of the beliefs not only of their partner's church but also of their own church. In a recent ecumenical group with pastors from six different Christian denominations, I was horrified to hear pastors admit openly they did not know much about the teachings of one another's churches. If pastors do not know what their brothers and sisters in Christ believe, how will their congregations ever know? But know Sarah and Philip, and every other interchurch couple, must if they hope ever to grow together religiously in marriage. Each must understand not only her and his own tradition but also that of the other, so they can come to understand and appreciate one another as fully as possible and respond to their children's questions about their two churches. For this to happen, both need to be educated ecumenically, not just in the few weeks preceding their wedding but also throughout their married life together. As the incidence of interchurch marriage continues to increase, the demand for this kind of religious education will increase accordingly. Mutual ignorance is not a good basis for any marriage, least of all an interchurch marriage.

It is now widely recognized that theology cannot be done in isolation from the cultural context in which it is done; a contemporary theology of interchurch marriages cannot be done without hard scientific data about interchurch marriages. To obtain this data, a national, randomized study of same-church and interchurch marriages was conducted by the Center for Marriage and Family at Creighton University in 1997. Approximately one-third of all respondents were in interchurch relationships at the time of their engagement,[24] a significant percentage. Fewer interchurch than same-church respondents reported they had any marriage preparation and, of those who had marriage preparation, fewer interchurch respondents reported it addressed religious issues related to their relationship and the raising of their children. In an earlier Center for Marriage and Family study of the impact of marriage preparation, interchurch couples, who randomly comprised 39 percent of that study population, complained that the marriage preparation offered to them minimally sought to prepare them for the challenges of a specifically interchurch marriage.[25]

Marriage preparation is a key learning moment, a natural rite of passage, in a couple's life. It can also be a key religious moment. In the culture of divorce that presently holds sway in the Western world, the churches are challenged to make interchurch couples, now a significant number of all marrying couples, a priority population. Only 24 percent of interchurch respondents who reported that religious issues were addressed in their marriage preparation reported having received specific material dealing with their different religious backgrounds. Those engaged in the marriage preparation of interchurch couples must do better to tailor their educational approach to the interchurch character of a couple's relationship. Programs should highlight religious faith and practice as an important part of marriage, as indeed it is,[26] and provide couples with strategies to deal with their religious differences. Such marriage preparation may be done best when the denominations of the two partners are both represented. The continuing and scandalous Christian problem is not that Christians of different denominations are falling in love and marrying in large numbers, but that the Christian church continues to be rent into different, sometimes unseemly competing, denominations. Only when Protestant and Catholic congregations come to understand and truly respect each other's faith and teachings will they be in a position to provide the marriage preparation interchurch couples require for their marriage to be successful.

In his 1981 letter *On the Family,* Pope John Paul II urged the Catholic Church to "promote better and more intensive programs of marriage preparation to eliminate as far as possible the difficulties many married couples find themselves in, and even more to favor the establishing and maturing of successful marriages" (n. 66). All the churches, not just the Catholic Church, are challenged to promote marriage, to prepare young people for their marital vocation, and to do all in their power to uphold the permanence of marriage. They are specifically challenged by interchurch couples to create preparation programs that make diverse Christian faith and practice an ongoing part of their marriages. That this is an important challenge for the churches is evident from the fact that the faith of parents is a critical factor in the religious education of their children. It is an even more critical factor in the religious education of interchurch children.

One other factor obliges the churches to a greater commitment to interchurch marriages. The Creighton interchurch study joined a growing list of studies demonstrating that interchurch couples are at greater risk than same-church couples for marital instability. Same-church respondents had a statistically significant lower percentage of divorce (12.7 percent) than interchurch respondents (20.3 percent). Two things, however, are to be noted here. The first is that, though the percentage of divorce was higher for interchurch than for same-church respondents, both percentages were significantly lower than the percentages commonly reported for the study's time frame, that is, approximately 40 percent.[27] Since every respondent in the study identified with a Christian denomination at the time of engagement, the sample may be more religiously oriented than the general married population. Since religious affiliation is associated with a lower risk of divorce,[28] the greater religiousness of the sample may account for the lower percentage of divorce. There is another message here for marriage preparation providers: religion makes a difference in a marriage, even when there are two different churches involved, as there are in an interchurch marriage. Religion can be a bonder in a marriage, binding the spouses together as a coupled-We; or it can be divisive, keeping the spouses apart from the joint religious activities they ought to share. Here is another place where genuinely ecumenical marriage preparation can help.

The second thing of note in the divorce statistics above is that, when a long list of other variables was taken into account, being in an interchurch marriage per se was not a major predictor of marital instability. This suggests that it is not interchurch marriage per se that puts interchurch couples at greater risk for marital instability but other factors that may accompany the interchurch status of the marriage. Three such factors were found to be major: the religious differences between interchurch couples, the limited joint religious activities they shared, and their families' approval or non-approval of their choice of spouse. If churches wish to contribute to the improvement of the declining attractiveness, quality, and stability of marriage, these findings suggest three concrete areas where they might profitably concentrate their efforts in marriage preparation and enrichment programs: the managing of religious differences, the promotion of joint religious activities, and the managing of parental influence. Religious differences and joint religious activities are areas of focus for both same-church and interchurch couples, but they are especially critical for interchurch spouses since they tend to report greater religious differences and fewer joint religious activities.

Two other findings by the Creighton study should be noted by the churches. The first is that interchurch respondents had, on average, lower religiosity scores than same-church respondents.[29] Religiosity, or level of religious attitude and practice, was assessed by a variety of factors, personal faith, personal church involvement, joint religious activities, sense of belonging to a local congregation, strength of denominational identity, religion as a strength in the marriage, emphasis on religion in raising children, commitment to Christ, and having participated in adult religious education. The *average* scores of interchurch respondents on all these items, both individually and collectively, were lower than the *average* scores of same-church respondents. I underscore *average* here to introduce an important caveat. Neither same-church nor interchurch individuals are homogeneous groups. Not all churches are alike, not all lawyers are alike, and not all interchurch or same-church individuals are alike. When respondents were divided into groups of high, medium, and low religiosity, there were interchurch individuals in the high religiosity group and same-church respondents in the low religiosity group, though only 15 percent of interchurch individuals were in the high religiosity group compared to 40 percent of same-church respondents. It is evident, nevertheless, that the pervasiveness of religiosity differences show that churches have much work to do to bind interchurch families to them.

The preceding conclusion is supported by the second item to be noted. Fewer interchurch than same-church respondents were very satisfied with the clergy with whom they came in contact. Satisfaction with clergy was related to clergy awareness of needs, sensitivity to people of other denominations, and commitment to helping interchurch couples deal with their marital and religious lives, and this suggests three areas where churches and their clergy need to examine their attitudes and behaviors. Clergy need to welcome interchurch couples when they attend church services or other activities, and they need to invite them to attend more activities than simply church services.

The family is the first and most vital cell of any society, the Christian family is the first and most vital cell of the church. The future of both society and church, in John Paul's felicitous phrase, "passes through the family."[30] It is in the family, which Chrysostom urged spouses "to make a church"[31] and Augustine called "domestic church" and "little church,"[32] that children learn to value or not to value Christ, Christ's gospel, and Christ's church. If for no other reason than the honest religious nurturing of their children, interchurch couples need to strive to understand and respect each other's faith as fully as possible. Only when they mutually understand and respect both faiths can their children consult both of them on both faiths, eliminating the divisive strategy of consulting mother on one faith and father on the other. Understanding and respecting the other spouse's faith might also ensure that nothing explicitly or implicitly derogatory about that faith will ever be said around the children. There are enough sources of potential conflict in marriage without multiplying them.

When we were talking about the children they hoped one day to have, Sarah surprised me with a sudden outburst of anger, blurting out that she would not agree to have Philip sign any document promising their children would be raised Catholics. Her father, she added, who was and still is a Lutheran, had to sign such a document when he married her Catholic mother and had been very angry at the Catholic Church, and her mother, ever since. She was astonished when I told her that neither she nor Philip would have to sign anything. When her parents were married in 1969, it was the law of the Catholic Church that such a written promise be given by the Protestant partner. It is no longer the law. In 1970, Pope Paul VI freed the non-Catholic partner of every declaration and promise concerning children born of the marriage. The Catholic partner is now required to promise *orally* "to do all in my power" to share her (his) faith with the children by having them baptized and raised as Catholics. This promise is simply an assurance given by the Catholic partner that she (he) understands her obligations; it makes explicit in a human fashion, *humano modo,* an obligation already existing by the fact that they are Catholics. Sarah retained a certain amount of anger and unease at the fact that such a promise is required, but both Pope Paul VI and Pope John Paul II have words to soothe her.

After having stated that the Catholic partner in an interchurch marriage is obligated *"as far as possible* to see to it that the children are baptized and brought up" in the Catholic faith, Paul VI added what the Catholic Church takes for granted, namely, the question of the children's faith is not a question for the Catholic partner alone. Their children's education is a responsibility of both parents, "both husband and wife are bound by that responsibility," Paul VI teaches, "and may by no means ignore it."[33] John Paul II reiterates the difficulty that arises here between interchurch couples and reaffirms the Catholic Church's modern celebration of religious freedom. This freedom could be violated, he teaches, "either by undue pressure to make the partner change his or her beliefs or by placing obstacles in the way of the free manifestation of these beliefs by religious practice."[34] John Paul here is simply repeating the Second Vatican Council's reaffirmation of an ancient Catholic teaching that "parents have the right to determine, in accordance with their own religious beliefs, the kind of religious education their children are to receive."[35]

The Catholic Church acknowledges that the education of children is the right and duty of *both* parents and is not to be reserved to one parent over the other, even if that parent happens to be a Catholic. The promise now required of a *Catholic* partner in an interchurch marriage specifies that she (he) *"will do all in my power"* to ensure that children are raised Catholic. It does not, because it cannot, guarantee that they *will in fact* be raised Catholic. Every decision about children in every marriage, including the decision about their religious upbringing, is a decision, the Catholic Church teaches, for both parents, never for the Catholic parent alone. Why then, Sarah wanted to know, did she still have to promise to do all in her power to ensure the children were raised Catholic? So that both she and Philip would be fully conscious of her obligations as a Catholic, not so that Philip would be required to surrender his parental rights.

There is another group of people to be considered in the project of an interchurch marriage, namely, the parents of the prospective bride and groom. All of us derive from a family of origin and all of us are marked by that family, no matter how free and individual we believe we are. I cannot tell you how often I have heard the comment, "My parents would never approve of me marrying a Catholic or a Presbyterian or a whatever." This perceived tension between parents and an adult child frequently is one more source of stress in premarital decisions, and marriage, interchurch or not. Something must be done to reduce that stress before it becomes intolerable. Parents may have concerns about the differences between churches and, therefore, also between their child and the one she or he is marrying. They may fear loss of faith through change of religious affiliation or indifference. They may worry about where the wedding will take place, what church the couple will attend, what faith their grandchildren will be reared in. They may cause great irritation, both before and after the wedding, by trying to convert the spouse not of their denomination. They need a good talking with to dispel their doubts, their fears, their worries, their tensions.

Since they do not always keep up with change, parents frequently need to have explained to them the change in attitudes between the Christian churches. They need to have explained to them the importance of their different faiths to the prospective spouses and that each not only loves the other but also respects the faith of the other. They need to know their children have already discussed the things that are bothering them, have come to mutually acceptable and respectful decisions about them, and want their parents to join them and support them in the project that is their marriage. Sarah told me that, when she told her parents she was going to marry Philip, they responded that she was facing a difficult task but they would do everything they could to be supportive. Philip, on the other hand, told me his father was very unhappy he was planning to marry a Catholic. Their very different levels of tension provided me with concrete evidence of the importance of embracing families of origin into the process of choosing an interchurch partner.

If there is one thing I have learned over the years of working with couples, it is that a stable and successful marriage takes time. It takes time for two individuals to come to know, appreciate, and respect one another; it takes time for them to come to value one another; it takes time for them to attain mutual love and communion; it takes time for them to become one body. If I was given the opportunity to offer one piece of advice to an interchurch, or any other, couple, it would be this: give your marriage time. I once asked a Missouri Synod Lutheran woman, who had been married to a Catholic for thirty-eight years, what was the most rewarding or most difficult time in her marriage. Her reply surprised me: "It depends what stage of marriage you are talking about." She explained that in the beginning of their marriage, she and her husband had wasted endless hours trying to convert one another, then had gradually come to understand and respect one another's commitment to religion, and had finally come to love one another precisely as *Lutheran* and *Catholic*. "I grew to understand," she said, "that loving John meant loving a Catholic." There is a wise message for all of us, and perhaps also for all of our churches, in that comment.

I have already cited Pope John Paul's 1982 comment to interchurch couples in York cathedral: "You live in your marriages the hopes and the difficulties of the path to Christian unity." His comment can stand as an overall summary of everything that can currently be said about interchurch marriages. Marriage is always a time of hope and difficulty, a time of gift and challenge, a time when families lovingly unite or angrily divide. John Paul suggests that interchurch marriages mirror the hopes and the difficulties of the churches as they come to know, appreciate, and respect one another as Catholic, as Presbyterian, as Baptist. I agree they do that and suggest they also do more. Interchurch couples who take the time required to know, appreciate, love, and respect one another, and thus become one "coupled-We," not only mirror the paths of the churches as they too seek to become one but they also mark out the path by which the churches can reach their goal. The path is not an easy one, for it is not a path that leads necessarily to the conversion of one spouse to the denomination of the other, though about

43 percent of spouses in the Creighton study did change religious affiliation to become same-church. Rather, it is a path that leads to mutual respect, mutual appreciation, mutual trust, mutual love, and mutual unity in diversity. That is the only path that will lead to the fulfillment of Jesus' great prayer for humankind: "That they may all be one" (John 17:21). Oneness for all couples, all churches, and all nations is a challenging goal; it is a goal that takes time. It is also a goal toward which many interchurch couples are now mapping out the way. "He, who has ears to hear, let him hear" (Matt. 11:15; Mark 4:9; Luke 8:8).

Questions for Discussion

1. Do you see any real difference between the terms "mixed marriage" and "interchurch marriage"? In the current context of mutual ecumenical respect, which do you think is preferable? Why?

2. What do you think of Philip's argument? "If Sarah and I are united in baptism and marriage blessed by both our churches, how can those same churches separate us for the Holy Communion of the lord's table?" Would you be scandalized in any way if Christian churches that shared the same faith in the presence of Jesus in Holy Communion also shared communion at the Lord's Table?

3. The Catholic Church has established four conditions for the sharing of Holy Communion with other Christians: the person is unable to have recourse to a minister of his or her own church, must ask for communion on his or her own initiative, must manifest Catholic faith in the sacrament, and must be properly disposed. How do you understand and evaluate these conditions?

4. It is well established by research that interchurch marriages have a greater risk of instability than same-church marriages. If this is true, what should the churches do about interchurch marriages?

5. Do you believe that marriage preparation is a key learning moment in a couple's life? If it is, how should the couple approach it, and how should the churches approach it, especially in the case of interchurch marriage?

Chapter 23

Interreligious Marriage

A Personal Reflection

R. R. Reno

On a Saturday morning in January, the bright Midwestern winter light falls across my daughter's brown hair, pulled back in a tight, neat bun. Rachel is surrounded by familiar faces. Larry Raful is at her left, Marcel Kahn to her right, and Emil Berkovits is floating behind her with a smile that would make a father proud. My wife, my mother-in-law, and my daughter's great-grandmother are next to Rachel, just to her right. Their faces are strangely unfocused, as if bewitched by the music of Rachel's voice, looking at nothing in particular in the space between Rachel's focused eyes and the Torah scroll she is reading. Rachel's face is serene with the isolation of concentrated attention.

The moment is elongated in my mind as I watch from the second pew. Everyone seems frozen in place, black and white and almost faceless, fading, while at the center of the scene, the center of the synagogue, and, as the sun's rays drape and illumine her, seemingly the center of the cosmos, Rachel is vibrant with color. Her shoulders are covered with a shimmering cloth. She has a silver pointer the size of a large pen in her hand and she is following the verses as she chants them in Hebrew, tracing out the figures of musical ornament that she has learned for singing this portion of the scriptures. My parents are behind me, along with sisters and brother, nieces and nephews, and row after row of friends who fill the sanctuary. My son is holding my hand. His face is a mixture of adulation and encouragement like a small boy at the baseball stadium who turns his heart to his favorite pitcher in his wind-up. I can hear no children whispering, no bodies shifting in the pews. My daughter's voice is omnipotent in my consciousness, neither quiet nor loud but all-penetrating. The words echo with eternity.

We are all sitting, as is the custom for seven segments of the Torah recited during worship on the Sabbath. But now we stand. *Vay'daber elohim et kol-had'varim ha'eleh leimor.* I do not know Hebrew. It is music to me, music of words saturated with the ages. It is Rachel's bat mitzvah, and she has been practicing this recitation at home, so I know that we are standing because we have come to Exodus 20:1: "Then God spoke all these words." The words God spoke and that my daughter will speak again are the Ten Commandments. We stand to receive them as they were received in the wilderness of Sinai and as they have been received by countless generations.

I am standing and receiving, but I confess that just as I cannot understand the Hebrew, or understand it only in outline, only in its spiritual meaning, I am baffled by who I am and where I am. My daughter is thirteen. At her age, I was confirmed in the Church of the Redeemer in Baltimore, Maryland. I still remember the hands of Bishop Doll on my head. "Defend, O Lord, this thy child with thy heavenly grace...." And had I been defended? So much spoke against the petition of Bishop Doll in my memory. Shortly after my confirmation I rushed to Carthage and its hissing cauldrons of illicit loves. Fantasies of immortality clouded my judgment and stoked my arrogance. I used commitment as a device for spiritual adventure, savoring what I imagined to be my boldness as a mark of achievement. I sharpened my mind as a warrior might sharpen his sword: to rush the citadels and slay my adversaries. I was eager for the bravery of seeking, but I was untrained and unprepared for finding, or being found. I threw myself into quests without caring for the direction. I conjured grails to which I might pledge myself.

On this day at Beth El Synagogue in Omaha, Nebraska, my daughter is the mouthpiece of the words God spoke. The scroll lives in her voice:

Anochi adonai eloheycha asher hotzeiticha me'eretz mitz'rayim mibeyt avadim lo-yih'yeh l'cha elohim acherim al-panay:

I am the LORD your God, who brought you out of the land of Egypt, out of the house of slavery: you shall have no other gods before me.

Love may not conquer all, but it has felled many young men. I was one so felled. But providence used more than the errands of Cupid to divert me from my path and put an end to my self-congratulating seeking. At the very point in my life when faith in Christ started to take root in my heart and mind and I was forced back upon myself, I fell in love with Juliana, a Jewish woman. Make no mistake. There was nothing about Yale University in 1985 that made such a love difficult or even noteworthy. Our lives were full of common experiences and common aspirations, and in that bastion of American liberalism, one could easily imagine a Jew marrying a Christian — after all, religion is a lifestyle choice. Eros may level many barriers, but American liberalism has its own power. It is like a cultural neutron bomb. The structures of ethnic and religious culture are left standing, but they are emptied of life. Far more unlikely was a Young Republican to marry a Women's Studies major than a Christian a Jew. No, for us, the complications of love were of the universally personal sort. Both of us were in bondage to a desire that was driving us toward a renunciation of possibilities: I shall be yours and no other's. In our own ways we struggled against the straightjacket, but we failed to escape the limitations of our own love, and we were joyful in the failure.

Lo-ta'aseh l'cha fesel:
You Shall Not Make for Yourself an Idol

After we decided to get married, we visited Jim Ponet at the Yale Hillel. He is a generous man, a passionate man. He told Juliana that as one committed to Jewish law he was obligated to tell her that what she wished to do was prohibited by God. "As a man," he said, "I wish you the best of luck."

Jim's response was representative. Contemporary rabbis live in the same pluralistic world as do all of us. They accommodate and resist; they exercise pastoral discretion and stand firm where they can. For Jews, intermarriage is an issue of fundamental importance, and, as we discovered, there are very, very few rabbis who will marry Jews to Christians. We had no interest in seeking out one of the few, for neither Juliana nor I wished to live our religious lives on the edges of our traditions. Both of us were just beginning to seek the centers, to accept the confines of orthodoxy just as we were accepting the limitations of desire in marriage. And my wife and I decided that a neutral, secular wedding between Judaism and Christianity would be the worst possible place to be married, for we had no intention of having a neutral, secular marriage. So my wife put herself and her family where they did not want to be: in front of the altar upon which Christians offer the sacrament of the sacrifice of Christ, surrounded by stained-glass windows of Jesus and his disciples. We were pronounced husband and wife in the name of the Father, and of the Son, and of the Holy Spirit. The opposite of neutrality is conflict. In the moment she became my wife, Juliana suffered the first blow.

Lo tissa et-shem-adonai eloheicha:
You Shall Not Take the Name of the
Lord Your God in Vain

We had no more interest in a neutral child than a neutral wedding, and we certainly did not want to tear the child in two by pretending that we could raise him or her as both a Jew and a Christian. I remember the conversation well. "The children will, of course, be raised Jewish," remarked Juliana one day. I looked at her and said with coldness, "What do you mean, raised Jewish? You do not go to synagogue. You do not keep kosher. I am not going to keep my children from baptism just so that they can be raised as bagels-and-the-*New-York-Times*-on-Saturday-morning Jews. If you become a religious Jew, then I am willing to promise that I will support you in raising the children as religious Jews."

I had made a promise I did not think I would need to keep, but I had underestimated my wife, or maybe God. That Saturday she marched down the street to the Hillel *minyan.* She announced that we were buying new plates and would keep a kosher kitchen. She was willing to marry me in a church, but she was not willing to see her children baptized. The first blow had awakened her, and she saw that the way forward in her life would require a deepened seriousness about what it means to be a Jew. Now I was to learn what it meant to be a resident alien in my own kitchen, an onlooker and supporter of her determined decision to burrow into the encompassing word of God's commandments.

Zachor et-yom hashabbat l'kad'sho:
Remember the Sabbath Day and Keep It Holy

Circumcision is a ruthlessly physical act. I remember waves of emotion that swept over me as my eight-day-old son lay screaming and the rabbi recited the prayers and the doctor wielded his scalpel. My mind was utterly disordered by the visceral reality of the event, but one thought came and it has so lodged itself in my memory that I am very nearly consumed by it to this day. It was a thought of self-doubt, a worry about the invisibility of my faith. How many times had I come to the altar of my church to receive the bread and wine? How many times had I confessed my sins and received absolution? How many children had I seen baptized with water and anointed with oil? I cannot count the times, and in each instance, I have felt the truth of the promise of Christ: I will be with you until the end of the age. He is with us, in our hearts and on our lips. So I had come to believe as my own path had paralleled my wife's turn of deepened immersion in the religious life. And yet, there, in the sterile environment of an outpatient room at the hospital, I watched the circumcision and saw God's word in the flash of the knife marking my son's flesh — so physical, so immediate, so shockingly intimate, so permanent. Christ was in my heart and on my lips, but was I unmarked in my flesh, unchanged in the brute reality of my life?

Kabed et'avicha v'et-imecha:
Honor Your Father and Your Mother

At the circumcision of my son, I felt the blow and it was more terrible than I could have imagined. It was the blow of judgment on my head. I do not mean guilt about anti-Semitism. That is an easy guilt for most American Christians, a guilt that makes one feel superior for being self-critical and progressive. No, this was a painful moment of self-recognition, for I now felt a terrible question that I could not answer. Where was I marked in my flesh? Where had God's commandment set me apart and marked me as Christ's own? Do we, no, I cannot hide, do I make the commandments of God empty emphemera, "spiritual" and pious commitments that the currents of culture erode and obliterate the moment I leave the church? Compassion is a humane sentiment. To seek justice is a noble goal. "Peace on earth and goodwill toward men" — these were watchwords of the liberal institutions that had educated me, institutions with no particular commitment to Christianity. My daughter cannot eat cheeseburgers, and her friends find this remarkable. Her very mouth is trained and set apart day-by-day. And me? Jesus teaches that what goes into the mouth is not important. What matters is what comes out. And yet what comes out of my mouth seems so generic, so easily molded into the progressive platitudes of our age. I am afflicted with a singular worry. Christianity, the faith of my forefathers, the basis and hope for my efforts to be faithful to God — is my inheritance the fuel for the neutron bomb for which American liberalism and its pious neutralities are but the trigger mechanism? Is the Christianity that accommodates interreligious marriage a religion that clothes indifference with the rhetorical dress of inclusion and tolerance?

Lo tir'tzach: You Shall Not Murder

A few years later I decided to participate in a reading group at my wife's synagogue. The rabbi was to lead a discussion of *Halakhic Man* by Joseph B. Soloveitchik. I had never heard of Soloveitchik, but I got the book and read it. The book enthralled me, not the least because Soloveitchik's description of the halakhic path of concretion seemed to me a beautiful and poetic evocation of the Christian belief in the incarnation. "When the Holy One, blessed be He, descended on Mount Sinai," writes Soloveitchik, "He set an eternally binding precedent that it is God who descends to man, not man who ascends to God. When he said to Moses, 'And let them make Me a sanctuary, that I may dwell among them' (Ex 25:8), He thereby revealed the awesome mystery that God contracts His divine presence in this world." Again, he writes, "Holiness, according to the outlook of Halakhah, denotes the appearance of a mysterious transcendence in the midst of our concrete world, the 'descent' of God, whom no thought can grasp, onto Mount Sinai, the bending down of a hidden and concealed world and lowering it onto the face of reality." The vision of divine kenosis captivated me. "Halakhic man, with his unique mode of understanding, declares: the higher longs and pines for the lower." Yes, I said to myself as I read, a thousand times Yes. Soloveitchik drew my attention to Ecclesiastes 12:11 and the nails that fasten divine wisdom to concrete reality. Indeed, I thought to myself, the nails are so strong that divine wisdom is fastened even to the cross of concrete suffering and death.

My head was spinning with insight into how my wife's attempts to conform to halakhic requirements had been teaching me the truth of Philippians 2: "Let the same mind be in you that was in Christ Jesus, who, though he was in the form of God, did not regard equality with God as something to be exploited, but emptied himself, taking the form of a slave, being born in human likeness. And being found in human form, he humbled himself and became obedient to the point of death — even death on a cross." She was humbling her spiritual aspirations, even to the point of taking the food that enters her mouth as a matter of spiritual significance. She was nailing her spiritual journey to the concrete reality of life. Yet in my reveries of insight and convergence, the glistening knife of circumcision flashed and the blow was struck again.

Throughout his analysis, Soloveitchik juxtaposes the way of halakhic concretion with the spiritual quest of those who seek to transcend the world, those who wish to climb the ladder of being and kick it away when they reach the Eternal. Soloveitchik sees how this spiritual quest creates a fissure in the religious life, one that turns all thought to the heavenly while leaving the world to its own devices: "Let the dead bury the dead." In a rare moment, he allows himself to address Christianity directly, and he reveals his worry about the spiritual consequences of a faith that is interested in circumcising the heart while leaving the body unmarked: "How many noblemen bowed down before the cross in a spirit of abject submission and self-denial, confessed their sins with scalding tears and bitter cries and in the very same breath, as soon as they left the dim precincts of the cathedral, ordered that innocent people be cruelly slain." It was a line written in the early 1940s as the Europe from which Providence had delivered Soloveitchik was consuming his community with a furious fire of murderous desire. How many noblemen indeed? When I read that sentence I was overcome with the failure of Christianity. Did Christ come to circumcise our hearts, only to leave our bodies free to indulge our lusts for power and domination? I thought of my daughter and son. Their mother was training their hands not to mix milk with meat so that the will of the LORD might be done, on earth as it is in heaven. Hands so trained, I thought, would not so readily take up the sword to slay the innocent, even if their hearts burned with murderous desire. Their hands were being pierced with the nails of divine intention day after day. And my hands, what of them?

Lo tin'af: You Shall Not Commit Adultery

Recently, my denomination, the Episcopal Church, has been in the news. We have ordained a gay bishop whose current partner, ex-wife, and daughter joined in the ceremony of consecration. As a so-called "conservative," I was asked to participate in a Canadian Broadcast Company radio show to discuss the whole affair with some liberal proponents of the gay bishop's ordination. The radio host made a good effort to address the issues, but like all media events, we traded sound bites and the segment ended. I left the studio and went out onto the street. In my mind's eye I was back at my son's circumcision. The day was warm, but I was chilled to my bones with horror. Have I been honest with myself about modern Christianity? Not only has my church rejected the need to mark the body with the knife of circumcision, it has rejected the very idea that God's commandments can shape or control how we use our bodies. Nothing needs to be submitted to God other than the fine sentiments of the heart. I despaired of an invisible Christianity. Did St. Augustine imagine this when he wrote, "Love and do what you will"? I recalled Soloveitchik: "A subjective religiosity cannot endure. And all those tendencies to transform the religious act into pure subjectivity, negate all corporeality and all sensation from religious life and admit man into a pure and abstract world, where there is neither eating nor drinking, but religious individuals sitting with their crowns on their heads and enjoying their own inner experiences, their own tempestuous, heaven-storming spirits, their own hidden longings and mysterious yearnings — will in the end prove null and void." I offered a prayer of petition to God. You have come to us in the human flesh of the man Jesus of Nazareth, but we have insisted upon seeking to obey you without regard to our flesh. Forgive us, O Lord, for we have rendered your Word null and void.

Lo tig'nov: You Shall Not Steal
Lo-ta'aneh v'reia'cha: You Shall Not Bear False Witness
Lo tach'mod: You Shall Not Covet

None of these memories are consciously with me as my daughter completes the tenth commandment and we sit down to hear the rest of her recitation of Exodus 20. Nonetheless, I am crying. My daughter is a beautiful, mature, well-spoken young lady. She is slipping from my grasp and into her own adulthood. I am proud of her, and the awe of God's words mingles with my awe of her self-possession. Did I ever really hold her in the first place? From the moment my wife marched off to synagogue that first Saturday to lay the foundations for her daughter, to receive the foundation laid centuries before Rachel was even born, I was already letting her go.

But my tears come for deeper reasons. Jesus teaches us that we must be able to hate our mothers and fathers, brothers and sisters, for his sake. My daughter loves me very much, but she is very conscious that this day of her bat mitzvah is as a hating of her father. She was bitter about the fact that I could not be with her mother at her side as she entered into the most intimate fellowship possible with God — to be His voice to His people through the reading of Torah. She was angry and she cried about it in the months of preparation prior to the bat mitzvah, but neither the rabbi, nor her mother, nor I could give her what she wanted. Indeed, I did not want to give her what she wanted, for her desire was that obedience to God would not require the pain of renunciation, would not require the visible marks on our bodies, the visible, public mark of distance between me in the pews and her before the congregation. And now, she is before me. She is being ravished by the concentration necessary to chant the ancient Hebrew. She is being drawn near to God. I can only witness. I cannot be by her side to hold onto the hems of her garments as she rises upward with each flourish of the canticle of recitation.

My daughter is feeling the full blow of intermarriage. Why can't we all go together? Why can't all the people she loves journey toward the LORD, linked arm and arm? Why is God setting a daughter against her father? I know these are her thoughts, and because I love her so much, I feel her anguish as the knife of circumcision cuts into her heart. She is entering into the narrow way of obedience, and for all the joy of that day and the rapture of her voice into the very voice of the Ten Commandments, I cannot join her. My absence, which is forced upon her, is marking her. She knows I support her every word with my spirit, even though I could understand none of them, but I cannot support her with my voice in the prayer before the reading. I cannot touch her gently before she reads. God is cutting me away from her as he had cut away my son's foreskin, not to harm or destroy or denigrate, but to sanctify her as a woman called to Him as a Jew, a Jew who is set apart from the nations into which I must, of necessity, recede.

As I recede and she is drawn away, I am basked in light, for she is aglow on this day. I have failed, she has failed, to escape the limitations of divine love, and we are joyful in our failure. Adorned with dawn's dew of adulthood, she is radiant. She is a light to her father, a citizen of the nations. Her voice continues to sing the ancient words. Her face shines. Cut away from me, she is taking up a pair of tongs. She is pulling out the living coals of the divine word. She is flying toward me. The liquid fire of her voice touches the lips of my unclean heart. Oh, the depth of the riches and the wisdom and knowledge of God!

Questions for Discussion

1. Discuss some of the challenges that may confront a couple in an inter-religious marriage. What are some creative ways for resolving these challenges?

2. How can one be faithful to one's Christian religious convictions (e.g., as expressed in John 14:6: "I am the way and the truth and the life. No one comes to the Father except through me") as well as to one's spouse and children within an interreligious marriage, especially where the children are raised in a different tradition?

3. In what ways has a liberal, pluralistic culture facilitated or frustrated interreligious marriages?

Chapter 24

The Sacramentality of Marriage as a Hermeneutic for Health Care Ethics

Gerard Magill

The purpose of this essay is to discuss how the meaning of marriage can help us understand Catholic ethics in general and health care ethics in particular. That is, the meaning of experience in married life can shed light on the meaning of varied life experiences in ethics, especially in the realm of health care. I emphasize health care because of the shared role of "care" in marriage and health-related issues.

This inquiry is divided into three sections. The first section offers a brief explanation of my general thesis or argument; in this section I discuss the role of the shared experience of life and love between wife and husband in the sacramental meaning of marriage. The second section presents an explanation of the theory behind my argument; in this section I consider how the sacramentality of marriage can be a helpful hermeneutic (a sort of lens so to speak) for interpreting Catholic ethics. The third section then applies my analysis to health care ethics; in this section I examine an important and emerging issue in health care to suggest new possibilities for discourse in Catholic ethics.

The Thesis

Michael G. Lawler's many works on sacrament and on marriage celebrate the symbolic meaning of married love in the life of the church. He identifies two levels of meaning in the symbol of marriage: the mutual covenant of the couple's loving communion (the foundational level of meaning) as the representation of the love between Christ and the church (the sacramental level of meaning).

> In every symbol there are . . . two levels of meaning. . . . The foundational level in a sacramental marriage is the loving communion for the whole of life between a man and a woman who are disciples of Christ and members of the Church. The symbolic or sacramental level is the representation in the communion of the communion of life and love between Christ and the Church. This two-tiered and connected meaningfulness is what is meant by the claim that marriage between

Christians is a sacrament. In a truly Christian marriage . . . the symbolic meaning takes precedence over the foundational meaning.[1]

The final sentence in this quote emphasizes the symbolic meaning of marriage. The point here is that any sacrament entails an action pointing to other meanings that embrace and celebrate divine grace. In the sacrament of marriage the couple's covenant of love points to Christ's love for the church that specifically bestows divine grace upon their married life, thereby fostering the life of the church. In this sense, the sacrament of marriage is a prophetic symbol:

> In symbol-language, a sacrament is a symbolic action which points beyond itself to meanings which it proclaims, realizes, and celebrates; in theological language, it is an action which contains and confers the grace it signifies.[2]

The conferring and celebration of grace in sacramental marriage is not only for the couple but also for the church. Sacramental marriage is a prophetic symbol in the sense that God's grace fosters both the couple and life of the church.

> Marriage is not only a reality of social law; it is also a reality of grace. Lived in faith, marriage appears as a two-fold reality. On the one hand, it bespeaks the mutually covenanted love of this man and this woman. . . . On the other hand, it prophetically symbolizes the mutually covenanted love of God and God's people.[3]

In sum, the symbolic meaning we attribute to married life is that sacramental marriage celebrates Christ's love for the church. And that celebration confers God's grace upon the couple to transform their own covenant of love and thereby contribute to the life and transformation of the entire church. In other words, the personal experience of the couple in marriage elicits much deeper meaning than their own covenant of love. The deeper meaning is that the very personal and intimate experience of their marriage elicits God's grace to transform their own lives and simultaneously the life of the church. It is this deeper meaning that the phrase "sacramentality of marriage" highlights.

Of course, God's grace does not come upon the married couple like a spoonful of cream on a cake, clearly distinct and very noticeable. Rather, divine grace imbues human nature akin to pouring wine into a saucepan while cooking: as the wine flavors all the ingredients bringing out their flavor, grace imbues all our humanity to transform us entirely in a highly subtle yet comprehensive way. The deeper meaning of sacramental marriage is that God's grace utterly transforms the couple's personal experience to enrich their love and the life of the church.

Simply, the sacramentality of marriage invites us to identify the deeper meaning of the marriage covenant experience as a grace-filled opportunity that can radically transform the couple and the church. In the next section, I explain how this insight can be very helpful for Catholic ethics today.

The Theory

The theory of this essay is that the sacramentality of marriage can be a hermeneutic for ethics, especially in health care. By a "hermeneutic" I simply mean a sort of lens that enables us to interpret ethics differently, just as wearing prescription lenses can help us see reality properly. That is, the sacramentality of marriage (by eliciting a deeper meaning for the covenant experience of married love) provides a sort of lens for Catholic ethics to seek a deeper meaning for the human experiences that we encounter. The deeper meaning that we seek in Catholic ethics is to identify in and through our ethical actions a more profound significance aligned to divine grace. For example, giving money to someone begging on the street simply to impress the person we are with is quite different from the same action when done out of solidarity with the poor. The deeper meaning of the act of charity in the latter case can be interpreted in light of the biblical invitation to help the needy with the concomitant promise of God's grace to foster our compassion and care. As with marriage, the deeper meaning here entails an understanding of God's grace that transforms both the life of the moral agent (as occurs with the couple in marriage) and the life of the church.

At first glance, this theory seems straightforward in the sense of encouraging us to interpret our ethical actions with deeper meaning, including the celebration of God's grace to transform the moral agent and the church. For example, the tradition of "virtue ethics" focuses upon the transformation of the moral agent and society by the ethical actions that we have undertaken. By doing the right action we become good or virtuous people, and in turn society becomes a better community. And the more virtuous we become the more morally right actions we are capable of performing. In this sense, the theory I am presenting is straightforward. However, the theory also raises a more complicated issue for Catholic ethics that will now be discussed.

The more complicated issue that needs to be discussed is how we understand normativity in Catholic ethics. This is an issue of hermeneutics itself. Previously I referred to hermeneutics as a sort of lens for interpreting reality. My point here is to argue that Catholic ethics needs a better sense of hermeneutics if we are to detect and celebrate God's grace in our daily experiences. Hence, I propose that the sacramentality of marriage not only functions as a hermeneutic (or interpretative lens) for Catholic ethics but also encourages an important role for hermeneutics in Catholic ethics. Therefore, we should ask what sort of role hermeneutics can have in Catholic ethics.

The most important contribution hermeneutics can have in ethics is to interpret our practical experiences deeply as we develop ethical norms to guide church and society. I have explained that a deep interpretation of the experience of marriage can elicit a sacramental understanding of God in the lives of the married couple. Likewise, ethics needs to interpret the meaning of our human experiences more deeply as grace-filled moments before God. As mentioned earlier, this approach to ethics can enhance a sense of virtue in our lives. However, the point I discuss here is quite distinct from the tradition of "virtue ethics." My point here is that our ethical experiences, if interpreted deeply, can contribute to the formulation of new ethical norms to guide us. Using technical vocabulary in ethics, I am discussing the relation between descriptive ethics and normative ethics. Descriptive ethics studies what people do and why they act in specific ways (for example, how many people support capital punishment and why they do so). Normative ethics studies what people should do based on principles and theories (for example, the church condemns the use of capital punishment in most cases out of respect for human life). The challenge of hermeneutics in ethics is to bridge descriptive ethics and normative ethics more effectively than has been the case.

Hermeneutics in ethics invites us to interpret deeper meaning in our ethical actions, especially when those actions may be grace-filled opportunities. This focus upon hermeneutics in ethics can help our increasingly diverse populace to discern normative practices in culturally complex situations. For example, in health care ethics today there is an increasing sensitivity to the role of descriptive ethics to provide relevant empirical data for normative analysis. Moreover, health care has become very attentive to the importance of population perspectives in order to track patterns across large groups rather than focusing merely on diagnosing diseases among individual patients. This propensity to interpret the meaning of empirical data among large populations fits well with the Catholic emphasis upon the common good as the context for respecting the human person. Hence, hermeneutics in ethics invites us to interpret our actions (as a basis for norms) by focusing more upon their deeper meaning, especially when they occur commonly and extensively. And as we pursue this quest for deeper meaning in our ethical actions, the metaphor of conversation can be very helpful.

Cardinal John Henry Newman in the nineteenth century emphasized the importance of grasping the depth of meaning in our language and lives. This occurs by interpreting data in a manner that opens up new possibilities previously unrecognized. A century later David Tracy adopted a similar approach when discussing the text as bearing a surplus of meaning (poetry is a good example) whose ongoing interpretation re-creates new possibilities for different cultures. Tracy described this hermeneutical process as conversation in which we encounter moments of recognition where truth is both disclosed and concealed.[4] This metaphor of conversation recognizes that discourse can be ambiguous when the participative character of language fosters open-ended discourse. Only by recognizing a multiplicity of voices in ethics conversation can we hope to perceive the depth of meaning that we seek (as a basis for norms).

This metaphor of conversation encourages sensitivity to human experience, especially from the perspectives of historicity and subjectivity. In this regard, feminist scholars emphasize the multiplicity of lived experience to express diversity and difference while celebrating mutuality and relationality.[5] Above all, the metaphor of conversation fosters a sense of solidarity that is crucial for the Catholic tradition in general and Catholic ethics in particular. Solidarity exhorts us to decipher our activities in community perspectives as we seek to elicit their deeper meaning as grace-filled moments that provide the basis for ethical norms.

Let me now summarize the theory that I am proposing here. The sacramentality of marriage reveals a deeper meaning for the marriage relationship by celebrating the grace-filled reality of married life. This understanding of the sacramentality of marriage provides a hermeneutic or lens for Catholic ethics to seek the deeper meaning of our ethical experiences as grace-filled opportunities that provide the basis for ethical norms.

Hence, the sacramentality of marriage helps to clarify an important role that hermeneutics can have in Catholic ethics.

Application

Sensitivity to hermeneutics in ethics can help our increasingly diverse populace to discern normative behavior from practical experiences in culturally diverse situations. This discernment calls for a closer affinity between descriptive ethics and normative ethics in the following sense: to interpret the deeper meaning of our ethical activities we need to understand the relevant empirical data prior to establishing or further developing ethical norms. Moreover, grasping the empirical data in a reliable manner may require a focus upon population perspectives — an approach that fosters conversation and enhances solidarity. This grasp of empirical data from population perspectives can give deeper meaning to our practical experiences as grace-filled moments as we develop our normative approaches in Catholic ethics. This final section of this chapter applies the thesis and theory to an important and emerging issue in health care ethics that has an impact on normative guidelines in Catholic teaching.

The issue is that of surrogacy after the process of in-vitro fertilization. There are two related reasons for the church's prohibition of surrogacy in Catholic teaching. On the one hand, the process of in-vitro fertilization has been forbidden by Catholic teaching insofar as it separates the unitive and procreative dimensions of sexuality within marriage. The church teaches that even couples suffering from infertility may not avail themselves of this procedure. A very large number of babies have been born globally using this technology after the birth of Louise Brown on July 25, 1978, just over twenty-five years ago. On the other hand, surrogacy entails the use of a third person in the procreative process insofar as the natural mother of the in-vitro fertilization embryo is unable to bring a pregnancy to term:

Catholic teaching opposes such a use of a surrogate womb in its defense of the meaning of marriage and procreation.

Typically, in the process of in-vitro fertilization several embryos are created by fertilizing multiple eggs with sperm. However, only one or a few are implanted in the mother's womb, thereby often leaving several for future use. The embryos that are not implanted are frozen to make them available at a later time for the couple. Because many couples choose not to use the so-called "spare" embryos, a large number of such embryos have accumulated in fertility clinics. It is estimated there could be as many as 400,000 frozen embryos in fertility clinics across the United States that will not be used for procreation by the original parents.

Independent of the ethics of in-vitro fertilization, health care ethicists debate what would be an appropriate destiny for these frozen "spare" embryos. In the Catholic tradition, some argue that a proper course of action is thawing the embryos and letting them die. This would be akin to legitimately withdrawing life support (e.g., a ventilator) that is either futile or overly burdensome at the end of life. It is argued that thawing these embryos entails a similar process. That is, retaining the embryos in a frozen state is deemed to be either futile (they will never develop in a pregnancy process) or overly burdensome (such as the cost to society to continue the freezing process). So, withdrawing the freezing process is akin to justifiably withdrawing life-sustaining treatment. This is a reasonable argument, seeking to respect the dignity of the embryo, which Catholicism is open to accepting.

Another option is to use the "spare" embryos for embryonic stem cell research in the quest to develop effective therapies for many debilities and diseases in society, such as Alzheimer's, Parkinson's, etc. Certainly, there is a great deal of investment in current research on stem cell therapies today. Because of the versatility of embryonic stem cells, research on them has become a very promising dimension of molecular medicine, especially given the recent breakthrough in genetics with the completion of the map of the human genome in spring 2003. Because embryonic stem cells can develop into almost any other cell type (bone, skin, organs, etc.), they offer great hope in the development of therapies for many different diseases (gene-linked and otherwise). So promising is this research that many scientists are discussing the possibility of pursuing human cloning to develop embryos that can be used to harvest stem cells for research purposes. This technology raises a vast array of ethical dilemmas, not least the creation of human embryos for research purposes.[6] For our purposes here, it is important simply to note that the process of harvesting embryonic stem cells necessitates the destruction of the embryo. Hence, from the perspective of Catholic teaching, such research is deemed unacceptable. That is, the use of "spare" human embryos for stem cell research is forbidden because the harvesting process entails destroying the human embryo.

Fortunately, there is a third option that may be an appropriate destiny for "spare" frozen embryos. This option is especially pertinent in light of the analysis of this chapter. The frozen embryos could be "rescued" if we take another look at the ethics of surrogacy to discern a deeper meaning for the experience. In the United States it is estimated there are 6–10 million infertile couples (12–20 million individuals) affected in some manner by infertility. Nor surprisingly, there are many infertile couples that seek to adopt but are unable to do so, often because of the limited number of adoption babies. Such couples could become "rescue" parents of frozen embryos through an "early adoption" process — the process of surrogacy (assuming, of course, that pregnancy is feasible). In this scenario, surrogacy refers to the obvious fact that the adopting mother is different from the natural parents whose sperm and egg created the embryo. The advantages of surrogacy in this circumstance are obvious: frozen embryos are rescued through the pregnancy process; and the parents fulfill their marriage by having a child or children. The surrogacy process necessarily involves a full period of pregnancy by the mother. Hence, the sense of pregnancy and giving birth to their own child further deepens the meaning of their adoption. Unfortunately, for Catholic couples, the problem with this approach is that the Catholic Church forbids surrogacy.

The analysis presented in this essay is intended to shed light on this prohibition in order to suggest the possibility of doctrinal development around church teaching against surrogacy. Specifically, I am suggesting that a better understanding of the empirical data can encourage a development of church doctrine on surrogacy. That is, we can seek to build a better bridge between descriptive ethics (empirically, what couples are making ethical decisions to pursue, etc.) and normative ethics (what couples should decide as ethical) on surrogacy in these circumstances.

The growing number of frozen embryos in fertility clinics indicates an increasing need to resolve the ethical conundrum around the destiny of these embryos. This need presents an opportunity for Catholic doctrine to develop its normative teaching with a clearer understanding of the empirical data based on the perspectives of so many infertile couples willing to rescue these embryos in an early adoption process. These many couples with their infertile conditions, along with the large number of "spare" frozen embryos, represent what I have described previously as a population health scenario. The circumstance of surrogacy by a married couple that *seeks to rescue* frozen embryos through an early adoption process appears to have a deeper meaning than the process of surrogacy (forbidden by the Catholic Church) that *sets out to create* human embryos for an infertile person or couple.

Now what does this deeper meaning entail? Certainly, surrogacy in such rescue circumstances can be a grace-filled moment that celebrates the sacramentality of marriage by embracing the reality of a child or children whose destiny is otherwise doomed. Of course, it would be difficult to argue that any specific couple would have an obligation to rescue "spare" frozen embryos through surrogacy. Yet heroism may be abundantly evident when couples choose to adopt in this manner.

When empirical data reliably informs us that many infertile couples (as a health population) can resolve their infertility by early adoption of frozen embryos, normative ethics should engage this adoption experience as an important learning moment. The grace-filled experience of many couples struggling to celebrate their sacrament of marriage by welcoming a child or children provides an invitation for doctrinal development on surrogacy in the normative teaching of the church.

The invitation here is especially important from the perspective of solidarity with the poor, in this case couples suffering infertility and embryos destined otherwise to death. Using the metaphor of conversation, we have an amazing opportunity to gain practical insight into the deeper meaning of married love that is willing to rescue these frozen embryos via the surrogacy process. If we can bring together descriptive ethics (empirically, what couples are making ethical decisions to pursue, etc.) and normative ethics (what couples should decide as ethical) on surrogacy we may be able to witness a genuine development of the church's moral doctrine. And this development is very likely to celebrate the experience of the faithful as sacramental, grace-filled moments of ethical insight for church teaching.

Conclusion

The general thesis of this essay (section one) is that the sacramentality of marriage invites us to identify the deeper meaning of the marriage covenant experience as a grace-filled opportunity that can radically transform the couple and the church.

The specific theory of the chapter (section two) is that the sacramentality of marriage can be a hermeneutic for health care ethics, hence the title of the chapter. By a "hermeneutic" I simply mean a sort of lens that enables us to interpret ethics differently. That is, the sacramentality of marriage (by eliciting a deeper meaning for the covenant experience of married love) provides a sort of lens for Catholic ethics to seek a deeper meaning for the human experiences that we encounter. And the deeper meaning that we seek in Catholic ethics is to identify in and through our ethical actions a more profound significance aligned to divine grace. That is, the sacramentality of marriage provides a hermeneutic or lens for Catholic ethics to seek the deeper meaning of our ethical experiences as grace-filled opportunities that provide the basis for ethical norms.

The application of this thesis and theory (section three) indicates that the sacramentality of marriage helps to clarify an important role that hermeneutics can have in Catholic ethics. Sensitivity to hermeneutics in ethics can help our increasingly diverse populace to discern normative behavior from practical experiences in culturally diverse situations. This discernment calls for a closer affinity between descriptive ethics and normative ethics in the following sense: to interpret the deeper meaning of our ethical activities we need to understand the relevant empirical data prior to establishing or further developing ethical norms. Moreover, grasping the empirical data in a reliable manner may require a focus upon population perspectives — an approach that fosters conversation and enhances solidarity. This grasp of empirical data from population perspectives can give deeper meaning to our practical experiences as grace-filled moments as we develop our normative approaches in Catholic ethics. In this regard an important and emerging topic in health care ethics (surrogacy to rescue frozen embryos) is ripe for doctrinal development in Catholic doctrine. If that development occurs it is very likely to celebrate the experience of the faithful in solidarity with the poor as sacramental, grace-filled moments of ethical insight for church teaching.

Questions for Discussion

1. What is the deeper meaning that the sacramentality of marriage brings to human experience?

2. What does it mean to say that the sacramentality of marriage can be a hermeneutic for Catholic ethics?

3. What does it mean to say that doctrinal development can celebrate the experience of the faithful as grace-filled moments of ethical insight for church teaching?

4. What is meant by doctrinal development in Catholic moral teaching?

Appendix

Theology 350

Marriage in the Catholic Tradition

Description

The purpose of this course is to investigate marriage in the Catholic tradition as it originated in scripture, evolved historically and theologically in the Roman Catholic Tradition, and is lived in the twenty-first century. To that end, the course will be divided into three parts: (1) Marriage in Scripture and Early Christianity; (2) Marriage and Tradition; and (3) Marriage and Contemporary Experience.

Course Objectives

- To understand the institution of marriage chronologically in a variety of historical contexts.

- To understand the New Testament treatment of marriage in light of the Old Testament history of that institution.

- To understand Catholic sacramentality and how such sacramentality has evolved and changed.

- To understand the place of marriage within the church as a whole.

- To understand the contemporary challenges to Catholic marriage in terms of cohabitation, interchurch and interfaith marriages, and other cultural realities.

Text

Todd Salzman, Thomas Kelly, and John O'Keefe, eds., *Marriage in the Catholic Tradition* (New York: Crossroad, 2004).

I. Marriage in Scripture and Early Christianity

Week 1:   The Many Faces of Marriage throughout History: An Overview

Week 2:   Collins, "Marriage in the Old Testament" (chap. 1)

Simkins, "Marriage and Gender in the Old Testament" (chap. 2)

Malina, "The Meaning(s) of Purposeful Non-Marriage in the New Testament" (chap. 3)

Week 3: Marriage Texts in the New Testament: The Importance of Understanding in Context

Week 4: Collins, " 'And the Greatest of These Is Love' " (chap. 4)

Calef, "The Radicalism of Jesus the Prophet: Implications for Christian Family" (chap. 5)

Week 5: Cahill, "Equality in Marriage: The Biblical Challenge" (chap. 6)

O'Keefe, "Marriage Is Good, but Celibacy Is Better: The Mixed Legacy of the Early Christian Understanding of Marriage" (chap. 7)

Week 6: Early Church Monasticism, Asceticism, and Consequences for Marriage. Topics to include: stoicism and sexuality, Greek dualism, early church cosmologies

II. Marriage and Tradition

Week 7: Catholic Sacramentality: Foundations and Understandings

Week 8: Buckley, "The Bond of Marriage" (chap. 8)

Roberts, "Christian Marriage: A Divine Calling" (chap. 9)

Cooke, "*Casti Connubii* to *Gaudium et Spes*: The Shifting Views of Christian Marriage" (chap. 10)

Week 9: Salzman, "Friendship, Sacrament, and Marriage: The Distinction between Christian Marital Friendship and Non-Christian Marital Friendship" (chap. 11)

Heaney-Hunter, "Toward a Eucharistic Spirituality of Family: Lives Blessed, Broken, and Shared" (chap. 12)

Week 10: Knieps-Port le Roi, "Sacramental Marriage and Holy Orders: Toward an Ecclesial Ministry for Married People" (chap. 13)

Kelly, "Sacramentality and Social Mission: A New Way to Imagine Marriage" (chap. 14)

III. Marriage and Experience

Week 11: Contemporary Sexuality and Sociology of the Family: New Challenges Need New Solutions

Week 12: Risch, "Cohabitation: Integrating Ecclesial and Social Scientific Teaching" (chap. 15)

Faulhaber, "Engagement: A Time to Discern, a Time to Build" (chap. 16)

McDonagh, "Vulnerable to the Holy: Meditating on Friendship, Sex, and Marriage" (chap. 17)

Week 13: Wright, "The Christian Spiritual Life and the Family" (chap. 18)

Rubio, "Living the Dual Vocation of Christian Parenthood" (chap. 19)

Brenninkmeijer-Werhahn, "Married and Aging: A Value to Society" (chap. 20)

Week 14: Bourg, "Marriage and Non-Practicing Catholics" (chap. 21)

Lawler, "Interchurch Marriages: Theological and Pastoral Reflections" (chap. 22)

Reno, "Interreligious Marriage: A Personal Reflection" (chap. 23)

Week 15: Magill, "The Sacramentality of Marriage as a Hermeneutic for Health Care Ethics" (chap. 24)

The History of Marriage as a History of Change: Future Directions? Possible topics: same-sex unions and church teachings; civil law and ecclesial law: separate but equal?

Frequently Asked Questions

1. What is polygamy and how long did it last? (chap. 1)

2. How is marriage in the Bible different from marriage today (chaps. 1–6)

3. Were men and women considered equal in the Bible? (chaps. 1, 2, 6)

4. Why does the church think celibacy is holier than marriage? (chaps. 3, 6, 7)

5. Have Christians always married out of love? (chaps. 2, 4, 6, 10)

6. Was the early church against marriage and sex? (chap. 7)

7. Why did Jesus not marry? (chaps. 3, 5)

8. Why does the church think sex belongs only in marriage? (chaps. 7, 9, 17)

9. Who were the key influences on Catholic teaching about marriage? (chaps. 7, 8–10, 13)

10. Can we find the modern ideal of the family in the Bible? (chaps. 1, 2, 3, 5)

11. Has the church's teaching on marriage changed over time? (chaps. 10, 14)

12. Has marriage always been a sacrament? (chaps. 10, 11)

13. What does it mean to say that marriage is a sacrament? (chaps. 8–14)

14. Do Catholic married couples have to have children? (chaps. 19, 20)

15. Why are so few saints married? (chap. 7)

16. What does the church say about divorce? (chap. 8)

17. Is living together good practice for marriage? (chap. 15)

18. Is marriage a call from God? (chaps. 9, 12, 14)

19. Can a Catholic marry a person from a different denomination or religion? (chaps. 21, 22)

20. Is being married holy? (chaps. 7, 9, 12, 14)

21. Should wives submit to their husbands? (chaps. 2, 6)

22. Why are so many people in the New Testament unmarried? (chap. 3)

23. How long should an engagement last? (chap. 9)

24. Should wives stay home and take care of the children? (chaps. 5, 19)

25. Should non-practicing Catholics be allowed to marry in the church? (chap. 21)

26. Has the church's view of women changed over time? (chap. 10)

27. If marriage is a sacrament, where do we experience God in it? (chaps. 9–12, 14, 17–19)

28. Should your spouse be your friend? (chaps. 11, 17)

29. What is the primary ministry of married life? (chaps. 14, 19, 20)

30. Is love in the Bible the same thing we mean by love today? (chap. 4)

31. What is official church teaching about marriage? (chaps. 8, 9, 22)

32. Why is there so much divorce today? (chap. 15)

33. How do I know who I am supposed to marry? (chap. 9)

Notes

1. Marriage in the Old Testament (John J. Collins)

1. Mark 10:6–9, citing Genesis 1:27 and 2:24. Compare Matthew 19:3–9.

2. On the contractual view of marriage, see further J. J. Collins, "Marriage, Divorce and Family in Second Temple Judaism," in L. G. Perdue, J. Blenkinsopp, J. J. Collins and C. Meyers, *Families in Ancient Israel* (Louisville: Westminster John Knox, 1997), 104–62; D. Instone-Brewer, *Divorce and Remarriage in the Bible: The Social and Literary Context* (Grand Rapids: Eerdmans, 2002), 1–19.

3. See B. Porten, *Archives from Elephantine* (Berkeley and Los Angeles: University of California Press, 1968).

4. For references, see Collins, "Marriage, Divorce and Family," 111.

5. The book of Tobit is usually dated to the Hellenistic period, that is, to the third or second century B.C.E.

6. Middle Assyrian Laws, 41, in M. Roth, *Law Collections from Mesopotamia and Asia Minor* (Atlanta: Society of Biblical Literature, 1997), 169.

7. See R. de Vaux, *Ancient Israel I: Social Institutions* (New York: McGraw-Hill, 1965), 26–29.

8. The pharaoh is said to give the city of Gezer as a dowry to his daughter when she married Solomon (1 Kings 9:16), but the pharaoh was not following Israelite custom.

9. Josephus, *Antiquities* 17.14; *Jewish War* 1.477.

10. For detailed discussion, see G. P. Hugenberger, *Marriage as Covenant: A Study of Biblical Law and Ethics Governing Marriage, Developed from the Perspective of Malachi* (Leiden: Brill, 1994).

11. Compare Sirach 25:25–26: "If she walks not by your side, cut her away from your flesh with a bill of divorce."

2. Marriage and Gender in the Old Testament (Ronald A. Simkins)

1. The problems encountered when labeling Israelite society as "patriarchal" are discussed thoroughly by Carol Meyers, *Discovering Eve: Ancient Israelite Women in Context* (New York: Oxford University Press, 1988), 24–46.

2. See also the discussion in Ronald A. Simkins, *Creator and Creation: Nature in the Worldview of Ancient Israel* (Peabody, Mass.: Hendrickson, 1994), 91–117.

3. Although early Christian writers (e.g., Justin, Ambrose, Gregory of Nyssa, Augustine) have debated whether procreation takes place before the Fall (the eating of the fruit of knowledge), such debates were theological without sound biblical exegetical methods and presupposed the unity of Genesis 1–3. Critical biblical scholarship, however, has recognized that Genesis 2:4b–3:24 was written independently of and earlier than Genesis 1:1–2:3 (attributed to the Priestly writer). Only in the later Priestly story are humans commanded "be fruitful and multiply" (Gen. 1:28). The Yahwist tale gives no indication of procreation until after the human couple eats the fruit.

4. See especially the "Great Hymn to Khnum," trans. Miriam Lichtheim, *Ancient Egyptian Literature*, vol. 3: *The Late Period* (Berkeley: University of California Press, 1980).

5. Siegfried Morenz, *Egyptian Religion* (Ithaca, N.Y.: Cornell University Press, 1973), 183–84.

6. See especially Phyllis Trible, *God and the Rhetoric of Sexuality* (Philadelphia: Fortress, 1978), 94–105. A critique of Trible's interpretation is given by Susan S. Lanser, "(Feminist) Criticism in the Garden: Inferring Genesis 2–3," *Semeia* 41 (1988): 67–84.

7. *Webster's Third New International Dictionary* defines "merism" as "a figure of speech in which a totality is expressed by two constitutive parts."

8. On the interpretation of the "knowledge of good and evil," see Claus Westermann, *Genesis 1–11* (Minneapolis: Augsburg, 1984), 242–45; Howard N. Wallace, *The Eden Narrative* (Atlanta: Scholars Press, 1985), 115–32; and Robert A. Oden, "Divine Aspirations in Atrahasis and in Genesis 1–11," *Zeitschrift für alttestamentliche Wissenschaft* 93 (1981): 213.

9. This view of procreation continues to be embraced by some peoples in the Mediterranean region. See Carol Delaney, *The Seed and the Soil: Gender and Cosmology in Turkish Village Society* (Berkeley: University of California Press, 1991).

3. The Meaning(s) of Purposeful Non-Marriage in the New Testament (Bruce J. Malina)

1. My Creighton colleague Michael Lawler has devoted much of his scholarship to the study of Christian marriage for more than thirty years. I dedicate this brief study on non-marriage to him with the hope that it rounds out the picture.

2. Emmanuel Todd, *The Explanation of Ideology: Family Structures and Social Systems*, trans. David Garrioch (Oxford: Basil Blackwell, 1985).

3. Bruce J. Malina, *The New Testament World: Insights from Cultural Anthropology*, 3rd ed. (Louisville: Westminster John Knox, 2001), 143–15.

4. Cora Lutz, ed. and trans., *Musonius Rufus "The Roman Socrates"* (New Haven: Yale University Press, 1947), 86.

5. Bruce J. Malina, *Christian Origins and Cultural Anthropology: Practical Models for Biblical Interpretation* (Atlanta: John Knox, 1986), 68–97.

6. Georg Fohrer, "Die Gattung der Berichte über symbolische Handlungen der Propheten," *Zeitschrift für die alttestamentliche Wissenschaft* 64 (1952): 101–20.

7. Lutz, *Roman Socrates*, 87.

8. Plutarch, *Moralia*, 140B.

9. See Josephine Massyngberde Ford, "St. Paul, the Philogamist," *New Testament Studies* 17 (1970/71): 338–46.

10. Epictetus, *Discourses*, III 22, 69–72.

11. See Jacques Dupont, *Marriage et divorce dans l'Évangile: Matthieu 19, 3–13 et parallèles* (Brugges, Belgium: Abbaye de Saint-André, 1959).

12. Carmen Bernabé, "Of Eunuchs and Predators: Matthew 19:1–12 in a Cultural Context — Critical Essay," *Biblical Theology Bulletin* (Winter 2003): 128–34.

13. *Hermas*, I.v.1.

14. Cf. Mark 12:18–27; Matthew 22:22–33; Luke 20:27–40; and esp. 1 Corinthians 7:25ff. on "virgins," i.e., the once-married childless young women.

15. *Hermas*, IV.iv.1.

16. See Bruce J. Malina, *On the Genre and Message of Revelation: Star Vision and Sky Journeys* (Peabody, Mass.: Hendrickson, 1995).

4. *"And the Greatest of These Is Love"* (Raymond F. Collins)

1. The extant "First Letter to the Corinthians" was at least Paul's second piece of correspondence with them. See 1 Corinthians 5:9. Among recently published commentaries on 1 Corinthians is my own *First Corinthians* (Collegeville, Minn.: Liturgical Press, 1999).

2. The name "chiasm" is derived from the Greek letter chi, whose X-shape symbolizes the inverted relationship of the literary units in the passage.

3. See 1 Corinthians 12:3–11, 28, 29–30; see also 1 Corinthians 1:3–7.

4. The first attested use of the term in ancient literature is to be found in 1 Corinthians 7:7.

5. Paul's original letter was not divided into chapters and verses. The New Testament was divided into chapters by an archbishop of Canterbury during the thirteenth century. When greater attention is paid to the way that Paul himself composed his letter, it is clear that the unit on love goes from 1 Corinthians 12:31 to 1 Corinthians 14:1. The phrase, "strive for the gifts," identifies the passage as a discrete literary unit, using the technique of *inclusio*, "ring construction."

6. See 1 Corinthians 14:23, 26, "come together" (*synerchomai*).

7. Had the medieval division of the New Testament into chapters and verses been done in a somewhat different fashion, the words "the greatest of these is love" (1 Cor. 13:13b) might have been included as part of 1 Corinthians 14:1. Had that been the case, the parallelism between 1 Corinthians 13:13 and 1 Corinthians 14:1, the "parentheses" around Paul's discussion of love, would have been even more apparent than it presently is.

8. Twelve verbs in the first person are used in these six verses.

9. In 1 Corinthians 13:8, Paul lists the gift of prophecy before the gift of tongues, just as he had done in 1 Corinthians 12:10, 28, 30. He is a good rhetorician and begins his reflection by writing first about the gift that the Corinthians overrate, tongues (1 Cor. 13:1). When he resumes the line of reflection in 1 Corinthians 13:8–13, Paul starts with the gift that he believes to be the most important, namely, prophecy (1 Cor. 13:8).

10. Paul's switch from the use of the first person in 1 Corinthians 13:1–3 to the use of the third person in 1 Corinthians 13:4–7 and then back again to the first person in 1 Corinthians 13:8–13 is one of the characteristic features of his chiasm.

11. *Sygkrisis* in Greek.

12. It is not only in *Symposium* 197 A–E that Plato personifies love; he also does so in other places of his works. See, for example, *Symposium* 203D, where Plato says that "love is dashing," and *Timaeus* 69D, where he writes that love is ready for any undertaking.

13. See Plutarch, "Table Talk," 5.1, *Moralia* 622C–623A.

14. See "Table Talk," 5.1, *Moralia* 622C.

15. Ibid., 622D.

16. One of my doctoral students, Paul Williamson, M.D., is currently researching the poetic qualities of this passage.

17. An alternate reading cited in a footnote of the NRSV, "body to be burned" is probably the better rendition of Paul's text. See Collins, *First Corinthians,* 476–77.

18. See *Gaudium et Spes,* n. 48 §2; *Catechism of the Catholic Church,* n. 1535.

19. See 1 Corinthians 7:7.

20. See 1 Corinthians 12:12–26.

21. See *Lumen Gentium,* n. 11, *The Catechism of the Catholic Church* (rev. ed.), n. 1656.

5: The Radicalism of Jesus the Prophet (Susan A. Calef)

1. Underlying this "single issue" approach to the Bible is a crucial, and in my estimation, dubious assumption, namely, that the root cause of the nation's social and moral ills is the decline of the two-parent, male-headed household. The deterioration of the family structure, I would argue, is symptomatic of a much deeper problem having to do with the root values of modern American culture, namely, individualism and materialism, and the cultural preoccupation with entertainment and entitlement.

2. Critical study of the Bible indicates that biblical families were quite different from modern American families in form, function, and values. Moreover, even those biblical texts that explicitly deal with marriage and family hardly speak univocally on the subject or in an edifying fashion; see Susan A. Calef, "The Shape of Family and Family Values: 'The Bible Tells Me So,' or Does It?" in *Religion and Family,* ed. R. Simkins (Omaha, Neb.: Creighton University Press, forthcoming).

3. It is true that in the Second Temple period prophets of the past were primarily remembered as miracle workers and predictors of future events. Recent study of prophecy, however, has illumined the complexity of prophecy in ancient Israel. Thus, biblical scholars now distinguish between early and later "classical" prophecy and within the latter, between preexilic, exilic, and postexilic prophecy; and they are increasingly wary of treating all prophets as if they had the same relationship to political and cultic institutions, the same message, or the same status in society. On prophecy, see Joseph Blenkinsopp, *A History of Prophecy in Israel: From the Settlement in the Land to the Hellenistic Period* (Philadelphia: Westminster, 1983); also John Barton, *Oracles of God: Perceptions of Ancient Prophecy in Israel after the Exile* (New York: Oxford University Press, 1986).

4. On the Spirit in prophetic utterance, see Ezekiel 2:2–3; 3:12; 8:3; 9:24; 11:1, 4; Haggai 2:5; Zechariah 4:6; 7:12; also Trito-Isaiah contains a famous reference to the spirit of Yahweh as the inspiration behind his prophecy: "The spirit of the Lord GOD is upon me, because the LORD has anointed me; he has sent me to bring glad tidings to the lowly, to heal the brokenhearted, to proclaim liberty to captives and release to prisoners; to announce a year of favor from the LORD" (Isa. 61:1). On the call and commission of prophets, see Hans Walter Wolff, "Prophecy from the Eighth through the Fifth Century," in *Interpreting the Prophets,* ed. James L. Mays and Paul J. Achtemeier (Philadelphia: Fortress, 1987), 14–26.

5. In the Bible, "justice" often occurs in tandem with "righteousness." In biblical texts "justice" is the establishment of the right and of the person in the right by legal procedures in accordance with the will of God; "righteousness" is the quality of life in relationship with others in the community that results in justice. On the biblical understanding of justice, see John R. Donahue, *"What Does the Lord Require?" A Bibliographical Essay on the Bible and Social Justice* (St. Louis: Institute

of Jesuit Sources, 2000). For references to justice, see Amos 2:6–4:13; 5:10–6:14; Isaiah 1:10–17, 21–26; 3:13–15; 5:8–23; 10:1–4; 32:1–8; Micah 2:1–11; 3:9–12.

6. Because of the complex tradition and composition history of the four canonical Gospels, scholars do not assume that everything contained in the Gospels represents the actual words and deeds of Jesus; thus, ordinarily a distinction is made between the Historical Jesus and Jesus as portrayed in either all four Gospels (the Gospel Jesus) or in a particular Gospel (e.g., the Markan Jesus, the Lukan Jesus, etc.). Throughout this essay, unless indicated otherwise, the term "Jesus" refers to the latter, i.e., the Jesus of the Gospels. For the purposes of this essay, it is not necessary to distinguish between the two, since it is the Gospel Jesus, not any particular scholarly reconstruction of the Historical Jesus, who is canonical, and so, authoritative, in the lives of Christians.

7. He is regarded as prophet in the eyes of the people: Matthew 16:14; 21:11; cf. 26:68; Mark 6:15; 8:28; 14:65; Luke 7:16; 9:8, 19; John 4:19; 9:17. C. H. Dodd presented fifteen reasons that Jesus was popularly regarded as a prophet; see "Jesus as Teacher and Prophet," in *Mysterium Christi: Christological Studies by British and German Theologians,* ed. G. K. A. Bell and D. Adolf Deissmann (London: Longmans, Green and Company, 1930), 53–66. Most Historical Jesus researchers have concluded that Jesus ought to be understood as a prophet of some kind. A few reject the majority view that Jesus should be understood as an eschatological prophet.

8. Throughout this essay, biblical quotations are my own translations.

9. Luke emphasizes that the entirety of Jesus' life and mission, beginning with his conception (1:35), is lived in response to the Spirit. For a concise review of the references to Spirit in Luke-Acts, see John Navone, *Themes of St. Luke* (Rome: Gregorian University Press, 1970), 151–69.

10. See also 13:35, which refers to Jesus as "the one who comes in the name of the Lord."

11. See also Acts 2:22, in which Peter's reference to the signs and wonders that God did through Jesus also evokes the memory of Moses the prophet.

12. See, e.g., Mark 1:15 and Matthew 4:17. Based on frequent reference to the kingdom of God in the Synoptic Gospels, most Historical Jesus researchers agree that the coming kingdom was central to the vision and mission of the Jesus movement. Under the influence of the alternative Matthean phrase "kingdom of heaven," Christians misconstrue it as an otherworldly reality. Although aspects of Jesus' understanding of the phrase are the subject of scholarly debate, it is clear that he understood it as the dynamic rulership of God in this world. See Bruce Chilton, *Pure Kingdom: Jesus' Vision of God* (Grand Rapids: Eerdmans, 1996).

13. It is worth noting that after the sending and return of the Seventy-Two, Jesus refers to what appears to be a prophetic vision, "I watched Satan fall like lightning from heaven" (10:18). In early Judaism the visions of prophets were closely connected with their proclamations. Such a relationship may well have existed between the anticipatory vision of Jesus' defeat of Satan in Luke 10:18 and his proclamation of the imminence of the reign of God. On this point, see David E. Aune, *Prophecy in Early Christianity and the Ancient Mediterranean World* (Grand Rapids: Eerdmans, 1983), 163.

14. See also Matthew 13:24, 31, 33, 44, 45, 47; Mark 4:26, 30.

15. He also teaches his disciples to pray, "your kingdom come" (11:2); and to the Pharisees, asking when the kingdom of God will come, Jesus replies, "The coming of the kingdom of God cannot be observed, and no one will announce 'Look, here it is,' or 'there it is.' For behold, the kingdom of God is among you" (17:20–21).

16. Gospel traditions attest that Jesus' relation to his own family was strained, and for good reason. In a society in which all goods were limited and the family was the locus of production, loss of a productive male entailed severe economic cost. Furthermore, a son's abrupt abandonment of family and property constituted shameless disregard of the divinely ordained obligation to honor parents (Exod. 20:12; Deut. 5:16; Prov. 23:22–25; Sir. 3:1–16, esp. v. 16). Such deviant behavior on the part of a son was a threat to family honor, one to which Jesus' family responds (Mark 3:20–21). For an analysis of the cultural values of honor and shame in Jesus' relations with his family, see Bruce J. Malina, *Social-Science Commentary on the Synoptic Gospels* (Minneapolis: Fortress Press, 1992), 212–13.

17. For example, in his interaction with a man concerned with inheriting eternal life, Jesus reaffirms God's prohibition of adultery and the obligation to honor parents (Luke 18:18–23). According to Mark (7:9–13) and Matthew (15:3–6), Jesus attacks religious leaders for failing to uphold the divinely sanctioned obligation to care for elderly parents (Exod. 21:17; Lev. 20:9; Deut. 5:16); in addition, his prohibition of divorce by either partner (Mark 10:1–12) strongly reaffirms marital relations. Numerous gospel narratives recount Jesus' compassionate outreach to families in need. Frequently, he responds to distraught parents of a sick child, e.g., raising Jairus's daughter (Luke 8:40–56 par.) and raising a widow's son (Luke 7:11–17), and heals Simon Peter's mother-in-law (Luke 4:38–39 par.). Additional examples may be found in other Gospels: exorcising the Canaanite woman's daughter (Matt. 15:21–28) and healing a royal official's son (John 4:46–54). He also responds to sisters, Mary and Martha, grieved by the death of their brother Lazarus (John 11:1–44). Also worth noting is the Johannine account of the crucifixion according to which Jesus, from the cross, entrusts his widowed mother to the care of the so-called "beloved disciple," thereby fulfilling his filial duty by providing for her care (John 19:25–27).

18. Because the Gospels in their final form are the product of a complex process of composition, they contain traditions in tension. The so-called hard or "radical" sayings of Jesus reflect the stringent demands that he made of a select group of persons whom he called to join in his itinerant mission of proclaiming the imminence of the reign of God. Other traditions clearly presuppose the existence of adherents who remained settled in their homes. Thus, gospel traditions indicate that his contemporaries embraced and supported his mission on behalf of the reign of God in different ways. Also, it should be noted that, given the centrality of kinship relations in the ancient Mediterranean world, Jesus' relativization or deprioritization of blood kinship ties was undoubtedly troubling to his contemporaries. However, it is not without precedent in the ancient context. Recent studies of family in the New Testament identify Greco-Roman and Jewish precedents for Jesus' attitude and conduct; on this see esp. Stephen C. Barton, *Discipleship and Family Ties in Mark and Matthew* (Cambridge: Cambridge University Press, 1994), 23–56.

19. "Fictive kinship" or pseudo-kinship, a term used by social scientists, refers to the ways in which societies link people who are not blood relatives into family-like relations.

20. In the ancient Mediterranean, "the poor" are those who suffer both economic poverty and powerlessness. Biblical justice, far from being "blind" or impartial, is partial to the poor, especially the widow, the orphan, and the stranger.

21. In Luke, Jesus' public ministry begins not with his proclamation of the imminence of the kingdom as in Mark 1:15 and Matthew 4:17 but with Jesus' citation of Isaiah 61:1–2 (Luke 4:18–19). This does not mean, however, that the kingdom of God is not a prominent feature of the Lukan Gospel. Within the Lukan narrative, the shorthand for Jesus' mission is "the reign of God is at hand for you" (10:9). That mission is given to the Twelve (9:1–2, 6) and the Seventy-Two (10:9).

22. Unlike modern economies in which goods and services are assumed to be in unlimited supply, in preindustrial agrarian economies such as ancient Palestine, all goods are in limited supply and already distributed; therefore, acquisition was understood as stealing from another. Thus, to be labeled "rich" was not only a statement about economics but a social and moral one as well; see Malina, *Social-Science Commentary,* 324.

23. This hoarding of the bountiful harvest, which clearly involves a surplus that far exceeds his needs, violates the spirit of laws in the Torah; see, e.g., Deuteronomy 15:7–11; 24:19–22.

24. The rich man's egocentric isolation is manifest in his inner dialogue with its repeated occurrence of "I" and the absence of even a single reference to anyone outside himself, including God: "What shall I do, for I do not have space to store my harvest?" (12:17); "This is what I shall do . . . " (12:18); "I shall tear down . . . " (12:18); "I shall store . . . " (12:18); "I shall say to myself . . . " (12:19). The rich man is evidently oblivious to what this bountiful harvest might mean for others and to what God wills in these circumstances.

25. God's word in 12:20 in effect exposes the illusion of self-sufficiency, for the man could die at any time, and confronts him with the reality of his utter dependence on God; hence, the need to be rich in what matters to God or to provide for oneself "treasure in heaven" (12:33).

26. See Luke T. Johnson, *Sharing Possessions: Mandate and Symbol of Faith* (Philadelphia: Fortress, 1981); Walter Pilgrim, *Good News to the Poor: Wealth and Poverty in Luke-Acts* (Minneapolis: Augsburg, 1981); John Gillman, *Possessions and the Life of Faith: A Reading of Luke-Acts* (Collegeville, Minn.: Glazier/Liturgical Press, 1991).

27. It is worth noting that the famous parable of the prodigal son features a pair of brothers whose relationship is threatened by resentment over one brother's squandering of family possessions and over the father's use of the family's fattened calf in celebration of the profligate son's return (15:11–32); see esp. vv. 12–13, 29–31.

28. For example, "I hate, I despise your festivals, and I take no delight in your solemn assemblies. Even though you offer me your burnt offerings and grain offerings, I will not accept them. . . . But let justice roll down like waters, and righteousness like an ever-flowing stream" (Amos 5:21–24). See also Amos 4:4–5; Isaiah 1:11–16.

29. The woe-formula associated with prophetic speech appears elsewhere in Luke; see also 6:24–26; 10:13; 11:43–44, 46–47, 52.

30. Although 23:34a does not occur in the oldest papyrus manuscripts, it has been received and treated by the church as part of the canonical text; hence, its inclusion here.

31. Candidates suggested by scholars include the breaking of the bread and sharing of the cup at the Last Supper, the cursing of the fig tree, the feeding of the multitude, the messianic entrance into Jerusalem, the sending of the Twelve, the giving of symbolic names to the disciples, the miracles, the purification of the Temple, the choice of the Twelve, Jesus' table fellowship with tax collectors and sinners, and the walking on water; see Morna D. Hooker, *The Signs of a Prophet: The Prophetic Actions of Jesus* (Harrisburg, Pa.: Trinity Press International, 1997).

32. On table fellowship in Luke, see Navone, *Themes,* 11–37; Eugene Laverdiere, *Dining in the Kingdom of God: The Origins of the Eucharist according to Luke* (Chicago: Liturgy Training Publications, 1994).

33. In the coherence of word and deed that is characteristic of him in Luke, Jesus issues teachings about table fellowship consistent with his practice. For example, his advocacy of an unconventional, even scandalous guest list, composed not of "your friends or your brothers or your relatives or rich neighbors" but of "the poor, the crippled, the lame, and the blind" (14:12–13), challenges the status consciousness and reciprocity ethos dictating that persons invite people like themselves, that is, social equals who could repay them in kind.

34. See Julie Hanlon Rubio's essay, "Living the Dual Vocation of Christian Parenthood," chapter 19 in this volume.

35. Isaiah 58:6–10 and Matthew 25:34–40 are the scriptural sources for the teaching on the seven corporal works, which address the physical needs of the neighbor: feed the hungry, give drink to the thirsty, clothe the naked, visit the imprisoned, shelter the homeless, visit the sick, and bury the dead. The seven spiritual works of mercy address spiritual and emotional needs: admonish the sinner, instruct the ignorant, counsel the doubtful, comfort the sorrowful, bear wrongs patiently, forgive all injuries, and pray for the living and the dead.

36. Walter Brueggemann, *Testimony to Otherwise: The Witness of Elijah and Elisha* (St. Louis: Chalice Press, 2001), 3.

6: Equality in Marriage (Lisa Sowle Cahill)

1. Pius XI, *Casti Connubii* ("On Christian Marriage"), in *Papal Teachings: Matrimony,* selected and arranged by the Benedictine Monks of Solesmes (Boston: St. Paul Editions, 1963), 234.

2. Ibid., 258–59.

3. John Paul II, "Letter to Women," *Origins* 25, no. 9 (1995): 137, 139–43, nn. 2, 3, 6.

4. John Paul II, *Familiaris Consortio,* nn. 22–23.

5. John Paul II, "Letter to Women," n. 12.

6. John Paul II, *Familiaris Consortio,* n. 23.

7. Ibid., n. 25.

8. For more on this debate, see Elizabeth A. Johnson, ed., *The Church Women Want: Catholic Women in Dialogue* (New York: Crossroad, 2002).

9. An exception here might be a very few roles assigned by physical capacity.

10. Michael Lawler, *Marriage and the Catholic Church: Disputed Questions* (Collegeville, Minn.: Liturgical Press, 2002), 15.

11. For a discussion of Ephesians 5 as a basis for the Catholic view of sacramental marriage, see ibid., 5–16.

12. Carolyn Osiek, "The Bride of Christ (Ephesians 5:22–33): A Problematic Wedding," *Biblical Theology Bulletin* 32, no. 1 (Spring 2002): 29.

13. Meredith Halpin, "Feminist Theology and Ethics: The Household Codes," weekly paper for Boston College TH 534 Feminist Theology and Ethics (January 2003).

14. National Conference of Catholic Bishops, *When I Call for Help: A Pastoral Response to Domestic Violence against Women* (Washington, D.C.: United States Catholic Conference, 1992), 6–7. A copy may be obtained through the Web site of the United States Conference of Catholic Bishops (www.usccb.org).

15. In 1998, the Southern Baptist Convention, the nation's largest Protestant denomination, approved an amendment to its basic statement of faith that declared that women should "submit graciously" to their husbands (Marie Griffith and Paul Harvey, "Wifely Submission: The SBC Resolution," *Christian Century* 115, no. 19 [July 1, 1998]: 636).

16. Russ Dudrey, " 'Submit Yourselves to One Another': A Socio-Historical Look at the Household Code of Ephesians 5:15–6:9," *Restoration Quarterly* 41, no. 1 (1999): 44.

17. John Paul II, "Letter to Families," *Origins* 23, no. 37 (1994): 653–54, n. 19.

18. U.S. Bishops, "Follow the Way of Love: Pastoral Message to Families," *Origins* 23, no. 25 (December 2, 1993): 439–40.

19. Lawler, *Marriage and the Catholic Church*, 5–6.

20. Sandra M. Schneiders, *Written That You May Believe: Encountering Jesus in the Fourth Gospel* (New York: Crossroad, 1999), 93.

21. See Elisabeth Schüssler Fiorenza, *In Memory of Her: A Feminist Theological Reconstruction of Christian Origins* (New York: Crossroad, 1983).

22. David L. Balch, "Household Codes," in *Anchor Bible Dictionary*, ed. Gary A. Herion and David N. Freedman, vol. 3 (New York: Doubleday, 1992), 318–20.

23. Angela Standhartinger, "The Origin and Intention of the Household Code in the Letter to the Colossians," *Journal for the Study of the New Testament* 79, no. 1 (2001): 129.

24. Osiek, "Bride of Christ," 35.

25. Schüssler Fiorenza, *In Memory of Her*, 30–33.

26. Karl Olav Sandnes, "Equality within Patriarchal Structures: Some New Testament Perspectives on the Christian Fellowship as a Brother- or Sisterhood and a Family," in *Constructing Early Christian Families: Family as Social Reality and Metaphor*, ed. Halvor Moxnes (New York and London: Routledge, 1997), 150–65.

7: Marriage Is Good, but Celibacy Is Better (John J. O'Keefe)

1. Language defending the superiority of celibacy is still easy to find in official church documents. For example, Pope John Paul II defended the traditional sense of the superiority of celibacy in the Apostolic Exhortation *Familiaris Consortio*, n. 16, published in 1981.

2. For a favorable reading of Augustine, see Margaret Miles, *Desire and Delight* (New York: Crossroad, 1991).

3. Cf. Elizabeth Clark, "Vitiated Seed and Holy Vessels: Augustine's Manichean Past," in *Images of the Feminine in Gnosticism*, ed. Karen King (Philadelphia: Fortress, 1988).

4. J. N. D. Kelly, *Jerome: His Life, Writings, and Controversies* (New York: Harper & Row, 1975).

5. Jerome, *ep.* XXII.

6. See Sandra Schneiders, *The Revelatory Text* (San Francisco: Harper, 1991).

7. Peter Brown, *The Body and Society: Men, Women, and Sexual Renunciation in Early Christianity* (New York: Columbia University Press, 1988), 6.

8. In addition to Brown, see also Douglas Burton-Christie, *The Word in the Desert: Scripture and the Quest for Holiness in Early Christian Monasticism* (New York: Oxford University Press, 1993).

9. See W. H. C. Frend, *Martyrdom and Persecution in the Early Church* (Grand Rapids, Mich.: Baker, 1965).

10. Cassian, *Institutes,* 11.18.

11. Cyril of Alexandria, *Third Letter to Nestorius,* 11.

12. David Hunter, *Marriage in the Early Church* (Minneapolis: Fortress, 1992), 22.

13. See B. R. Rees, ed. and trans., *The Letters of Pelagius and His Followers* (Rochester, N.Y.: Boydell Press, 1991).

14. Robert Markus, *Saeculum: History and Society in the Theology of St. Augustine* (New York: Cambridge, 1988).

15. Hunter, *Marriage in the Early Church,* 20–25.

16. John Chrysostom, *On Marriage and Family Life* (Crestwood, N.Y.: St. Vladimir's Seminary Press, 1986), 43–64.

8. The Bond of Marriage (Timothy J. Buckley, C.S.S.R.)

1. Timothy J. Buckley, C.S.S.R., *What Binds Marriage?* (London: Continuum, 2002).

2. Michael Lawler, *Marriage and the Catholic Church: Disputed Questions* (Collegeville, Minn.: Liturgical Press, 2002).

3. See James A. Coriden et al., eds., *The Code of Canon Law: A Text and Commentary* (New York: Paulist Press, 1985), 808.

4. *Gaudium et Spes,* n. 48.

5. Joseph Gredt, *Elementa Philosophiae Aristotelico-Thomistico,* vol. 2 (Barcelona: Herder, 1946), 121, 135.

6. Michael Lawler, *Marriage and Sacrament: A Theology of Christian Marriage* (Collegeville, Minn.: Liturgical Press, 1993), 38.

7. *The Code of Canon Law,* 808.

8. The single theoretical exception to that requirement is the case of the accidents of bread and wine which, after consecration, exist in Eucharist though not in their proper subject. In *S.T.,* III, q. 77, a. 1, Aquinas appeals to a "miracle" to explain this exception.

9. Lawler, "On the Bonds of Marriage," in *Marriage and Sacrament,* 68–69.

10. *DTC: Dictionnaire de théologie catholique.*

11. This is Örsy's reference to *The Code of Canon Law.*

12. Ladislas Örsy, *Marriage in Canon Law: Texts and Comments; Reflections and Questions* (Leominster: Fowler Wright, 1988), 204–5.

13. Lawler, *Marriage and Sacrament,* 74.

14. Kevin T. Kelly, *Divorce and Second Marriage* (London: Chapman, 1996), 73.

15. Sheila Rauch Kennedy, *Shattered Faith* (Dublin: Poolbeg Press, 1997).

16. Ibid., 196.

17. I dealt with this idea in some detail in an article, "Caring for the Remarried," *Priests and People* (August–September 1995): 325–30.

9: Christian Marriage: A Divine Calling (William P. Roberts)

1. For a similar theme to examine, see Julio Hanlon Rubio's essay, "Living the Dual Vocation of Christian Parenthood," chapter 19 in this volume.

2. See Todd Salzman's essay, "Friendship, Sacrament, and Marriage: The Distinction between Christian Marital Friendship and Non-Christian Marital Friendship," chapter 11 in this volume.

10. Casti Connubii to Gaudium et Spes (Bernard Cooke)

1. *Acta Apostolicae Sedis*, 22 (1930): 539ff.

11. Friendship, Sacrament, and Marriage (Todd A. Salzman)

1. Michael Lawler, *Marriage and the Catholic Church: Disputed Questions* (Collegeville, Minn.: Liturgical Press, 2002), 140–61.

2. Marcus Tullius Cicero, *De amicitia* (On Friendship), trans. E. S. Shuckburgh, *Letters of Marcus Tullius Cicero with His Treatise on Friendship and Old Age* (New York: P. F. Collier, 1925), nn. 1–27.

3. Ibid., n. 6.

4. Ibid., n. 5.

5. Søren Kierkegaard, *Works of Love: Some Christian Reflections in the Form of Discourses*, trans. Howard and Edna Long (New York: Harper & Row, 1964).

6. Anders Nygren, *Agape and Eros* (New York: Harper & Row, 1964).

7. Gene Outka, *Agape: An Ethical Analysis* (New Haven, Conn.: Yale University Press, 1972).

8. Edward Vacek, *Love, Human and Divine: The Heart of Christian Ethics* (Washington, D.C.: Georgetown University Press, 1994), xvi.

9. Ibid., 307.

10. Aelred of Rievaulx, *Spiritual Friendship*, trans. M. E. Laker (Kalamazoo, Mich.: Cistercian Publications, 1977), 3:2.

11. These four characteristics are taken from Marie Aquinas McNamara, *Friendship in Saint Augustine* (Fribourg: University Press, 1958).

12. Paul J. Wadell, *Friendship and the Moral Life* (Notre Dame, Ind.: University of Notre Dame Press, 1989), 100.

13. Gilbert Meilaender, *Friendship: A Study in Theological Ethics* (Notre Dame, Ind.: University of Notre Dame Press, 1981), 17.

14. Aelred of Rievaulx, *Spiritual Friendship*, 3:5; 3:54.

15. Ibid., 1:1.

16. Ibid., 1:21.

17. Ibid., 1:70.

18. Aquinas, *S.T.*, I-II, q. 65, a. 5.

19. Ibid., q. 108, a. 4.

20. Adrian Thatcher, *Marriage after Modernity: Christian Marriage in Postmodern Times* (New York: New York University Press, 1999), 235.

21. Karl Rahner, "Marriage as Sacrament," in *Theological Investigations*, vol. 10, trans. David Bourke (New York: Seabury Press), 202 (emphasis in original).

22. Lawler, *Marriage and the Catholic Church*, 48–50.

23. Aelred of Rievaulx, *Spiritual Friendship*, 1:1.

24. See James A. Coriden et al., eds., *The Code of Canon Law: A Text and Commentary* (New York: Paulist Press, 1985).

25. I am indebted in this section to John T. Noonan's treatment of Aquinas on marital friendship. See "Maxima Amicitia," in Congresso internazionale Tommaso d'Aquino nel suo settimo, *L'agier morale* (Rome: Edizioni domenicane italiane, 1977), 344–51.

26. Aelred of Rievaulx, *Spiritual Friendship*, 1:21.

27. *The Code of Canon Law*, c. 1057.

28. Gustave Martelet, "Sixteen Christological Theses on the Sacrament of Marriage," in *Contemporary Perspectives on Christian Marriage*, ed. Richard Malone and John R. Connery (Chicago: Loyola University Press, 1984), 46.

29. *Catechism of the Catholic Church*, n. 2204.

12. Toward a Eucharistic Spirituality of Family (Joann Heaney-Hunter)

1. www.agreeley.com/homilies96/June0996.html.

2. See Wendy Wright's essay, "The Christian Spiritual Life and the Family," chapter 18 in this volume.

3. John Paul II, *Familiaris Consortio*, n. 49.

4. *Lumen Gentium*, n. 11, and *Sacrosanctum Concilium*, n. 10.

5. Monika Hellwig, *The Eucharist and the Hunger of the World* (New York: Paulist Press, 1976), 9.

6. Edward Schillebeeckx, *Christ the Sacrament of the Encounter with God* (New York: Sheed and Ward, 1963), 97–100.

7. Ronald Rolheiser, *The Shattered Lantern: Rediscovering a Felt Presence of God* (New York: Crossroad, 2001), 175–204.

8. Henri Nouwen, *Life of the Beloved* (New York: Crossroad, 2002).

9. John Paul II, *Familiaris Consortio*, n. 42.

10. John Chrysostom, "To a Young Widow 3," *Nicene and Post-Nicene Fathers*, vol. 9, series 1, www.ccel.org/fathers2/NPNF1–09/npnf1-09-15.htm#P728_458375.

11. Beginning with the Second Vatican Council, the church moved from an understanding of marriage as contract to marriage as covenant. See, for example, *Gaudium et Spes*, n. 48. There are problems, however, in relating contemporary marriage to biblical covenant due to the inherent inequality found in the relationship between God and the Israelites. It is important to remember the essential element of covenant — that God loves God's people unconditionally. Unconditional love is at the heart of the marriage covenant.

12. Margaret Farley, "The Meaning of Commitment," in *Perspectives on Marriage*, ed. Michael Warren and Kieran Scott (New York: Oxford University Press, 1993), 110–22.

13. Ronald Rolheiser, *The Holy Longing: The Search for a Christian Spirituality* (New York: Doubleday, 1999), 140.

14. Richard Rohr, "Epiphany: You Can't Go Home Again," www.americancatholic.org/Messenger/Jan2001/Feature3.asp. This stance is also central to Ignatian spirituality, particularly in the maxim "Find God in all things." See, for example, *Complementary Norms to the Constitutions of the Society of Jesus*, Norms, Part

VI, Sect. 5, Ch. 1, n. 223.3 in *The Constitutions of the Society of Jesus and Their Complementary Norms* (St. Louis: Institute of Jesuit Sources, 1996), 255.

13: Sacramental Marriage and Holy Orders (Thomas Knieps-Port le Roi)

1. See, for example, John Paul II, *Familiaris Consortio*, n. 16; *Catechism of the Catholic Church*, n. 1620.
2. *Lumen Gentium*, n. 1 (emphasis added).
3. Ibid., n. 48.
4. Ibid., n. 5.
5. See Karl Rahner, *The Church and the Sacraments* (New York: Herder & Herder, 1963).
6. Ibid., 77.
7. See *Catechism of the Catholic Church*, nn. 1210–11.
8. See Timothy Buckley's essay, "The Bond of Marriage," chapter 8 in this volume.
9. See *Presbyterorum Ordinis*, n. 2; *Lumen Gentium*, nn. 10 and 28.
10. Quoted in *Lumen Gentium*, n. 32.

14. Sacramentality and Social Mission (Thomas M. Kelly)

1. *Lumen Gentium*, n. 31.
2. Ibid.
3. Ibid., n. 36.
4. John Paul II recognizes this as well. "The Pastors, therefore, ought to acknowledge and foster the ministries, the offices and roles of the lay faithful that find their foundation in the Sacraments of Baptism and Confirmation, indeed, for a good many of them, in the Sacrament of Matrimony" (*Christifideles Laici*, n. 23).
5. John Paul II, *Familiaris Consortio*, n. 1.
6. Ibid., n. 2.
7. Ibid., n. 5.
8. Ibid., n. 11.
9. Ibid., n. 12.
10. Ibid., n. 13 (emphasis added).
11. See Timothy Buckley's essay, "The Bond of Marriage," chapter 8 in this volume.
12. See below.
13. John Paul II, *Familiaris Consortio*, n. 17.
14. Ibid., n. 42.
15. Ibid., n. 43.
16. Ibid., n. 44.
17. Ibid., n. 47.
18. Ibid., n. 51.
19. Ibid.
20. Ibid., n. 56.
21. Ibid., n. 68 (emphasis added).
22. Michael G. Lawler, *Secular Marriage, Christian Sacrament* (Mystic, Conn.: Twenty-Third Publications, 1985), 66.

23. See Florence Bourg's essay, "Marriage and Non-Practicing Catholics," chapter 21 in this volume.

24. Michael Himes, "The Instrinsic Sacramentality of Marriage: The Theological Ground for the Inseparability of Validity and Sacramentality in Marriage," *The Jurist* 50, no. 1 (1990): 215.

25. I am thinking of Platonism, neo-Platonism, and their derivative movements.

26. John Paul II, *Familiar Consortio*, n. 17.

27. Michael Himes, *Doing the Truth in Love* (New York and Mahwah, N.J.: Paulist Press, 1995), 108.

28. In "The Intrinsic Sacramentality of Marriage" Himes states the following: "Because grace is everywhere, it must be attended to somewhere. Certainly we are accustomed to this in our treatment of 'sacred space' and 'sacred time.' Consecrating a particular place does not mean that all other places are profane; celebrating a particular day or season as holy does not mean that all other times are unholy. Because *this* place and *this* time can be especially designated as sacred, they provide us with somewhere and somewhen to attend to what is true everywhere and at all times" (214).

29. It is a love, roughly translated by St. Thomas, as one that effectively wills the good of the other. *Agape* found its way into medieval theology as *caritas*, what Aquinas defines as the effective willing of the good of the other. "Dicendum quod secundum Philosophorum in VIII Eth., non qui libet amor habet rationem amicitiae, sed amor qui est cum benevolentia; quando scilicet sic amamus aliquem ut ei bonum velimus" (*S.T.*, II-II, q. 23, a. 1, respondeo). According to Florence Bourg in *Where Two or Three Are Gathered: Christian Families as Domestic Churches* (Notre Dame, Ind.: University of Notre Dame Press, 2004), Rahner, like Aquinas, links love of God and love of neighbor. See *S.T.*, II-II, q. 25, a. 1; q. 26, a. 7. For a deeper inquiry into the perichoresis of *agape, philia,* and *eros* within married love, see my article "An Integrated Theology of Married Love," *LOGOS, A Journal of Catholic Thought and Culture* 5, no. 1 (2002): 76–103.

30. For example, one never knows if the rich young man ever came back to Jesus again (Mark 10:17–22), but it is clear from the biblical text that Jesus had no problem in letting him walk away. Jesus' willingness to confront the rich young man on the main idol in his life was agapic love in action. The good of the young man was realized because he learned what was keeping him from a right relationship with God.

31. Rahner would designate this as "sacrament in general." "Marriage as Sacrament," in Karl Rahner, *Theological Investigations* 10 (New York: Seabury Press, 1974), 200. John Paul II recognizes that it is necessary to speak of sacraments "generally," at times. In *The Theology of Marriage and Celibacy* (Boston: Daughters of St. Paul, 1986) he states the following: "Until now, indeed, we have used the term 'sacrament' (in conformity with the whole of the biblical-patristic tradition) in a sense wider than that proper to traditional and contemporary theological terminology, which means by the word 'sacrament' the signs instituted by Christ and administered by the Church, which signify and confer divine grace on the person who receives the relative sacrament" (266–67). And later, "In relationship to this rather restricted meaning, we have used in our considerations *a wider and perhaps also more ancient and fundamental meaning of the term 'sacrament.'* The letter to the Ephesians, and especially 5:22–23, seems in a particular way to authorize us to

do so. Here sacrament signifies the very mystery of God, which is hidden from all eternity, however, not in an eternal concealment, but above all, in its very revelation and actuation (furthermore: in its revelation through its actuation)" (267).

32. Michael Lawler quotes Juan Alfaro and argues that faith is necessary for the sacramentality of marriage, with faith including "knowledge of a saving event, confidence in the Word of God, man's humble submission and personal self-surrender to God, fellowship in life with Christ, and a desire for perfect union with Him beyond the grave. Faith is man's comprehensive 'Yes' to God's revealing himself as man's savior in Christ" (*Marriage and the Catholic Church: Disputed Questions* [Collegeville, Minn.: Liturgical Press, 2002], 45). Lawler remarks that this is a less intellectualist conception of faith than earlier understandings and represents a "minimalist" reading as well.

33. Himes states the following: "In these seven sacramental events the Church sees its life so richly expressed that they serve as words of self-expression through which the Church 'selves.' As such, they are occasions when the Church exercises itself so fully they communicate the triumphant grace of Christ which grounds the Church's existence. They can therefore be said to signify and so effect grace *ex opere operato*" ("The Instrinsic Sacramentality of Marriage," 215–16).

34. Much of this section is indebted to the analysis of sacramentality and the particular angle of the theologian Rev. Michael Himes, "The Intrinsic Sacramentality of Marriage," 199.

35. Augustine of Hippo, *De Doctrina Christiana*, 2, 1, 1 (CSEL 80, 33). "Signum est enim res, praeter speciem quam ingerit sensisbus, aliud aliquid ex se faciens in cogitationem venire.... "

36. Aquinas, *S.T.*, III, q. 62, a. 1, ad 1: "Et inde est quod, sicut communiter dicitur, [sacramentum] efficiunt quod figurant."

15. Cohabitation (Gail Risch)

1. See, for example, Lisa Sowle Cahill, "Marriage: Developments in Catholic Theology and Ethics," *Theological Studies* 64 (2003): 78–105; Michael G. Lawler, *Marriage and the Catholic Church: Disputed Questions* (Collegeville, Minn.: Liturgical Press, 2002), 162–92; Center of the American Experiment, Coalition for Marriage, Family and Couples Education, Institute for American Values, *Why Marriage Matters: Twenty-One Conclusions from the Social Sciences* (New York: Institutes for American Values, 2002).

2. Michael G. Lawler, "Faith, Praxis, and Practical Theology: At the Interface of Sociology and Theology," *Horizons* 29 (2002): 199.

3. For an explanation and discussion of reception see ibid., 199–224.

4. Pontifical Council for the Family, *Family, Marriage, and "De Facto" Unions* (Washington, D.C.: United States Catholic Conference, 2001), 1.

5. Ibid., 1–2.

6. R. Kelly Raley, "Recent Trends and Differentials in Marriage and Cohabitation: The United States," in *The Ties That Bind: Perspectives on Marriage and Cohabitation,* ed. Linda J. Waite (New York: Aldine de Gruyter, 2000), 20; see also Lynne M. Casper and Philip N. Cohen, "How Does POSSLQ Measure Up? Historical Estimates of Cohabitation," *Demography* 37 (2000): 237–45; Kathleen Kiernan, "European Perspectives on Union Formation," in *Ties That Bind,* ed. Waite, 40–58; John Ermisch and Marco Francesconi, "Cohabitation in Great Britain: Not for Long,

but Here to Stay," *Journal of the Royal Statistical Society: Series A* 163 (2000): 153–71; Larry Bumpass and Hsien-Hen Lu, "Trends in Cohabitation and Implications for Children's Family Contexts in the United States," *Population Studies* 54 (2000): 29–41; Pamela J. Smock, "Cohabitation in the United States: An Appraisal of Research Themes, Findings, and Implications," *Annual Review of Sociology* 26 (2000): 1–20.

7. Bumpass and Lu, "Trends in Cohabitation," 7.

8. See ibid., 29–41; Michael J. Brien, Lee A. Lillard, and Linda J. Waite, "Interrelated Family-Building Behaviors: Cohabitation, Marriage, and Nonmarital Conception," *Demography* 36 (1999): 535–51; Deborah Roempke Graefe and Daniel T. Lichter, "Life Course Transitions of American Children: Parental Cohabitation, Marriage, and Single Motherhood," *Demography* 36 (1999): 205–17; Kathleen Kiernan, "The Rise of Cohabitation and Childbearing outside Marriage in Western Europe," *International Journal of Law, Policy, and the Family* 15 (2001): 1–21; Wendy D. Manning and Nancy S. Landale, "Racial and Ethnic Differences in the Role of Cohabitation in Premarital Childbearing," *Journal of Marriage and the Family* 58 (1996): 63–77; R. Kelly Raley, "Increasing Fertility in Cohabiting Unions: Evidence for the Second Demographic Transition in the United States?" *Demography* 38 (2001): 59–66; Howard Wineberg and James McCarthy, "Living Arrangements after Divorce: Cohabitation versus Remarriage," *Journal of Divorce and Remarriage* 29 (1998): 131–46; Daniel Lichter and Deborah Graefe, "Parental Cohabitation, Marriage, and Single Motherhood: Life Course Transitions of American Children," paper presented at the 1997 Annual Meetings of the Population Association of America; Wendy D. Manning and Pamela J. Smock, "Children's Living Arrangements in Unmarried Mother Families," *Journal of Family Issues* 18 (1997): 526–44.

9. Bumpass and Lu, "Trends in Cohabitation," 8.

10. Committee on Marriage and Family, National Conference of Catholic Bishops, *Marriage Preparation and Cohabiting Couples: An Information Report on New Realities and Pastoral Practices* (Washington, D.C.: United States Catholic Conference, 1999), 4.

11. Ibid., 6.

12. Ibid., 16.

13. For an explanation of physicalism and personalism, see Richard M. Gula, *Reason Informed by Faith: Foundations of Catholic Morality* (Mahwah, N.J.: Paulist Press, 1989), 63–74, 231–49.

14. The National Marriage Project, *The State of Our Unions: The Social Health of Marriage in America* (New Brunswick, N.J.: National Marriage Project, Rutgers University, 2003), 24–25. See also Don S. Browning, *Marriage and Modernization: How Globalization Threatens Marriage and What to Do about It* (Grand Rapids: Eerdmans, 2003); Ermisch and Francesconi, "Cohabitation in Great Britain," 153–71; Kathleen Kiernan, "The Rise of Cohabitation and Childbearing outside Marriage in Western Europe," *International Journal of Law, Policy, and the Family* 15 (2002): 1–21.

15. Smock, "Cohabitation in the United States," 3.

16. M. D. Bramlett and W. D. Mosher, "Cohabitation, Marriage, Divorce, and Remarriage in the United States," National Center for Health Statistics, *Vital Health Statistics* 23 (2002): 12.

17. The National Marriage Project, *The State of Our Unions*, 25; Bumpass and Lu, "Trends in Cohabitation," 35.

18. For a summary of reasons for cohabitation see the National Marriage Project, *The State of Our Unions 2001*; Smock, "Cohabitation in the United States," 1–20.

19. An explanation of the complexity of statistical analyses by which divorce rates are calculated, as well as the analyses of factors that may affect marital stability, are beyond the scope of this article.

20. See Bramlett and Mosher, "Cohabitation, Marriage, Divorce, and Remarriage" for a comprehensive study and discussion of factors related to the likelihood of cohabitation and relationship dissolution among women.

21. Smock, "Cohabitation in the United States," 5.

22. Bramlett and Mosher, "Cohabitation, Marriage, Divorce, and Remarriage," 2, 28–32.

23. Ibid., 32. See also Ann Berrington and Ian Diamond, "Marriage or Cohabitation: A Competing Risks Analysis of First-partnership Formation among the 1958 Birth Cohort," *Journal of Royal Statistical Society: Series A* 163 (2000): 127–51.

24. See W. G. Axinn and A. Thornton, "The Relationship between Cohabitation and Divorce: Selectivity or Causal Influence?" *Demography* 29 (1992): 357–74; W. G. Axinn and J. S. Barber, "Living Arrangements and Family Formation Attitudes in Early Adulthood," *Journal of Marriage and the Family* 59 (1997): 595–611; and M. E. Clarkberg, *The Cohabitation Experience and Changing Values: The Effects of Premarital Cohabitation on the Orientation Towards Marriage, Career, and Community, BLCC Working Paper, No. 99–15* (Ithaca, N.Y.: Cornell Employment and Family Careers Institute: Cornell University, 1999).

25. Renata Forste and Koray Tanfer, "Sexual Exclusivity among Dating, Cohabiting, and Married Women," *Journal of Marriage and the Family* 58 (1994): 124–26. See also Lynn Jamieson et al., "Cohabitation and Commitment: Partnership Plans of Young Men and Women," *Sociological Review 2002* 50 (2002): 356–77.

26. Linda L. Waite, "Cohabitation: A Communitarian Perspective," in *Marriage in America: A Communitarian Perspective*, ed. Martin King Whyte (Lanham, Md.: Rowman & Littlefield, 2000), 26. See also Susan Brown and Alan Booth, "Cohabitation versus Marriage: A Comparison of Relationship Quality," *Journal of Marriage and the Family* 58 (1996): 668–78; Susan Brown, "Cohabitation as Marriage Prelude versus Marriage Alternative: The Significance for Psychological Well-Being," unpublished manuscript, Bowling Green University, Bowling Green, Ohio, 1998.

27. Steven Nock, "A Comparison of Marriages and Cohabiting Relationships," *Journal of Family Issues* 16 (1995): 53.

28. Brown and Booth, "Cohabitation versus Marriage," 674.

29. Waite, "Cohabitation: A Communitarian Perspective," 26 (emphasis added).

30. Lawler, *Marriage and the Catholic Church*, 166.

31. Jay Teachman, "Premarital Sex, Premarital Cohabitation, and the Risk of Subsequent Marital Dissolution among Women," *Journal of Marriage and Family* 65 (2002): 453.

32. Robert Schoen, "First Unions and the Stability of First Marriages," *Journal of Marriage and the Family* 54 (1992): 283–84.

33. Susan McRae, "Cohabitation: A Trial Run for Marriage?" *Sexual and Marital Therapy* 12 (1997): 259–73.

34. Ruth Weston, Lixia Qu, and David de Vaus, "Premarital Cohabitation and Marital Stability," Paper presented at the HILDA Conference, University of Melbourne, Australia, 2003.

35. Joshua R. Goldstein, "The Leveling of Divorce in the United States," *Demography* 36 (1999): 409, 414.

36. Tim B. Heaton, "Factors Contributing to Increasing Marital Stability in the United States," *Journal of Family Issues* 23 (2002): 406.

37. For a discussion of contemporary social changes and the context in which cohabitation is best examined see Arland Thornton and Linda Young-DeMarco, "Four Decades of Trends in Attitudes toward Family Issues in the United States: The 1960s Through the 1990s," *Journal of Marriage and Family* 63 (2001): 1009–37; Whyte, ed., *Marriage in America;* Waite, *The Ties That Bind;* Arlene S. Skolnick and Jerome H. Skolnick, *Family in Transition* (New York: Longman, 1999); Paul R. Amato and Alan Booth, *A Generation at Risk: Growing Up in an Era of Family Upheaval* (Cambridge, Mass.: Harvard University Press, 1997).

38. Michael Murphy, "The Evolution of Cohabitation in Britain, 1960–95," *Population Studies* 54 (2000): 43–56; Faith Monique Nicole and Cynthia Baldwin, "Cohabitation as a Developmental Stage: Implications for Mental Health Counseling," *Journal of Mental Health Counseling* 17 (1995): 386–97.

39. Teachman, "Premarital Sex, Premarital Cohabitation," 447, 453.

40. Adrian Thatcher, "When Does Christian Marriage Begin? Before or after the Wedding?" in *Moral Issues and Christian Responses,* ed. Patricia Beattie Jung and Shannon Jung, 7th ed. (Toronto: Thomson Wadsworth, 2003), 82–86. See also Adrian Thatcher, "Living Together before Marriage: The Theological and Pastoral Opportunities," in Adrian Thatcher, ed., *Celebrating Christian Marriage* (Edinburgh: T & T Clark, 2001), 55–70.

41. For a comprehensive history of Christian marriage, the role of cohabitation, betrothal, and entry into marriage, and discussion of marriage in contemporary society, see Adrian Thatcher's highly acclaimed *Marriage after Modernity: Christian Marriage in Postmodern Times* (Sheffield, U.K.: Sheffield Academic Press, 1999). See also Michael G. Lawler, *Marriage and Sacrament: A Theology of Christian Marriage* (Collegeville, Minn.: Liturgical Press, 1993), 52–72, and Reg Harcus, "The Case for Betrothal," in Thatcher, *Celebrating Christian Marriage,* 41–52.

42. Thatcher, "When Does Christian Marriage Begin?" 111.

43. For extended discussion of the retrieval of the betrothal tradition, see Adrian Thatcher's *Living Together and Christian Ethics* (Cambridge: Cambridge University Press, 2002), and Michael G. Lawler's "Cohabitation and Marriage in the Catholic Church: A Proposal" in idem, *Marriage and the Catholic Church,* 162–92.

44. Thatcher, *Marriage after Modernity,* 120–24; Thatcher, *Living Together and Christian Ethics,* 211–36; and Lawler, *Marriage and the Catholic Church,* 77–87, 162–92.

16. Engagement (Gregory M. Faulhaber)

1. John Paul II, *Familiaris Consortio,* n. 66.

2. U.S. Census Bureau, "Number, Timing, and Duration of Marriages and Divorces: 1996," February 2002, www.census.gov/populationwww/socdemo/marr-div .html.

3. U.S. Census Bureau, "U.S. Adults Postponing Marriage," www.census.gov/ Press-Release/www/2001/cb01-113.html.

4. The PMI (Pre-Marital Inventory) is the oldest of these marriage preparation instruments, put forward by the Bess Associates in 1975. PREPARE (Premarital

Personal and Relationship Enrichment) was next, first issued by David Olson and his Minnesota colleagues in 1977. The Archdiocese of Omaha, Nebraska, developed FOCCUS (Facilitating Open Couple Communication, Understanding and Study) in 1984.

5. Paul Giblin, "Premarital Preparations: Three Approaches," *Pastoral Psychology* 42, no. 3 (1994): 148–49.

6. See Raymond Collins's essay, " 'And the Greatest of These Is Love,' " chapter 4 in this volume.

7. *The New Revised Standard Version of the Holy Bible* (New York: Oxford University Press, 1989).

8. *Catechism of the Catholic Church* (Mahwah, N.J.: Paulist Press, 1994), nn. 2360–63.

9. *Gaudium et Spes,* n. 48.

10. *Familiaris Consortio,* nn. 17–64.

11. Vincent Genovesi, *In Pursuit of Love: Catholic Morality and Human Sexuality,* 2nd ed. (Collegeville, Minn.: Liturgical Press, 1996), 147.

12. NCCB Marriage and Family Committee, "Marriage Preparation and Cohabiting Couples: Information Report," *Origins* 29, no. 14 (September 16, 1999): 213, 216.

13. Ibid., 217–18. More recent studies, however, demonstrate a decline in the direct correlation between cohabitation and divorce. See Gail Risch's essay, "Cohabitation: Integrating Ecclesial and Social Scientific Teaching," chapter 15 in this volume.

14. From my limited study of this issue I find this to be true, but not universally supported by all research. A 2001 study by Oklahoma State University observed that those who attended religious services regularly (at least once a month) were more likely to be very happy in their marriages (72 percent) than those who seldom or never attended religious services (52 percent). This survey also reported that those who were more frequent in attendance at religious services were significantly less likely to have been divorced (OSU Bureau for Social Research, "Marriage in Oklahoma: 2001 Baseline Statewide Survey on Marriage and Divorce," www.okmarriage.org/pdf/survey, 24–26). However, a 1999 study of the Barna Research Group did not support this view. Their survey of some four thousand adults discovered a higher divorce rate among Christians than atheists and concluded that religion was no preventive for divorce (Virginia Culver, "Study: Religion no Divorce Preventive," *Denver Post,* January 8, 2000, B-6).

17. Vulnerable to the Holy (Enda McDonagh)

1. Michael Lawler, *Marriage and the Catholic Church: Disputed Questions* (Collegeville, Minn.: Liturgical Press, 2002).

18: The Christian Spiritual Life and the Family (Wendy M. Wright)

1. I have explored the questions raised in this brief article in more depth in *Sacred Dwelling: A Spirituality of Family Life* (New York: Crossroad, 1st ed., 1989; Leavenworth, Kans.: Forest of Peace, 2nd ed., 1994) and *Seasons of a Family's Life: Cultivating a Contemplative Spirit at Home* (San Francisco: Jossey-Bass, 2003).

2. See Ron Simkins's essay, "Marriage and Gender in the Old Testament," chapter 2 in this volume.

3. See Joann Heaney-Hunter's essay, "Toward a Eucharistic Spirituality of Family: Lives Blessed, Broken, and Shared," chapter 12 in this volume.

4. See my "The Charism of Parenting," in *Retrieving Charisms for the Twenty-first Century, Proceedings of the Charisms for the Twenty-first Century Symposium*, ed. Doris Donnelly (Collegeville, Minn.: Liturgical Press, 1999), 85–102.

5. See Thomas Kelly's essay, "Sacramentality and Social Mission: A New Way to Imagine Marriage," chapter 14 in this volume, for his discussion of sacramentality.

19: Living the Dual Vocation of Christian Parenthood (Julie Hanlon Rubio)

1. Michael G. Lawler, *Marriage and Sacrament: A Theology of Christian Marriage* (Collegeville, Minn.: Liturgical Press, 1993), 6.

2. Ibid., 103.

3. Ibid., 104.

4. Julie Hanlon Rubio, *A Christian Theology of Marriage and Family* (New York: Paulist, 2003).

5. Florence Caffrey Bourg, *Where Two or Three Are Gathered: Christian Families as Domestic Churches* (Notre Dame, Ind.: University of Notre Dame Press, 2004).

6. Linda Woodhead, "Faith, Feminism, and the Family," in *The Family, Concilium,* ed. Lisa Sowle Cahill and Dietmar Mieth (Maryknoll, N.Y.: Orbis, 1995), 45.

7. See Susan Calef's essay, "The Radicalism of Jesus the Prophet: Implications for Christian Family," chapter 5 in this volume.

8. Lisa Sowle Cahill, *Family: A Christian Social Perspective* (Minneapolis: Fortress, 2000), 29.

9. See Bruce Malina's essay, "The Meaning(s) of Purposeful Non-Marriage in the New Testament," chapter 3 in this volume.

10. For further discussion, see Richard Horsley, *Sociology of the Jesus Movement* (New York: Crossroad, 1989), and Peter Brown, *Body and Society: Men, Women, and Sexual Renunciation in Early Christianity* (New York: Columbia University Press, 1988).

11. Andrew Jacobs, "A Family Affair: Marriage, Class, and Ethics in the Apocryphal Acts of the Apostles," *Journal of Early Christian Studies* 7, no. 1 (1999): 106.

12. See Brown, *Body and Society,* 33–44.

13. See John Paul II, *Familiaris Consortio,* n. 16.

14. See my "The Dual Vocation of Christian Parents," *Theological Studies* 63, no. 4 (2002): 802–6.

15. The list is adapted from Jaine Carter and James D. Carter, *He Works She Works: Successful Strategies for Working Couples* (New York: Amacom, 1995), 4–5. A similar, more optimistic study is Rosalind C. Barnett and Caryl Rivers, *She Works He Works: How Two-Income Families Are Happier, Healthier, and Better-Off* (San Francisco: HarperSanFrancisco, 1996).

16. Betty L. Broom, "Parental Sensitivity to Infants and Toddlers in Dual-Earner and Single-Earner Families," *Nursing Research* 47, no. 8 (May–June 1998): 162–70.

17. See Scott Coltrane, *Family Man: Fatherhood, Housework, and Gender Equity* (New York: Oxford, 1996); and Diane Ehrensaft, *Parenting Together: Men and Women Sharing the Care of Their Children* (New York: Free Press, 1987).

18. Ellen Galinsky, *Ask the Children: What America's Children Really Think about Working Parents* (New York: William Morrow, 1999).

19. See Don Browning et al., *From Culture Wars to Common Ground,* 2nd ed. (Louisville: Westminster John Knox, 2000), 317.

20. Arlie Hochschild with Anne Machung, *The Second Shift* (New York: Avon, 1989).

21. Joseph Pleck argues that men actually do 34 percent of housework, not 20 percent, in "Are 'Family Supportive Employer Policies' Relevant to Men?" in *Men, Work and Family,* ed. Jane C. Hood (Newbury Park, Calif.: Sage, 1993), 220.

22. See Ronald J. Burke, "Effects of Sex, Parental Status, and Spouse Work Involvement in Dual-Career Couples," *Psychological Reports* 87 (2000): 919–27, who finds that men are still working longer hours than women and doing less housework; Michelle L. Frisco and Kristi Williams, "Perceived Marital Happiness, and Divorce in Dual Earner Households," *Journal of Family Issues* 24, no. 1 (January 2003): 51–73, where the authors find that perceived fairness in the division of housework is associated with higher levels of marital happiness, which is linked to lower levels of divorce; Daphne Stevens, Gary Kiger, and Pamela J. Riley, "Working Hard and Hardly Working: Domestic Labor and Marital Satisfaction among Dual Earner Couples," *Journal of Marriage and Family* 63 (May 2001): 514–26, agree that predicting satisfaction is difficult and may be related to factors other than the actual number of hours worked.

23. Kristin M. Perrone and Everett L. Worthington Jr., "Factors Influencing Ratings of Marital Quality by Individuals within Dual Career Marriages: A Conceptual Model," *Journal of Counseling Psychology* 48, no. 1 (2001): 3–9. The authors found that coping mechanisms had some mitigating effects on key stressors.

24. See Florence Caffrey Bourg, "Family Economics and the Lay Theologian," panel presentation at the Catholic Theological Society of America annual meeting, June 6, 2003.

25. Penny Edgell Becker and Phyllis Moen, "Scaling Back: Dual-Earner Couples' Work-Family Strategies," *Journal of Marriage and Family* 61 (November 1999): 995–1007.

26. Francine M. Deutsch, *Halving It All: How Equally Shared Parenting Works* (Cambridge, Mass.: Harvard University Press, 1999).

27. Ehrensaft, *Parenting Together,* 165.

20: Married and Aging (Aldegonde Brenninkmeijer-Werhahn)

1. In 1982 in Vienna the UN organized its first world assembly on aging. In 1998 Kofi Annan, the UN Secretary General, declared the World Day of the Older Person, and in April 2003 the UN held its second world assembly on aging, in Madrid. See also Pope John Paul II, *Familiaris Consortio;* Bishop Anthony Pilla, "The Needs and Talents of the Aged," *Origins* 14, no. 21 (November 8, 1984): 328–34; The Church of England General Synod, *Aging,* November 1990; Pontifical Council for the Laity, *The Dignity of Older People and Their Mission in the Church and the World,* February 1999; John Paul II, *Letter to the Elderly,* October 1, 1999.

2. Pastoral letter of the U.S. Conference of Catholic Bishops: *Blessing of Age: A Pastoral Message on Growing Older within the Faith Community,* in *Origins* 29, no. 25 (December 2, 1999).

3. *Signum* (Documentation and Information Service for Religious) 28/7 (July 12, 2000).

4. Ben E. Dickerson and Derrel Watkins, "Empowering through Faith: The Age Crescendo: The Oldest-Old and Their Families," *Family Ministry* 15, no. 4 (Winter 2001): 31–43.

5. Anne Forbes, "Age as Opportunity," *Priest and People* 12, nos. 8–9 (August–September 1998): 304.

6. Pope John Paul II, *Letter to the Elderly*, 13.

7. Ovid, *Metamorphoses* VIII, AD 8, quoted in Helge Rubinstein, ed., *Oxford Book of Marriage* (Oxford: Oxford University Press, 1990), 323–25.

8. Ibid.

9. See the collection Adrian Thatcher, ed., *Celebrating Christian Marriage* (Edinburgh and New York: T & T Clark, 2001), especially the article by Margaret A. Farley, "Marriage, Divorce and Personal Commitments," 355–72. See also in the same collection my further discussion of this topic in "Lifetime as a Virtue: Changes in Marriage over Time," 201–18.

10. Terry D. Hargrave and Suzanne Midori Hanna, *The Aging Family: New Visions in Theory, Practice and Reality* (New York: Brunner/Mazel, 1997), 184.

11. Ibid., 26 and 186.

12. Romano Guardini, *Die Lebensalter: Ihre ethische und pädagogische Bedeutung* (Würzburg, 1953; reprint, Mainz: Grünewald, Topos Taschenbuch 160, 1990), 77.

21: Marriage and Non-Practicing Catholics
(Florence Caffrey Bourg)

1. Sociologists typically measure Catholic affiliation by Mass attendance or by asking whether persons consider themselves Catholic. In a guide for Catholic ministers who field wedding requests from "marginal" Catholics, Joseph Champlin defines marginal Catholics broadly as those who "have only a tenuous link with the parish. This fragile bond is manifested when persons seeking a sacrament either overtly reject a major church tenet, or do not participate weekly at Sunday Mass, or seldom receive communion or penance, or rarely volunteer for church activities, or never formally register with a particular parish.... There are, naturally, degrees of marginalization. The case of the person who has not been to church in ten years differs greatly from that of the individual who goes regularly to mass, but chooses not to affiliate or become involved with any parish. The challenge presented by the latter to the priest, deacon, or pastoral leader is rather minimal; the challenge offered by the former is quite substantial" (Joseph M. Champlin, *The Marginal Catholic: Challenge, Don't Crush* [Notre Dame, Ind.: Ave Maria Press, 1989], 18).

2. Ibid.; Dean Hoge et al., *Young Adult Catholics: Religion in the Culture of Choice* (Notre Dame, Ind.: University of Notre Dame Press, 2001); Dean Hoge et al., *Converts, Dropouts, Returnees: A Study of Religious Change among Catholics* (New York: Pilgrim Press, 1981); Mitch Finley, *It's Not the Same without You: Coming Home to the Catholic Church* (New York: Doubleday, 2003), chap. 7.

3. Pierre Hegy and Joseph Martos, *Catholic Divorce: The Deception of Annulments* (New York: Continuum, 2000); Carrie Kemp, *Catholics Can Come Home Again: A Guide for the Journey of Reconciliation with Inactive Catholics* (New

York: Paulist Press, 2001), 163–76; Lorene Duquin, *Could You Ever Come Back to the Catholic Church?* (New York: Alba House, 1997), 117–38.

4. The most significant predictors of church involvement among a 1997 sample of adults aged twenty to thirty-nine and previously confirmed in the Catholic Church were (1) whether the person married a Catholic spouse, and (2) whether the person (if now married) attended the same church as the spouse. The researchers clarify, "No one should conclude that the act of marrying a non-Catholic by itself explains a religious change. This is because people who marry outside their faith have less commitment than average to their own faith. Such people feel less loyalty to their faith than others, and when they subsequently marry outside the faith, the interfaith marriage is only part of the explanation for any later behavior. In the case of our sample members who married non-Catholics, on average they were less Catholic to start with. . . . How many of the exits from Catholicism were directly due to these interfaith marriages? After reviewing the interviews we guess that it is about one-third of the non-Latinos and one-fourth of the Latinos" (Hoge et al., *Young Adult Catholics*, 97–98).

Somewhat different results come from a recent study of interchurch marriages among Christians of different denominations (IC), same-church marriages (SC), and relationships that were initially interchurch but became same-church (IC-to-SC). "IC respondents had lower church attendance than SC respondents at engagement, and their attendance remained lower, but the *change* in church attendance over time for the two groups was not significantly different. IC-to-SC respondents were significantly more likely than both SC and IC respondents to increase church attendance and to strengthen denominational identity between engagement and interview. The one area where interchurch individuals might be at more risk for drift is in terms of changing to no religious affiliation. Although the numbers are small, a higher percentage of respondents who were initially interchurch at engagement (3.3 percent) changed to no religious affiliation than respondents who were same-church at engagement (0.3 percent)." Lee Williams and Michael Lawler, "Religious Heterogamy and Religiosity: A Comparison of Interchurch and Same-Church Individuals," *Journal for the Scientific Study of Religion* 40, no. 3 (2001): 476.

On the link between intermarriage and (generally lower) religiosity among previous generations of Catholics, consult Hoge et al., *Converts, Dropouts, Returnees*, chapter 4.

5. Tom Smith, "American Catholics," General Social Survey 1998 (University of Chicago: National Opinion Research Center, 1999), cited in Hoge, *Young Adult Catholics*, 1. U.S. Catholics numbered 55 to 60 million in 1995 (estimates from Joseph Harris, "Supply, Demand, and Parish Staffing," *America* 180, no. 12 [April 10, 1999]: 16–21; James Davidson, "Outside the Church: Whom Catholics Marry and Where," *Commonweal* [September 10, 1999]: 14–16; Andrew Greeley, *The Catholic Myth: The Behavior and Belief of American Catholics* [New York: Charles Scribner's Sons, 1990], cited in Finley, *It's Not the Same without You*, 6). According to Greeley, since 1960 there has consistently been about 15 percent of the U.S. "Catholic" population who were raised as church members but no longer consider themselves Catholic — at least 9 million people today. In Europe, average attendance at Sunday Mass is 10 percent, compared to about 30 percent in the U.S. (Hegy and Martos, *Catholic Divorce*, 4).

6. Hoge et al. found 64 percent of young adult confirmands agreed with the statement, "One can be a good Catholic without going to Mass." They note that a similar 1997 study found 73 percent of young adults agreeing with this statement (*Young Adult Catholics,* 54–55).

7. Ibid. The researchers explain that because the survey group was limited to confirmands and not all Catholics are confirmed (they estimate that in the 1980s 30–40 percent of Latino youth were confirmed and 60–70 percent of non-Latino youth), this sample is likely to be more religious over their lifetimes than the general young adult U.S. Catholic population. Yet because this study was limited to young adults and young adulthood is the most common age to forego religious worship, this sample is expected to be less active than the Catholic U.S. population overall.

8. Ibid., 252–53.

9. The difference from Greeley's 15 percent figure may be because Hoge's study was limited to confirmands. Of those who said they were no longer Catholic, only 3 percent of Latinos and 4 percent of non-Latinos reported no religion; most are members of other religions. This group attends church, on average, more regularly than those who remained Catholic (ibid., 45).

10. Ibid., 70–71.

11. Rutgers University National Marriage Project, "Age at First Marriage," (2003); online see http://marriage.rutgers.edu/Publications/SOOU/TEXTSOOU2003.htm# AgeatFirstMarriage.

12. Still, unconfirmed Catholics are probably less active in parish life than those profiled in Hoge et al., *Young Adult Catholics.*

13. "Canonical form" refers to the requirement of church law (that is, canon law) that baptized Catholics have marriage vows witnessed by an ordained Catholic minister (bishop/priest/deacon) plus two additional witnesses. "Dispensations" allow for weddings witnessed by ministers of other religious communities. If Catholics marry without canonical form or dispensation from it, the marriage is considered invalid for purposes of church law.

14. Davidson, "Outside the Church," 15. Harris, "Supply, Demand," cites different numbers (from an unidentified source): 327,317 Catholic marriages in 1950, 302,919 in 1995.

15. Davidson ("Outside the Church") notes this increasing trend. For instance, in a 1995 national telephone survey, he found 40 percent of Catholics born between 1961 and 1977 reported they were/had been married to a non-Catholic. According to the *Official Catholic Directory,* the intermarriage rate was 33.5 percent in 1985 and 30.8 percent in 1995. The most reasonable explanation seems to be that Catholics who marry persons of other religious traditions are increasingly marrying in weddings not authorized by their own church.

16. Working from Harris's figures, Hegy and Martos remark: "Had all the Catholics who married in 1995 done so in the Catholic Church, there would have been about 687,000 Catholic weddings instead of 303,000. What happened to the missing 384,000 newlyweds who did not show up at Catholic parishes? . . . Knowing that approximately 45 percent of all marriages in the United States are second marriages involving at least one divorced person, and knowing that between 80 and 90 percent of divorced Catholics do not obtain annulments so they can remarry in the Catholic Church, we can be virtually certain that many of the missing 384,000 were prevented

from having a Catholic wedding by the church's marriage laws. If this situation continues, the U.S. Catholic Church will be losing perhaps half its newlyweds every year. Moreover, since rejected divorced Catholics are less likely to foster the Catholic faith in their children, the church is likely to lose the children of these marriages as well" (*Catholic Divorce*, 2).

17. See examples in Champlin, Kemp, Hegy/Martos, Duquin, and Finley.

18. Official Catholic guidelines say eucharistic sharing is possible for interchurch couples in exceptional situations, but there is not consensus about which situations these are. See Michael Lawler's essay, "Interchurch Marriages," chapter 22 in this volume, and Ernest Falardeau, "The Church, the Eucharist, and the Family," *One in Christ* 33, no. 1 (1997): 20–30.

19. Hoge et al., *Young Adult Catholics,* 47.

20. Ibid., 77.

21. Asked if they had read the Bible at home within the previous two years, "yes" responses among Latinos were 50 percent of occasional churchgoers and 41 percent of non-attending Catholics; among non-Latinos, 48 percent of occasional churchgoers and 29 percent of non-attending Catholics (ibid., 76–78).

22. Ibid., 154.

23. Ibid., 76–77.

24. Such obstacles are not unique to Catholics, of course. See Williams and Lawler, "Religious Heterogamy and Religiosity," 476.

25. Hoge et al., *Young Adult Catholics,* 15. For scrutiny of this trend, see Lawrence Cunningham, "Stairways to Heaven," *Notre Dame Magazine* (Autumn 2002), at www.nd.edu/~ndmag/au2002/cunningham.html.

26. Cunningham, "Stairways to Heaven."

27. Figures were as follows: Non-Latinos — 71 percent of occasional attendees and 63 percent of non-attending; Latinos — 73 percent of occasional attendees and 59 percent of non-attending.

28. J. Z. T. Pieper, "An Opportunity for Religious Growth? A Study of Marriage Preparation in Two Belgian Dioceses," *INTAMS Review* 9, no. 1 (Spring 2003): 17–29.

29. In Pieper's sample, 67 percent consider themselves members of the Catholic Church, 14 percent not members, 19 percent are uncertain. Thirteen percent attend Mass weekly, 15 percent go once/month, 45 percent a few times annually, and 27 percent almost never. Respondents were asked whether they agreed/disagreed with these statements: #1, "I try to apply my faith and vision of life to my daily life"; #2, "My faith and vision of life are the foundation of my life"; and #3, "In my life I experience the presence of the Divine." For question #1, 60 percent were in complete or basic agreement; for #2, 43 percent, and for #3, 48 percent ("An Opportunity," 18–19).

30. Key source texts are Vatican II, *Gaudium et Spes,* nn. 47–52; Pope John Paul II, *Familiaris Consortio; Catechism of the Catholic Church,* nn. 1601–66. All of these sources are available at the Vatican Web site, www.vatican.va.

31. "The response of faith to questions about your new future" (58 percent); "What the Bible has to say about marriage" and "God's support and help for marriage" (45 percent); "Faith in daily married life, e.g., praying together" (43 percent); "The meaning of the life of Jesus for marriage" (42 percent); "Participation in church

life" (35 percent); "Talking with other couples about faith and church" (32 percent); "Working with other married couples on the world's problems, e.g., peace and development" (25 percent) (Pieper, "An Opportunity," 22).

32. "You marry in the church because many other people do so" scored lowest (12 percent); "I married in the church because it is important for my parents/in-laws" scored third-lowest (29 percent) (ibid., 20).

33. Hoge et al., *Young Adult Catholics,* reports 95 percent of 848 respondents answering "yes" to the question, "Would you want a child of yours to receive any religious instruction?" (58).

34. Robert Barry, "Marriage as a Sacrament for Generation X?" unpublished essay, 5.

35. Hoge et al., *Young Adult Catholics,* chapters 1, 2, and 6.

36. Ibid., 219–20.

37. Consult sources cited in note 30 and sections of this volume devoted to scripture and tradition for in-depth treatment of sacramentality, validity, indissolubility, etc.

38. The word "recipient" reinforces the idea that a sacrament is a "thing" passively received at a specific moment. Many contemporary theologians, to accentuate ongoing, active roles of the parties involved in a sacramental event, avoid the word "receive" and prefer "participate." Tension between these schools of thought will be evident when we examine whether inactive Catholics can marry sacramentally. See Thomas Kelly's essay, "Sacramentality and Social Mission: A New Way to Imagine Marriage," chapter 14 in this volume.

39. Before canonical form requirements existed, marriages were considered valid by virtue of the couple's consent, even without witnesses. Catholic bishops found themselves refereeing disputes about who was or wasn't married because there weren't always effective civil authorities to do so. To curtail this problem, the canonical form requirement was instituted at the Council of Trent (1545–63).

40. The church doesn't authorize a civil ceremony, because baptized Catholics are obligated to canonical form. But those who don't intend what the church intends cannot marry sacramentally. Canon 1055.2 may imply they cannot marry at all, but this contradicts the premise of a right to marry.

41. The National Marriage Project recently found 94 percent of never-married singles agreed that "when you marry you want your spouse to be your soul mate, first and foremost" ("The State of Our Unions 2001: Who Wants to Marry a Soul-Mate?" at http://marriage.rutgers.edu/Publications/SOOU/TEXTSOOU2001.htm).

42. Ladislas Örsy, "Faith, Contract, Sacrament, and Christian Marriage: Disputed Questions," *Theological Studies* 43 (1982): 385.

43. John Paul II, *Familiaris Consortio,* n. 68.

44. Lawler, *Marriage and the Catholic Church,* 51–52.

45. Örsy, "Faith, Contract, Sacrament, and Christian Marriage," 386.

46. Michael G. Lawler, *Secular Marriage, Christian Sacrament* (Mystic, Conn.: Twenty-Third Publications, 1985), 66–67; cf. Örsy, "Faith, Contract, Sacrament, and Christian Marriage," 391ff.

47. Champlin, *The Marginal Catholic;* Susan Wood, "The Marriage of Baptized Nonbelievers: Faith, Contract, and Sacrament," *Theological Studies* 48 (1987): 279–301.

48. Wood, "The Marriage of Baptized Nonbelievers," 295.

49. I agree with Lawler that Wood is wrong when she says a couple can share the church's intention for marriage of baptized Christians "even if the couple would wish to exclude the sacrament" (Lawler, *Marriage and the Catholic Church*, 51; Wood, "Marriage of Baptized Non-Believers," 300).

50. Michael Skelley, *The Liturgy of the World: Karl Rahner's Idea of Worship* (Collegeville, Minn.: Liturgical Press, 1991).

51. I have more fully articulated how concepts of sacrament and charity overlap in *Where Two or Three Are Gathered: Christian Families as Domestic Churches* (Notre Dame, Ind.: University of Notre Dame Press, 2004), chapters 9 and 11.

52. Barry, "Marriage as a Sacrament for Generation X?" 24–25. Words in brackets reflect prior sections of Barry's essay.

53. Ibid., 19–20.

54. With forty thousand U.S. annulments annually, usually based on immaturity at the time of marriage (Hegy and Martos, *Catholic Divorce*, 2), those who take the annulment system seriously cannot help but wonder if their marriage could be considered invalid.

55. At one of the most meaningful Catholic wedding liturgies I've attended, the bride, a divorcee, selected the parable of the prodigal son as the Gospel reading. The homilist explained that meeting her husband was a sign to her that God had given her a second chance. The bride's choice of this Gospel took maturity and courage. (By contrast, she was hardly involved in the annulment of her first marriage, which was petitioned by her ex-husband.) Could the church's ministers enable more people to be so thoughtful in planning their wedding liturgies?

22: *Interchurch Marriages (Michael G. Lawler)*

1. This essay is a revised version of one that appeared in *INTAMS Review* 6 (2000): 199–214; it is also reprinted with permission from Michael G. Lawler, *Marriage and the Catholic Church: Disputed Questions* (Collegeville, Minn.: Liturgical Press, 2002).

2. Howard M. Bahr, "Religious Intermarriage and Divorce in Utah and the Mountain States," *Journal for the Scientific Study of Religion* 20 (1981): 251–61; Dean R. Hoge and Kathleen M. Ferry, *Empirical Research on Interfaith Marriage in America* (Washington, D.C.: United States Catholic Conference, 1981); Tim B. Heaton, Stan L. Albrecht, and Thomas K. Martin, "The Timing of Divorce," *Journal of Marriage and the Family* 47 (1985): 631–39; Tim B. Heaton and Edith L. Pratt, "The Effects of Religious Homogamy on Marital Satisfaction and Stability," *Journal of Family Issues* 11 (1990): 191–207; Larry L. Bumpass, Teresa Castro Martin, and James A. Sweet, *Background and Early Marital Factors* (Madison, Wisc.: Center for Demography and Ecology, 1989); Evelyn L. Lehrer and Carmel U. Chiswick, "Religion as a Determinant of Marital Stability," *Demography* 30 (1993): 385–404.

3. See George Kilcourse, *Double Belonging: Interchurch Families and Christian Unity* (New York: Paulist Press, 1992).

4. See Center for Marriage and Family, *Ministry to Interchurch Marriages: A National Study* (Omaha, Neb.: Creighton University, 1999), 20–34.

5. *Lumen Gentium*, n. 8.

6. John Paul II, *Ut Unum Sint*, n. 13.

7. *Gaudium et Spes*, n. 48.

8. "Eucharistic Sharing in Interchurch Marriages and Families: Guidelines from the German Bishops," *Journal of the Association of Interchurch Families* 6 (1998): 10.

9. Ibid., n. 2 (my emphasis).

10. Ibid., n. 5.

11. *Blessed and Broken: Pastoral Guidelines for Eucharistic Hospitality* (Brisbane, Australia: Archdiocese of Brisbane, 1995), 7.

12. *One Bread One Body: A Teaching Document on the Eucharist in the Life of the Church and the Establishment of General Norms on Sacramental Sharing* (London: Catholic Truth Society, 1998).

13. See Michael G. Lawler, *Marriage and Sacrament: A Theology of Christian Marriage* (Collegeville, Minn.: Liturgical Press, 1993), 7–12.

14. *Directory on Ecumenism for Southern Africa*. This document may be found at www.sacbc.org.za/ecume.htm.

15. Ibid., nn. 6, 3, 7.

16. *The Tablet*, October 16, 1999.

17. *AAS* 54 (1962): 792.

18. *Directory on Ecumenism for Southern Africa*, nn. 6, 3, 8.

19. H. Denzinger and A. Schoenmetzer, eds., *Enchiridion Symbolorum Definitionum et Declarationum de Rebus Fidei et Morum* (Fribourg: Herder, 1965), n. 1652.

20. Ladislas Örsy, "Interchurch Marriages and Reception of Eucharist," *America*, October 12, 1996, 19.

21. Peter Lombard, *Liber Sententiarum* 4, dist. 1, cap. 4; Thomas Aquinas, *Summa Theologica*, III, q. 60, a. 1; Michael G. Lawler, *Symbol and Sacrament: A Contemporary Sacramental Theology* (Omaha, Neb.: Creighton University Press, 1995), 33–35; *Lumen Gentium*, n. 1.

22. *Sacrosanctum Concilium*, n. 59.

23. *Unitatis Redintegratio*, n. 8.

24. *Ministry to Interchurch Marriages*, 15, 139. This percentage was replicated in the more recent Center for Marriage and Family study, *Time, Sex, and Money: The First Five Years of Marriage* (Omaha, Neb.: Creighton University, 2000). See also *Catholic Engaged Encounter Renewal: 1999 Follow-Up Project* (Washington, D.C.: Georgetown University, 1999), 3.

25. Center for Marriage and Family, *Marriage Preparation in the Catholic Church: Getting It Right* (Omaha, Neb.: Creighton University, 1995).

26. S. L. Albrecht, H. M. Bahr, and K. L. Goodman, *Divorce and Remarriage* (Westport, Conn.: Greenwood Press, 1983); Vaughn R. A. Call and Tim B. Heaton, "Religious Influence on Marital Stability," *Journal for the Scientific Study of Religion* 36 (1997): 382–92; Heaton and Pratt, "The Effects of Religious Homogamy on Marital Satisfaction and Stability," 191–207; Lehrer and Chiswick, "Religion as a Determinant of Marital Stability," 385–404.

27. Theresa Castro Martin and Larry Bumpass, "Recent Trends in Marital Disruption," *Demography* 26 (1989): 37–51; Andrew J. Cherlin, *Marriage, Divorce, Remarriage* (Cambridge, Mass.: Harvard University Press, 1992); Norval D. Glenn, *Closed Hearts Closed Minds: The Textbook Story of Marriage* (New York: Institute for American Values, 1997).

28. See the works cited in n. 26.

29. This finding was replicated independently for a different sample population in Center for Marriage and Family, *Time, Sex, and Money.*

30. John Paul II, *Familiaris Consortio,* n. 75.

31. John Chrysostom, *In Gen. 6,* 2, *PG* 54, 607.

32. Augustine, *Epist. 188,* 3, *PL* 33, 849.

33. *Matrimonia Mixta, AAS* 62 (1970), 259.

34. John Paul II, *Familiaris Consortio,* n. 78.

35. *Dignitatis Humanae,* n. 5.

24: *The Sacramentality of Marriage (Gerard Magill)*

1. Michael G. Lawler, *Marriage and Sacrament: A Theology of Christian Marriage* (Collegeville, Minn.: Liturgical Press, 1993), 14–15.

2. Michael G. Lawler, *Symbol and Sacrament: A Contemporary Sacramental Theology* (New York and Mahwah, N.J.: Paulist Press, 1987), 205.

3. Michael G. Lawler, *Family: American and Christian* (Chicago: Loyola Press, 1999), 95.

4. David Tracy, *Plurality and Ambiguity: Hermeneutics, Religion, and Hope* (San Francisco: Harper & Row, 1987), ix, 18, 20–28, 66; *The Analogical Imagination: Christian Theology and the Culture of Pluralism* (New York: Crossroad, 1981), 446–57.

5. Karen Lebacqz, "Difficult Difference," *Cambridge Quarterly of Healthcare Ethics* 7 (1998): 25; Catherine Mowry LaCugna, ed., *Freeing Theology: The Essentials of Theology in Feminist Perspective* (San Francisco: HarperSanFrancisco, 1993).

6. Gerard Magill, "The Ethics Weave in Human Genomics, Embryonic Stem Cell Research and Therapeutic Cloning: Promoting and Protecting Society's Interests," *Albany Law Review* (Summer 2002): 701–28.

Glossary

Agape: Greek word meaning love in the New Testament; refers to the unconditional absolute self-gift of God.

Allocentric: From the Greek, meaning centered on others.

Annulment: A juridical declaration that a canonically valid marriage never existed between two people.

Ascetic: One who practices asceticism.

Asceticism: Radical self-restraint for religious purposes. Practitioners of asceticism in ancient Christianity fasted frequently, renounced sexual activity, and renounced material possessions for the sake of spiritual insight.

Betrothal: Engagement with the intention to marry.

Biblical Narrative: The written account of the lived reality and experience of God's presence in the human community most fully recognized and realized in the Incarnation.

Canon Law, Code of: The official body of church law most recently revised and promulgated in the Roman Catholic Church in 1983.

Casti Connubii ("On Christian Marriage," 1930): Encyclical letter of Pope Pius XI addressing the issue of artificial contraception and asserting the primary ends (procreation and education of children) and the secondary ends (unitive) of marriage.

Catholic Social Thought: The application of biblical notions of justice and solidarity to contemporary social and economic realities. The church has a long history of this thought, though it has only been formalized in encyclicals beginning with Pope Leo XIII's *Rerum Novarum* ("On the Condition of Workers," 1891).

Celibacy: A way of life characterized by a person's perpetual renunciation of marriage for the sake of the reign of God.

Many of the definitions in this glossary are taken from Richard P. McBrien, general ed., *The Harper Collins Encyclopedia of Catholicism* (New York: HarperSanFrancisco, 1995).

Charism: A spiritual gift given to individuals or groups for the good of the community. The word was introduced with theological meaning by Paul. "To each is given the manifestation of the Spirit for the common good. . . . All these [gifts] are activated by one and the same Spirit, who allots to each one individually just as the Spirit chooses" (1 Cor. 12:7, 11).

Chiasm (Chiasmus): A literary term that refers to an inverted parallel arrangement of themes or ideas arranged concentrically around a main point found at the center of the literary unit.

Cohabitation: When two people are living together sharing all the dimensions of married life, including sexual relations, without being married. It is a de facto union where there may or may not be the intention to marry.

Covenant: An unconditional relational agreement between two parties based on fidelity and exclusivity.

Culture of Youth: A social tendency glorifying youth and its preservation and vilifying the aging process in terms of physical appearance, medical needs, relational capacities, and productivity.

Debitum: Traditional Latin term referring to the conjugal debt whereby a spouse could demand sex and, out of justice and the demands of the marriage contract, the other spouse could not refuse the request.

Descriptive Ethics: This type of ethics describes the context and circumstances surrounding an ethical issue as well as what people do and why they act in specific ways.

Dialectic: The practice of systematically and logically examining ideas or concepts, often by question or answer, or by comparing and contrasting two realities, ideas, or concepts, to determine their validity and truth.

Discipleship: To be a follower of Christ and all that entails spiritually, relationally, and morally.

Domestic Church: The Christian family as a sacred and holy community, which "constitutes a specific revelation and realization of ecclesial communion" (*Familiaris Consortio*, n. 21).

Dual Career: Where two spouses pursue full- or part-time career aspirations, but are not necessarily committed to the vocation of public discipleship.

Dual Vocation: Parents have at least two callings; one is to procreate and educate children, the other is to work toward the common good of the wider human community or public discipleship. Both flow from discipleship and living out one's Christian commitment.

Dualism: A term with multiple meanings referring to diverse doctrines that posit some form of coexisting, opposing principles, entities, forces, or distinctions (e.g., spirit and matter) as basic components of the world or of human life.

Ecclesial: Adjectival form of *ecclesia*. From the Greek for "church" or "community." Hence, "ecclesial" means "pertaining to church matters."

Ecclesiology: The study of the church.

Efficacious Grace: Often referred to as "sanctifying grace," the effect of the self-communication of God by which we are made holy, transformed into "participants of the divine nature" (2 Pet. 1:4).

Engaged Encounter Weekend: This program was developed by the Catholic Church to prepare engaged Christian couples in their marital journey and focuses on communication skills, spiritual and personal needs, and the nature of commitment in marriage.

Eschatological: Adjectival form of the word "eschatology." Eschatology is the branch of theology that considers both the nature and fulfillment of God's promises at the end of time.

Eucharist: "Thanksgiving," the sacramental celebration of the Paschal Mystery (i.e., Christ's dying and rising for humankind) in a context of praise and thanks for all that God has done and continues to do for humanity.

Eucharistic Sharing: Sharing of communion in interchurch marriages and the denominational, sacramental, and relational complexities involved with this sharing.

Familiaris Consortio (Apostolic Exhortation on the Role of the Christian Family in the Modern World, 1981): This document published by Pope John Paul II encourages married Catholics to model fidelity, mutual love, and service to the wider community, thereby modeling a countercultural view of marriage.

Gaudium et Spes (Pastoral Constitution on the Church in the Modern World, 1965): In this Vatican II document the church reformed the previous distinction between the primary end (procreation) and secondary (unitive) ends of marriage. For the first time, the unitive dimension was placed on equal footing with procreation, laying the foundation for a more personalist view of marriage.

Grace: God's free and forgiving self-communication that enables humans to share in God's love.

Hermeneutics: The theory and/or practice of interpretation, particularly of biblical texts.

Hillel: An important Jewish sage who lived in the first century B.C.E. He is usually discussed at the same time as Shammai, a contemporary with whom he frequently disagreed.

Household Codes: Passages in the New Testament that give explicit instructions about how to manage relationships between men and women and parents and children. The most famous of these is Paul's admonition in Ephesians 5 that women should be submissive to their husbands.

Immediate Marriage Preparation: This is a specific term used by Pope John Paul II to indicate the period of marital preparation during a couple's engagement.

Indissolubility: The teaching that a valid, sacramental marriage cannot be dissolved.

Interchurch Marriage: A marriage between spouses from two Christian denominations, where each spouse participates in varying degrees in her or his own church and, to some degree, in the spouse's church, and in which both spouses take an active part in the religious education of their children.

Interreligious Marriage: A marriage between spouses from two different religious traditions (e.g., a Christian and non-Christian tradition). *See also* Interchurch Marriage.

Intrinsic Sacramentality: A manifestation of God's power and love in space and time, not tied to official actions or liturgies of the church.

***In Vitro* Fertilization:** The extracorporeal fertilization of an ovum in a petri dish (*vitro* means glass) and its subsequent transfer to the uterus.

Juridical: Of or relating to the law, jurisprudence.

Kenosis (*kenotic*)**:** A Greek term meaning "emptying," which refers to Jesus' emptying of his divinity through the Incarnation.

Kingdom of God: An image of God's sovereign authority and its consequences. The emphasis in the image is on the activity of God's rule, not the realm over which it is exercised.

Laity: The Christian faithful. This term refers to the vast majority of the Catholic Church, the faithful, who are consecrated to the Lord by the sacraments of initiation (Baptism, Eucharist, and Confirmation).

Lex Dubia: Law based on uncertainty.

Magisterium: From the Latin *magister* meaning "to teach." The teaching authority of the Catholic Church on faith and morals, consisting of the pope and bishops and informed by all the Catholic faithful, including theologians.

Marriage Bond: The Second Vatican Council spoke of this bond in personal language. "The intimate partnership (or relationship) of married life and love ... is rooted in the conjugal covenant of irrevocable personal consent" (*Gaudium et Spes,* n. 48).

Martyr: From the Greek word meaning "witness." Martyrs are people who are killed because of their religious beliefs. Martyrs are usually contrasted with "confessors," individuals who suffer persecution for their beliefs but who survive.

Matter and Form: Matter is the reality underlying all visible things before they are determined to be this or that kind of thing. Form is that reality that allows for the identification of matter as this or that kind of thing.

Mishna: Codified collection of oral Jewish law.

Mixed Marriage: *See* Interchurch Marriage.

Non-Practicing Catholics: Those who were baptized Catholic, but have very limited or no participation in the worshiping community.

Normative Ethics: A type of ethics that uses theories and principles to explain and justify what people ought to do.

Ontological: An argument or position usually articulated in terms of being or an intrinsic relationship.

Opus Operantis (*Ex Opere Operantis:* "from the work of the doer"): Expression used in sacramental theology to refer to actions or merits of the minister or recipients of the sacrament, in contrast to God's own action in and through the sacraments.

Opus Operatum (*Ex Opere Operato:* "from the work done"): Expression used in the theology of the sacraments to emphasize that, since God is the chief agent of the sacrament, the sacrament can never fail to celebrate the salvation promised in Christ provided that it is celebrated under proper conditions.

Pater Familias: Latin phrase describing the father as the head of the household. Many ancient (as well as contemporary) cultures were highly patriarchal and households were dominated by fathers.

Patriarchal: The social system wherein one's status is directly proportional to one's relationship to the oldest male in the clan.

Patriarchy: Term used to describe the dominance of society by men.

People of God: This concept reflects the predominant communion ecclesiology or understanding of the nature and structure of the church developed at Vatican II and found in *Lumen Gentium*. It asserts that, based on baptism and the gifts of priest, prophet, and king, all of the faithful share in the ongoing discernment of truth regarding faith and morals. This ecclesiology is contrasted with a hierarchical, top-down ecclesiology in the pre–Vatican II church.

Pericope: A term used by New Testament scholars to describe a small section of text singled out for interpretation. Pericopes are usually larger than verses. They are small units of meaning.

Personalism: A foundational concept of Catholic moral theology that assesses the morality of actions and motives in terms of how they either facilitate or frustrate human dignity or the human person integrally and adequately considered.

Philia: Greek word meaning friendship love in the New Testament.

Physicalism: A criticism often leveled against Catholic sexual teaching that the physical or biological structure of an act determines the morality of an act. This reflects a biological interpretation of natural law rather than a personalist view that focuses on the *meaning* of acts for human persons and relationships.

Polygamy: Marriage of a spouse to multiple spouses.

Polygyny: Marriage of a man to two or more wives.

Preexilic: A term for Old Testament studies to refer to a period in Israelite history known as the *exile*. The exile lasted from 597 to 538 B.C.E. The *preexilic* period differs significantly from the *postexilic* period.

Prenuptial: The engagement period that precedes marriage.

Q: A hypothetical document from the first century that some scholars believe once existed. "Q" helps to explain the presence of common material in the Gospels of Matthew and Luke that does not appear in Mark. The name

"Q" is not ancient, but a scholarly term taken from the first letter of the German word for "source" (*Quelle*).

Religious: Men or women who publicly profess religious vows (poverty, chastity, and obedience) and live with one another in community.

Rhythm Method: A form of "natural" contraception that relies upon a calendar calculation of fertility based upon menstrual cycles.

Sacrament: Any manifestation of God's power and love in space and time. Usually refers to the seven sacraments of the Roman Catholic Church, though sacramentality is never limited to just those seven.

Scholasticism: A method of intellectual inquiry that was prominent until the sixteenth century in Western medieval thought, especially in universities. Scholasticism is described by M.-D. Chenu as "a rational form of thinking, consciously and voluntarily working from texts it held to be authoritative" (*Toward Understanding St. Thomas*, 63).

Shammai: An important Jewish sage who lived in the first century B.C.E. He is usually discussed at the same time as Hillel, a contemporary with whom he frequently disagreed.

Spiritual-Embodiedness: One dimension of personalism that emphasizes the intrinsic link between matter and spirit, thus denying much of the dualism (matter is evil, spirit is good) that has plagued Christian tradition, especially in human sexuality.

Spirituality: The individual and communal lived reality of one's relationship with God.

Stem Cell Research: Stem cells are human embryonic *totipotent* cells (capable of becoming any tissue in the body) or *pluripotent* cells (somewhat differentiated and only capable of becoming some cells or tissues in the body), experimented upon and destroyed with the hopes of discovering cures for such diseases as Alzheimer's and diabetes. The ethical issues surrounding this research focus on when human life begins, and if it is ever morally acceptable to destroy innocent human life to further science, and perhaps cure diseases.

Substance and Accidents: Substance is a philosophical concept derived from Aristotle that describes pure existence independently of changeable "accidents" inhering to it. Thus, substance is the pure existence of a thing while accidents are the outward appearance of something perceptible to our senses and often change.

Surrogacy: To elect to have another woman carry one's child due to an inability to conceive or carry a fetus to term.

Symbol: Something through which something other than itself is incarnated and encountered. A symbol runs deeper than a mere sign, which arbitrarily points to some other thing extrinsic to itself.

Table Fellowship: Phrase used by New Testament scholars to describe the human phenomenon of eating with others. Who one eats with says much about what one values. Hence, part of the radical message of Jesus was that he ate with (kept table fellowship with) sinners and other marginal people in Jewish society.

Transubstantiation: Official Catholic teaching on the nature of the Eucharist. Namely, the substance of bread and wine is transformed into the substance of the body and blood of Christ. This is often referred to as the "real presence" in the Eucharist.

Valid Marriage: A juridical classification asserting that when a marriage is contracted between a male and a female baptized person, a sacramental marriage exists.

Vatican Council II: The twenty-first general council of the Roman Catholic Church (October 11, 1962–December 8, 1965). The council is regarded as the most significant religious event since the sixteenth-century Reformation and certainly the most important of the twentieth century. The Italian term that defined the council was *aggiornamento,* or updating, designating Pope John XXIII's wish to update Catholic theology in light of "the signs of the times."

Vocation: The inclination toward a particular state of life that the Christian accepts as a call from God.

Yahweh: A name used for God in the Old Testament. It was revealed to Moses, to whom God is identified as "I am who I am" (Exod. 3:14) — a wordplay on Yahweh.

Yahwist: The term used to describe the primary author or authors of the first five books of the Bible. The use of the term "Yahweh" to refer to God distinguishes this author(s) from the other main source, usually referred to as the "Priestly" source. In Old Testament studies these sources are called "J" and "P," respectively.

About the Editors

Todd A. Salzman received his Ph.D. in Christian Ethics at the Katholieke Universiteit Leuven, Belgium, 1994. He teaches sexual ethics, foundations of Christian ethics, and biomedical ethics at Creighton University.

Thomas M. Kelly received his Ph.D. from Boston College in 1999. Currently he is assistant professor of theology and the director of the M.A. in Ministry Program at Creighton University. Dr. Kelly has published nationally and internationally on philosophical hermeneutics, systematic theology, and marriage and social ethics.

John J. O'Keefe received his M.T.S. from Weston School of Theology in 1987, and his M.A. and Ph.D. in Early Christian Studies from the Catholic University of America in 1990 and 1993. Specializing in patristic theology, O'Keefe has particular interests in early Christian biblical interpretation and doctrinal development.

Index

Of Related Interest

Richard Gaillardetz
A DARING PROMISE
A Spirituality of Christian Marriage

Most Catholic books on marriage either take a therapeutic approach, or they treat it in romantic and lofty terms far removed from ordinary experience. This book offers a refreshing alternative. Gaillardetz, a prominent theologian and popular speaker, teaches that marriage sets a couple on a spiritual journey that promises romance and intimacy but also involves moments of fear, loneliness, and regret. He invites couples to celebrate their romance, but also to recognize that moments of loneliness and emptiness are equally a part of the fabric of married life — and part of the Paschal Mystery to which every Christian is called.

0-8245-1935-3, $16.95 paperback

Joann Heaney-Hunter and Louis Primavera
UNITAS
Preparing for Sacramental Marriage

Based on the Rite of Christian Initiation for Adults, this marriage formation program is designed to help couples appreciate the importance of sacramental marriage in their lives and in the life of the wider church community.

Unitas Leader's Guide: 0-8245-1755-5, $19.95 paperback

Unitas Couples Workbook: 0-8245-1756-3, $14.95 paperback

Unitas Videotapes (set of 3): 0-8245-1757-1, $99.00

Please support your local bookstore,
or call 1-800-707-0670 for Customer Service.

For a free catalog, write us at

THE CROSSROAD PUBLISHING COMPANY
16 Penn Plaza, 481 Eighth Avenue
New York, NY 10001

Visit our website at
www.crossroadpublishing.com
All prices subject to change.

crossroad